The Cambridge Companion to the Organ

This Companion is an essential guide to all aspects of the organ and
its music. It examines in turn the instrument, the player and the
repertoire. The early chapters tell of the instrument's history and
construction, identify the scientific basis of its sounds and the
development of its pitch and tuning, examine the history of the organ
case, and consider the current trends and conflicts within the world
of organ building. Central chapters investigate the practical art of
learning and playing the organ, introduce the complex area of
performance practice, and outline the connection between organ
playing and the liturgy of the church. The final section explores the
vast repertoire of organ music in relation to the instruments for
which it was written, focusing on a selection of the most important
traditions. The essays, all newly commissioned, are written by experts
in their field, making this the most authoritative reference book
currently available.

Nicholas Thistlethwaite is author of *The Making of the Victorian
Organ* (1990).

Geoffrey Webber is Precentor and Director of Studies in Music at
Gonville and Caius College, Cambridge, and author of *North German
Church Music in the Age of Buxtehude* (1996).

Cambridge Companions to Music

The Cambridge Companion to Brass Instruments
Edited by Trevor Herbert and John Wallace
0 521 56243 7 (hardback)
0 521 56522 7 (paperback)

The Cambridge Companion to the Clarinet
Edited by Colin Lawson
0 521 47066 8 (hardback)
0 521 47668 2 (paperback)

The Cambridge Companion to the Recorder
Edited by John Mansfield Thomson
0 521 35269 X (hardback)
0 521 35816 7 (paperback)

The Cambridge Companion to the Violin
Edited by Robin Stowell
0 521 39923 8 (paperback)

The Cambridge Companion to the Piano
Edited by David Rowland
0 521 47470 1 (paperback)
0 521 47986 X (paperback)

The Cambridge Companion to Bach
Edited by John Butt
0 521 45350 X (hardback)
0 521 58780 8 (paperback)

The Cambridge Companion to Berg
Edited by Anthony Pople
0 521 56374 7 (hardback)
0 521 56489 1 (paperback)

The Cambridge Companion to Chopin
Edited by Jim Samson
0 521 47752 2 (paperback)

The Cambridge Companion to Handel
Edited by Donald Burrows
0 521 45425 5 (hardback)
0 521 45613 4 (paperback)

The Cambridge Companion to Schubert
Edited by Christopher Gibbs
0 521 48229 1 (hardback)
0 521 48424 3 (paperback)

The Cambridge Companion to the

ORGAN

EDITED BY
Nicholas Thistlethwaite and Geoffrey Webber

CAMBRIDGE
UNIVERSITY PRESS

PUBLISHED BY THE PRESS SYNDICATE OF THE UNIVERSITY OF CAMBRIDGE
The Pitt Building, Trumpington Street, Cambridge CB2 1RP, United Kingdom

CAMBRIDGE UNIVERSITY PRESS
The Edinburgh Building, Cambridge CB2 2RU, United Kingdom http://www.cup.cam.ac.uk
40 West 20th Street, New York, NY 10011–4211, USA http://www.cup.org
10 Stamford Road, Oakleigh, Melbourne 3166, Australia

First published 1998

Printed in the United Kingdom at the University Press, Cambridge

Typeset in Adobe Minion 10.75/14 pt, in QuarkXPress™ [SE]

A catalogue record for this book is available from the British Library

Library of Congress cataloguing in publication data

The Cambridge companion to the organ / edited by Nicholas
  Thistlethwaite and Geoffrey Webber.
      p.   cm. – (Cambridge companions to music)
    Includes bibliographical references (p.   ) and index.
    ISBN 0 521 57309 2 (hardback). – ISBN 0 521 57584 2 (paperback)
    1. Organ.   2. Organ music – History and criticism.
  I. Thistlethwaite, Nicholas.   II. Webber, Geoffrey.   III. Series.
  ML550.C35   1998
  786.5 – dc21   97-41723 CIP

ISBN 0 521 57309 2 hardback
ISBN 0 521 57584 2 paperback

Contents

Figures

Acknowledgements

The editors would like to express their thanks to the following individuals, institutions and firms who have kindly made photographs available for this volume:

Stephen Bicknell (2.1, 2.2, 2.3, 2.4, 2.5, 2.6); John Brennan (5.9); The British Library (1.1); Gerard Brooks (18.2); Flentrop Orgelbouw (5.17); Fotografia Lensini Fabio (10.1); Dean and Chapter of Gloucester Cathedral (13.1); Volkmaar Herre (5.5); The Holtkamp Organ Company (5.16); The Jakobikirche, Hamburg (15.1); Alan Lauffman (5.15); John Mainstone (3.1); George Taylor (6.1); Pierre Vallotton (5.1, 5.2, 5.3, 5.4, 5.7, 5.8, 5.10, 5.11, 12.1, 14.1, 16.1, 16.2); Klaus Walcker-Mayer (5.13).

Musical examples from editions in copyright have been reproduced from publications by the following:

Bärenreiter (17.1, © 1993); Editions Bornemann (18.2, 18.3); Editions Chanvrelin (18.1); Editions Henry Lemoine (18.5); C. F. Peters Corporation (20.6, © 1980, used by permission of C. F. Peters Corporation on behalf of Henmar Press Inc.); F. E. C. Leuckart (17.3); Möseler Verlag (17.4, © 1978); Musikverlag Alfred Coppenrath (17.2, © 1973); Stainer & Bell (19.6, © 1916 Stainer & Bell, London, England); Schott & Co. (19.4, © 1914 Schott & Co. (London) reproduced by permission); Theodore Presser Co. (20.5, © 1969 Societé des Editions Jobert, used by permission of the publisher; sole representative U.S.A. Theodore Presser Company); Warner Bros. Communication (20.2, 20.3, 20.4).

Contributors

Graham Barber is Professor of Performance Studies, Department of Music, University of Leeds, and Senior Tutor in Organ Studies, The Royal Northern College of Music.

Stephen Bicknell is the author of *The History of the English Organ* (Cambridge 1996).

Gerard Brooks is Associate Director of Music, All Souls, Langham Place, and Organist, St James' Church, Clerkenwell, London.

Geoffrey Cox is Associate Professor at the Australian Catholic University, and Assistant Organist at St Patrick's Cathedral, Melbourne.

James Dalton is former Organist and Tutor in Music at The Queen's College, Oxford.

Edward Higginbottom is Organist and Tutor in Music at New College, Oxford.

Christopher Kent is Senior Lecturer in Music at the University of Reading and coordinator of The Lady Susi Jeans Centre for Organ Historiography.

John Mainstone is Head of the Department of Physics at the University of Queensland, Brisbane, Australia.

Kimberly Marshall, formerly Dean of Postgraduate Studies at the Royal Academy of Music, London, is Associate Professor of Music at Arizona State University.

Andrew McCrea is a music tutor for London University's Extra-Mural Department (Birkbeck College), and the Open University. He is also Assistant Librarian to the Royal College of Organists.

Douglas Reed is Professor of Music and University Organist at the University of Evansville, Indiana.

Patrick Russill is Head of Choral Direction and Church Music at the Royal Academy of Music, London and Organist of the London Oratory.

Christopher Stembridge lives and works in Italy, where he holds regular courses on historic organs in Arezzo, Brescia and Siena.

Nicholas Thistlethwaite is a member of the Music Faculty, University of Cambridge, and author of *The Making of the Victorian Organ* (Cambridge 1990).

Geoffrey Webber is Precentor and Director of Studies in Music at Gonville and Caius College, Cambridge.

David Yearsley is Assistant Professor of Music at Cornell University, New York State.

Preface

But oh! what art can teach,
What human voice can reach,
The sacred organ's praise?
Notes inspiring holy love,
Notes that wing their heavenly ways
To mend the choirs above.
JOHN DRYDEN ('A SONG FOR ST CECILIA'S DAY', 1687)

For Dryden there was no doubt: the organ had no equal in the exercise of music. Indeed, throughout the ages the organ has been granted an elevated status in the minds of both writers and musicians. Its most lofty eminence has been in association with the patron saint of music, St Cecilia, who, in W. H. Auden's description, 'constructed an organ to enlarge her prayer'. Medieval writers appealed to the Book of Psalms, or to Psalm commentaries by the Church Fathers, arguing that there was no more worthy instrument for the praise of God. Later writers saw other opportunities for relating the instrument to things monumental or even elemental. The seventeenth-century polymath Athanasius Kircher represented the six days of creation as an organ, illustrating each as a stop on an instrument which as an ensemble depicted the *Harmonia nascentis mundi* (the harmony of the world's creation). Such noble metaphors are only rarely balanced by more temporal references, though the earliest printed book on the organ, Arnolt Schlick's *Spiegel der Orgel-macher und Organisten* (Mirror of Organ-builders and Organists) of 1511 refers not just to its role in praising God and assisting singing, but also to its capacity to provide refreshment for the human spirit and its woes. But in general, the organ rests unimpeachable as the King of Instruments, an epithet enunciated by Praetorius, Mozart and many others.

But there is also a negative side to this stereotype of the organ as that 'wond'rous machine' (to use another description by Dryden). For the instrument placed above all others and reflecting the harmony of whole creation may perhaps have little to say at the mundane level of human feelings and emotions. In the vocabulary of many a writer through the ages the organ simply thunders, swells, peals or throbs, echoing only a limited field of human experience. At best, this manner of description is complimentary, but at times the sentiment seems less positive, as when Tennyson wrote that 'the great organ almost burst his pipes, groaning for power', or as in the following couplet by the eighteenth-century poet John Wolcot: 'Loud groaned the organ through his hundred pipes, / As if the poor machine had got the gripes.' But players of most musical instruments hope to appeal to a varied palette of human emotions, and there can be little reason for the organist to be satisfied with a lesser challenge. To make music on the organ, to communicate effectively through music rather than merely to provide an ecclesiastical atmosphere, carries great responsibilities for both the organ builder and the performer. The builder must ensure that the instrument functions properly and that the wind supply matches the demands of the player (as J. S. Bach was so keen to do when he examined new instruments), whilst the organist must ensure that the music is given shape and form, not degenerating into a seamless stream of sound. This latter difficulty lies behind perhaps the most famous criticism of the organ uttered this century – Igor Stravinsky's comment that 'the monster never breathes'. In this regard it is salutary to recall that in only a fraction of the instrument's history has the wind supply been provided by mechanical means. Perhaps when one person or indeed several people were required to pump the wind into the pipes, organists may have perceived more keenly their machine as a living musical instrument. In his brief poem 'On the Musique of Organs', the early seventeenth-century poet Francis Quarles portrays organ music as a partnership between blower and player: 'They both concurre: Each acts his severall part, / Th'one gives it *Breath*; the other lends it *Art*.' Today that breath is available at the end of an electric switch, but players do well to remember the ultimate source of their music-making, as they work to breathe life into the music forming in their minds or in the musical notes laid out before them.

The organ's credentials as a versatile musical instrument have thus continually been under threat. But in recent times the organ has faced an even greater challenge with the rise of devices (in the shape of an organ console) that electronically reproduce recorded sound. In these the breath that gives life to the music has been extinguished altogether; the wind supply, portrayed by Michael Praetorius as the 'soul of the organ', has been cut off. Seduced by a cheaper initial outlay, many committees have embraced an electronic instrument that becomes obsolete against a newer and better model almost as soon as it arrives. But although such instruments have their particular role to play, it is a testament to the value of the traditional instrument that so few organ firms have been forced out of business by the rise of electronic substitutes. New organs are still being built in large numbers across the world, either in churches or in concert halls or private residences. But if the general future of the traditional pipe organ seems for the moment secure, its future lines of development are far from clear. Both the instrument and its music face many questions about style and function which have no simple or single answer. The history of

organ building and playing is one of more or less continuous parallel progression with the occasional crossing of boundaries between the principal
schools, but after the watershed of the early part of this century when the
organ could get no larger without repeating itself, and when the organist
had come to imitate all the orchestra had to offer, this continuity col-
lapsed. The restoration of old instruments and the building of new
instruments according to old principles has become commonplace,
reflecting the wider interest in historically aware musical performance,
and the natural symbiotic relationship between the instrument and its
music has thus largely broken down. There is no current prevailing single
style of organ building, and there is no current prevailing single style of
organ composition. As a natural component of the current climate of cultural eclecticism this need not signal a major crisis for the organ, but it
certainly raises challenging questions regarding the way the organ and its
music will develop in the next century.

This Companion is designed as a general guide for all those who share
Dryden's enthusiasm for the organ. The early chapters tell of the instrument's history and construction, identify the scientific basis of its sounds
and the development of its pitch and tuning, examine the history of the
organ case and consider current trends and conflicts within the world of
organ building. In the central chapters the focus changes to the player:
here the practical art of learning the organ is considered, encompassing
both elementary and advanced problems, the complex area of performance practice is introduced, and the relationship between organ
playing and the liturgy of the church is outlined. In the final section of the
book, the emphasis turns to the vast repertoire of organ music, high-
lighting a selection of the most important traditions. Every chapter in the
book should be read as an introduction to the subject it treats, and it is
hoped that the bibliography will encourage readers to pursue their own
particular interests. Other books in this series published by Cambridge
University Press have dealt with instruments considerably younger and
less multifarious than the organ, and the reader is encouraged to accept
the limitations of the book's scope with understanding. In particular,
certain areas of repertoire have been omitted entirely or barely mentioned, as is the case with the music of the late medieval and early renaissance periods and of the contemporary sphere. Moreover, the desire to
treat certain areas in reasonable detail has inevitably led to the exclusion
of important areas of the repertoire within the principal period covered
between *c*1550 and 1950, such as the Italian school after Frescobaldi or the
romantic and modern Scandinavian repertoire. But the specific intention
of the repertoire chapters, however restricted in scope, is to consider the

development of organ music within each school in relation to the development of the instrument itself. Many books and articles have been written which concentrate principally on the developments of either organ building or of organ music in isolation. In reality the two aspects have developed in tandem, and at times the ambitions of organ players may have dictated changes in organ design, whilst at others the technological advances of the designers have presented new challenges and possibilities to composers and players. This book attempts to respect the mutual dependency of organ builder and organ player, so that even if the modern player is unable to play a particular piece on the most appropriate type of organ, he or she will be able to understand to a fair extent the music as it was conceived for a particular school of organ design and thus be able to re-interpret it as required on the instrument available. Similarly, the examination of the role of organ playing in the liturgy helps to explain the development of particular organ schools where understanding the function of the organist as improviser illuminates the nature of the written-down, composed repertoire.

The editors offer their thanks to all the contributors who so willingly parted with their time and expertise, but owe a particular debt to Stephen Bicknell, who – besides contributing three chapters – undertook the arduous and protracted task of assembling the illustrations. Our thanks also go to our respective Tessas, and to all others who have helped or encouraged the project, including Joseph Alcantara, Gavin Alexander, Robin Goodall, Lynda Stratford and Pierre Vallotton. To Penny Souster, Lucy Carolan and other members of staff at Cambridge University Press we must extend our grateful thanks for much helpful advice and a great deal of patience.

1 Origins and development of the organ

Nicholas Thistlethwaite

Organ ... the name of the largest, most comprehensive, and harmonious of musical instruments;
on which account it is called 'the organ', *organon*, 'the instrument' by way of excellence.
(Charles Burney, writing in A. Rees, *The Cyclopaedia, or Universal Dictionary of Arts,*
Sciences, and Literature, London 1819)

Although modern etymologists would question Burney's appropriation
of a Greek word with a general meaning (*organon* seems to have meant a
tool with which to do a job of work) for so specific a purpose, it would be
hard to deny that the pipe organ in its most developed form is structurally
the largest, and (for sheer variety of effect) musically the most comprehensive of all instruments. And if by 'harmonious' is meant the capacity to
order diverse elements and bring them into concord with one another for
a common purpose, then Burney's claim for the organ, with its multiplic-
ity of sound-producing and mechanical parts, can surely be sub-
stantiated.

At its most basic, the organ is a simple wind instrument. It consists of a
grooved chest supporting a set of pipes, bellows to supply wind to the
pipes, and some sort of mechanism to cause the pipes to sound. Though
such simplicity is now rare it perfectly well describes the sort of organ
depicted in medieval illuminated manuscripts (Figure 1.1). The path
from such modest instruments to giant modern organs boasting four or
five keyboards, 32' pipes, dozens of registers, sophisticated stop controls
and electrical blowing apparatus encompasses a complex and fascinating
process of development in which music, technology, architecture, liturgy,
industrial organisation and changing taste all play a part.

Certain things follow from this long historical development.

First, at any given period, styles of organ throughout Europe (and it is
Europe with which we are principally concerned before 1850) varied
considerably. Fifty years ago it was widely assumed that any pre-nineteenth-century German organ was suitable for the performance of Bach.
Today, we are becoming more aware of the distinct characteristics of
organs built in Swabia and the Rhineland, Hamburg and Westphalia – and
perhaps none of them is altogether appropriate for Bach, who spent most
of his working life in Thuringia and Saxony. Repertoire must be related
carefully to the type of instrument for which it was conceived: not

Figure 1.1 A detail of an illuminated initial from a Book of Hours of King Alfonso V of Naples (Aragon, 1442; British Library MS Add. 28962, fol. 281v). This portrayal of a positive organ appears immediately below a scene depicting the celebration of a mass in the royal chapel of the Aragonese court, and is probably indicative of the type of instrument used in such circumstances.

because this determines how it must be played today (which it does not) but because it offers an opportunity to understand more fully the intentions of the composer and the experience of the original player. From this informed position intelligent decisions can be made about modern performance.

Secondly, historic organs (with few exceptions) possess their own building history. We still know little about the 'ageing' process as it affects organs; change must be assumed in the molecular structure of pipe metal, and that may affect the tone. More obvious is change brought about by human intervention. Compasses, temperament, pitch, wind pressure and voicing are all matters that can be altered relatively easily in response to changing fashion, even when more drastic alterations are avoided. Nor is restoration necessarily a guarantee of authenticity. Old organs restored in the 1950s and 60s are now being restored again. (The famous F. C. Schnitger organ of 1723–6 in St Laurents, Alkmaar was restored by Flentrop in 1947–9, and again in 1982–6 to more exacting standards.) Whether current restoration techniques will be regarded as adequate in another fifty years time remains to be seen. Claims to historical correctness should always therefore be treated with some caution, though few old organs will fail to yield some valuable insights for the player.

Thirdly, with a documented history going back at least a thousand years, and an archaeological history spanning six centuries – setting aside such fragmentary remains as the cache of medieval organ pipes found at Bethlehem (Williams 1993: 348–9) and the earlier Graeco-Roman organ found at Aquincum in Hungary (Perrot 1971: 109–16) – the organ has benefited from a succession of technological innovations. At the end of the medieval period new techniques of carpentry, metalwork and bellows-making were exploited by organ builders for their own purposes (Williams 1993: 314–35). Four hundred years later, their successors were using steam-driven machinery in their workshops, and experimenting with pneumatics and electricity (Thistlethwaite 1990: 61, 351–61). Today, many organ builders take advantage of computer technology in both the design (computer-simulation in the drawing office) and equipping (multi-level memory systems, playback facilities, transmission) of organs. This suggests the wisdom of keeping an open mind about such technological developments. The pneumatic lever, for instance, is an integral feature of the nineteenth-century Cavaillé-Coll organ, which itself inspired an important school of organ composers at least in part because of the flexibility the pneumatic motors gave to these ambitious instruments. For the same reason, contemporary console developments in new organs are not to be condemned out of hand just because there is no precedent for them in the organ's earlier history. Probably the strongest objection that can be made to them is that they can seem to diminish the gap between the legitimate pipe organ and a variety of electronic keyboard instruments which endeavour to reproduce its effects.

In the following chapters, a good deal of attention will be devoted to particular repertoires and the instruments for which they were written. It may therefore be found helpful to have a brief summary of the organ's historical evolution with special reference to those technological innovations which created new opportunities for composers and performers, and which, taken together, assist us in defining the genius of this 'largest, most comprehensive, and harmonious of musical instruments'.

The medieval organ

The origins of organ technology and the type of instruments to which it gave rise in the earlier medieval period have been discussed elsewhere, notably by Jean Perrot (1971) and Peter Williams (1993). Here, it must suffice to say that organs had found their way into churches by the end of the tenth century, when several Anglo-Saxon monasteries (Malmesbury, Ramsey, Winchester) are known to have possessed them. However, their construction and the uses to which they were put (signalling devices, like bells; the expression of jubilation in the liturgy?) remain obscure.

Organs gradually spread throughout Europe, though the date of reception and the degree of mechanical sophistication must have varied considerably from one region to another. Probably the Benedictine order, with its interest in the useful arts, technology and science, played an important part in disseminating knowledge about organs. If so, it should not surprise us that the most comprehensive account of organ-building before the fifteenth century was written by a monk named Theophilus, who seems to have lived in what later became Westphalia in the period 1110–40. His treatise (which is part of a much longer work entitled *Diversarum Artium Schedule*) describes the manufacture of copper pipes, a wind-chest with seven or eight notes, wooden sliders projecting from the chest and lettered so that the player knew which note he was sounding, bellows, a wind collector (*conflatorium*) and a hollow wooden duct to convey wind to the chest (Perrot 1971: 232–52).

The evolution over the next three centuries of this simple (but in its own terms doubtless effective) sound-producing instrument into the early modern organ with its multi-ranked *Hauptwerk*, a *Rückpositiv* with separately-drawn registers, Pedal *trompes* (bourdons), extensive key-board compasses and a variety of pipe constructions was a complex process which there is not space to discuss here (but see Williams 1993: 336–57). However, certain crucial developments need to be briefly mentioned.

The *soundboard* is a large box on which the pipes are mounted, and which supplies them with wind. In early organs, wind was admitted to the pipes by means of sliders running in grooves beneath each pipe or set of pipes and operated directly by the player. By *c*1400 (possibly earlier) pallets had made their appearance. A small wooden clack-valve was located beneath each groove; when the player caused this pallet to open, wind entered the groove and the pipe(s) sounded. The connection between key and pallet was made by means of linkages known as trackers, and with the development of rollerboards to convey the action sideways it became possible to arrange the pipes in a different sequence from that dictated by the keyboard. It also enabled organ builders to make larger soundboards and to accommodate more and bigger pipes on them. Ultimately, these technological developments encouraged the multiplication of soundboards in an instrument; sometimes they were connected to a single keyboard, but in north-west Europe after *c*1450 it became

increasingly common to find organs with two or three keyboa
Pedal division.

Meanwhile *sliders* found a new role in enabling the pla
individual registers or groups of pipes. The large chur
later medieval period incorporated massive chorus
which each note sounded multi-ranked unisons and
de Zwolle (*c*1450) describes organs with between s
to a note (inevitably including much duplicatio
some attempts were being made to split up th
pipes, for example, a division into three: prin
pitched mixture, high-pitched mixture. By making s
sliders running at right angles to the grooves, organ builders
the means of shutting off groups of pipes. Only after 1500 did 'stop
to be thought of as bringing registers on rather than shutting them off.

In some parts of Europe (notably Italy) a second set of pallets was preferred to the slider. Each note of a register had its own spring-loaded
pallet which opened when the player brought the stop on. As soon as the
player released the lever or knob the springs closed the pallets, silencing
the register. Soundboards of this type were known as *spring-chests*. They
were seldom made outside Italy after the sixteenth century.

Keyboards and *compasses* evolved in response to the changing technology of soundboards and actions, and the desire of musicians to play
polyphony. It is not known whether keys were ever 'thumped' with the
whole fist as used to be suggested, but there can be little doubt that the
early organs with their crude engineering would require some force to
operate, whether the player pulled sliders or pressed keys. Theophilus's
organ had seven or eight notes operated by sliders. Over the next three
centuries compasses gradually expanded, the diatonic scale with B♭ added
to accommodate plainsong giving way after *c*1300 to (sometimes incomplete) chromatic compasses. By *c*1450 a compass of rather more than
three octaves (F–a^2) was widespread, though pitch varied greatly, and
some of these organs were undoubtedly transposing instruments. An
example was Anthony Duddyngton's new organ for All Hallows, Barking,
London (1519); the keyboard had C as its lowest key, but the note it
sounded was F (5′) or FF (10′). It is important to realise that compasses
and keyboards are not necessarily all that they appear to be in the years
before 1650, and sometimes later.

The introduction of pallets in place of sliders enabled organ-builders
to develop keyboards which could be both elegant in appearance and
subtle in action. The Halberstadt keys (Figure 1.2) perhaps represent a
transitional phase (the upper set still resemble the pull-push levers of
earlier illustrations) but another picture in Praetorius's *Syntagma*

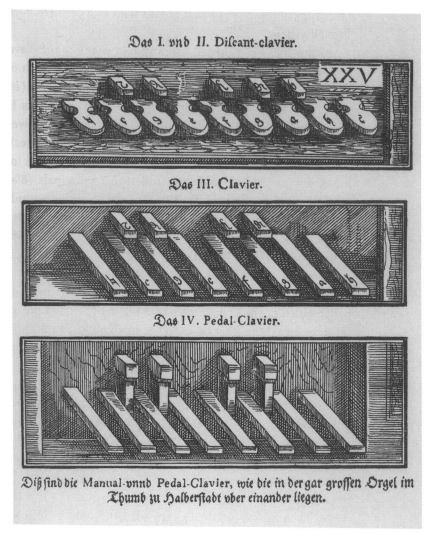

Figure 1.2 An illustration from Michael Praetorius's *Syntagma Musicum* of 1619, showing the manual and pedal keyboards of the organ at Halberstadt Cathedral, which he believed to date from the work of Faber in 1361.

musicum (Figure 1.3) shows a style of keyboard for the *Rückpositiv* at the Aegidienkirche, Brunswick (1456) which would not change radically before the nineteenth century.

Other significant developments included the appearance of new *pipe forms* including reeds (the earliest firm evidence is *c*1450) and wooden registers (possibly at a similar period, though equally possibly much earlier). In part this was due to increasing confidence in the manufacture of pipework, in part to the growing taste for novel tonal colours (in some regions, at least) to which Arnolt Schlick's *Spiegel der Orgelmacher und*

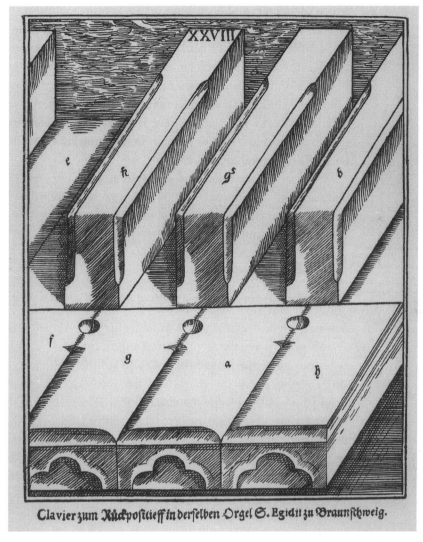

XXVIII

Clavier zum Rückpositieff in derselben Orgel S. Egidii zu Braunschweig.

Figure 1.3 The *Rückpositiv* keyboard of the organ at the Aegidienkirche in Brunswick (1456) from Praetorius's *Syntagma Musicum*; note that the keys approximate to the modern form.

Organisten (Mainz 1511) was later to bear impressive testimony. *Organ cases* probably began to appear in the thirteenth century (Williams 1993: 322–3). If organs were not located on the floor near the singers – as most positive organs were – they would be placed in wooden galleries from which the organist could command a view of the liturgical action (reflecting the organ's growing importance in liturgy). These instruments whether raised or at floor level required architectural treatment, and surviving cases such as those at Sion (*c*1435), the Jakobikirche, Lübeck (*c*1480) and San Petronio, Bologna (1474–83) illustrate the relish with which carpenters and decorative artists approached the task. The design of *bellows* must have been refined to meet the needs of the large organs being built by the mid-fifteenth century, though little is known about this. Small forge-bellows made of animal skins gave way to larger wedge-bellows with ribs and boards, raised by levers. Ropes seem also to have been used, but whatever the method, the fact that the wind was fed directly into the chest must have led to considerable unsteadiness of speech – a problem that was not overcome until the introduction of the reservoir in the eighteenth century.

Yet for all its imperfections, the technology of the early modern organ was essentially complete by *c*1450. It is a remarkable tribute to medieval enterprise and craftsmanship that no significant innovations in the basic design of the organ were made for the next three centuries.

The early modern organ (1500–1740)

Any scrutiny of organ schemes from the first half of the sixteenth century reveals great diversity of practice. Despite this, two 'families' of organ types can be distinguished. In Italy and southern France, organs with a single keyboard, spring chests and separately drawn registers were the norm; this 'southern' type was also influential in parts of Spain and southern Germany. In the north (the Netherlands, northern France, Scandinavia and much of Germany) larger organs with two or three keyboards, multiple chests, pedals, multi-ranked principal choruses and an extensive selection of colour stops – often imitations of other instruments – were common. (A variant of this 'northern' type was found in Spain during the years of Spanish rule in the Netherlands.)

The sixteenth century was a period of intense activity and bold experimentation in organ building. Builders explored, refined and extended the techniques of their medieval forebears to meet new demands. In many wealthy towns of northern Europe organs became status symbols, provided, maintained and played under the direction of the civic authorities; tonal novelties, daring mechanical layouts and splendid casework were deployed to add lustre to the town's reputation.

Organ builders often travelled widely in pursuit of work and new ideas. In particular, builders from the Low Countries – that cradle of European organ building – worked extensively outside their native region. Hendrik Niehoff built influential organs in Hamburg (1550) and Lüneburg (1552), Nicolaas Niehoff at Cologne (1573). Nicolaas Maas spent the majority of his working life (1590–1615) in Denmark. The Brebos family built important organs in Spain (1579–92) whilst Jan and

Matthijs Langhedul and Crespin Carlier laid the foundations of the French classical organ in the years to either side of 1600. Altogether, these Dutch and Flemish craftsmen had a vital influence on the regional schools of organ-building which (like the corresponding nation states) had begun to emerge before the end of the sixteenth century.

Organ-building was not unaffected by politics (the existence of the Habsburg Empire facilitated a free trade in ideas between craftsmen and artists within its borders). But it was more immediately and directly influenced by religious change – of which there was a great deal in the sixteenth and seventeenth centuries. The upheavals of the Protestant Reformation and Catholicism's spirited response, the Counter-Reformation, had profound implications for the role of the organ in worship (see below, Chapter 9). Design is driven by function, and the particular ecclesiastical demands of the different traditions played a major part in determining the character of regional organ schools.

This can be illustrated by comparing four different organ cultures.

The Netherlands experienced some destruction of organs in the riots of 1566, and more were removed from churches in succeeding years under the influence of the Calvinists. However, the fact that they were usually the property of the town helped to protect many organs, and although the Reformed Church at first refused to countenance their use in worship, in most towns they continued to be played before and after the service and in weekday recitals that had long been a feature of Dutch municipal life. So organs were built and repaired, and distinguished players such as J. P. Sweelinck were able to exploit the resources of the Dutch organ (weighty *plenum*; flutes, reeds and imitative registers in *Rugpositief* and *Bovenwerk*; Pedal solo stops) in variations on psalm tunes, decorated transcriptions of vocal pieces, and improvisations (Peeters and Vente 1971: 88–122).

In England, by contrast, the Puritans (radical Calvinists) had all but succeeded in having organs banned from churches in 1563. They failed, but organ building languished for most of Elizabeth's reign until the emergence in the 1590s of a party determined to restore something of 'the beauty of holiness' to the worship of the Established Church. The primary role of organs built under its influence was the accompaniment of the surviving cathedral and collegiate choirs in the daily services of Matins and Evensong. The instruments were correspondingly unadventurous. They lacked pedals, and relied instead on long manual compasses. Most had a single keyboard with five or six stops, though the occasional provision of a Chair Organ extended the scope a little. There were no mixtures, mutations or reeds, but duplication of chorus registers was usual. Such an instrument provided adequate accompaniment for a small group of singers and permitted the performance of short voluntaries – which was all that was required (Bicknell 1996: 69–90).

Lutheranism had no single view about the appropriateness of organ music in worship. Where it was permitted (perhaps the majority of Lutheran churches) the organist was encouraged to play preludes – sometimes at considerable length – before the congregation sang an unaccompanied chorale. Interluding between verses, *alternatim* performance, and choir accompaniment were also common requirements. The organs of northern and central Germany, with their large Pedal divisions, massive *plenums*, and subsidiary manuals stocked with flutes, mutations and reeds, equipped the organists for a multitude of liturgical tasks, and the strongly marked distinction of pitch, placement and tone between the different departments was particularly valuable in an instrument required to be so versatile.

The French organ also relied upon colour and contrast, but for different reasons. France had remained within the Catholic fold, and French organs were required to accompany the mass and other liturgical offices, performing music in which plainsong themes figured prominently. In particular, the organ performed movements of the mass in alternation with voices (see Chapter 9). Solo registrations were functionally important for 'bringing out' a plainsong theme (hence, for example, the *Tierce en taille*, the flûtes and trompettes 8′ of the Pédale, the popularity of the *Cornet* and the appearance of short-compass solo divisions – Écho and Récit – in the early seventeenth century) and rigid conventions grew up concerning the use of particular registrations for particular movements of the mass. 'Every stop in a French organ of about 1700 came to have an appointed purpose' (Williams and Owen 1988: 105) and this purpose was entirely dictated by liturgical use.

These brief summaries give an indication of the highly specific background to the emergence of regional schools of organ construction, design, composition and performance in post-Reformation Europe. They will be discussed more fully below, in relation to the repertoires. Many of the organ types they fostered came to maturity in the second half of the seventeenth century: the Hamburg *Werkprinzip* organ in the work of Arp Schnitger (*fl.* 1666–1719), the French classical organ at the hands of Pierre and Alexandre Thierry and Robert Clicquot (from the 1650s), the Spanish baroque organ with its horizontal reeds and echo organs made by various builders after 1680, and the English long-compass organ developed – in conscious rivalry with one another – by Bernard Smith and Renatus Harris during the 1670s and 80s. In other parts of Europe taste, relative affluence, liturgical priorities, musical innovation and news of developments elsewhere had an impact on local traditions. By 1700 a comparison of organs in leading European cities would reveal extraordinary contrasts of scale, disposition, effect and function, and yet, despite unmistakable regional characteristics and local preferences (suspended key actions in France, separate Pedal cases in Hamburg, *en chamade* reeds in Spain and Portugal) the *technology* of the organ remained essentially that inherited from the late-mediaeval builders. Some innovations had been tried (couplers, ventils, tremulants, toy stops, transmission) and, of course, tonally, the organ of 1700 was radically different from that of 1500 in many respects, but the technology was essentially the same and provided a foundation upon which the leading builders of the late seventeenth century raised regional organ cultures of great refinement and distinction.

In the period which was to follow, however, players and builders alike would increasingly feel its limitations.

The Golden Age, 1740–90

By the mid-eighteenth century, certain trends were manifesting themselves in many parts of Europe which serve to distinguish the period from what came before and anticipate developments in the nineteenth century. Inevitably, their impact varied considerably from one region to another, and some traditions changed only slowly (Holland after 1770) or scarcely at all (England before 1820). Yet in most places priorities shifted decisively between 1710 and 1750. Generalisations are dangerous, but it would not be too wide of the mark to say that in Protestant communities there was a desire for more power (perhaps in response to the increasing use of the organ in congregational accompaniment) whereas in Catholic areas the new taste was for colour effects – solo flutes, strings, undulating registers, imitative reeds, echo departments, percussion stops and other musical gadgetry. Both trends radically revised the balances between different departments of the organ (as compared with, for example, the classic *Werkprinzip* scheme) and the fashion for intensity of effect, supported by the growing practice – made possible by more resourceful wind systems – of drawing handfuls of stops all at once, led in many areas to the superseding of the discriminating registration practices of previous generations.

Although large organs were by no means unknown before the eighteenth century (Schnitger's 1687 organ for the Nicolaikirche, Hamburg had sixty-seven stops) the period saw the construction of numerous instruments which impress by their sheer size, tonal range, complexity of action and monumental visual effect. They are to be found across Europe.

Christian Müller's Haarlem organ (1735–8) with its sixty stops; the Hamburg Michaeliskirche (1762–7) by J. G. Hildebrandt with a 32′ front and fifteen-stop *Brustwerk*, François Thierry's five-manual for Notre Dame, Paris (1730–33); Christ Church, Spitalfields, London (Richard Bridge, 1730) with its sixteen-stop Great containing duplicated trumpets; Toledo Cathedral (José Verdalonga, 1796–7) with enclosed and unenclosed reeds from 32′ to 2′ pitch – these represent a breed of organ which, in the course of the eighteenth century, attained a novel degree of scale and sophistication.

Some of the most spectacular organs were those of southern Germany and Austria, particularly the organs of the great abbey churches. This was an area which had always favoured colour stops (Schlick's *Spiegel* is early evidence), and the taste was sustained by the requirement that the organist play quiet interludes at various points during the mass. The logical conclusion was an instrument like Gabler's *Chororgel* at Weingarten (1739): the eleven-stop *Hauptwerk* contained seven 8′ registers (Prinzipal, Violoncello, Salizional, Hohlflöte, Unda maris, Coppel and Quintatön), the second division was an Echo of 'quiet and pleasant stops', and (characteristically for this region) there was not a reed or mutation in sight. Gabler had the opportunity to expand his repertoire of fanciful colour stops when he built the west-end organ at Weingarten – including, for example, a flageolet of ivory, conical pipes made of cherrywood, bells and glittering multi-ranked mixtures – but its fame is as much due to its astonishing visual effect, the cases appearing suspended in mid-air, supported by cherubim and angels, and surrounded by light from the windows behind (see Figure 5.11).

Gabler's concern with colour, and his desire to make the organ a more flexible musical instrument, was reflected elsewhere in Europe. Even in Protestant regions the period saw a move towards subtlety, refinement and tonal variety which in some instances (G. Silbermann at Freiberg, 1710–14; J. Moreau at Gouda, 1733–6) involved drawing on French ideas. In all but the most conservative areas less and less importance was attached to providing balanced choruses in all departments; 'terracing' of dynamics offered the possibility of those dramatic contrasts for which a taste steadily developed during the course of the century. The same taste was the ultimate beneficiary of Jordan's 'invention' of the Swell (St Magnus the Martyr, London Bridge, 1712); this offered the prospect of greater expressiveness – initially for a handful of short-compass stops, later for the entire organ (Samuel Green at St George's Chapel, Windsor, 1790) – and other peripheral traditions (Italy, Spain) also experimented with echoes, swells and tonal novelties.

Power, too, was increasingly sought. When in 1738 J. C. Müller rebuilt the 1724 Vater organ in the Oude Kerk, Amsterdam he took steps to improve the wind supply, increased the pressures, doubled chorus ranks in the treble, added further ranks to the mixtures, re-made the reeds and added stops to strengthen the *plenum*. Perhaps Vater's organ was not a very good organ anyway. But these were the sorts of changes builders were making all over Europe in order to enhance the organ's power. The Bavokerk at Haarlem (1735–8) with its big mixtures and more chorus reeds than would have been found a generation earlier is indicative of the same trend, and Zacharias Hildebrandt's Naumburg organ (1743–6) – approved (perhaps inspired) by J.S. Bach – is remarkable for its strength of tone (especially in the bass) allied to brilliant mixtures and solid reeds. But then Hildebrandt was a pupil of Gottfried Silbermann, who at the Dresden Hofkirche (1754) specified a *Hauptwerk* of 'large and heavy scaling' to be supported by a 'forceful and penetrating' Pedal. Even in the rather different circumstances of France, where organs were not required to accompany hearty congregational singing, the introduction of the Bombarde division (Notre Dame, Paris, 1733), the doubling of 8′ Trompettes, the addition of 8′ and 4′ chorus reeds to the Positif, and the gradual expansion of the Pédale bore witness to similar priorities.

All of this testifies to the emergence of preoccupations which were to become central to the evolution of the organ in the nineteenth century.

The triumph of technology (1790–1890)

By the end of the eighteenth centry, the aspirations of the builders had overtaken the available technology. The Weingarten organ, for instance, with its five manual and two pedal departments strewn (apparently effortlessly) across the west end of the church, and played from what may have been the world's first permanent detached console, must have presented formidable problems of action layout to its builder. It was to be another century before the technology was invented which would assist organ-builders in managing long tracker runs to huge soundboards, and a further generation on from that before builders were released altogether from the need to connect keys to pallets with levers and rods.

Priority in introducing the pneumatic lever is disputed (Thistlethwaite 1990: 351–7) but there is no doubt that it was the Englishman C. S. Barker and the great French builder Aristide Cavaillé-Coll who first brought it to a reliable form. It was used in Cavaillé-Coll's earliest triumph, the organ for St Denis (1841), in which pneumatic motors, located between key and pallet pull-down, assisted what was otherwise a complete tracker system, enabling the builder to increase the number of chests and raise wind pressures. Pneumatic levers were widely used in the largest organs in France, England and Germany within three decades. The next development was tubular-pneumatic action, in which the motion of the player was transmitted not by way of wooden rods but by air under pressure travelling through lead tubes and inflating motors connected to the pallet pull-downs. (An early but imperfect version was made by P. Moitessier during the 1840s.) By freeing the builder to arrange chests, console and mechanism in hitherto unconventional ways, this form of action was of the greatest use to a builder such as the Englishman Henry Willis (1821–1901), confronted with an organist's demand for a large organ and the architect's refusal to accommodate it. By pioneering the division of a cathedral organ on either side of the choir at St Paul's, London in 1872, Willis at once overcame a difficulty and created an opportunity for abuse which other builders and players were quick to exploit. The system was popular in England, where it was extensively made between 1875 and 1925. Electric action was the next logical step. The possibility of using electro-magnets to open pallets had been recognised as early as the 1840s by Wilkinson, an English builder, but it was not until the collaboration of Péschard and Barker in the 1860s that a workable electro-pneumatic system was made. Organs powered entirely by electric actions appeared in Paris and London in 1868, and New York in 1869. Electric action became particularly important in the USA through the pioneering work of Hilborne Roosevelt (1849–86); by the 1890s most companies were experimenting with it, and it was in the States that Robert Hope-Jones (1859–1914) found the welcome for his improved electric action that had been largely denied him in England.

A revealing snapshot of the state of organ technology in the 1880s is afforded by a comparison of three instruments that competed for the title of 'the largest organ in the world'. E. F. Walcker's 124-stop organ for the Riga Dom (1883) had mechanical action with some assistance from pneumatic levers. Roosevelt's 114-stop instrument for the Cathedral of the Incarnation, Garden City, Long Island (also completed in 1883) had rather more than half its stops on electric action, whilst Hill & Son's *magnum opus*, Sydney Town Hall (1889), with 126 stops and the famous 64′ reed, had mechanical coupling, pneumatic levers to the Great and tubular-pneumatic action to all other departments.

Innovation equipped the builders of the nineteenth century with the technology they needed to pursue objectives (power, dramatic contrasts, orchestral registrations, proliferation of chests, detached keyboards, the physical separation of divisions of the organ) already to be identified in the most ambitious instruments of the previous century. Console gadgetry, novel soundboards (e.g. the German *Kegellade*, or cone chest), steam-powered, hydraulic or electric blowing machines, horizontal bellows to steady the wind (widely used in England after 1800), dispersion of reservoirs throughout the organ, ventils (for admitting or denying wind to selected chests and fundamental to an understanding of the French nineteenth-century organ), pneumatic thumb pistons (patented by Henry Willis in 1851 and equally essential to an understanding of the English organ of the period), relief pallets to reduce the weight of touch, crescendo pedals (including the *Rollschweller*, implied in many of Reger's registrations), sforzando pedals – these, and a multitude of other 'improvements' provided the technological foundation upon which to erect a nineteenth-century organ aesthetic. It represented a considerable achievement – the transformation of a technology little altered in funda-mentals for three centuries – but at a price: although the organist had greater resources at his command and more control over registration, he had less control over key touch and might (particularly in England and the USA) be separated by a considerable distance from the sound-pro-ducing parts of his instrument.

The musical character of the organ which this technology made possi-ble paradoxically expressed both the fulfilment of the ideals of pro-gressive eighteenth-century builders and their eclipse. E. F. Walcker's important organ for the Paulskirche, Frankfurt (1827–33) continued the fashion for massive choruses with thickening quints, a 32′ *Hauptwerk* and solid reeds. The fourteen-stop Swell and the generous provision of south German colour stops (strings, dulcianas and flutes) is a further link with tradition. However, the free reeds and Pedal mutations owe something to the 'simplification system' pedalled around Europe by the Abbé Vogler in the 1780s and 90s, and the divided Pedal section (with two pedal boards, one above the other) served a contemporary preoccupation with dynamic variation. Other German builders might prefer more conservative tonal schemes (J. F. Schulze, Marienkirche, Lübeck, 1858; F. Ladegast, Merseburg Cathedral, 1855) but Walcker's Frankfurt organ sketched the lines along which German organ-building would run in the nineteenth century and foreshadowed the firm's later mammoth organs for Ulm (1856), Boston (1863) and Riga (1883).

In England, something more radical was needed. Under the influence of the Bach revival on the one hand, and the taste for orchestral transcrip-tions on the other, William Hill (1789–1870) introduced the 'German System' organ – an instrument with C-compasses, 16′ manual choruses and a comprehensive Pedal Organ. Tonally, it represented a fusion of traditional English choruses, 'German' flutes and strings, and modern reeds. The latter included Hill's invention, the ophicleide or tuba mirabilis – a solo reed of commanding power, speaking on around 10″

wind pressure (Birmingham Town Hall, 1840). Other builders looked to France for inspiration (Gray & Davison at the Crystal Palace, 1857) until Henry Willis finally solved the quest for power and orchestral colour with his organs for the Alexandra Palace (1868) and the Royal Albert Hall (1871).

The organ built by Cavaillé-Coll for St Denis still owed much to the French classical tradition. Five years later (1846), at La Madeleine, Paris, the debt was much less apparent. The proliferation of harmonic stops (flutes and reeds), the inclusion of strings and a céleste, the disappearance of cornets and mutations, the transformation of the Positif into a mixtureless colour department, and the provision of ventils for the various *jeux de combinaison* all pointed to the romantic-symphonic organ of the 1850s and 60s. With its immaculately blended *jeux de fonds*, peerless reeds (harmonic, and with varying pressures throughout the range), luxurious consoles and finely engineered actions, this instrument has good claim to be regarded as the summit of the nineteenth-century organ-building achievement, not least because (unlike Willis's instruments) it inspired a school of distinguished organist-composers.

Epilogue: the romantic twilight (1890–1950)

It may seem both churlish and arbitrary to dismiss several decades of European and American organ building in what must appear little more than an addendum. The fact remains, however, that by the 1890s influences were making themselves felt which increasingly separated the organ from much of its legitimate repertoire. Hope-Jones's reduction of the organ to a series of extreme tonalities controlled from an electric console bristling with accessories prepared the way for the cinema organ. G. A. Audsley's *The Art of Organ-Building* (New York 1905) revelled in the *minutiae* of the voicing, construction and design of the romantic organ, whilst asserting the desirability of extensive enclosure including even a portion of the Pedal. On both sides of the Atlantic, builders exploited the technical possibilities of electric action, among them, the construction of unit chests enabling one set of pipes to be made available at several pitches. (It was in the tradition of Vogler and his 'simplification system', and appealed to factory organ builders anxious to build cheap organs.)

Some leading firms of the nineteenth century continued to build distinguished organs in their respective house styles – Hill in London, Cavaillé-Coll (under Mutin) in Paris, Sauer in Frankfurt among them. For them all, the First World War proved a watershed. Others endeavoured to take the romantic-orchestral organ on a stage further from the work of the great nineteenth-century masters. In England, Harrison & Harrison dominated the scene, whilst on the other side of the Atlantic, Ernest M. Skinner and John T. Austin developed a more thoroughgoing orchestral instrument. Yet despite the undoubted integrity of the best organs of this period there were those who felt that the true nature of the organ had become obscured. Albert Schweitzer was one of the first, and the views he expressed in the early 1900s paved the way for that gradual and often painful recovery of 'true principles' which is discussed in Chapter 6.

2 Organ construction

Stephen Bicknell

The craft of organ building remains today essentially the same as it was during the development of the organ in the middle ages. Although machinery can be employed to save time and perform repetitive tasks, the core crafts of woodwork and metalwork remain at the heart of the industry. Moreover, although the metal pipes are the most distinctive feature of an organ, it is the wooden structure of the instrument that absorbs the bulk of the organ builder's time and effort. Wood remains an astonishingly useful and versatile material. Weight for weight, it is stronger than steel. Despite the alarming deforestation of the planet, a conscientious workshop can find supplies of many different species and grades of timber from renewable sources. Timber is the ideal material for custombuilding anything; with relatively simple equipment it can be formed into virtually any shape and adapted to almost any purpose – including, in organ building, complex air-tight components containing many moving parts.

The structure of an organ consists of a frame (usually still of solid timber, though some builders use steel) and a case. Very often, especially in small instruments or those inspired by historic precedent, the frame and case are integrated in a monocoque structure. In the Anglo-American tradition of the nineteenth and early twentieth centuries organ builders did not concern themselves much with casework – its design often left to architects and its construction to specialist joiners – but still used wood for supporting framework. Even an organ with no case, such as those built by Walter Holtkamp and others with the pipes on open display (midtwentieth century) will still have the familiar wooden structure within.

The various components that occupy the interior of the instrument can take many forms, and have been subject to continuing change and development during the course of the organ's long history.

We may start with the lungs of the organ – its winding system. An organ requires a copious supply of air at a pressure only a little higher than that of the atmosphere. Organ wind is typically at only about 50 to 100 mm water-gauge. Supplying an organ with enough air has never been a great problem (even a large eighteenth-century organ could be blown by two or three men at the feeder bellows); but finding a way of making the supply steady has been more of a challenge.

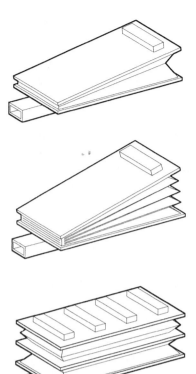

Figure 2.1 Three types of bellows commonly found. From top to bottom: single-fold diagonal bellows typical of northern Europe in the seventeenth and eighteenth centuries; multi-fold diagonal bellows typical of classical practice in France and the south; the horizontal bellows with inverted folds developed in England round 1800 and used extensively thereafter in many countries.

Weighted diagonal or 'wedge' bellows, filled one after the other and allowed to drop under their own weight, are the traditional solution (Figure 2.1). Almost universal until the mid-nineteenth century, they are now being made again, especially in organs designed for the performance of pre-romantic music. The musical results of using diagonal bellows vary a great deal, but their inherent unsteadiness is not always a defect, and at its best the slight fluctuations in pressure and therefore pitch give a beautiful and complex result not unlike the sound of many players in an instrumental ensemble.

The English developed the horizontal bellows in the early nineteenth century, and it is the preferred winding system for instruments catering for the romantic repertoire. The horizontal bellows is more properly a reservoir, used for storing wind supplied by feeder bellows or a blowing motor. With this system it becomes possible to supply wind at different pressures to different parts of the organ: a reservoir weighted to provide the highest pressure required in the organ can be connected to others via control valves reducing the pressure by stages. Horizontal reservoirs may be found in single-rise and double-rise forms, the latter usually having one set of ribs folding inwards and one outwards, cancelling out the tendency of the pressure to drop as the bellows collapses. The wind supply may be further steadied by the introduction of small *concussion bellows* or *winkers* (Am.) on the wind trunks; these are small sprung bellows that act as shock absorbers.

The development of more sensitive control valves for the wind system has made it possible to reduce the size of reservoirs, and ultimately to install them as compact wind regulator units in the soundboard or chest itself. The most commonly used of these is the *schwimmer* regulator, popular with most European neo-classical builders at one time or another over the last forty years. The schwimmer regulator gives, at low cost, a wind supply of astonishing steadiness; so steady in fact as to be considered lifeless and mechanical by some builders, who have therefore retained, or re-introduced, traditional bellows or reservoir systems.

Today wind for an organ is rarely supplied by mechanical labour; the task is usually performed by an electric motor driving a fan.

Each manual or pedal keyboard is usually represented by a separate *soundboard* or *chest* (Am.) inside the organ. On this stand the various ranks of pipes representing the stops brought into play by the performer. Each receives wind at the appropriate pressure for that division. Inside the soundboard there is a valve or *pallet* for each note on the keyboard: the linkage between pallet and key is the *key action*. When a key is pressed, the pallet opens and wind is admitted to a channel corresponding to that note. When the key is released a spring under the pallet closes it and raises the key again.

On each soundboard there must be a mechanism for isolating or silencing individual ranks to allow the performer to choose which he wishes to sound and which to remain silent. The traditional and most widespread system is that provided by slider soundboards (Figure 2.2). The pallet admits wind to a channel that supplies all the pipes for that note. Each rank is arranged in note order over the channels in the soundboard. A perforated slider between the top of the soundboard or *table* and the *upperboards* or *toeboards* (Am.) is linked to the stop knob, and can be moved so that it either admits wind to the pipes above (on) or prevents them from speaking (off).

In a large or complex organ there may be more than one soundboard per division, as well as subsidiary chests, all of which require their own mechanism. Alternatives to the slider soundboard are the archaic *spring chest*, found especially in the organs of Italy, and various forms of *sliderless chest*. Sliderless chests – in which every pipe has its own valve linked to the key action for that note and in which the ranks are brought into play by admitting wind to a channel for that stop – were developed in the nine-

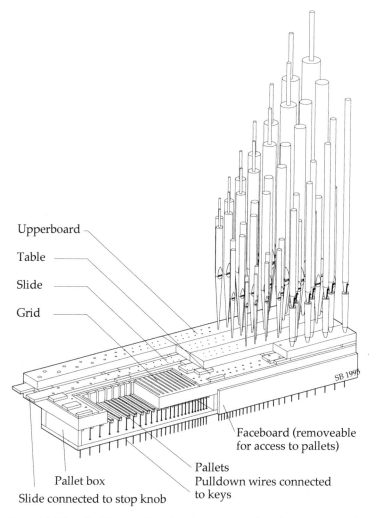

Upperboard
Table
Slide
Grid

SB 1995

Faceboard (removeable
for access to pallets)

Pallets
Pulldown wires connected
to keys

Pallet box
Slide connected to stop knob

Figure 2.2 View of a slider soundboard partly cut away to show the construction. The example shown has four slides, one for each of the following stops (from back to front): Chimney Flute 8′, Principal 4′, Octave 2′, Krummhorn 8′. The pipes in this example are arranged in diatonic order, the basses at the ends and the trebles in the middle. Only the pipes of the lowest notes on one side are shown.

teenth century, the best-known early type being the cone-valve chest or *Kegellade* introduced by E. F. Walcker of Ludwigsburg. Through the nineteenth and early twentieth centuries further types of sliderless chest were devised, many of them to patent designs. Other well known types are the *Roosevelt* chest, named after the American organ builder Hilborne Roosevelt (1849–86) who invented it, and the *Pitman* chest, developed by E. M. Skinner around 1900 and still highly prized in parts of the American organ building industry.

Though it is possible to link the many small valves in a sliderless chest

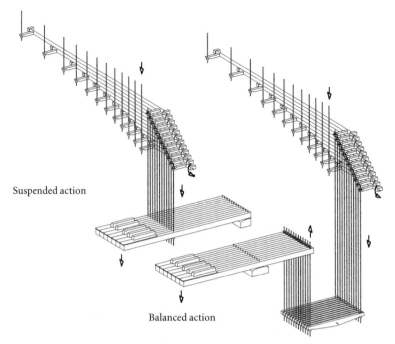

Figure 2.3 The two main types of mechanical key action. Left: suspended action, with the key pivoted at the tail and the action pick-up forward of the half-way point. Right: balanced action, with the key pivoted near the centre and the action pick-up at the tail. The use of a rollerboard between the keys and the soundboard allows the notes to be spread into a more convenient spacing or order.

with a mechanical action this is in fact rarely done, and the use of sliderless chests usually presupposes a non-mechanical key action. The slider chest is difficult to design and make and, until the use of man-made materials in its construction became practical and widespread after *c*1950, it was not well suited to extremes of temperature and humidity. However, the provision of one channel per note is considered to assist blend and, of course, automatically gives absolute unanimity of speech. The sliderless chest is cheaper and allows a much faster stop-action; it is typically associated with late romantic instruments where quick changes of registration are considered desirable.

The key action provides the link between keyboard and soundboard (Figure 2.3). At its most simple, the key is pivoted at the tail. From the key a wire or wooden *tracker* rises directly to the pallet. This is known as *suspended action*. If the spacing of the pallets on the soundboard is wider than the keyboard, then the trackers may need to be fanned or splayed. If, as in all but the smallest organs, the pipes on the soundboard are arranged symmetrically, rather than in chromatic order, then a *rollerboard* is needed to transfer the movement laterally and rearrange it into soundboard order.

Suspended action is associated with particular types of organ: early instruments in general, and the organs of the French, Spanish and Italian classical schools. It is used today by some builders who appreciate its simplicity and the precise and responsive touch it offers.

It is also possible to provide a key pivoted in the middle, with the key action picking up off the tail: a *balanced action*. From the key tail the movement is transferred via a tracker or sticker to a row of levers or *backfalls* to the soundboard. Again there may be a rollerboard if required. Mechanical key actions of the balanced or suspended types may be made to change direction by introducing further sets of backfalls or *squares* (small bell-cranks). The pedal keys, where provided, operate in a similar way to the manuals. Further developments include *couplers*, making it possible to play two separate departments from one keyboard.

In the middle of the nineteenth century it became possible to harness the power of the wind already in the organ to assist the key action: especially useful in large organs where the key action was becoming increasingly heavy. At first, pneumatic power was used in conjunction with mechanical linkages: the *pneumatic lever* or *Barker lever*. Here the mechanical action from the keys admits wind via a valve to a small pneumatic power bellows or *motor*. This is connected in turn to the soundboard pallet by mechanical linkages. The appearance is essentially similar to an all-mechanical action, only the bank of pneumatic motors or *Barker machine* interrupting the link between key and soundboard.

Replacing the mechanical linkages with small-bore tubing – the message travelling down the tube as a charge of air – gave late-nineteenth century builders much greater flexibility in arranging the internal components of the organ. Such systems were understood in the early nineteenth century, but did not start appearing regularly until the end of the 1860s, usually still in conjunction with mechanical couplers. By the mid-1880s the English builders were developing all-tubular actions in which even the couplers were pneumatically actuated. This tubular pneumatic action comes in many different forms, each builder developing his own system. Broadly speaking the various types may be divided into charge pneumatic actions – the earlier, simpler variety – and exhaust pneumatic actions – more complex and arguably more sophisticated. In the charge action pressing the key admits air under pressure to the tube, and this charge operates a small bellows or *pneumatic motor* that opens the pallet. In the exhaust system the key opens a valve at the end of the tube allowing a motor enclosed in the wind at the other end to be exhausted to the atmosphere, causing it to collapse and open the pallet as before. Intervening small motors or *relays* are used to improve speed and repetition.

As a result of much experiment in the second half of the nineteenth century it eventually became possible to replace the pneumatic tubing with an electric cable: by 1900 electro-pneumatic actions (the opening of the pallet still effected by a pneumatic motor) were being attempted on a regular basis. Their success depended on the use of precision-made magnets in which the armature acted also as the valve of the primary pneumatic; on the use of low voltages which made low demands on batteries (until they were replaced by generators); and on the development of self-cleaning key contacts. All-electric key action has always been rare, being mostly restricted to very small organs and one or two American firms who have made a speciality of the technique. In the heyday of electro-pneumatic action, from 1920 to 1960, it became usual for almost all the mechanical functions of the organ to be carried out through electrical switchgear, even if the final stages of the movement remained pneumatic.

Since 1960 there has been a considerable revival of the use of all-mechanical actions. The application of modern engineering to the design of pallets and to the development of low-friction bearings has made it possible to provide all-mechanical actions even in quite large instruments without producing an unduly heavy touch, though sometimes the quality of touch is maintained by using pneumatic assistance (*balancers*) in the bass. A limited number of builders resort to electric action for the manual couplers. A further refinement in modern times has been the introduction of self-regulating actions, which are able to react to changes in climatic conditions, taking up the slack in the key action as the major components expand and contract with changes in temperature and humidity.

The stop action links the stop knobs at the keys with the soundboards or chests within, allowing different ranks of pipes to be brought into play. A simple mechanical system of squares and rods may be used. With such systems it is possible to introduce a limited range of devices to allow groups of stops to be changed quickly, usually by pressing a pedal. Amongst these are registration devices found in Iberia, where stops on subsidiary chests may be silenced by pressing a pedal controlling a single isolating slider; similar devices are found in England where they were called *shifting movements*. The more elaborate French *ventil* system works in a similar way; individual sections of the organ have wind admitted to them only when the appropriate *pédale de combinaison* is pressed, allowing new registrations to be prepared in advance and brought into play when required. A *composition pedal* is usually a mechanical device that moves the stop knobs according to certain pre-determined combinations.

The introduction of pneumatics allowed further refinements. By 1851

Willis in England had developed a pneumatic stop action in which rapid changes of registration could be effected at the press of a button or *thumb piston,* mounted in the keyslip; this system is now widespread. By 1890 some organs were provided with a limited kind of memory system, allowing the organist to reset the combination of stops brought into play by combination pedals or pistons. The advent of electro-pneumatic mechanisms allowed much more sophisticated systems for stop changing, and all-electric adjustable combinations become a feature during the 1930s, eventually to be transistorised in the 1960s and finally reduced to programmable silicon chips in the 1980s. There is now a movement in some quarters towards the simplicity and reliability of all-mechanical systems.

Keys, pedals, stops all meet under the player's control at the *console* or *keydesk*; simple in early organs, but increasingly complex after 1850 and in those modern instruments not specifically built in imitation of historic styles. With the advent of pneumatic and electro-pneumatic actions it has become possible to detach the console from the organ itself (as well as spreading the instrument into different and sometimes unlikely parts of the building); the console then becomes a highly sophisticated piece of apparatus in its own right.

In English organs from 1712 onwards an important feature has been the *swell box,* completely enclosing one or more soundboards and the pipes that stand on them (probably derived from similar though more simple devices in Spanish and Portuguese organs). The front of the swell box consists of movable shutters connected to a pedal, allowing the organist to make the sound louder or softer. The use of the swell spread to the rest of the organ-building world in the nineteenth century and is now a widespread feature. The obvious value of such a device in performing romantic music means that instruments that are built for the perfomance of a wide repertoire may have two or more departments enclosed. In the large, sprawling organs found in parts of the English-speaking world, especially North America, enclosure in swell boxes may extend to almost all divisions of the organ.

Finally, the pipes. From the middle ages the most common material for organ pipes has been an amalgam (not strictly speaking an alloy) of tin and lead, sometimes with traces of other metals such as bismuth, copper or antimony. An alloy with a high proportion of tin is hard and can be polished, especially useful for front pipes. Pipe metal is cast in sheets, usually on a stone casting bench. The parts of the pipe are cut out of the sheet, beaten into shape round a former or *mandrel,* and then soldered together. Pipes can also be made out of wood, again with the possibility of choosing a particular species of timber to help in the production of a particular tone quality. Metal pipes are also sometimes made of zinc or copper,

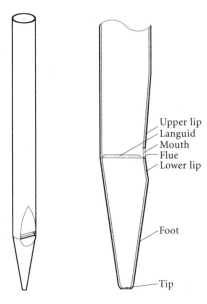

Upper lip
Languid
Mouth
Flue
Lower lip

Foot

Tip

Figure 2.4 A typical open flue pipe of the principal family. Left: general view. Right: section through mouth and foot.

usually with an eye to economy, and other materials as diverse as glass, ivory, aluminium and paper have occasionally been used.

The backbone of organ sound is a chorus of cylindrical open metal pipes (Figure 2.4) playing at various different pitches from each key. The principal chorus of the modern organ is distantly descended from the medieval *Blockwerk*. Perhaps related to the early medieval practice of sung *organum*, a melody sung in parallel fourths or fifths, perhaps because of an intuitive understanding of the rudiments of harmonics, the *Blockwerk* chorus might include ranks pitched at the fifth as well as unisons and octaves. As the scale ascended and it became more difficult to make small pipes for the higher-pitched ranks, these might break back to lower pitches duplicating other ranks. The various pipes at different pitches reinforced the natural harmonic structure of the unison: the complex interplay of harmonic corroboration between pipes harmonically related to one another is one of the most characteristic features of organ sound.

Once the development of soundboard mechanisms allowed the *Blockwerk* to be split up into individual ranks, these would each represent a particular pitch: unison, octave, octave quint, superoctave etc. Remaining high partials might be grouped together as a *Mixture* stop, each key playing a cluster of small pipes. In a modern organ each rank is identified by a characteristic name and by the length in feet of the speaking part of the longest pipe in the rank, indicating its pitch. Unison pitch on the modern keyboard, with C as its lowest note, is described as 8′ pitch, and this standard is almost universal today, though other pitches were once current and are important to the earlier English organ. Note that a second pipe twice as long as the first will have a frequency half that of the first, sounding exactly an octave lower; thus the use of length to identify pitch is easy to understand at a glance. A simple organ chorus might consist of:

Principal	8′	Unison = first partial
Octave	4′	One octave higher = second partial
Quint	$2\frac{2}{3}$′	One octave and a fifth higher = third partial
Superoctave	2′	Two octaves higher = fourth partial
Mixture	IV	Four pipes per note, various harmonics

The Mixture, following the pattern of the early *Blockwerk*, will emphasise high harmonics at the low end of the keyboard; as the notes ascend these may break back successively to lower harmonics, duplicating the other pitches. A scheme for the four-rank mixture shown above might be:

C–B 12 notes				$1\frac{1}{3}$′	1′	$\frac{2}{3}$′	$\frac{1}{2}$′
c–b 12 notes			2′	$1\frac{1}{3}$′	1′	$\frac{2}{3}$′
c¹–b¹ 12 notes		$2\frac{2}{3}$′	2′	$1\frac{1}{3}$′	1′
c²–b² 12 notes	4′	$2\frac{2}{3}$′	2′	$1\frac{1}{3}$′
c²–top note	8′	4′	$2\frac{2}{3}$′	2′

As well as unisons and quints it is also possible to introduce third-sound ranks or *tierces*, representing the fifth harmonic in the series. Sub-unisons are also common. Other more remote harmonics, especially the seventh and ninth partials, have been explored in the twentieth century.

During the middle ages considerable effort was expended on developing new pipe forms to answer the demand for variety of timbre. Pipes might be made tapered rather than cylindrical. It was found that by stopping the end of a pipe it could be made to sound an octave lower than an open pipe of the same length, with a change in the tone (we now know that the harmonic structure of a single stopped pipe includes only the odd-numbered partials). The use of different alloys or even of wood further varied the possibilities.

To these *flue* pipes, whether open or stopped, were added *reed* pipes (Figure 2.5), in which a brass tongue vibrating against an opening in a tube (the *shallot*) generates the sound, amplified and controlled by a *resonator*.

The extensive variety of pipe forms thus produced (Figure 2.6) required a vast repertoire of names, some practical, some fanciful. Many are descriptive of a supposed comparison to another instrument: thus amongst the flue stops we find various kinds of flute; amongst the reeds *Trumpet*, *Bassoon* or *Fagott*, *Oboe* and *Krummhorn*, and even the *Vox*

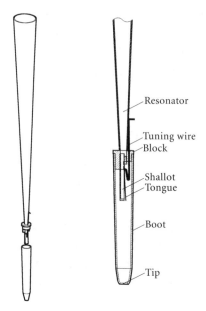

Resonator

Tuning wire
Block

Shallot
Tongue

Boot

Figure 2.5 A typical reed pipe of the Trumpet family. Left: general view with the boot removed; right: section through boot, block and base of resonator showing shallot, tongue and tuning wire in position.

Tip

humana. Other names are descriptive of form – the *Chimney Flute* or *Rohrflöte* has indeed got a chimney on each pipe; some are evocative (*Tuba mirabilis, Voix célestes*); others esoteric (*Terpodion, Zauberflöte*); some mysterious (*Vox Candida; Omphiangelon*). Nomenclature has no recognised limits, and beyond identifying the characteristic traditions of each organ-building nation there is little in the way of taxonomic science at work.

The precise manufacturing dimensions of the pipes may be varied almost infinitely, and the art of determining details of form, construction and especially diameter of pipes from bass to treble, or from one rank to another, is known as *scaling*. This has always required a degree of appreciation of mathematics, even at a time when literacy itself was not taken for granted.

The organ builder has a free hand in deciding what stops or ranks of pipes to provide in an organ. He may draw up a list of stops or specification that reflects current fashion, the intended use of the organ he is building and his own artistic intentions.

When the pipes are put into the organ, they are *voiced*: the exact tone and speech of each must be adjusted and balanced with the rest of the organ. The scaling of the pipes will determine certain broad features of the sound – for example the diameters of the pipes, the width of the mouths compared to the diameters, and so on. Pipes of a large relative diameter will give a broader sound and/or greater power; pipes of a smaller diameter will be keener in sound and/or softer. Decisions about

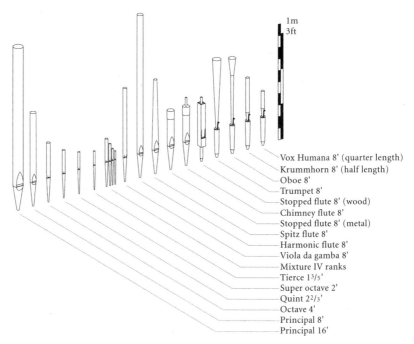

1m
3ft

Vox Humana 8' (quarter length)
Krummhorn 8' (half length)
Oboe 8'
Trumpet 8'
Stopped flute 8' (wood)
Chimney flute 8'
Stopped flute 8' (metal)
Spitz flute 8'
Harmonic flute 8'
Viola da gamba 8'
Mixture IV ranks
Tierce 1^3/$_5$'
Super octave 2'
Quint 2^2/$_3$'
Octave 4'
Principal 8'
Principal 16'

Figure 2.6 Various forms of organ pipe. All the pipes shown play c^1 (middle c) – the length, in feet, given after the name of an organ stop indicates the nominal length at the lowest note on the keyboard, C.

wind-pressure, the layout of the pipes in the organ and the position of the organ in the building will also have a significant impact. The process of voicing allows considerable further leeway in determining the finished sound, as well as adding a final polish to the instrument. As pipe metal is soft and can easily be bent or cut with a knife, adjustments are physically quite easy to make, though requiring great skill of hand, eye and ear. The precise height to which the mouth of a flue pipe is cut in relation to the width is a vital factor – the *cut-up*. The vast repertoire of voicing techniques includes manipulation of the upper and lower lips, the languid and the foot-hole, chamfering the upper lip, nicking the languid and/or lower lip, introducing slots of various dimensions near the top of the pipe, and so on. All these techniques are for flue pipes: reeds have their own extensive battery of voicing methods, much attention being lavished on the proportions and shape of the shallot and the exact thickness, hardness and curvature of the brass tongue, as well as on the form, scale and length of the resonator.

As the voicing progresses the pipes will be brought gradually nearer to their final pitch, until they are finely tuned. At its simplest, pipes are flattened by making them longer, sharpened by making them shorter. This may also be achieved on smaller open pipes by hitting them with a brass cone: flaring the end of the pipe sharpens; closing the end of the pipe flattens. Tuning may also be achieved with flaps, caps, cylindrical tuning slides and slots. Stopped pipes are tuned by moving the stopper or by shading the mouth with soft metal *ears*. Reeds are tuned at the tuning spring on the tongue, though the exact length of the resonator is also important in securing the right pitch and tone, and some resonators are equipped with some form of regulation.

In a large organ of several thousand pipes it will be appreciated that the possibilities afforded by the design of the organ and its specification, its layout and construction, and the materials, scaling and voicing of the pipes are almost endless. From this bottomless store of variety and invention arises the fact that no two organs are remotely similar to each other. The organ builder creates a completely individual and new musical instrument at every attempt. Herein lies the enduring fascination of the organ and the special importance of its history.

3 The physics of the organ

John Mainstone

Introduction

The ancient Greek philosopher Zeno of Citium (*c*335–263 BC) tells us that the reason we have two ears and only one mouth is so that we may hear more and speak less. We could dismiss this utterance from the founder of the Stoics in Athens as mere wishful thinking on the part of one who argued that the elements of physics and logic must serve the element of ethics; we might even declare it to be rubbish! Paradoxically, there are some grains of truth in his statement. Two ears do hear more than one; we experience *binaural summation*. At least for moderate intensities, a sound heard in two ears at once does seem to be about twice as loud as the same sound heard in one ear only. Our hearing system must obviously be 'wired' differently from our seeing system – closing one eye does not change the brightness of the scene in front of us. Nevertheless, binaural summation really has little to do with the main purpose of the two-eared system we have inherited.

We have two ears so that we may hear more, but in the late twentieth century AD the word 'more' has to be interpreted in a subtle way. Our ears allow us to use, quite unconsciously, very small time differences (and, at high frequencies, intensity differences) associated with the binaural reception of sound, for location and discrimination within a complex acoustic environment. A solo violin or clarinet represents a localised source of sound for the listener, who is able to recognise the particular type of instrument through its tone quality or timbre. The whole orchestra acts as a distributed source, with a number of different mechanisms (bowing, striking, blowing and so on) contributing to the production of the total sound output. Each mechanism tends to have a characteristic initial transient, which assists the ear–brain system in its identification of the source.

The organ must also be regarded as a distributed source, even if the pipes are confined to one organ case, but the basic mechanism for sound production is the same throughout the instrument – blowing. The array of open and stopped pipes, some metal and some made of wood, which constitutes the organ is able to produce sounds possessing a very impressive range of timbre. Our ear–brain system allows us to make a distinction between the sound from flue pipes and reed pipes, and within the flue-pipe family between diapason, flute and so-called *string* pipes.

Over the years many different materials have been tried in the construction of organ pipes. It has been found that what is of prime importance is high mechanical rigidity of the pipe walls, resulting in negligible sound radiation from them when the pipe speaks; the material itself has only a minor effect on the tone quality of the pipe. Such rigid pipe walls will also produce minimal disturbance to the acoustic standing wave pattern in the pipe, which is integral to the pipe excitation. A rectangular pipe constructed from thin metal will generally not satisfy this criterion, even though a cylindrical pipe made of the same material does so. For rectangular pipes the organ builder uses thick wooden walls, of well-seasoned timber. The tin-lead alloys sometimes known as 'organ metal' (having a range of about 30–90 per cent tin) which are used for most metal pipes have to be malleable enough to allow easy nicking when voicing is being carried out, yet hard enough not to collapse when the pipe is placed in a vertical position, unsupported except at the foot.

If tone quality is not determined to any great extent by the pipe material itself, we must look to other physical parameters for explanations. A set of pipes corresponding to the compass of the organ keyboard, containing a range from relatively long and large-diameter pipes down to very narrow short pipes can be made to exhibit a uniform tone quality. This assemblage is known as a *rank*, the organ having *diapason* or *principal* ranks as its tonal foundation. Another rank, with different tone quality, might have much narrower pipes throughout (giving string tone) or a set of broader pipes with narrow mouths and softly voiced, producing a flute tone. Flute pipes may even be tapered towards the top, rather than cylindrical. Yet other ranks which have varying forms of conical pipe provide distinctive *reed* tones. Since the perceived timbre of an instrument reflects the characteristic admixture of fundamental and partials (overtones) present in the sound, the art of the organ builder must lie in the achievement of the appropriate mix by judicious choice of such physical parameters as the pipe geometry, the wind pressure and the dimensions of the mouth opening.

From the point of view of the basic physics, organ pipes are of two kinds. The first is the flue pipe (Fig. 2.4), in which an air jet traversing the mouth of the pipe drives the resonant modes associated with a cylindrical tube (or one with a square, or even rectangular, cross-section). The second is the reed pipe (Fig. 2.5), where a lightly damped metal reed is tuned to the frequency of the note which is to be played, and a conical or cylindrical tube acts as an essentially passive acoustic resonator (i.e. it determines the loudness and tone quality).

It would be unwise to imagine that any treatment of the physics of the organ could do more than suggest a rather basic framework for understanding a highly complex situation. The very presence of other pipes within an organ case can have a significant effect on the sound produced by a particular pipe or rank of pipes. It is not unknown for considerable re-voicing of 'interior' ranks to be required after the installation of the display pipes, particularly where, for instance, an 8', 4' and 2' chorus is involved. In addition, the acoustic radiation pattern for the sound coming from an open pipe, having sources at both the mouth and the open end, is quite different from that for the closed pipe, which has a single radiating source at the mouth. The further the listener is away from the organ in a reasonably 'live' acoustic environment, the more such subtleties in the source will be masked by the response of the auditorium. A recording made with microphones placed quite close to the pipes, however, may well give the listener an impression of the organ which is markedly different from that gained in situ.

Sound waves

Sound involves motion. For sound to travel through the air, air molecules have to be set in motion. At room temperature these molecules are already moving very energetically with an average speed comparable with that at which sound travels in air. Yet the human ear can detect sound on the threshold of hearing involving a molecular motion with a vibration amplitude which matches typical atomic dimensions – less than 10^{-10} m.

A musical sound begins with a vibrating source which either directly (as in the case of a drum) or indirectly (as in the violin) disturbs the adjacent air in a periodic manner, alternately compressing it and then allowing it to expand again. The air molecules in proximity to the source, having been set vibrating, are able to compress and then release the next layer of molecules in the same periodic fashion, and so on. The result is a wave which travels out from the source, able to transmit energy without the need for any net transfer of matter. An individual particle simply vibrates backwards and forwards in the direction of propagation of the wave, which is therefore known as a *longitudinal* wave. Most of the waves propagating in a stretched string, on the other hand, are *transverse* waves because the individual particles oscillate in a plane perpendicular to the direction of propagation of the wave itself.

A small parcel of air repetitively displaced by about as little as one hundredth of a millimetre either side of its equilibrium position as the 'compressions' and 'rarefactions' due to the sound wave affect it, would be associated with the loudest sound actually tolerated by the human ear. On the threshold of audibility the amplitude of the oscillation is some one million times less than this! It might seem strange, then, that we can hear the *ppp* of the Swell strings, say, without an accompanying buzz or hiss in our ears arising from the thermal motion of the air molecules as they dart backwards and forwards and collide with one another. The answer lies in the *ordered* nature of the molecular motion which is produced by the musical tone, compared with the random, chaotic thermal motion – to which our ear–brain system is, rather fortunately, not sensitive.

For a mechanical wave to propagate through a medium, that medium must possess both inertia (mass) and elastic properties. In the case of the longitudinal sound waves the basic elastic requirement is that the medium be compressible. Air is certainly compressible, as we can easily demonstrate through observation of phenomena encountered in every-day life. Sound can also travel through water quite readily, implying that it too is compressible to some extent. The same is true for solid materials such as steel or rock.

A detailed knowledge of the inertial and elastic properties of the air, and some facility with thermodynamics, enables the prediction that at a temperature of 15°C sound should travel at a speed $v = 340$ m s^{-1}, at sea level; in fact this is in agreement with experiment. Specification of the temperature turns out to be very important, for it is the dependence of the speed of sound on the ambient temperature which ultimately leads to significant tuning problems with organ pipes, since v turns out to be directly proportional to $\sqrt{T}$, where T is the absolute or Kelvin temperature (0°C = 273 K, and each °C step corresponds to 1 K). Over a range of temperature from 0°C to 30°C the speed of sound in air would be expected to rise from about 331 m s^{-1} to about 349 m s^{-1}.

A wave is a periodic (in most cases) disturbance within a medium, or along a boundary between two media, such that a snap-shot taken at a particular instant would show the disposition of the wave in space and hence allow determination of the wavelength λ; monitoring of the time variation of the disturbance at a particular location would enable the period T (and hence frequency f, the reciprocal of the period) to be found. The speed of the wave, its frequency, and its wavelength are related through

$$v = f\lambda,$$

implying that over one period T the wave advances one wavelength λ. When a longitudinal acoustic wave is produced by a single tone, its wavelength is the spacing between successive compressions or successive rarefactions (Figure 3.1).

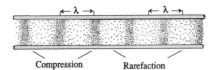

Compression   Rarefaction   Figure 3.1

The sound from a speaking pipe reaches the ear via a travelling wave, but within the pipe itself the acoustic disturbance takes the form of a 'standing' wave. Such a standing wave can arise whenever a travelling wave is reflected back on itself. For both open and stopped pipes this reflection takes place at the upper end of the pipe, but clearly under quite different conditions in the two cases, viz. from a rigid boundary in the stopped pipe and a 'free' boundary in the open pipe.

Standing waves

Reflection from a rigid boundary

There cannot be any *net* movement of the air molecules in the direction perpendicular to a completely rigid boundary when reflection of a wave occurs. Any air particle motion due to the incident wave is exactly cancelled, at all times, by that due to the reflected wave at this point on the boundary, which thus becomes a particle displacement *node*. One quarter of a wavelength ($\frac{\lambda}{4}$) away from the rigid boundary the incident and reflected waves reinforce one another to produce a particle displacement *antinode*, the amplitude of the oscillation at this antinodal point being a maximum at all times. At a distance of $\frac{\lambda}{2}$ from the boundary the conditions again correspond to a displacement node, i.e. zero disturbance at all times; a further $\frac{\lambda}{4}$ away, and another antinode position is reached. A spatial pattern of regularly varying amplitude of particle oscillation, marked by nodes (N) and antinodes (A) which are $\frac{\lambda}{4}$ apart, is set up as the two waves propagating in opposite directions traverse the medium. The net effect of the superposition of the travelling waves is to produce a 'standing' wave with a structure NANANA . . . as distance from the boundary increases. Within a *stopped* (i.e. one end closed) organ pipe such standing waves may be set up.

Reflection from a free boundary

Whilst reflection of a wave from a rigid boundary is easy to visualise, it is perhaps a little harder to see why a 'free' boundary will also allow reflection of a wave. Actually the wave has to be laterally constrained – as in a pipe – if such free boundary reflection (from an open end) is to occur. The ratio D/λ, where D is the pipe diameter, is crucial. For $D \gg \lambda$ the waves essentially pass straight out of the end of the tube, suffering virtually no reflection at all. If $D \ll \lambda$, the waves which actually emerge from the open end are 'diffracted' over a wide angle, so that the propagation conditions outside are greatly different from those inside the pipe. Consequently most of the energy is reflected back into the pipe. It is clear that the open end cannot impose much constraint on the particle motion and so represents a particle displacement antinode, quite the opposite of what occurs with a rigid boundary. The standing wave which ensues has a similar spatial pattern to the closed-end case, with nodes and antinodes λ apart, but in the sequence ANANAN....

In theory the pressure 'amplitude' at a closed end will be a maximum (because the molecules influenced by the incident wave experience maximum change of momentum during the wave reflection process) and correspondingly at an open end it will be zero. In practice the pressure node at an open end does not coincide with the physical boundary, but instead lies just outside. This factor assumes quantitative significance when related to the 'end-correction' for the open end of an open organ pipe, and the analogous correction for the mouth of both the open and the stopped pipe. The physical length of the pipe itself is not that used for detailed calculations of its acoustical characteristics.

The requirement that there be an ordered pattern of nodes and antinodes in both the open and the stopped organ pipe imposes major restrictions on the conditions under which each is able to resonate, and thus give rise to a stable sound.

Resonant modes of a cylindrical tube

Cylindrical tube of length ℓ open at both ends

A wave disturbance generated in a tube open at both ends will be reflected from the ends, at which the conditions are those of a particle displacement antinode (or pressure node). The simplest standing wave possible under these constraints is one which has a single displacement node at the mid-point, the pattern ANA occupying the whole length ℓ. Since nodes and antinodes are $\frac{\lambda}{4}$ apart, the antinodes at the open ends of the tube will have to be $\frac{\lambda}{2}$ apart, requiring $\ell = \frac{\lambda}{2}$ or $\lambda = 2\ell$. The first known public statement of this important relationship between the wavelength λ of the sound produced when such a tube is excited in its fundamental mode and the length ℓ of the tube was given somewhat tentatively by Newton in the first edition of his *Principia*, published in 1687. It appears that Huygens had probably come to the same conclusion about the $\lambda = 2\ell$ relationship independently.

The pattern ANA, which we now recognise as corresponding to the *fundamental* for the open tube, is not the only solution satisfying the requirement of having an antinode at each end. For example, the pattern ANANA should be equally acceptable, as also should ANANANA, and so on. These patterns represent the resonant modes of the tube, whose frequencies may be readily deduced:

$$\text{ANA} \qquad \text{1 node} \qquad \ell = \frac{\lambda_1}{2} \qquad f_1 = \frac{v}{\lambda_1} = \frac{v}{2\ell}$$

$$\text{ANANA} \qquad \text{2 nodes} \qquad \ell = \lambda_2 \qquad f_2 = \frac{v}{\lambda_2} = \frac{v}{\ell}$$

$$\text{ANANANA} \qquad \text{3 nodes} \qquad \ell = 3\frac{\lambda_3}{2} \qquad f_3 = \frac{v}{\lambda_3} = 3\frac{v}{2\ell}$$

$$\text{ANANANANA} \qquad \text{4 nodes} \qquad \ell = 2\lambda_4 \qquad f_4 = \frac{v}{\lambda_4} = 2\frac{v}{\ell}$$

The frequencies of these modes may be written as

$$f_1 = v/2\ell, \quad f_2 = 2v/2\ell, \quad f_3 = 3v/2\ell, \quad f_4 = 4v/2\ell, \dots f_n = nv/2\ell.$$

The frequencies of the overtones $f_2, f_3, f_4 \dots f_n$ represent integral multiples of f_1, i.e. they are exact harmonics of the fundamental. Both the even harmonic series (second, fourth, sixth ...) and the odd harmonics (third, fifth, seventh ...) are included in the overall spectrum.

Cylindrical tube of length ℓ closed at one end

A similar analysis, but taking into account the necessity for a particle displacement node at the closed end and an antinode at the open end, leads to patterns of the form AN, ANAN, ANANAN.... The fundamental mode is characterised by the requirement that $\ell = \frac{\lambda}{4}$. The first overtone, with the ANAN pattern, requires $\ell = 3\frac{\lambda}{4}$. Thus its wavelength is $4\ell/3$, whereas that of the fundamental is 4ℓ. The corresponding frequencies are therefore in the ratio 3:1, implying that the first overtone is the third harmonic of the fundamental. In fact the even harmonics are entirely missing, and the frequency spectrum consists of the fundamental and the odd harmonic series only.

When the two tubes are compared it is clear that for the same length ℓ, the one which is open at both ends has a fundamental at the frequency

$f_{1\,open} = v/2\ell$ which is twice that found when one end is closed, $f_{1\,closed} = v/4\ell$. The closed tube therefore sounds, in terms of pitch intervals, one octave below the open tube of the same length. The latter is much richer in harmonics, and the quality or timbre of the sound produced is distinctly 'brighter'.

In both open and closed tubes the wavelength λ is determined by the pipe length ℓ, which is relatively insensitive to temperature change. The frequency f which corresponds to that λ, however, increases quite appreciably with increasing temperature because the speed of sound v is proportional to $\sqrt{T}$. The result is a *sharpening* of the pitch as the temperature rises, and a problem with the tuning of the flue pipe ranks relative to the reeds.

Conical tubes

The behaviour of a conical tube with little or no truncation of the apex, but in any case closed at the narrow end, matches very closely that of a cylindrical tube of the same length open at both ends: all harmonics are present. The half-wavelength conical resonators commonly used for certain of the reed stops exploit this characteristic. As the truncation of the apex becomes more severe, the harmonic nature of the overtones is lost, but the higher frequency modes resemble the odd-harmonic structure of the 'closed' cylindrical tube.

Flue-pipe excitation

A representation of the mouth structure for a typical cylindrical metal flue pipe is shown above in Figure 2.4. The mouth opening is cut into a section of the pipe wall which has been flattened. An air jet flow is produced when air under pressure – typically 0.5 to 0.8 kPa – enters the foot of the pipe and is forced to emerge from the flue slit, travelling in the direction of the upper lip. The first real attempt to study the interaction between this jet and the oscillating air column was made by Sir John Herschel in 1830. Helmholtz and Rayleigh both tried to solve the problem in a slightly more quantitative manner later in the nineteenth century; they came to differing conclusions as to the precise mechanism of the interaction. Their models are generally referred to as the 'volume drive' and the 'momentum drive' mechanisms respectively.

The Helmholtz argument is that if the jet is to contribute maximum energy to the air column oscillation, the volume of flow into the pipe represented by the jet input has to be a maximum. Entry of the jet into the pipe has to occur at those times when the acoustic pressure is a maximum, and the acoustic oscillatory flow is therefore zero. Rayleigh argued that maximum energy transfer from jet to pipe should occur when the acoustic pressure at the point of entry is zero, and hence the acoustic flow is a maximum. The instants specified for greatest effectiveness of each of these mechanisms are separated by one quarter of the oscillation period T of the air column. A helpful analogy is that of the child's swing, which may be induced to oscillate with a constant amplitude by pushing in the right direction when it is at an extremity (Helmholtz) or when moving at its maximum speed at the bottom of the arc (Rayleigh). Modern laboratory measurements indicate that the Helmholtz mechanism is predominant under normal conditions, but that both mechanisms certainly play a part when the whole range of pipe speaking conditions is examined.

In order to give it a high degree of stability, the jet flow is made deliberately turbulent rather than laminar (streamline). During its passage across the mouth, the jet broadens and also slows down. In fact the flow velocity in its central plane has to be inversely proportional to the square root of the distance from the flue slit. When the pipe is speaking steadily, there will be a strong acoustic flow in and out of the mouth, with the result that the jet is subjected to a strong transverse oscillatory motion. At the flue slit itself the net transverse motion of the jet must obviously be zero at all times. The only way in which this can happen is for an equal and opposite motion to be imposed on the jet at the slit. This means that a disturbance which is characterised by the acoustic frequency spectrum of the flow in the mouth has to move up the jet once it has been initiated at the slit. The result is a sinuous oscillation in the jet, which travels upwards at around half the speed of the jet. That speed is not constant, because there is deceleration. If energy is to be supplied to the air column to overcome the losses due to the combined effects of viscosity, heat flow, acoustic radiation and so on, the timing of the arrival of each pulse-like burst inside the lip is crucial.

The sinuous oscillation grows in amplitude roughly exponentially as it propagates along the jet, so long as its wavelength is considerably greater than the width of the jet. This condition provides a natural selective filter, ensuring that only the low frequency components in the original disturbance reach the upper lip with a large amplitude. These components then dominate the acoustic flow oscillations. The tip of the jet traverses the lip (horizontally) with a simple harmonic motion corresponding to the fundamental frequency of the pipe, unaffected by the contributions to the acoustic flow in the mouth which are made by the higher-order modes. This does not mean that the jet flow into the pipe is 'sinusoidal' at the fundamental frequency. The flow has a complex waveform, with flat tops and bottoms due to its saturation whenever it is directed entirely either inside or outside the pipe. This is just the condition for the waveform to be rich in harmonics of the fundamental. The fact remains, however, that whereas the pipe is an active element in the generation of the fundamental, it behaves essentially as a passive resonator for the higher harmonics.

If the upper lip were to be placed exactly on the centre-line of the jet, the even harmonics could easily be suppressed, leading to an undesirable situation with an open pipe, which has a full set of harmonic resonances. In practice, therefore, the jet is directed slightly outside the lip and the open pipe is able to respond to a harmonically rich jet inflow under normal speaking conditions, and to behave as a mode-locked system, thus ensuring a steady output waveform.

Reed pipes

In an organ reed pipe, the reed itself is a thin flexible brass tongue which closes against the shallot (see Figure 2.5 above). Tuning is accomplished by varying the vibrating length of the tongue by means of a stiff wire which presses it firmly against the shallot. In general the longer the tongue, the lower the frequency. Air under pressure enters the foot of the pipe and passes through the opening in the shallot, setting the reed-tongue into its characteristic vibrational mode. The pipe, which may be conical or cylindrical, acts as an essentially passive resonator in its role of determining the loudness and timbre, since the sharply resonant reed is hardly affected by the actual tuning of the pipe. A conical pipe which is half a wavelength long supports all the harmonics generated by the reed, and hence is the appropriate resonator for a Trumpet stop. The vibrating reed has the effect of making the narrow end of the conical resonator behave as if 'closed'.

End-corrections and scaling

The effective length for a cylindrical open flue pipe of length L is $L^1 = L + e + m$, where e is the end-correction for the open end and m is that for the mouth of the pipe. At low frequencies $e \sim 0.6\ r$, where r is the radius of the pipe, but it decreases smoothly as the frequency increases. For the higher-order modes of the pipe where the behaviour is largely that of a passive resonant filter, e is less significant. The correction m is much harder to quantify, but is generally rather larger than e (perhaps by as much as five times) at the low frequency end. The net effect of the end-corrections is to produce a significant sharpening of the upper resonances of the pipe, which are thus de-tuned with respect to the fundamental. In the case of the stopped pipe, m is the only end-correction to be applied.

An extension of these ideas leads to the conclusion that the ratio of diameter to length for the pipes in a rank should be kept constant – they should be geometrically similar. This implies doubling the radius of the pipe every octave, or 'doubling on the twelfth pipe'. In practice this is not very satisfactory; the bass pipes need to be narrower, the treble pipes wider, than this rule suggests. Organ builders have developed rules of thumb to try to ensure reasonable tonal similarity across a whole rank. It is interesting that when the physicist calculates the quality factor Q expected for the various resonant modes of the pipe (a quantitative indicator of the sharpness of the resonance, and hence of the relative amplitude of response), typical modern scaling with doubling on about the sixteenth pipe turns out to have fairly good theoretical justification. For those who are a little sceptical, perhaps this is a case where our ears should be allowed to make the final judgment.

For further reading see Campbell and Greated 1987, Coltman 1969, Fletcher and Rossing 1991, Fletcher and Thwaites 1983, Mainstone 1992, and Sumner 1973.

4 Temperament and pitch

Christopher Kent

Temperament

It is not improbable that a high proportion of the readership of this book
will have accepted early in their musical education the principle of an
octave being divided into twelve semitones of equal size, implicit within
this being the notion of enharmonic notes and equal temperament
tuning. Yet the second half of the twentieth century has seen an increasing
preoccupation on the part of musicians with matters relating to heightened stylistic awareness in performance. Amongst players and makers of
keyboard instruments quests for 'historically informed' or 'authentic'
performances include the issues of pitch and temperament. For the
organ, unlike the pianoforte, equal temperament tuning has been the
universal norm for barely a century, but the current desire for enlight-
ened performances of the pre-romantic repertoire has seen the
rehabilitation of historically appropriate systems of tuning. As the keyboard instrument with the widest repertoire, the organ also has the
richest heritage of historic instruments and artefacts. The issue of
temperament is therefore of considerable significance with regard to
restorations and for new instruments which seek to replicate historical
styles.

The scope of this chapter is such that it can only attempt to provide an
introduction to the concept and history of a very large and complex
subject. The plan is threefold: first, to consider the principles of temperament, secondly, to consider three historically important systems (equal
temperament, mean-tone temperaments, irregular temperaments), and
thirdly, to consider the subject chronologically in relation to the repertoire and modern performance conditions.

Much of the literature of temperament is mathematical and theoretical, describing systems which may not have seen practical application. In
reality, gulfs existed between theory and practice, and many musicians
tuned, or expected instruments to be tuned, to match their own particular
requirements. It may therefore be risky, if not simplistic, to argue an
association between one composer or repertoire area and a particular
temperament. Although today's electronic tuning aids and electrically
driven winding systems make the exploration of different temperaments

relatively easy, their subtleties may still be undermined by changes in temperature and humidity.

The need for temperament arises from a physical property of the notes of the harmonic series in which the cardinal consonances (i.e. the octave, fifth and major third) are pure intervals. A comparative understanding of different temperaments requires a convenient mathematical method of measuring the sizes of intervals. This can be achieved either through ratios, as employed by Pythagoras (*fl. c*570–540 BC) and Ptolemy, an octave being 1:2 as represented by the doubling of the frequency (e.g. a = 220 Hz and a^1 = 440 Hz) and the diatonic scale thus:

C	D	E	F	G	A	B	c
1	9/8	5/4	4/3	3/2	5/3	15/8	2

or, as is customary today, by measurements in cents, where an equally tempered semitone = 100 cents, as introduced by Ellis in his translation of Helmholtz's *Sensations of Tone* (1885).

Through experiments with a monochord it became evident to Pythagoras that a cycle of twelve pure ascending fifths through seven octaves (i.e. C–G–D–A–E–B–F♯–C♯–G♯/A♭–E♭–B♭–F–C) would result in a sharpwards 'overshoot' of almost a quarter of a semitone (23.46 cents). This is commonly known as the 'Comma of Pythagoras'. The practice of temperament exists to assimilate this overshoot by making all or some consonances slightly impure. For example, the system known as equal temperament dictates a uniform flattening ('tempering') of each fifth by $\frac{1}{12}$ of the Pythagorean comma (1.955 cents), as well as the tempering of thirds and sixths. This latter necessity arises from the fact that a sequence of three pure ascending thirds (e.g. C–E–G♯–B♯) falls flat of a pure octave by an error of 41.06 cents, known the Lesser Diesis, whereas four pure minor thirds descending (C–A–F♯–D♯–B♯) are sharp of an octave by an excess of 62.57 cents, known as the Greater Diesis. Equal temperament enables all keys to be uniformly serviceable, all intervals except the octave being slightly out of tune, but it fails to provide the contrasts in key character implicit in unequally tempered systems.

Equal temperament may have been advocated in theory by Aristoxenus (*c*350 BC) and was first employed during the sixteenth century by some players of fretted instruments such as the lute and viol. Notwithstanding its endorsement by Zarlino (1588), the ageing Frescobaldi (late 1630s) and Froberger, it met with differing responses from organists, organ builders and theorists: it was advocated by Mersenne (1637), it was held at arm's length by some, and became a subject of intense discourse among others.

The practice of mean-tone temperament stems from the 'Syntonic

Comma' or the 'Comma of Didymus.' Here, a sequence of four pure fifths through two octaves and a pure major third (i.e. C–G–D–A–E = 701.955 cents × 4 = 2807.82 cents) results in a sharpwards overshoot when the same interval is calculated over two octaves and a major third (i.e. C–C–E = 1200 cents × 2 + 386.14 = 2786.314 cents). The difference between them (i.e. 21.506 cents, only slightly smaller than the Pythagorean Comma) is known as the Syntonic Comma. Some regular systems of mean-tone temperament are designed to accommodate this excess.

In quarter comma mean-tone, widely used in Europe during the sixteenth and seventeenth centuries, eleven intervals of the cycle of fifths are flattened (696.58 cents) by $\frac{1}{4}$ of the Syntonic Comma, leaving a very sharp ('wolf') interval between G♯ and E♭ (737.64 cents). There are eight out of twelve pure (or 'just') major thirds and the same number of minor sixths, but augmented fourths and minor sevenths are consistently inaccurate. The major keys of: C, D, F, G, A and B♭ and the minor keys of d, g, and a are excellent. E♭, E, c, c♯, e, f♯ and b are mediocre, but D♭, F♯, A♭ and B, e♭, f, g♯ and b♭ are unusable. In fifth comma mean-tone eleven of the cycle of fifths are flattened by $\frac{1}{5}$ of the Syntonic Comma with the 'wolf' also between G♯ and E♭; only four keys are unusable (D♭, F♯, A♭ and e♭). It was used extensively from the mid-seventeenth century in England (chamber organ at Wollaton Hall; see Bicknell 1982) and in France, where it gave excellent tunings in the keys stemming from the eight liturgical modes, *viz.* I (d), II (g), III (a), IV (e), V (C), VI (F), VII (D), VIII (G), as in the *Livres d'Orgue* of Jacques Boyvin (1649–1706). A sixth comma mean-tone temperament associated with the organ builder Gottfried Silbermann (1683–1753) has eleven fifths flattened by $\frac{1}{6}$ of the Pythagorean Comma with a similar 'wolf' in which the keys of D♭, F♯, A♭ and e♭ are unusable. Table 4.1 gives a comparative table of the key qualities in quarter, fifth and sixth comma mean-tone systems.

Irregular temperaments contain pure and tempered intervals with the errors of the Pythagorean and/or Syntonic commas being accommodated by varying amounts. They give access to greater ranges of keys than regular mean-tone systems. One of the most familiar is Werckmeister III (*Musicalische Temperatur*, Frankfurt and Leipzig, 1691). Here, the Pythagorean Comma is absorbed by flattening four fifths of the cycle: C–G, G–D, D–A and B–F♯, leaving the remaining eight pure. There are also six pure minor sevenths and six pure major seconds. Five of the thirds are purer than those of equal temperament. The keys of C, e, F, a and B♭ are very good; d, E♭, e♭, G, g♯, b♭ are better than in equal temperament; c♯, D, E, f, f♯, A and b are inferior to equal temperament, and c, D♭ and F♯ are generally poor.

Table 4.1

The key qualities of three systems of mean-tone tuning compared

In each equally tempered scale the errors total 49 cents if compared with
the measurements for the acoustically pure intervals. Thus the lowest
figures in the tables below (reckoned in each case from the tonic upwards),
drawn from the study by Padgham (1986), signify particularly good
intonation and the highest very poor intonation.

| | Temperament | | | | | |
| | 1/4 comma | | 1/5 comma | | 1/6 comma | |
Key	Major	Minor	Major	Minor	Major	Minor
C	32	73	30	58	33	57
D♭	164	82	126	69	111	65
D	32	32	30	30	33	33
E♭	63	145	50	106	49	96
E	63	63	58	58	57	57
F	32	114	30	86	33	80
F♯	145	63	115	58	103	57
G	32	32	30	30	33	33
A♭	195	113	145	89	127	80
A	32	32	30	30	33	33
B♭	32	114	30	86	33	80
B	104	63	86	58	80	56

The suggestion that organs were tuned to the Pythagorean system
from the medieval period until the advent of mean-tone systems at the
end of the sixteenth century may be ill-founded (Padgham 1986: 93).
Pythagorean tuning (as codified by Arnaut de Zwolle, c1450) gives pure
octaves, fourths and fifths, whilst eight out of the twelve major thirds are
intolerably sharp, but Bartolomeo Ramos de Pareia (*Musica practica*,
Bologna, 1482) in relating tuning to compositional practice with lists of
'good' and 'bad' intervals (major and minor semitones, whole tones,
major and minor thirds) suggests a less severe system. Split keys were
applied at Lucca Cathedral, Italy (1484) for the major and minor semitones (e.g. A♭/G♯), and also to the da Prato organ (1475) at San Petronio,
Bologna, in 1528 (restored in 1982: [Adamoli *et al.*] 1982). By 1496,
Franchinus Gaffurius (*Practica Musicae*, Milan) noted that organists were
in the habit of slightly flattening fifths 'by a very small and hidden and
somewhat uncertain quantity' (Riemann 1898, trans. 1962: 282–90).

Arnolt Schlick (1511) described an ingenious hybrid method of

Ex. 4.1 Sweelinck, *Mixolydian Fantasia*

(a)

(b)

(c)

tuning, apparently the first to encompass every note of the chromatic scale, which entailed both the tempering of fifths (ten flattened and two sharpened) and thirds (twelve sharpened). Barbour (1951) describes this as an irregular temperament with aspects of both the equal and mean-tone systems, and Lindley (1980) as 'an artful variant of regular meantone with major thirds slightly larger than pure'. Schlick was also pragmatic enough to concede that some organists might prefer a less compromising regular mean-tone system, such as those prescribed for the harpsichord by Aaron (1523) and for the clavichord by Santa María (1565).

Quarter comma mean-tone was first codified mathematically, and described as 'un novo temperamento' by Zarlino in 1571; in Germany it was termed 'Praetorianische Temperatur' after the description by Michael Praetorius in *De organographia* (1619). Some of its qualities can be appreciated in the *Mixolydian Fantasia* (No. 8 in M. Seiffert's edition) by Sweelinck (1562–1621), as illustrated by Example 4.1. In (a) the major third of the triad of G is perfect, but the fifth is flat by a quarter comma, and there is inequality in the sizes of the semitones: C–C♯ is narrower than C♯–D; in (b) the predominantly pure minor sixths and almost pure major sixths add lustre to Sweelinck's sequences, and in (c) there are strong harmonic contrasts, the purity of E and a versus the piquancy of the chord B.

Praetorius in his *Syntagma Musicum* (1619) recommended the adding of trills to camouflage such imperfections in intonation. Quarter comma mean-tone, with its predominance of pure major thirds, is well suited to cornet solos, sesquialtera mixtures or the *Récit de Tierce*. From 1682/3 until 1879 the Father Smith organ at the Temple Church, London, used by John Stanley (1712–86) had split keys (E♭/D♯ and A♭/G♯) to facilitate the keys of E♭ and E.

Andreas Werckmeister (1645–1706), author of *Orgel-Probe* (Frankfurt and Leipzig, 1681/1698), devised several irregular 'well-tempered' systems permitting unrestricted access to all keys. The high proportion of pure fifths (eight out of twelve) in his third system enhance quint mixtures and mutations. Latterly it has been widely applied to new instruments. A collection which relates well to this system is the *Hexachordum Apollinis* (Nuremberg 1699) of Pachelbel (1653–1706) where the key scheme employs its five purest keys (C, e, F, a and B♭) and others with distinctive characteristics (d, G, g, f and A♭) as follows:

Aria	Tonic	Modulation
I	d	F
II	e	G
III	F	C
IV	g	B♭
V	a	C
VI	f	A♭

The re-tuning of Buxtehude's two organs in the Marienkirche, Lübeck in 1683, (over a period of thirty-six days) to a 'new temperament' of Werckmeister (Snyder 1987: 84) has altered the perspective of temperament questions posed by some passages in his music (e.g. Praeludium in F♯ minor BuxVW 146, bb. 49–90). Before this, the lack of holograph MSS had prompted discussions as to whether copyists from central Germany had transposed the music from the original keys that were purer in 'Praetorianische Temperatur' (see Beckmann 1987).

J. S. Bach lived at the time of the greatest plurality in tuning systems. His contemporaries Johann Georg Neidhardt (c1685–1739, Kapellmeister in Königsberg) and Georg Andreas Sorge (1703–78, organist in Lobenstein) each advanced different methods of subtly nuanced unequal temperament. They also advocated a range of systems, simple for rural churches, increasingly sophisticated for municipal churches and of the greatest finesse for courts. There is no evidence to suggest that Bach preferred any one particular system of temperament, nor is it ever likely that any single scheme of tuning can be devised to address satisfactorily every facet of his demanding harmonic and melodic language. Bach is believed to have worked pragmatically; like most professional musicians of his age he tuned by ear, rather than according to a mathematical system: 'In tuning harpsichords he knew how to temper so exactly and correctly that all keys sounded handsome and agreeable' (Mizler 1754: 172–3). There is no reason to suspect that his mature requirements for the organ were any different. Indeed, his writing for the instrument in some contexts may not suggest the acceptance of any modulatory or chromatic limitations.

Neidhardt devised several good temperaments in which all keys are serviceable. These, particularly his system of 1724 (*Sectio Canonis Harmonici*, Königsberg 1724) in which only the key of E major is indifferent though not unbearable, were approved of by Kuhnau, Bach's predecessor as Kantor at the Thomaskirche. Referring to Bach's work with the organ builder Zacharias Hildebrandt at the Wenzelkirche, Naumburg (1743–6), Bach's son-in-law, J. C. Altnikol wrote: 'In tempering he follows Neidhardt and one can modulate very well in all keys without presenting the ear with anything repugnant – which for today's taste in music is the most beautiful' (Dähnert 1962, p. 115; cited by Lindley 1985).

Although it may be tempting to consider the chromaticisms and enharmonic pivot of bb. 32–9 of the Fantasia in G minor (BWV 542) as a suggestion of equal temperament, these progressions, often revolving around diminished sevenths (i.e. accumulations of minor thirds), can be reasonably related to Werckmeister III (Williams 1984: 186, 191), where five of the minor thirds are as in equal temperament, and all but one of the remainder are slightly flatter. The chromaticisms of the *Kleines harmonisches Labyrinth* (BWV 591), although scarcely attributable to Bach (Williams 1980: 281–2), are a measure of the fascination that unrestricted temperaments held for his contemporaries and successors. Table 4.2 compares the key qualities of Werckmeister III and Neidhardt (1724).

The challenge of Bach's style has motivated several recent researchers to evolve their own 'well tempered' systems. One such example, by Mark Lindley, is applied to the organ by Goetze & Gwynne at St Helen Bishopsgate, London (1995).

In eighteenth-century France, the two *Tempérament Ordinaire* tunings were derived from the quarter and sixth comma mean-tone systems respectively. In the first system, as reconstructed by Mark Lindley, there were probably six or seven flattened fifths, three or four pure fifths and two or three sharp ones. The second system (Padgham 1986: 79–82) gives excellent tunings for the keys of C, D, F, G and A and varying degrees of piquancy elsewhere. Eb, F#, Ab and B are uncomfortable, but Bb, c#, d, e and a are better in quality than in equal temperament. The major and minor thirds vary sharpwards and flatwards of the equal temperament norms, and this gives subtle variety to tierce-based registrations.

Table 4.2

The Key qualities of two unrestricted irregular temperaments compared

Key	Werckmeister III Major	Minor	Neidhardt 1724 Major	Minor
C	**29**	65	**31**	53
D♭	64	53	55	51
D	53	47	47	53
E♭	47	47	53	55
E	53	35	61	41
F	**23**	53	**33**	45
F♯	70	53	57	43
G	47	59	**39**	55
A♭	59	47	55	57
A	53	**29**	55	47
B♭	**29**	47	43	47
B	59	53	57	41

Although both Werckmeister (*Musicalische Paradoxal-Discourse*, Quedlinburg 1707) and Neidhardt (*Gäntzlich erschöpfte mathematische Abteilungen . . .*, Königsberg 1732) approved of equal temperament in principle, they both preferred some variety in the tunings of major and minor thirds. The system as promulgated by Barthold Fritz (*Anweisung, wie man Claviere, Clavecins, und Orgeln, nach einer mechanischen Art, in allen zwölf Tönen gleich rein stimmen könne*, vol. II, Leipzig 1756) was approved by C. P. E. Bach (1762), who noted that equal temperament was more widely applied to mid-eighteenth century German clavichords and pianos than to organs. Further impetus to the spread of equal temperament followed with F. W. Marpurg (*Versuch über die musikalische Temperatur*, Breslau 1776). Although it was initally welcomed by Rameau (*Génération harmonique*, Paris 1737) on account of wider opportunities for modulation, it was less readily accepted in France during the later eighteenth century to the extent that the first organs of Cavaillé-Coll were tuned unequally (*c*1840).

The major nineteenth-century organ composers of mainland Europe were also pianists and their attidude to temperament was influenced by the already established equal tuning of the latter instrument. Yet it is interesting to note that Mendelssohn's Three Preludes and Fugues Op. 37

(composed 1835–7 and dedicated to Thomas Attwood of St Paul's Cathedral, London) do not make excessive demands of an unequal tuning system, whereas in the Six Sonatas Op. 65, particularly no. 1, there are more testing harmonic progressions (Kent 1990: 31–3). With the major organ works of Liszt and Franck – associated with the organs of Ladegast at Merseburg Cathedral (1859–62) and Cavaillé-Coll at St Clothilde, Paris (1859–60), respectively – equal temperament tuning is a prerequisite.

In England, equal temperament was also viewed cautiously and its imperfections became a source of contention (Williams 1968: 60). Experiments to allow the use of 'extreme keys' included an invention by Robert Smith (*Harmonics, or the Philosophy of Musical Sounds*, London, 1759) where, instead of divided sharps, a system of stop levers either side of the keyboard allowed the selection of separate pipes for the 'demitones' of C♯/D♭, D♯/E♭ and F♯/G♭ etc. It is likely that Smith's device was applied by Parker to the organ of the Foundling Hospital Chapel (1769) and there is a similar example in a chamber organ now in the Russell Collection at the University of Edinburgh.

By 1800 Samuel Wesley (1766–1837) noted that the pressure for a system which permitted the use of a greater number of keys had arisen from the appearance of much German music, and in his *Practical Tuner for the Organ or Pianoforte* (London 1819) Benjamin Flight Jun. (1767–1847) observed two systems: 'tuning by unequal temperament, is used for Church Organs . . . Pianofortes and Organs, used for the Concert-room, are tuned by equal temperament . . .' In the same source Flight described an unequal system very similar to quarter comma mean-tone (Kent 1990: 33). However, further to Flight's comment on the piano, it should be noted that it was not until 1846 that Broadwoods of London began to tune their instruments equally.

There was little general acceptance of equal temperament for organs in England until after the Great Exhibition of 1851. Of the fourteen organs displayed at this event only the instrument by Edmund Schulze was tuned equally. Although Hopkins (Hopkins and Rimbault 1855: 140–57) described both the unequal and equal systems, he, along with other disciples of German organs, advocated a change to the latter. The advanced harmonic language of the repertoire of Town Hall organists (transcriptions, and works with choir and orchestra), made this particularly desirable. The first Gray & Davison organ tuned to equal temperament left their works in 1853, the same year in which William Hill (1789–1870) used the system for the 'Grand Organ' erected in the Royal Panopticon, Leicester Square. Joseph Walker (1802–70) followed in 1856, but in 1863 Thomas Lewis (1833–1915) boldly claimed his organs to be 'the only English instruments that are tuned with a mathematically just temperament' (*Musical Standard* vol. 2, no. 31: 2 November 1863). Apparent opposition came from the mature S. S. Wesley (1810–76), in whose organ music there are some harmonically ambitious contexts that may arguably be related to an irregular and unrestricted temperament. Examples include the Prelude and Fugue in C♯ minor, Larghetto in F♯ minor, and bb. 57–65 and 85–8 of the Andante in F. A rare survival of such a tuning exists at Frilsham, Berkshire (Bower 1995) in an organ of *c*1860 by George Maydwell Holdich (1816–96). It is similar to the third system of J. P. Kirnberger (1721–83) in which the fifths C–G, G–D, D–A and A–E are flattened and those for E–B, B–F♯, D♭–A♭, D♯–A♯, remain pure (Bower 1995, and Padgham 1986: 68–9). However, it was typical of Wesley's contradictory personality to write passages in his early anthems (Horton 1993: xxvi-ii) which suggest that he may have been acquiescent towards equal temperament, as in *The Wilderness* (bb. 122–7), composed in 1832 for the re-opening of the organ in Hereford Cathedral as rebuilt by J. C. Bishop. (Yet it is known that at this time the instrument had not been tuned to equal temperament.)

Henry Willis (1821–1901), according to S. S. Wesley, was initially opposed to equal temperament, although he employed it by request at Carlisle Cathedral in 1856. His organ at St George's Hall, Liverpool was at first tuned unequally at Wesley's insistence, until W. T. Best's desire for equal temperament prevailed in 1867. The gradual adoption of equal temperament caused English organ builders to question the continued existence of tierce mixtures. William Hill compromised in his later instruments by terminating the Tierce rank at g (Thistlethwaite 1990: 244, 405). Although equal temperament had became common for new organs by the 1860s, the conversion of existing instruments was a slower process, the organ at Wells Cathedral remaining in unequal tuning until 1895.

Today, the increasing availability of a choice of temperaments demands judicious decisions of performers, particularly in relation to the romantic and twentieth-century repertoires. In an era of authenticities it may be as questionable to perform music conceived in terms of equal temperament, such as works by Liszt, Hindemith, Messiaen or Reger, on an instrument tuned to an eighteenth-century Italian temperament, as to deny the pertinence of a stylistically appropriate tuning for music of earlier periods.

Pitch

Although the evidence of history militates against the notion of any degree of standardisation of organ pitch there have been periods of greater stability than the past 150 years. For example, some pitch levels dating from the early sixteenth century remained in use for up to 300 years. Much historical data has been gleaned from dimensional and calligraphic studies of organ pipes, as well as from written sources, in which the publications of Alexander Ellis (1880) and Arthur Mendel (1968, 1978) remain seminal.

Arnolt Schlick (1511) gave two standards: one for an organ at F pitch, where a^1 has been estimated to have been in the range of 374–392 Hz, and a second for a C organ at $a^1 = 510$ Hz, pitched a fourth higher (or a fifth lower) than the F organ. Instruments within the range of Schlick's first (low) pitch were built in France and Italy until the middle of the nineteenth century. For example, Dom Bédos de Celles in *L'art du facteur d'orgues* (Paris 1766–78) establishes a^1 at 376.5 Hz and the tuning fork of the Versailles Chapel organ (1795), by Dallery & Clicquot, gives a^1 as 390 Hz.

A century after Schlick, Praetorius (1619) mentions three pitches for organs. First, he established a high pitch of medieval origin, giving the example of the organ at Halberstadt Cathedral (1361/1495), which he estimated to be a minor third higher than his second pitch. This was his *Cammer & Chor-Thon* pitch (for concerted music, sacred or secular), which he illustrated with an octave of organ pipes; the measurements of these indicate a^1 to have been 425 Hz at 15°C. This 'standard' pitch level remained in use for up to 300 years, being used for Ruckers harpsichords, and it is close to the tuning fork used by Handel in 1740 ($a^1 = 422.5$ Hz). A number of examples survive in English chamber organs of the eighteenth century, including those by John Byfield at Finchcocks and Snetzler at Kedleston Hall; both date from 1766 and are pitched at $a^1 = 425$ Hz. However, chamber organs built at the end of the eighteenth century show a slight rise in pitch (Attingham Park, Samuel Green 1788, $a^1 = 433.9$ Hz; Oakes Park, England & Son 1790, $a^1 = 431$ Hz).

The third organ pitch mentioned by Praetorius was a minor third lower than his second ('standard') pitch. This low pitch ($a^1 = c360$ Hz) was used in England for the 1611 Thomas Dallam organ at Worcester Cathedral played by Thomas Tomkins. As it was a fourth lower than the choir pitch (which was then a tone higher than Praetorius's 'standard'), the discrepancy was overcome by organists transposing accompaniments (up a fourth with a 5′ stop, or down a fifth with a 10′ stop), or by means of transposing keyboards. Referring to the Worcester organ, Tomkins's son, Nathaniel, explained in a letter of 1665 that a 10′ Open Diapason which sounded FF at choir pitch was played from the C key. This dual system of 'quire pitch' and 'organ pitch' existed in England throughout the sixteenth century and continued into the 1660s, when new organs began to be built with the pitch of the keys corresponding to that of the pipes (Gwynn 1985).

The higher organ pitch described by Schlick continued to be used until the seventeenth and eighteenth centuries. Its co-existence with the lower *Cammer & Chor-Thon* pitch required dual provision as in the Schnitger organ at the Jacobikirche in Hamburg (1690–93). Here the entire instrument was tuned to $a^1 = 490$ except for a Gedackt stop for continuo purposes which was a minor third lower at $a^1 = 411$. There are also English references to dual-pitch organs, as in the 'anthem stop' proposed for New College, Oxford (1661), or the 'one Recorder of tin unison to the voice' at York Minster (1634).

J. S. Bach was well accustomed to varying pitch levels. In his cantata performances at Weimar, the strings tuned to the high organ pitch, and the woodwinds transposed their parts. At the Thomaskirche, Leipzig it was the organ that was treated as a transposing instrument. He had inherited the arrangement established by Kuhnau in 1682, when the organ had been tuned sharp of *Cammer & Chor-Thon* (but differently from the *Chorton* pitch of the eighteenth century). This required Bach to continue Kuhnau's practice of transposing or writing some cantata organ parts one tone lower than the sound required so that they matched the lower pitch of the orchestra and harpsichord. The Schnitger organ that he played at the Katharinenkirche, Hamburg in 1720 was tuned a minor third higher (to high *Chorton* pitch) than the Silbermann instruments at *Cammerton* pitch that he played in Dresden in 1725, 1731 and 1736. The organ at the Marienkirche, Mühlhausen, rebuilt in 1738 by Johann Friedrich Wender, which Bach had been asked to visit three years earlier, had what appears to have been a transposing device, described as 'two chamber couplers, one for the large, and one for small chamber pitch throughout the entire organ'. The new organ at Naumburg which Bach and Gottfried Silbermann proved in 1746 was tuned to choir pitch.

In post-Restoration England, a conflict between low French and higher German organ pitches was evident in the work of Renatus Harris and Bernard Smith. Harris's organ at St Andrew Undershaft, London (1696) was tuned to $a^1 = 427.7$ Hz, whereas Smith's instrument at Durham Cathedral (1684–5) was at $a^1 = c474.1$ Hz (Ellis 1880, cited by Gwynn 1985: 70). An unaltered example of an organ at intermediate pitch ($a^1 = 446.7$ Hz), possibly of the late seventeenth century, exists at Wollaton Hall (Bicknell 1982: 57). There are a number of cases in which Smith's pitches were subsequently lowered, particularly his organ at Trinity College, Cambridge (1708), which was lowered to the pitch of an Italian tuning fork ($a^1 = 395.2$ Hz) in 1750. The sharpness of Smith's organ at St Paul's Cathedral was noted in the *English Musical Gazette* in

January 1819: 'It is a remarkable thing that all Schmidt's instruments were a quarter, and some even a half tone above pitch: this was so severely felt by the wind instuments, at the performances of the Sons of the Clergy, that they could not get near the pitch of the organ.'

The tendency for pitch to rise during the first half of the nineteenth century was led by European opera houses, most notably La Scala, Milan, where by 1856 it had exceeded $a^1 = 451$ Hz. The most successful attempt at moderation came with the French 'Diapason Normal' pitch of $a^1 = 435$ Hz, legally enforced by the Government in 1859 (though in practice the official tuning forks emerged at 435.5 Hz). In England, the organ of St James's Hall was re-tuned to this pitch for Barnby's 1869 season of Oratorio Concerts, but it was not until 1895, after much chaos and contradiction between organ and orchestral pitches particularly at provincial festivals, that the Philharmonic Society formally endorsed 'Diapason Normal' as the 'New Philharmonic Pitch'. Notwithstanding, the conversion of organs was a slow process: even the instrument in the Royal Albert Hall remained sharp of this standard until 1923, so in a performance of Bach's Mass in B minor in 1908 the organist H. A. L. Balfour had to transpose his entire part (Scholes 1944: 406–9). 'Diapason Normal' was generally adopted by organ builders for new instruments, as by Norman & Beard at the Usher Hall, Edinburgh in 1912.

Although first proposed as an international standard pitch in Vienna in 1885, the present-day norm of $a^1 = 440$ Hz was not followed by the British Standards Institution until 1938. In the period immediately following World War II many organs were raised to this new standard, as at Gloucester Cathedral in 1947. In 1955 and 1975 it was re-confirmed by the International Organisation for Standardisation, but as the century draws to a close there has been a tendency for standard orchestral pitch to rise again. Conversely, the requirements of early music ensembles playing period instruments have led to new continuo organs being tuned to historically correct pitches (e.g. $a^1 = 415$).

It is now very rare for an historic organ to have retained its original temperament or pitch; where either or both *do* survive, they are deserving of scrupulous conservation.

5 The organ case

Stephen Bicknell

The organ is unique amongst musical instruments in that it makes an architectural contribution to the building in which it stands. This is not solely on account of size: the layout and decoration of organ cases has traditionally been a branch of architectural design with its own grammar and traditions, but still allowing free interpretation according to changing fashions, local influences, and the skills of the designer and organ builder.

The organ case has an effect on the sound of the organ, though this may be difficult to define. For the neo-classical builders of the mid-twentieth century the revival of the traditional organ case – with side walls, back and roof – was an important argument in the ideology of organ reform. The casework was believed to focus the sound, assist the blend of the various ranks of pipes and project the sound into the room (usually down the main axis of the building). There is still considerable debate as to whether the organ case is essentially a passive structure, like a loudspeaker cabinet, or whether it has an active role as a resonator, bringing it more into line with other musical instruments where the body or soundboard is vital in creating power and timbre.

In practice many variations are possible, and as with other factors in the design and building of organs, success is not dependent on this element alone. If one allows that good organs exist in many forms and from many different periods, then one must acknowledge the success, on their own terms, of organs built in less than ideal cases or indeed without any case at all.

Indeed it seems that the early medieval organ had no case, the pipes being exposed to view as in the classical hydraulis, though not enough documentation survives to be certain. In 1286 the organ at Exeter Cathedral in England was the object of the expenditure of 4 shillings 'in expensis circa organa claudenda', and although it is not clear whether this 'clothing' of the instrument is truly a case or not, it is from this time onwards that organ casework becomes an entity in its own right. The earliest illustration of an organ case seems to be mid-fourteenth century (see Jakob *et al.* 1991), and this is more or less contemporary with the earliest surviving examples or fragments – the remains of positive organs from Sundre (1370) and Norrlanda (*c*1390) in Sweden (Kjersgaard 1987 and

1988), the organ case at Salamanca in Spain (variously dated from *c*1380 to *c*1500; de Graaf 1982), and the instrument usually described as the oldest organ in the world at Sion in Switzerland, dating from *c*1435 (Figure 5.1).

Why did casework become a necessary and integrally important part of the fully developed European organ tradition? The functional reasons are obvious enough: an instrument as delicate as an organ needed to be protected from interference, theft, the elements (not all churches had glazed windows throughout), dust and vermin (rats and mice are fond of bellows leather and will even gnaw their way through metal pipes when circumstances are propitious). As part of this need for protection, so the early organ also acquired doors which closed over the one remaining open face – the front. From this it is obvious that preparing the organ for use would have been something of a ceremony in its own right, not least because it would have required someone learned in the art to sit at the keys and others to pump the bellows.

As the use of music in the church is laden with symbolic meaning, so the very presence of the organ can be used as part of the symbolic apparatus and it becomes essential to ask which particular symbols may have been uppermost in the minds of those who commissioned these instruments and of those who made and installed them.

The organ at Sion, in its original form (the row of tall wooden pipes at the back is assumed to be a later addition), seems to have been typical. It is largely symmetrical, with the pipes arranged in towers with intervening flat compartments; the front itself is flat, with the pipes arranged in a tidy and ordered form – not necessarily the chromatic order of the notes on the keyboard. Decorative carving embellishes the case and carved shades relieve the row of naked pipe tops. The case is surmounted not just with carved decoration but in particular with crenellation. Finally it has a pair of doors that can close over the front, on which can be painted appropriate images. The same approach can be seen in other whole or part surviving instruments at Salamanca in Spain (fifteenth century?), at the Cathedral in Zaragoza in Spain (1443), at Calatayud in Spain (*c*1480), at San Petronio in Bologna, Italy (the gothic organ of *c*1480 partly hidden inside a later stone case), in the portative illustrated by Schlick (1511) and in representations of other organs now lost.

The crenellations or battlements are perhaps a clue to the iconography being evoked. The organ case houses a 'population' of pipes, all different from each other and quite individual in every respect, but all governed by an overall precise order (the notes of the scale determining the length of the pipes and the relative diameter scaling determining the quality of the sound). This is a neat model of the medieval world view, and one is

Figure 5.1 The organ on the west wall of the Cathedral of Notre Dame, Valère sur Sion, Switzerland, generally regarded as the oldest playable organ in the world. The case and much pipework date from *c* 1435 (though earlier dates have been mentioned); the present position and the wood pipes projecting behind the organ are the result of later changes. The doors over the face of a medieval organ are practical, keeping out dust and vermin and preventing accidental damage, but also emphasise the instrument's iconographic status – as would the doors of an altar-piece.

immediately struck by the idea of a parallel with the Augustinian notion of the City of God or with the image of the Heavenly Jerusalem; hence, perhaps, the battlements. The pipes are of course a representative example of God's creation on earth, all the more potent because their order and manufacture is governed by the semi-magical properties of mathematics and geometry. To the medieval mind there would have been a profound symbolic link between this and concepts such as the music of the spheres and the idea that through music fallen man may access, albeit in a transitory way, the pure truth of heaven.

The image of the organ as a model of a city is surprisingly useful, though it may seem at first to stretch a point. It helps explain the alternation of towers (or turrets) and flats (or walls); it gives an insight into how the craftsman gave a notional order to the many pipes standing in their house; it explains the application, in several languages, of terms normally reserved for body parts to the pipes themselves – the mouth, the foot, the lips, the tongue (languid) and so on. Indeed it helps to explain why some medieval organs have faces painted on the pipe mouths. It also helps to illustrate that there was a strong metaphysical vision of the organ and of its role in worship.

The simple iconography explained here was to survive as the basis of all organ case design right down to the present day: the alternation of towers and flats has survived every change in architectural or decorative fashion and is still the starting point for the design of an organ case many hundreds of years later, long after the original symbolism has been forgotten.

Part of the reason for this enduring pattern was sheer practicality. The medieval organ was inevitably a simple functional structure. Dividing the pipes symmetrically – involving the use of a rollerboard to transmit the movement of the key action sideways – distributed weight evenly, made the wind supply more consistent, and made the tuning easier (adjacent pipes speaking adjacent semitones will rarely speak in good tune with each other). The lower part of the organ was narrower than the part containing the pipes, for much the same reasons that call for the same plan in a timber-framed house. The overhang allows simple cantilevering of the upper structure and therefore larger overall dimensions, and gives plenty of room for access at ground level (Figure 5.2).

It was not long before the original plan, with all its forceful simplicity, was developed in order to celebrate in a more down-to-earth way the joys of decorative craftsmanship. To the modern mind the function of a musical instrument may be its sound. With the organ this is not the case: it is a total art object in which its size, scope, form, appearance, manufacture, installation and use are all part of the creative experience. For much

Figure 5.2 The organ at Oosthuizen in the Netherlands, built in 1530 by Jan van Covelen, probably in association with his pupil Hendrik Niehoff. The work of these two builders marks the emergence of the influential and innovative north Brabant school of organ building. This small instrument (one manual from F, seven stops) is an impressively little-altered survivor from the period, well-known for its powerful ringing chorus. The casework begins to bridge the gap between the last of flamboyant Gothic and the opening of new Mannerism, a style that was to have limitless potential in organ design.

of its life an organ is silent – and yet, through its appearance, it continues to make a vital contribution to the building in which it stands.

By the late medieval period, the flat-faced towers had begun to form groups; these were now often semi-circular or pointed in plan; battlements were joined by pinnacles or even carved cresting, both abstract and figurative; pipeshades lost their architectural quality and joined the riot of decoration (Figure 5.3). With all this celebration going on, the line drawn by the pipe mouths changed from straight (in early instruments) to contrary: as if imitating the rules of musical counterpoint the lowest pipes in a particular group usually have the shortest feet, and the higher pipes the longest.

With the coming of the renaissance the craft of organ building began to separate into its various national schools, most immediately obvious (from the point of view of case design and layout) in Italy.

For the Italian renaissance designer the 'building' housing the organ pipes mutated into a Roman triumphal arch – the connection with the former iconography being maintained in a new guise. Once established, this 'arch' pattern of case was to last, unchanged in principle, for the entire duration of the native Italian school of organ building (Figure 5.4). The instruments themselves never grew very big, and classical architecture and design ruled Italian taste in organ cases from the fifteenth century until modern times.

Meanwhile in northern Europe, particularly in an area centred round Hamburg (but with tendrils reaching as far as Poland in the North and Bohemia in the South), the development of a sophisticated and colourful style of organ building and the construction of many large instruments led to a style of organ case in which rigorous logic is applied to form, function and embellishment. A twentieth-century term describes organs of this type – the *Werkprinzip* (work-principle; explained below).

Once the idea of having an instrument of more than one manual was established, it was natural that some kind of visual and structural order should be sought for the various components. The relationship of one manual division to another was clear enough when the first positive organ was placed behind the back of a player seated at a larger fixed instrument. The organist could now turn round and play the 'baby' organ for contrast in pitch, placement and thus tone; from this developed the *Rückpositiv*. An organ further enlarged to include large *trompes* (bass pipes from which the pedal organ is ultimately derived) would display them as separate towers to right and left, with their own structure (Figure 5.5). Another small instrument, effectively a regal, might also be at the early player's command: from this developed a tiny division, with its own keyboard, placed behind or immediately above the music desk: the *Brustwerk*. In a

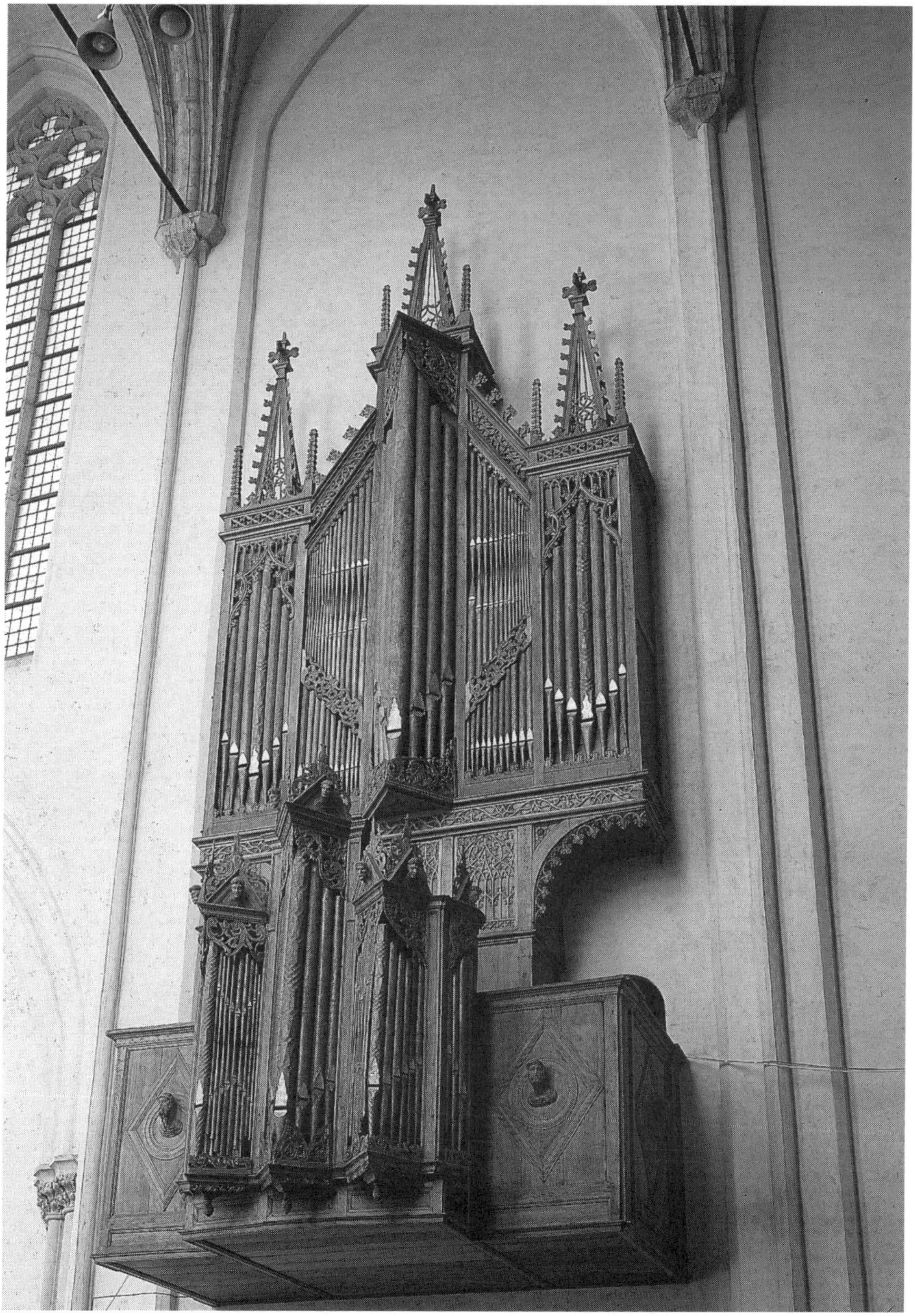

Figure 5.3 Organ case from St Nicolaas Utrecht, now in the Koorkerk, Middleburg (Netherlands). The main case was built in 1479–80 by Peter Gerritsz to house an instrument of the *Blockwerk* type (the chest survives). The smaller *Rugwerk* case was added in 1580, and shows a developing interest in casework elaborated in plan as well as in elevation, moving away from the castellated 'houses' of earlier instruments.

Figure 5.4 By the end of the middle ages the Italian organ was developing along lines different from the rest of Europe. This example at Santa Maria della Scala in Siena in about 1515, was built by a team of local craftsmen of which the organ builder was only one member. The classical case, in the form of a triumphal arch, had already become the standard form for Italian organs, and would remain so until modern times. The instruments, usually of one-manual only, were intended for a particular role in the celebration of the mass rather than for any ostentatious musical display, and remained modest in size.

Lübeck: Jacobikirche
(W. End)

A G Hill del.

Figure 5.5 The west-end organ of the Jakobikirche, Lübeck, Germany, as it existed prior to destruction by bombing during the second world war. Typical of ostentatious instruments in the prosperous cities on the coast of northern Europe, it also demonstrates the development of the *Werkprinzip* ideal during the sixteenth and seventeenth centuries. The flat-fronted main case (*Hauptwerk*) was built to house an organ of 1504; the more florid *Rückpositiv* dates from 1637, and the detached and separated pedal towers from 1673.

very large instrument the main *Werk* or *Hauptwerk* might have been split into two chests, lower and upper: the upper one became the *Oberwerk* (Figure 5.6).

Different combinations of these various *Werke* were possible: a two-manual and pedal organ might have *Hauptwerk*, *Rückpositiv* and Pedal or *Hauptwerk*, *Brustwerk* and Pedal, and so on with larger instruments. Because of the different sizes of the departments they naturally differed in pitch (or at least in pitch emphasis) from each other. A typical (but by no means universal) convention is to have the Pedal an octave lower than the *Hauptwerk* (therefore with front pipes twice as long), the *Rückpositiv* an octave higher (with front pipes half as long) and the diminutive *Brustwerk* an octave higher still (usually with the delicate *Schnarrwerk* of regal stops at the front where the pipes could be tuned easily – and often). However, this octave differentiation, though customary, is not a strict rule and there are many variations, especially in later examples from the eighteenth century.

The development of the *Werkprinzip* organ reached its peak in the work of Arp Schnitger (1648–1719); the cases of his organs are representative of the fully-developed Hamburg school (see Figure 15.1, p. 220). Schnitger's art reflected the rise of the independent Friesian middle-classes, and many of them stand in churches built with farmers' money. The Schnitger organ is not 'high' academic art: it is an extremely rich and sophisticated flowering of a folk art that had gained intellectual approval. His cases are exuberant and bucolic; the instruments themselves had popular appeal and the music making of the period must have made church worship almost irresistibly entertaining, as well as uplifting.

In surrounding areas there were variations on the theme. In the northern Low Countries the *Hauptwerk* (Dutch *Hoofdwerk*) and Pedal were more likely to be built in a single block, and organ builders were more likely to work with others on the case design (Schnitger seems to have designed almost all his cases himself). Whilst organs round Hamburg kept their gothic form intact (even though mouldings and carvings followed classical taste from the early seventeenth century onwards), further south organ cases began to incorporate more formal arrangements of pillars, entablatures and pediments – though keeping the arrangement of pipes in towers and flats and stopping short of the fully classical interpretation introduced by the Italians. In Catholic areas the dry intellectuality of the *Werkprinzip* was not followed with such precision; attached pedal towers are common and the *Rückpositiv* – where it appears – is often tiny.

In the Iberian states that make up modern Spain and Portugal the organ did not become the complex multi-keyboard instrument common

Figure 5.6 The case of the organ in the Marienkirche, Stralsund, Germany, built by F. Stellwagen in 1659. Though predating the work of Arp Schnitger, this is already a fully developed and exceptionally large *Werkprinzip* organ, with the various departments, *Hauptwerk*, *Rückpositiv*, *Oberwerk* and pedal, clearly identifiable in the complex mannerist design.

further north (perhaps partly because of a comparative shortage of good timber from which to make numbers of large soundboards for each department). Iberian organ casework tended therefore to remain as a single unit without pedal towers and with only the occasional *Rückpositiv* (*Cadireta*). The decorative scheme of these instruments, in keeping with progress in the architecture of the churches where they stood, moved in orderly progression from the gothic, through the renaissance, to the spectacular and mannerist local version of baroque classical taste known as *churrigueresque*. Spanish and Portuguese organs sometimes stand in pairs on either side of the choir, occupying the arches dividing the chancel from the aisles. They therefore have to be shallow and are usually flat in overall plan. Apart from the usual projecting towers, some three dimensional interest is provided by the provision of batteries of horizontal reed pipes (the *trompeteria*) from about the end of the seventeenth century onwards (Figure 5.7).

The full flowering of the French classical school of organ building took place in the late seventeenth and eighteenth centuries. In its mature form the French organ consisted of two large departments, the *Grand Orgue* and *Positif de Dos* (*Rückpositiv*); other manual divisions and the pedal organ were subsidiary. The French organ case is usually simple in overall form, having a large single-storey main case with the Positif in front (Figure 5.8). A typical French arrangement for the main case is to have five towers with four flats between, but there are variations including seven- and even nine-tower cases.

Prolonged religious and political upheavals in the British Isles prevented any coherent and long-lasting school of organ building from emerging until after the Civil War and Commonwealth of 1642–60. Even then, the English organ remained a small instrument until the nineteenth century. Perhaps the most individual feature of the English case is the application of high-quality cabinet making and the wide use of mahogany in the second half of the eighteenth century. The best examples have the exquisite quality of fine furniture, but executed on a grander scale (Figure 5.9).

In a general essay it is not possible to concentrate on the special features of individual instruments, though some useful comments will be found in the captions accompanying the illustrations in this volume. It is perhaps worth drawing attention to the best-known of all classical organ cases, that gracing the four-manual Christian Müller organ of 1735–8 in the Bavokerk, Haarlem in the Netherlands (Figure 5.10).

This is an immensely complex and sophisticated structure; it is also huge in scale, well over 20 metres tall (the largest pipes on display form the bass of a 32′ pedal stop). It was designed by Müller, working with Hendrick de Werff (the town architect), the painter Hendrick van Limborch and the carvers Jan van Logteren and Jan Baptist Xaverij (Wilson 1979: 29). The basic form of the case is still traditional, with alternating towers and flats reminding the viewer of the gothic origins of the organ. The execution is in opulent baroque taste and it is immediately

Figure 5.7 The Epistle organ in the Cathedral of Segovia, Spain, built in 1702. In 1772 it was
joined by an identically cased Gospel organ opposite, an arrangement typical of larger Iberian
churches. By the beginning of the eighteenth century the extraordinary *trompeteria* had also
become a standard feature: batteries of horizontally mounted trumpet (and regal) stops providing
spectacular aural and visual effects backed up by lavish baroque detailing in the casework. The
highly inventive and elaborate design typical of Iberian baroque was matched in the organs
themselves, which placed strong emphasis on solo and echo effects. Stops are usually divided to
operate in the treble or bass only. Manual departments are divided up amongst numbers of small
soundboards and sub-soundboards, linked by tubes: a method well suited to the hot southern
climate.

apparent that a strict mathematical system of proportion has been used to
lay out the whole, as in all good classical architecture. The result is as near
perfect as can be: balance, order and harmony are handled with truly
remarkable skill. The function of the various parts is immediately apparent, for this is an instrument still more or less in the *Werkprinzip* tradition
of northern Europe. The *Hoofdwerk* stands in the centre, with the
Bovenwerk above and the pedal divided in great towers on either side. The
Rugwerk stands on the gallery front, concealing the organist (whose role is
surely regarded as quite subsidiary to the music he makes).

It could be argued that the great *Werkprinzip* organ cases of the seventeenth and eighteenth centuries combine the structure of the medieval
craft of organ building with classical principles of design and decoration,

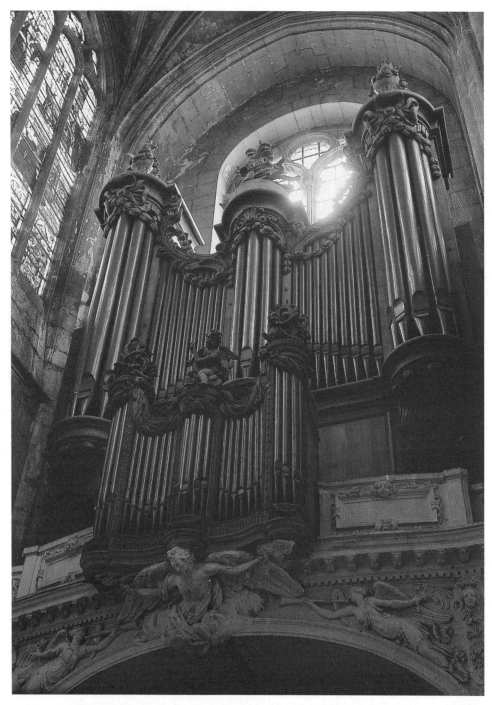

Figure 5.8 The organ in St Gervais, Paris, played by successive generations of the Couperin family, including François Couperin *le grand*. The case, dating essentially from 1758–9, incorporates some material from an earlier one of 1601.

Figure 5.9 The organ in the church of St Mary, Rotherhithe (then a riverside village on the south-east edge of London), built by John Byfield II in 1764-5. This modest three-manual instrument is typical of those that proliferated in prosperous town churches in England during the eighteenth century, built for the accompaniment of congregational psalm-singing and for the performance of solo voluntaries. The exquisite cabinet-made mahogany casework and gilded front pipes are typical of the period, as is an emphasis on sweet and refined tone.

Figure 5.10 The wealthy towns of the Low Countries vied with each other over the building of large new organs in the eighteenth century, vigorously displaying wealth, civic pride and craftsmanship of the highest order. The organ in the Bavokerk, Haarlem, the Netherlands, was built by the immigrant German Christian Müller in 1735-8, and is justly one of the most celebrated organs in the world. When new it was played on by the young Mozart. Despite some alterations in twentieth-century neo-classical taste, it still draws visiting organists from all over the world. The case, in which the traditional forms of towers and flats have been elaborated into a quasi-classical structure of immense complexity and subtlety, was designed by Hendrik de Werff, the town architect of Haarlem. It is painted deep red and heavily gilded, the front pipes being of polished tin. The design is notable for its confident application of harmonic proportion and, with pipes of 32′ speaking length in the façade, the total effect is one of unrivalled majesty.

the two moulded and controlled by a strong sense of rhetoric – a science which stood at the foundation of contemporary education and both intellectual and artistic endeavour. The result is an astonishingly powerful and independent branch of architectural decoration, well worth serious study in its own right. With the coming of baroque and rococo styles in the eighteenth century there was the potential for greater freedom, and in various places this was exercised to the full.

The case of the organ built by Josef Gabler in 1737–50 for the Benedictine Abbey at Weingarten in south Germany is astonishingly different from that at Haarlem, though they are almost contemporary (Figure 5.11). Here the vocabulary of classical design is treated with wild exuberance and freedom, while still retaining the principles of balance and harmony. The result, as far as the organ is concerned, is a riot of form and decoration: this remains the most spectacular organ case ever made. Full use is made of shapes as complex in plan as they are in elevation. The ideas of the *Werkprinzip* have been stretched to the limit: the parts of the organ are not just notionally separate from each other, they have actually exploded to allow the insertion of no less than six windows between different sections of the organ. There are two *Rückpositive* (one is a secondary Pedal section) and a diminutive *Kronwerk* high above the central window. The whole instrument (and only a few pipes in the case are dummies inserted for show) is played from a free-standing detached four-manual console in the centre of the gallery, from where devious and complex mechanical linkages spread out to the various independent sections.

While the baroque and rococo cases of south Germany show a delightful and quite untamed freedom of expression, in other countries the taste for more elaborate and dynamic decoration was mostly accommodated in organ cases of traditional layout and structure. Some of the best examples are to be found in France, standing as witness to the extravagant and accomplished artistic standards that marked the heyday of the *ancien régime* (Figure 5.12).

However, it was the advent of severe neo-classical taste at the end of the eighteenth century that at last began to break down the traditional appearance of the organ case and introduce some new and original forms. When François-Henri Clicquot built an organ for St Sulpice in Paris (completed in 1779), the case was designed by Jean-François Chalgrin (better known as the architect of the Arc de Triomphe) (Wilson 1979: 58–9). Chalgrin's case was no longer a composition of alternating towers and flats, but a version of a classical temple in which curtains of pipes of (apparently) identical length and diameter filled up the spaces between the giant columns. This is perhaps the most extreme example – there seem

Figure 5.11 In Catholic south Germany and Austria Counter-Reformation and rococo came together in some of the most astonishing organ designs ever created. Pre-eminent among them is the celebrated organ in the Abbey at Weingarten, Germany, built by Joseph Gabler in 1737-50. The organ is divided into sections round no less than six windows (the upper row of three visible here) in casework appearing as a reef-like encrustation on the west wall of the building. All sections function, including the two *Rückpositive* and the diminutive *Kronwerk* above the central window. The tonal disposition is as lavish and experimental as is the case, incorporating pipes made of glass and ivory and a number of entertaining musical toys, in addition to a tutti of *Blockwerk*-like scope but interpreted with delightful baroque prettiness.

Figure 5.12 The organ at the Cathedral of Poitiers, France, built by François-Henri Clicquot and his sons and completed in 1790. This instrument, one of the last completed before the Revolution, survives with few alterations and it exhibits the extraordinary richness and confidence of the French school at its very best. The whole organ is voiced on a pressure rather higher than would have been normal in other countries (here 125 mm water-gauge; 75–90 mm being more usual in the eighteenth century). The voicing of the reed stops is especially notable (details were published at the time of the organ's completion) and the *Grand Jeu* is an effect of considerable splendour and *éclat*.

to have been few other instances where an organ builder was persuaded to build an instrument behind an almost impenetrable wall of polished tin. However, the loss of the desire to show pipes in their natural order of length and diameter was significant, and it is a trend that can be seen right across the organ-building world.

While one might regret the decline of interest in an honest display of functional front pipes of natural length, there are many very fine neo-classical cases from the end of the eighteenth century and the first half of the nineteenth century. The cabinet maker's casework in England has been mentioned; the serenely calm painted and gilded cases of Sweden are also worthy of note. However, with the loss of an external expression of the organ's interior layout came a period of experiment and uncertainty. Some organ cases tried hard to be in some way novel or just strictly archi-tectural (i.e. actually looking like a building rather than merely symbol-ising one); the result varies from the odd (Michaeliskirche, Hamburg, J. G. Hildebrandt 1762–7) to the lumpen and ugly (Paulskirche, Frankfurt, E. F. Walcker 1827–33: Figure 5.13).

The result of this period of change is most apparent in the cases devel-oped in industrial Britain after 1850. While a few high-minded English writers and architects continued to defend the traditional organ case – at least in as much as it served to screen the mechanism and pipes in an architecturally acceptable way – various commercial and artistic pres-sures led most English organ builders to abandon the organ case alto-gether. At the Great Exhibition held in London in 1851 the organ exhibited by the firm of Gray & Davison (now in the church of St Anne Limehouse in east London) had no woodwork surrounding the pipes (Bicknell 1996: 244). Other builders soon followed this example.

There were different forces at work here. First, the commercial climate of nineteenth-century organ building led inevitably to economies: the British builders had to survive in an atmosphere of cut-throat competi-tion. Secondly, the gothic revival led to some small organs being built with no casework in the manner of the ancient portative; at some point the idea seems to have been appropriated to large organs also. Thirdly, in Britain there was no consistent tradition of building large organs, and the architectural vocabulary for clothing them had to be invented. Fourthly, in a country where industry was the life-blood of the economy the machine-like aspects of the organ were enthusiastically encouraged: it was natural to place the pipes on open display as they were the very com-ponents that made an organ so remarkable. By the time Henry Willis built his two great four-manual organs for the Royal Albert Hall and Alexandra Palace in London (1871 and 1875) he not only left them with no upper casework but also allowed the audience to see the inside pipes in their bare

Figure 5.13 The German organ of the early nineteenth century was the first to exhibit both romantic taste and a new scientifically informed approach to design and construction. Foremost amongst the first generation of romantic builders was Eberhard Friederich Walcker. This instrument, built for the Paulskirche in Frankfurt, Germany, in 1827–33, secured him an international reputation. New rational principles, some derived from the theories of Abbé Vogler, were extensively applied, even (presumably) affecting the design of the case. With no less than seventy-four stops this instrument opened the possibility of building organs far larger than had hitherto been possible, and by 1850 or so the magic figure of one hundred speaking stops was within sight.

functional order through arches made in the façade for the purpose (Bicknell 1996: 265, 267: Figure 5.14).

In the rest of the world the conventions of traditional casework held sway for longer, but were gradually eroded by the rampant eclecticism of nineteenth-century taste in design. There was certainly no connection between the layout of the organ and its appearance, as there had been in the past; the decline of the *Rückpositiv* as a separate cased division and the increased use of manual divisions enclosed in swell-boxes (and therefore having no pipes available for display) hastened the trend. Where traditional casework was still employed (as for instance in that designed by Dr A. G. Hill for the Hill & Son organ of 1890 in Sydney Town Hall) it was now solely as an architectural screen to the contents within.

From 1900 this was increasingly obvious in organs in the English-speaking world, where the widespread custom of installing organs in chambers (rather than as free-standing furniture) actually would have made it impossible to construct conventional casework. In many

Figure 5.14 Henry Willis's organ in the Alexandra Palace, London, completed in 1875. It replaced an almost identical instrument which went up in flames within a few days of its opening in 1873. This was one of London's grandest concert organs, with eighty-seven stops, six pneumatic pistons to each manual division, and a set of ventils in the French manner. The appearance was striking, with a massive wooden base supporting 32′ pipes and a large central archway affording a view of the Great pipework.

instances the visual component of the design consisted solely of arranging a curtain of front pipes in some kind of order. An organ by the American builder Hilborne L. Roosevelt for the First Congregational Church, Great Barrington (1883) illustrates the point (Figure 5.15).

With the start of a classical revival in the twentieth century came new attitudes towards the appearance of the organ. Though instruments built by proponents of organ reform were often classed as 'neo-baroque' or

Figure 5.15 The organ built by Hilborne L. Roosevelt in 1883 for the First Congregational Church, Great Barrington, Massachusetts, USA. The case was designed by the organ theorist and architect George Ashdown Audsley; its decorated pipes on open display are typical of both British and American organs in the second half of the nineteenth century. This instrument included one of the first successful electro-pneumatic key actions, though the limited capacity of the batteries used for the supply of current before the invention of the electric generator rendered that success somewhat intermittent. Tonal influences on the American organ of the period were cosmopolitan, but the basic layout and character owed much to origins as a colonial branch of the English school.

held to revive the artistic principles and character of a forgotten 'golden age' in organ building, it should not be forgotten that the first stirrings of revival are contemporary with the modern movement in design and architecture and reflect many aspects of the then fashionable functional approach.

This is most obvious in the work of the American builder Walter Holtkamp, whose most characteristic instruments from the 1930s onwards consisted of pipework entirely on open display (Figure 5.16), even to the extent of having the large pipes at the back and the smaller ranks of upperwork at the front (the exact opposite of traditional practice). When skilfully handled (and few builders other than Holtkamp himself ever took the trouble to cast a designer's eye over the effect of this functional array) the result is striking, original and harmonious, though the tonal disadvantages of having mixtures in such an exposed location have arguably never quite been overcome.

In northern Europe the pioneering neo-classical builders (notably Frobenius and Marcussen in Denmark and Flentrop in the Netherlands) sought more detailed inspiration from instruments that conformed to the *Werkprinzip* ideal (though in fact the term was itself coined in the twentieth century). The decorative details of seventeenth- and eighteenth-century cases were not considered to be of much interest, but the idea that the structure and appearance of the instrument should express its design and layout in visual terms became an important plank of their revolutionary argument. In this they were of course suggesting that form should strictly follow function, complying with the principles established by the Bauhaus and the new vanguard of designers and architects. For Danish builders, coming from a country where modern design was an everyday language understood by all, this was a natural path. Flentrop (trained by Frobenius) found another appreciative market in the Netherlands (Figure 5.17). By the 1950s and 60s the ideals were spreading through Germany and onto the international stage.

The revival of casework as part of the new 'classical' organ brought several perceived advantages. The organ was again protected from dust and interference. The relatively mild low-pressure voicing of the pipes could be heard to its best advantage enclosed in a cabinet with roof, walls and back, which tends to suppress high frequencies and boost lower ones.[1] The various manual departments all stood at the front of the organ where they could be seen and heard clearly; remotely placed divisions or departments enclosed in swell boxes were falling out of favour again.

Where such designs were executed with care the results were as splendid as anything created in previous centuries, although the absence of much in the way of decorative detail gives all good modern cases a Spartan

Figure 5.16 The twentieth-century classical revival in North America was spearheaded by two builders. G. Donald Harrison of the Aeolian-Skinner company drew from an eclectic inspiration. The organs of Walter Holtkamp were at once more Germanic and more strictly modern. In this instrument of 1950 at Crouse College Auditorium at the University of Syracuse the modern movement inspiration for the functional display of pipework is clear, and this was a hallmark of Holtkamp's most typical work. The key action was electro-pneumatic, and in this the American classical revival differed from its European equivalent, where mechanical action held sway. The habit of arranging the pipes with the smallest to the front, a break with tradition, accentuated the upperwork and mixture stops at the expense of the foundation, emphasising the anti-romantic character of instruments so treated.

Figure 5.17 The success of the first wave of the twentieth-century classical revival in organ building was largely due to the fine work of three builders: Marcussen and Frobenius in Denmark, and Flentrop in the Netherlands. This instrument, at Doetinchem in the Netherlands, built by Dirk Flentrop in 1952 illustrates well how the revived classical tradition was tempered by modern movement principles. The case is in fact treated more decoratively than most at this time. The underlying *Werkprinzip* layout is clearly visible, and indicates that this is a high-minded instrument eschewing all romantic influence.

and ascetic flavour – quite appropriate given the intellectual rigour and evangelistic fervour of the proponents of the new style. In the writings of Poul-Gerhard Andersen, a one-time employee of Marcussen and an experienced and successful case designer, one can see the importance of order, balance and proportion (Andersen 1956). Careful study of these guiding principles allowed adventurous designers to introduce some truly innovative patterns of case design, and several remarkable asymmetrical cases have been produced.

Sadly in the great majority of examples late twentieth-century organ builders saw no need to provide anything other than a series of wooden boxes of various shapes, starved of any guiding influence or decorative theme that might have given order or beauty to the result. A disappointingly large number of neo-classical organs are completely without any visual embellishment and in this they fall far short of the high ideals of the period they were intended to emulate.

In an age when materials are cheap and labour expensive, decoration of any kind is a luxury. Yet, in the second wave of organ revival, where a much closer interest in the stylistic qualities of old organs is taken for granted and where rigid adherence to modern movement ideals has been pushed firmly into the background, it has again been possible for organ builders to persuade their clients to pay for both the enclosing wooden structure of an organ case and its accompanying mouldings and carving. Nothing quite as opulent as Haarlem or Weingarten has been produced in the twentieth century, but we are at least permitted to enjoy the elaborate appearance of an organ as a feature in its own right. The next generation of craftsmen may well be able to press for a full revival of the traditional organ case and, as in the seventeenth and eighteenth centuries, indulge in a joyful and exuberant architectural expression of their art.

Further reading

The principles of case design are discussed in a number of influential modern texts of which the most accessible include Blanton 1957 and 1965, Andersen 1956/1969 and Klais 1990. A more historical approach will be found in Hill 1883–91, Servières 1928 and Wilson 1979.

6 Organ building today

Stephen Bicknell

Albert Schweitzer's status as a guru of twentieth-century organ building remains undiminished as the century draws to a close. The application of his intellect to an obscure musical craft remains a surprise to those who know him more as a philosopher, missionary and philanthropist. In fact the study of Bach and the organ was the major preoccupation of his early career and was a matter that he took as seriously as any other intellectual endeavour.

> The work and worry that fell to my lot through the practical interest I took
> in organ-building made me wish that I had never troubled myself about it,
> but if I did not give it up the reason is that the struggle for the good organ is
> to me a part of the struggle for the truth.   (Schweitzer 1931)

In this personal admission Schweitzer explains in the simplest possible terms why the organ, dependent on the technology and craft techniques of the middle ages and, at best, a complex and intractable means of making music, remains of enduring interest in a later age where entirely different technologies rule our daily lives (see Joy 1953: 186–213).

Twenty years ago – indeed perhaps at any time between 1930 and 1980 – it would have been obvious to explain Schweitzer's mission in terms of the classical revival: the *Orgelbewegung* or organ reform movement, built round the rediscovery of early instruments and the corresponding repertoire. In fact, though Schweitzer deplored the heaviness and (as he saw it) crudity of the average organ of *c*1900, he also had a message that links him to Ruskin and William Morris. Underlying his use of the works of Bach as a means to rediscovering the tonalities and balance taken for granted in the pre-romantic era is a keen sense of disappointment at the fact that organ building was ruled by commercial considerations. In fact, by 1900 the industrial ethos had invaded organ building to such an extent that the machine-like qualities of new instruments were as much a matter of pride and admiration as their artistic content. When Schweitzer visited the Cavaillé-Coll workshop in Paris in 1914 he saw the vast four-manual organ built for the Baron de l'Epée's castle in Biarritz in 1898, temporarily re-erected before delivery to the Basilica of Sacré-Coeur in Paris where it still stands. Schweitzer pronounced it the ideal instrument for Bach, despite its avowedly Wagnerian resources. The reason perhaps is this: the

Cavaillé-Coll workshop, by then run by Charles Mutin and, until the First World War, maintaining the standards established by the founder, was an artisan workshop not a factory. The sixty or so staff employed gave a sense of judicious artistry compared to the one hundred or more employees milling round a German or English organ plant at the same period. The materials remained luxurious, even extravagant, and each organ was given a personal and individual stamp by the French tradition of employing noted voicer-finishers to carry out the great task of '*harmonisation*' on site. In England Schweitzer's admiration was bestowed on the organs of Harrison & Harrison: instruments of deeply late-romantic character given a powerful artistic charge by the exquisitely detailed personal finishing of Arthur Harrison.

In this context it becomes clear that an important part of Schweitzer's message was his insistence that only the highest artistic standards were good enough for a musical instrument and that anything that smacked of standard commercial practice was deeply suspect. For some of the neo-classical builders inspired by Schweitzer, by the seminal conferences of the 1920s, by the rediscovery of old instruments and their associated repertoire this 'art' aspect was well understood, and in the instruments of Flentrop, Marcussen and Frobenius Schweitzer's concerns are well articulated – albeit with an overall impression of austerity spilling over from the emerging modern movement in design.

Schweitzer could not have anticipated that the modern movement would renew emphasis on function not decoration, and would highlight virtues of design and manufacture rather than those of pure art. None of the organ builders of the early classical revival escaped the influence of modernist thinking. In the work of the builders mentioned above the principles of modern design were executed to the highest standards of individuality and quality. In German-speaking Europe the picture was slightly different. Rudolph von Beckerath, the leading neo-classical builder in Germany after the Second World War, shared many sources of inspiration with his Scandinavian and Dutch colleagues, but did not have their visual sense, usually being content to interpret casework in the form of giant boxes reminiscent of commercial office blocks or even banks of loudspeakers. Rieger, Schuke, Ott, Klais, Kleuker and others celebrated the modern world with enthusiasm, incorporating new materials, experimental tonalities, and revelling in the opportunities offered by, for example, daring and radical layout or electric console gadgetry (even though mechanical key action had been revived for its twin virtues of simplicity and purity).

However, for the vast majority of organ builders, survival depended not on some great artistic statement but on good commercial sense. In

West Germany, for example, the post-war boom and the classical revival conspired to produce new organs in great numbers and to generally high standards. To say that there are relatively few bright stars in this galaxy of actvity would not be entirely unfair. With characteristic thoroughness German master organ builders are trained at a government college at Ludwigsburg and their style is somewhat homogenised as a result. Also, though the number of firms is many and their size modest (at least compared to a century ago), the commercial pressures of a boom period have meant that few have been encouraged to divert resources towards pure art – making such a statement at a time of stiff competition is simply too extravagant. One of the few styles to contrast with the norm of German organ building has come from the firm of Klais, where a more individual family tradition survived the neo-classical revolution. For those who still took refuge in romantic organ music (much decried by the hard-line classicists) the extraordinarily bold and rich palette of a big Klais proved the ideal vehicle for the full modernisation of great nineteenth-century works (see Klais 1975).

Though the classical revival may have been all-conquering in central northern Europe its activities were more than matched elsewhere. In America, where the organ building boom started before the Second World War and continued through it, commercial pressures were high. G. Donald Harrison and Walter Holtkamp pioneered the classicisation of the American organ, and the undeniable artistic quality of their instruments lies in the fact that both builders devoted their lives to tonal questions (although retaining the electro-pneumatic actions of factory organ building, and working in a manner that absolved them from all serious consideration of how to make an organ an object of architectural interest: the pipes were either hidden in chambers or totally exposed in a simple 'functional' display).

In France and Britain no economic boom ever quite managed to lift the organ industry out of a pattern of rebuilding and repairs into the world of organ building proper, and although it should be noted that in France the classical revival was more warmly received than it was in Britain, it is difficult to identify any twentieth-century builders of world class from either country (with the possible exception of Harrison and Harrison in the Arthur Harrison era). In Italy and Spain, where for much of the century the real pressure has been that of poverty, organ building has seemed still more halting and sporadic.

The continuing pressures of commerce on the one hand and modern design on the other have prevented organ building from continuing in the luxurious manner practised by Cavaillé-Coll in the nineteenth century or by Harrison and Harrison in the early twentieth. Even the most obviously artistic of the mainstream neo-classical organs of the period 1950–80 have few concessions to luxury and at every level the abiding impression is of austerity and restraint, even if sometimes carried out on a grand scale (for neo-classical organs in Britain, see Rowntree and Brennan 1975, 1979 and 1993).

Thus it has scarcely been possible to judge twentieth-century organ building in terms of artistic standards. There have been outstanding instruments, and the names of organ builders given above will give a clue as to where the masterpieces of the mid-twentieth century are to be found. However, the great majority of builders have stuck to their own local modern style, often displaying many virtues in design or manufacture, but rarely rising above the utilitarian virtues expected of any modern factory product.

Most analyses of our own period therefore tend to concentrate on the nature of the classical revival and judge progress and quality in terms of design virtues. The modernist approach is readily evident in the writings of Zachariassen (1969), Andersen (1956/1969) and Jancke (1977), in the organs of Flentrop and von Beckerath, and still more so in the futurism of Jean Guillou and German theorists such as Hans Klotz. Even to a writer like Peter Williams, where reference to a hypothetical 'golden age' in the past is maintained with dogged continuity, modernism is evident both in the concentration on the virtues of the *Werkprinzip* and in the determined exclusion from the Communion of Saints of anything with the remotest romantic taint.

Yet Williams's keen interest in the historic roots of the organ have permitted him to grasp an emerging new movement in organ building without quite realising that its most remarkable feature is the way in which it offers fulfilment to Schweitzer's hope of an artistic revival. Though the American organ building scene has remained for the most part a wholly commercial concern, a vocal minority has emerged to restate the 'art' position with more earnestness and intensity than any of their predecessors.

American tracker builders were keen to distance themselves from instruments that had classical tonal schemes but electro-pneumatic action and no real case – standard fare in the USA until arrival of a few European imports in the late 1950s. By 1970 it was clear that three were pre-eminent, Fisk, Noack and Andover. Of these three Charles Fisk rapidly became the most respected; though the instruments he built until his early death in 1983 (his colleagues continue his tradition under the Fisk name) were original and clearly modern in style, his deep intellectual awareness of the importance of history, his grasp of the underlying philosophy of style, and his totally individual approach to every organ building problem allowed him to stand head and shoulders above his contemporaries. By 1975 the emergence of John Brombaugh's first organs in close imitation of north German instruments of the early seventeenth century had further widened the picture and had brought a seriously 'authentic' builder into the limelight.

For Williams the work of Brombaugh – intractably correct in almost every historical detail – offered justification of his belief that the future of the organ lay in its past. The nearest equivalent in Europe lay in the work of Ahrend in Germany and Metzler in Switzerland, yet neither of these two builders could be seen to have escaped quite so far from the pure asceticism of modern movement principles. A Brombaugh organ had all the virtues of purity, plus elaborately carved historical casework, luxurious details executed in precious timbers, and many exuberantly cranky touches in direct imitation of the eccentricities of the renaissance and early baroque – amongst them unsteady or 'free' wind and unequal temperament. The fact that the success of the Brombaugh type quickly spawned a number of offshoots and imitators (Taylor & Boody, Paul Fritts, Ralph Richards and others) could easily lead one to believe that it was the *extent* of the authenticity that was their most distinguishing feature. In fact it may be worth arguing that the most significant element of their work is their success in reviving the notion of organ building as a total hand-craft enterprise in which the application of any economy in materials or decoration is seen as undesirable – if there is only a little money the customer gets a small organ, but still a very beautiful one.

Singular dedication to principles is not however the reserve of neo-classical builders, and the appearance late in the century of several 'art' builders with romantic leanings has shifted the picture a great deal.

The seminal instrument in this movement was the organ by Åckermann & Lund in the Katarina Kyrka, Stockholm, built in 1975 (since destroyed by fire) and incorporating some eighteenth-century and much nineteenth-century material. This was a thoroughly romantic instrument owing a very considerable debt to the work of Cavaillé-Coll. Regarded as a 'naughty treat' by many neo-classically trained players, it was nevertheless admired hugely for its sheer tonal beauty, conveyed very well in a number of recordings.

The Cavaillé-Coll 'bug' was already spreading quickly in 1976, and became even more apparent in 1984 when the young Dutch firm of van den Heuvel built, amid controversy, a mighty eighty-stop instrument at Katwijk-aan-Zee also inspired by Cavaillé-Coll. In these instruments and others it has become clear that the question of quality no longer resides in allegiance to a neo-classical ideal (and indeed may never quite have done so). In Britain, new organs by Mander have broken the classical mould, and in America the work of Rosales, Jaeckel, Noack and others confidently celebrates aspects of the romantic tradition.

Whatever these builders are up to, it has to be made clear that the majority picture is that of continuing commercial organ building, whether of relatively standardised encased tracker organs in Germany or of showy electro-pneumatic instruments in the United States and Canada. In North America, where the huge size and affluence of the continent allows a view of the entire potential of modern organ building, it may be that we have a glimpse into the future.

Between the commercial American organ builder and the manufacturer of the electronic substitute the differences are now slight. Both offer the same kind of tonal schemes and a similar playing experience, with the only significant and obvious contrast being the provision of pipes in the one and loudspeakers in the other. However, the difference between the joint armies of commercial organ building (both pipe and electronic) and the art builders is substantially clear and widening. At the pinnacle of the latter, perhaps, stands Munetaka Yokota, who built the Gottfried Silbermann-inspired organ for California State University at Chico using entirely local labour and materials, and working for several years on site just as a seventeenth- or eighteenth-century master might have done.

While this extravagantly slow but perfectionist method of working – and the patronage and patience required to sponsor it – may remain exceptional, the principles of care and attention to detail it illustrates are common to the highest levels of organ building round the world. Such instruments are often, but not always, related to a specific historical style. This need not necessarily be archaic – the appearance of strong romantic and contemporary influence in the work of Rosales or van den Heuvel is notable, as is the relaxation of the neo-classical rule that only mechanical action is acceptable. Fisk and van den Heuvel, amongst others, have revived the use of the pneumatic lever and, with renewed interest in the romantic repertoire and the large organs that go with it, there is a now a very real prospect that the debate over the virtues of electro-pneumatic action in 'art' organ building may revive. Elaborate and showy casework, complete with carving and decorative mouldings, is returning to organ building with a force and enthusiasm not seen since the middle of the nineteenth century. The most serious-minded builders have also been prepared to divorce themselves from the standardised pipework of the nineteenth- and twentieth-century organ factories, rediscovering the many constructional details that contributed to the art of voicing in the more distant past. The new (or revived) tonal worlds that have been opened up have been stimulating, and have stood well alongside the revival of slightly unsteady or 'live' bellows winding systems and experiments with unequal temperaments. Keen interest in the restoration of old organs, centred round the many surviving early instruments in Europe, has fuelled the new movement with its massive input of technical details and unfamiliar organ building recipes.

For the European builders who rose to fame during the pure classical revival of the 1950s and 60s the picture has changed. In Germany, the Netherlands and Scandinavia the local firms have built enough reliable new organs to have flooded their home markets. The old avant-garde, represented by firms such as Marcussen, Frobenius, Flentrop, von Beckerath, Rieger and others, has been obliged to take the international market seriously and to modify its former purist stance. All the firms mentioned have made attempts to introduce a more eclectic style, perhaps moving towards some of the romanticism evident in the work of Klais and joining the latter company in its international success. However, this has introduced an element of hard competitiveness not apparent a generation ago. Most of these companies have made only partial progress in the revival of more artistic casework, still using simple modern movement principles albeit sometimes overlaid with extra decoration. Nor have they cared to pursue the kind of detailed historical research that has distinguished some of the newer firms, tending to stick with ultra steady regulator wind systems, equal temperament, and the inherited conventions of neo-classical tonal schemes and pipework. With some the challenge of building really large multi-purpose organs has led to a ready acceptance of the idea that, though mechanical action may be desirable for individual departments, the manual couplers may be operated by a direct-electric system. This suggests a discontinuity in their logic – one that is being exploited by those prepared to reconsider the requirements of the romantic and modern repertoire from the ground up with an eye to technical and artistic consistency. For the more serious-minded builders mechanical action means mechanical coupling too – for exactly the same philosphical reasons – and, where an organ is too big to be operated mechanically, pneumatic assistance is now being explored as in the nineteenth century.

However, the joint production of these different groups adds up to a broader picture of world organ building, dominated by the surviving neo-classical builders and their post-modern progeny (the latter, incidentally, forming an exact parallel with the world of architecture, where the modernists appear to be in organised retreat from various waves of post-modern eclecticism, classicism and vernacularism). The countries of the old world still dominate in many ways. Germany (now incorporating the slightly different tradition of the former East Germany), the Netherlands and Scandinavia lead the field, with France and (at last) Great Britain entering the world picture. Organ building in Belgium, Iberia and Italy operates on a slightly smaller scale with fewer excursions into the international arena. Typical organ building companies are much smaller than they were a hundred years ago, a workforce of fifty representing a substantial and successful workshop, and with numerous firms as small as three or four staff making a significant contribution to the overall picture.

Outside Europe pockets of activity are to be found in Australasia and Japan. Japan has introduced the pipe organ with characteristic seriousness and thoroughness as part of its general cultural borrowing from the west, importing instruments in large numbers from the most famous European and American firms (Figure 6.1), and developing a small but interesting organ building industry of its own.

However, it is to North America that one must turn for the most stimulating and varied insight into the world of contemporary organ building. The market is huge, partly fuelled by the many rival religious denominations, competing openly for the financial support of their regularly attending members and operating at a level of professionalism that is the envy of their European counterparts (even in countries where the church is assisted by the state). The bulk of the market is one of intense commercial competition, and the most common North American organ is an instrument with electro-pneumatic action sold to the customer on the basis of the completeness of its paper scheme and the provision of an up-to-date console bristling with the latest gadgetry. Such instruments may be swelled in size by some extension or borrowing, may sometimes have electronic voices in place of expensive and space-consuming pedal basses, and may now be fitted with MIDI interfaces allowing an even wider exploration of modern musical technology. The largest instruments of this type may be split into several sections, with subsidiary or 'floating' antiphonal departments that can be switched in and out at will.

Alongside these instruments, where the purchaser's equation is clearly one that relates the number of stop knobs at the console to the expenditure in dollars, the custom-built electronic organ has had a very significant impact. As mentioned above, the two types of organ offer a very similar musical experience, the difference between those with pipes and those without not being as clear-cut as one might imagine – except to notice that a large custom-built electronic instrument is likely to cost less than half its counterpart with pipes and electro-pneumatic action.

A much smaller sector of the American market is occupied by the quite different instruments of the 'art' builders, who exist in considerable numbers despite the commercial pressures of the market as a whole (their prices are a prohibitive 50–100 per cent higher than those of the

Figure 6.1 The organ built by the American builders George Taylor and John Boody for Ferris Ladies College, Yokohama, Japan in 1989. The pipe organ has only existed in Japan since 1900, but since 1950 there has been considerable interest in the instrument and many organs have been built, usually in concert halls, and often ordered from the better-known European neo-classical builders. This instrument, built by one of the new wave of North American builders working in a well-researched and confident style based closely on historic principles, shows Japanese awareness of new trends. Such instruments have revived not just the elaborate casework but also the musical beauty of the finest instruments of the past, and have restored to the pipe organ some of the artistic and decorative qualities discouraged during the earlier classical revival.

commercial firms). The contribution of these companies, some of whom have already been mentioned, has revolutionised the world organ building scene, offering glimpses into a world of craft perfection and intellectual and artistic seriousness that exceeds even the bravest efforts of the neo-classical movement and goes some way to justifying the stance taken by Schweitzer at the beginning of the century.

Thus it is clear that the outstanding contribution to the craft is being made by those builders who are devoting their attention to fine details; as in any other period the names that will become part of future histories and will be identified by our descendants as the 'greats' are not those who are simply competing bravely for a market share (and this now includes the former avant-garde of neo-classical builders), but those who have secured their place through artistic endeavour. Until its recent closure the largest organ building concern in the world was claimed to be that of Möller of Hagerstown, Maryland USA, building eclectic unencased American Classic instruments at highly competitive prices. However, such a firm, despite its obvious influence and importance, could hardly be described as having made a contribution to the the progress of organ building – its entire operation was avowedly commercial and the many economies of manufacture prevented any attempt to convey an artistic message; moreover if there had been a message to convey it would have been a profoundly conservative one.

Those who are successfully making that attempt are no longer attracted only by the sounds of the seventeenth and eighteenth centuries. Their interests have widened to include much of the romantic (though still hardly daring to explore the palette offered by the symphonic organs of the later nineteenth and early twentieth centuries) and, moreover, to incorporate as an integral part of their work the provision of beautiful and artistic cases (these being a far cry from the bare undecorated boxes of the less handsome neo-classical organs). This decorative element is not merely the provision of expensive frills: a builder who can make a beautiful case shows a real vision of organ building in the round, where every aspect of design and construction makes a contribution to the success of the whole.

It is therefore not unreasonable to claim that the organ has recovered its position as a most remarkable hand-crafted object after its century-long affiliation with the worlds of industry, commerce and manufacture. This fact has a singular importance that lifts the pipe organ out of the world of music into a wider one of general artistic expression. To commission a new instrument and watch it arrive is, for the client, a unique experience and one that has no parallel in the modern world. This extraordinary object – arcane, complex and custom-designed – is the joint effort of a group of people whose hand skills are quite beyond the daily experience or comprehension of modern man. The process of installation, often lasting many months and culminating in the assiduous and individual tonal finishing of every one of several thousand pipes, is a notable performance in its own right. The resulting creation combines musical potential with a permanent architectural contribution. Few commissioned works offer such potential at a readily accessible level, especially today when fine art is hideously expensive and arguably very difficult for all but the expert to understand. Few works of art offer us the opportunity to listen, through the medium of music, to the individual, varied and complementary voices of their creators.

7 The fundamentals of organ playing

Kimberly Marshall

There is nothing remarkable about it. All one has to do is hit the right notes at the right time, and the instrument plays itself.

(Comment attributed to Bach by J. F. Köhler, *Historia Scholarum Lipsiensium*, p. 94; cited in Spitta 1880 ii: 744)

J. S. Bach's modest response to compliments on his organ playing is perhaps the most authoritative and succinct account of that art. However, playing 'the right notes at the right time' on the organ is more complicated than it may at first appear. Although organists do not produce the tone of their instrument and are unable to create variations of dynamics and timbre through touch, crafting a musical line from the static quality of organ sound demands an extremely sensitive approach to articulation and to timing the notes that make a musical phrase. The art of playing the organ resides almost exclusively in articulation and timing; these nuances are what distinguishes the organist's technique of touch from that of typists and stenographers, who are also concerned with striking the right keys. For the latter, the way the keys are depressed and released matters little as long as the text is captured in print as quickly as possible. In order to make music on the organ, however, a mechanical approach to accuracy is insufficient; the organist must cultivate different ways of depressing and releasing keys to create the musical nuances possible in other instruments where the tone is produced by the player.

The dynamic stability of the organ makes it ideal for the performance of counterpoint since each line is heard at approximately the same loudness and timbre throughout the compass of any combination of stops. It is not surprising that the instrument's most cherished repertoire is contrapuntal, because the independence of the parts is brought out by the uniformity of organ tone. The player's task is to articulate each line of polyphony so that it can be heard clearly, even in reverberant acoustical settings. The organist is like a one-person ensemble, or even orchestra, and this demands a finely tuned musical ear that can isolate individual voices. In many instances of two- or three- or four-part counterpoint, the voices are most clearly discernible when each is played on its own keyboard with separate rank(s) of pipes fulfilling the roles of separate instruments. In dense polyphonic textures, such as the six-part Ricercar from Bach's *Musical Offering*, the demands on touch are even greater. The musician who performs polyphonic scores of up to ten or more parts with both hands and feet must also possess great technical prowess over the instrument's multiple manuals and pedalboard. The following sections focus on the fundamental issues, both musical and technical, involved in playing the organ.

Position at the instrument

Most writers on organ technique stress the importance of a relaxed position at the console, with the body in the middle of the keyboard and the hands and feet poised lightly, as if floating, upon the keys and pedals. The spine should be straight, not stiff, with the head poised upright upon it. To find this ideal posture, one might imagine being a marionette that is gently pulled by a string from the top of the head; the axis of support from the two pelvic bones to the head enables the arms and legs to move freely over the keyboards and pedals, providing a centre from which the multifarious activities of organ playing can radiate. Artists practising and performing under pressure are prone to hunching the shoulders and bending the neck back, thereby breaking this vertical line and putting stress on muscles that are not designed to maintain a state of contraction for long periods. But this natural tendency should not be countered with another type of tension, such as pulling the shoulders back or pushing the chin down. Rather, the posture is achieved by finding the right alignment between body parts so that there is no unnecessary muscular strain and the limbs can move freely.

In the Preface to his first *Livre d'Orgue*, Guillaume-Gabriel Nivers explains: 'To play agreeably, you must play easily; to play easily you must play comfortably; and for this effect place the fingers on the keyboard gracefully, comfortably and evenly, curving the fingers a little, mainly the longer ones, to make them even with the shorter ones' (Nivers 1665: preface, n.p.). A natural relaxed position, where the hand is shaped like a cup with the fingers curved gently over the keys, is advocated throughout the technical literature. The wrist should be in line with the arm and hand. Diruta laments the 'poorly-trained hands' of organists who 'hold the arm so low that it is under the keyboard' making the hands seem as though they were 'hanging from the keys' (Diruta 1593: 5r; 1984: 53). He considers the most significant of all the rules to be that the arm must guide the hand, so that the hand and arm are always directly in front of the key that is sounding. In this way, the position of the hand is not distorted in lateral movements and the fingers remain parallel to the keyboard, ready to depress the keys. Diruta specifies that 'the fingers must press rather than strike the key, lifting only as much as the key rises'. Over two centuries later Forkel instructs those wishing to imitate J. S. Bach's keyboard playing 'that no finger must fall upon its key, or (as also often happens) be thrown on it, but only needs to be placed upon it with a certain consciousness of the internal power and command over the motion'. (David and Mendel 1945: 307). Organists who raise the hand unnecessarily to strike the keys lose control moving from one note to another, and this can produce choppy playing that undermines the fluid projection of melody. The extra time needed for the raised finger to reach the key also hinders the execution of fast passagework. Economy of movement permits greater virtuosity, and warnings against excess motion abound in the organ tutors of all times. The fingers should work independently with small gestures primarily from the joints. Agility and suppleness are more vital in organ playing than actual strength, and to maintain fine technical control one must avoid expending too much energy at the keyboard. These very features are stressed by Forkel in his description of Bach's organ technique: 'Seb. Bach is said to have played with so easy and small a motion of the fingers that it was hardly perceptible. Only the first joints of the fingers were in motion; the hand retained even in the most difficult passages its rounded form; the fingers rose very little from the keys, hardly more than in a shake [trill], and when one was employed, the other remained quietly in its position. Still less did the other parts of his body take any share in his play, as happens with many whose hand is not light enough' (David and Mendel 1945: 308).

Position at the pedals

In the preface to his influential *Ecole d'orgue*, Jacques-Nicolas Lemmens writes: 'If the organ is the king of instruments, let us observe that it is also the most complicated and the most difficult. The player must join to the movement of the hands that of the feet' (Lemmens 1862: 1). The performance of musical lines by the feet is what most obviously distinguishes the organ from other keyboard instruments. This physical co-ordination demands many hours of practice to develop a pedal technique that is fluent and assured. The organist's body should be positioned solidly on the bench, forward far enough to allow the legs to be easily pivoted to the right or left, as necessitated by the pedal line. The bench height is crucial to the comfortable position of the feet, with both heels and toes resting lightly on the pedals. (The benches of many historical organs are too high for the heels to lie on the keys, and in these cases it is very difficult to use the heels when playing.) The angle between the thigh on the bench and the shin leading down to the pedals should be at least 90° to prevent unnecessary tension in the thigh muscles. When intervals of about a fifth or less are being played, the legs should be held loosely together with the knees touching, but for larger intervals, the knees will separate naturally. Still, the legs generally move together and should execute melodic lines as a unit, like the fingers of a hand. Just as the arm guides the hand to position the fingers over the keys, so the leg guides the ankles and feet into position over the pedals. The feet move downwards from the ankle to depress and release the pedals with small efficient movements, like those used by the fingers to play the keys. The control over articulation will be better if one plays on the inside edge of each foot (only possible for the right foot in the upper half of the pedalboard and the left foot for the lower half), so the ankles should be turned in slightly to facilitate this. As with the fingers, the amount of motion is kept to a minimum, so that the feet remain close to the pedals at all times. Even J. S. Bach's greatest critic, Johann Adolph Scheibe, marvelled at the ease of his co-ordination between hands and feet: 'One is amazed at his ability and can hardly conceive how it is possible for him to achieve such agility, with his fingers and his feet, in the crossings, extensions, and extreme jumps that he manages without mixing in a single wrong tone or displacing his body by any violent movement' (David and Mendel 1945: 238).

Accents

The eminent virtuoso Charles-Marie Widor is said to have told his students that if he were to open the windows of his apartment in the middle of the night and play a short chord on the tutti of his house organ, no one would notice, but that a sustained chord on the softest stop would have his neighbours looking out to see what was wrong (Geer 1957: 106). Thus the master demonstrated a fundamental principle of organ playing: prolonging a sound intensifies its effect. This is especially true in a reverberant acoustic, but even in a dry room, surface reflection supports a sustained tone. Since organists cannot use dynamic variations to emphasise metrically or thematically important notes, they take advantage of acoustical properties to define pulse and to make accents. Preceding a note with silence or delaying a note rhythmically makes it stand out more vividly than others, while lengthening a note relative to others makes it sound stronger. The skilful use of silence and sound enables the organist to create the impression of upbeats and downbeats within a musical phrase.

Many treatises on music before the nineteenth century describe articulation as a way to clarify the succession of strong and weak beats within a musical pulse (Houle 1987: Chapter 5). The construction of most early music relies on short figures that maintain rhythmic flow in equally notated beats. But in performance, variations in importance must be made to avoid a monotonous succession of evenly spaced beats. As early as the sixteenth century, treatises on instrumental performance distinguish notes of equal value as 'good' or strong and 'bad' or weak, depending on their position within the metric pattern of the music. (Diruta 1593 is the first writer on keyboard music to make this distinction.) The international musician Georg Muffat explains in the preface to his *Florilegium secundum* (1698): 'Good notes are those that seem naturally to give the ear a little repose. Such notes are longer, those that come on the beat or essential subdivisions of measures, those that have a dot after them, and (among equal small notes) those that are odd-numbered and are ordinarily played down-bow. The bad notes are all the others, which like passing notes, do not satisfy the ear so well, and leave after them a desire to go on' (transl. from Houle 1987: 82). Successions of 'good' and 'bad' notes underscore the metre of a piece, with the first beat of each bar being the strongest note and the upbeat to the next bar the weakest. This hierarchy of good and bad notes extends to the subdivisions of the beat, so that in a group of four semiquavers the first and third (Muffat's 'odd-numbered' notes) are stronger than the second and fourth. The organist creates this metrical stress and release within each bar by lengthening the strong beats and shortening the weaker beats. F. W. Marpurg concurs with Muffat's statement that good notes are of longer duration: 'The good notes are called long and the bad, short, according to their intrinsic quantity [determined by the position the note occupies in the metric scheme]' (Marpurg 1756: 23).

It can be beneficial to compare musical structure to the forms used in speech. Each note is like a syllable: its attack resembles a consonant, while its duration is a vowel sound. Just as notes are organised according to beats, syllables are grouped together as words, and both words and musical beats constitute larger structures known as phrases. To be intelligible, language is accentuated by syllables with differing degrees of stress, just as the notes in a musical phrase must be articulated according to their metre. This is achieved on wind instruments by tonguing with different syllables to obtain varying attacks, and on stringed instruments by using different bowing techniques. (The historical information about these instrumental articulations is summarised in Erig 1979: 30–58.) Organists create a sense of metre by holding downbeats longer than upbeats, so that a passage notated in duple rhythm as $\frac{4}{4}$ ♩ ♩ ♩ ♩ might be performed as $\frac{4}{4}$ ♩ ♪. 𝄾 ♪. 𝄾 ♪ 𝄾 or even $\frac{4}{4}$ ♩ ♪𝄾 ♪ 𝄾 ♪𝄾. The subtle alteration of note values enables the organist to emphasise metrically or melodically important notes; the amount and type of alteration will vary greatly depending on the style of the music and the acoustic in which it is performed. The player must develop a keen ear and a flexible touch to adapt to these differences in performance, and this requires years of practice and attentive listening. A good exercise for experimenting with varied note values at the organ is to imitate the accentuation of a word or phrase by repeating a note with the same finger. 'Cambridge Companion to the Organ' would look something like this in rhythmic notation: ♩ ♪꜔♪ 𝄽 ♪꜔♫♩ ♪ 𝄽, but in organ playing it is possible to create much finer degrees of distinction, even imitating the minute differences in accentuation between individual voices. Once one is attuned to the rhythmic fluctuations within spoken phrases, the ear will easily guide the fingers in the performance of a musical phrase with a regular metre.

Lengthening a note relative to others makes it seem louder although it is played at the same dynamic level. Another way to create an accent on the organ is by delaying a note. This is ideal for emphasising the top note in a phrase or an unexpected dissonance, and it represents an important type of rhythmic flexibility that has characterised the performance of organ music for centuries. Such metric freedom can be used at specific times or more generally throughout a piece, when it is known as tempo rubato ('robbed time'). A melody played freely over an accompaniment in strict time is effective in performing homophonic textures. This type of rubato was greatly prized during the second half of the eighteenth century, when it was described by C. P. E. Bach (1753/rev. 1787: 161–2) and Daniel Gottlob Türk (1789/1982: 363–4). More relevant to organ performance is rubato that affects all parts of a composition as they move together freely in accordance with the mood and texture of the music. Such fluctuations of tempo were recommended by Frescobaldi in his preface to *Fiori musicali* (1635), and they later became a hallmark of romantic performance practice, where changing tempi reflected spontaneous expressions of emotion.

Attacks and releases

The tone and tuning of the organ are determined by the builder and pipe voicer, so that it is not possible to vary the quality or intensity of tone through touch, as on the clavichord or piano. Yet unlike these other keyboard instruments, where the sound fades as soon as the string has been struck, organ sound is maintained as long as the corresponding key is depressed. In addition to its notated duration, each note has a beginning and an end, and the quality of these attacks and releases is affected by the speed with which the pallet admits or stops the flow of wind to the pipes. Mechanical action transfers the depression and release of the key into the opening and closing of the pallet underneath the pipes. This control over the pallet enables organists, like players of wind instruments, to vary attacks and releases when shaping musical lines. Several of the different ways to connect any two notes are depicted in the table of organ articulations shown in Figure 7.1 (this table is based upon a diagram used by Harald Vogel in his teaching). Releases that are widely spaced produce a staccato effect, shorter breaks between the release of one note and the attack of the next create a non-legato, and no interruption of the sound between release and attack yields a legato line. Varying degrees of legato are achieved by overlapping the attack of each note with the release of the note preceding it. The ability to realise these subtle nuances of touch in the articulation of a musical line is the essence of organ playing.

Although written sources rarely provide unambiguous descriptions of organ playing, historical documents suggest that over time an increasingly close articulation between notes was used. Surviving sixteenth-century treatises suggest that the usual touch allowed the attacks and releases of each note to be heard. Santa María explains in *L'arte de tañer fantasia*: 'in the striking of the fingers on the keys, one should always lift the finger that has first struck before striking with the one immediately following, both ascending and descending. And one should always proceed thus, for otherwise the fingers will overtake one another, and with this overtaking of the fingers, the tones will overlap and cover one another as if one were striking 2nds. From such overlapping and covering up of one tone by another, it follows that whatever one plays will be muddy and slovenly, and neither purity nor distinctness of tones is achieved' (Santa María 1565: 38v; 1991: 97). This concern with clarity is echoed through the centuries, but rarely is the desirable relationship between notes so explicitly stated. Each note is fully released before the next is played, yielding the articulation depicted as 'structured legato' in the table of articulations. This is the predominant articulation to be used in music composed before the nineteenth century, allowing each note to be heard clearly without any silence breaking the musical line. There will nevertheless be fluctuations in the sound, created by the slight diminuendo of the release as the pallet closes and by the speaking noise of the following note as wind enters the pipe(s). These nuances create a vibrant musicality, although they may seem to break the 'legato line' for ears that are unaccustomed to hearing the attacks and releases of organ sound because of the overlapping articulations featured in later music.

The structured legato is most easily illustrated by the close repetition

Figure 7.1

Table of organ articulations

Key A   Key B

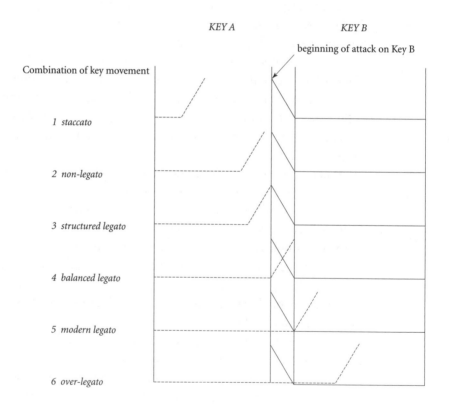

of a single note, where the release of the key leads immediately into the attack of the repetition. By repeating the note with the same finger, the organist develops a feeling for the depth of the keybed and the speed with which the pallet can be made to open and close. There should be no gaps between the notes, although the attacks and releases should be audible. This technique produces a relaxed feeling of being suspended on the key; weight is applied to depress the key, but the action will release the note as soon as the weight is removed, effectively pushing the finger back up with the key.

The next stage in learning the structured legato touch is to apply it to a series of consecutive notes using the same finger, as shown in the next exercise, where a scale is played with one finger only. Again, there should be no break in the sound of these scale passages, where the release of each note leads directly into the attack of the next. The player will feel the key rise up as the weight is removed, and the arm should guide the finger into the position for the next note:

To play a simple line beautifully, the hands and fingers must be relaxed so that the move from release to attack is effected smoothly and without effort. Diruta gives a useful analogy for this: 'When one slaps in anger, one uses great force, but when one wants to caress and charm one does not use force but holds the hand lightly in the way we are accustomed to fondle a child' (Diruta 1593: 5r; 1984: 53). Much control is required for this gentle touch, and the organist should listen carefully to the pipe speech in the acoustic to determine the most effective speed for the attacks and releases.

For performing diminutions, Diruta suggests a slightly closer connection between notes than that advocated by Santa María: 'Remember that the fingers clearly articulate the keys so that one does not strike another key until the finger rises from the previous one. One raises and lowers the fingers at exactly the same time' (Diruta 1593: 8r; 1984: 63). This articulation, where the release of one key and the attack of the next overlap, is illustrated in the table of organ articulations as the 'balanced legato', and it is ideal for the execution of ornamentation and slurred passages in early music. With this articulation, the initial transient noise of the subsequent pipe masks the release of the preceding note. Care must be given to fingering when using the balanced legato, since it is not possible to play consecutive notes with the same finger as in the articulations discussed above. One should imagine the slurred notes being played with one bow-stroke on a stringed instrument or with one breath on a wind instrument.

On the organ, this is reflected by partially obscuring the releases of each key by the following attack so that the notes sound closer together. Short figures taken from renaissance and baroque music can be employed to practise the technique.

Descriptions of keyboard touch by later writers such as Mattheson (1735: 72) and Türk (1789: 356; 1982: 345) suggest that the structured and balanced legato were still the usual approaches to articulating organ sound during the baroque. Forkel may be referring to a similar technique in his description of Bach's keyboard playing, where the finger is not raised perpendicularly, but glides off the forepart of the key by drawing the tip of the finger back towards the palm of the hand: 'In the transition from one key to another, this gliding off causes the quantity of force or pressure with which the first tone has been kept up to be transferred with the greatest rapidity to the next finger, so that the two tones are neither disjoined from each other nor blended together' (David and Mendel 1945: 38). This yields the proper amount of clarity without sacrificing lyricism in melodic projection. As late as 1775, Engramelle's instructions for pinning mechanical organs, based on the playing styles of renowned organists, call for a 'silence d'articulation' following every note of a performance (Engramelle 1775: 18).

The use of musical slurs increased greatly during the nineteenth century, when organ music became more melodically, rather than metrically, orientated. Already before Bach's death, the motoric rhythmic figuration and imitative polyphony of the baroque were giving way to the galant style, with its incorporation of more varied note values and elegant homophonic textures. Pleasing melodies were greatly prized in the new style, and with the advent of romanticism in the nineteenth century, the projection of expansive and emotive melodies became a central concern for all musicians. To imitate the singing line produced by the orchestra, where many instruments playing together created a flowing sound of unparallelled power, organists developed a closer overlapping articulation where each key was released only after the following note had been sounded. This is depicted as the 'modern legato' in the table of articulations. Neither attacks nor releases are heard because they are masked at either end by the sounding of the preceding and subsequent notes in a melody. The modern legato is ideally suited to the long, sinewy lines of romantic music, since it links together a series of pitches sounding at full force without any transient noises between them.

This is the articulation that formed the basis for the legato school of playing established by the Belgian organist Jacques-Nicolas Lemmens, whose technical ideas were adopted at the Paris Conservatoire and exerted enormous influence on organ performance worldwide through such disciples as Widor and Guilmant, and their students Vierne, Schweitzer, and Dupré. Lemmens provided a systematic description of the legato technique in his 1862 organ method, *Ecole d'orgue basée sur le plain-chant romain*. As implied by its title, the book's aim was to enable the organist to play the fluid melodies of Gregorian chant with ease and comfort. But the legato method is much more versatile than this might suggest; it can be applied successfully to most organ music written after 1750, providing great technical security on different types of action. The modern legato touch is well suited for tracker-pneumatic or electro-pneumatic actions where the organist has no control over the speed of attacks and releases, and it helps to compensate for imperfections in pipe voicing, such as delayed speech. But it does not work well on most seventeenth- to nineteenth-century instruments or replicas in which pipe voicing emphasises transient tones for attacks. The changes in musical style and organ-building that arose during the second half of the nineteenth century created a new aesthetic in performance, and the modern legato supplanted the structured legato as the usual way of articulating musical lines.

Fingering

To achieve control over the fundamentals of articulation and timing as discussed above, one must find the most expedient technical means of executing the notes in question. Throughout the long history of organ music there have been many systems of fingering, and each was designed to create the most natural way to perform a specific repertoire with appropriate nuance and accentuation. The general principle for systems before the eighteenth century was to find patterns of fingering that corresponded to the short motives of the music. For example, figuration comprising the interval of a third would be played by the index, third and ring fingers, regardless of which notes were included in the figure:

Longer figures such as scales would be divided into smaller groups and played with fingerings designed to stress metrically strong notes with 'strong' fingers. (Although the conception of strong notes was consistent in the different national styles of writing for the organ, different fingers were used as 'strong' fingers, so it is not possible to generalise here.) This resulted in paired fingerings, where the arm would guide the hand to a new position as the second finger of each pair released its key:

Such systems were very effective in rendering musical motives in the most frequently used keys, which did not exceed three or four sharps or flats, but as organist-composers began to modulate to more distant keys, a different type of fingering was developed to accommodate the more frequent use of black keys. Here, the thumb was turned underneath the fingers to lead the hand to a new position. J. S. Bach is often credited as the inventor of the 'thumb-under' system, which enabled him to play fluently in all the major and minor keys, as required by the Preludes and Fugues in his *Well-Tempered Clavier*. The first printed tutor to advocate modern fingerings exclusively was Lorenz Mizler's *Beginning Principles of Figured Bass*, published in Leipzig in 1739. But the earlier approach to fingering clearly remained in use concurrently with the new system, since C. P. E. Bach includes both ways to finger scales in his *Essay on the True Art of Keyboard Playing*:

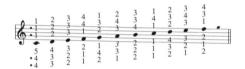

These variants demonstrate the transition from early to modern fingerings that was being made in the mid-eighteenth century, and they remind us that there is no one 'correct' fingering for any given passage. Rather, the organist must determine the most natural way to produce the type of sound desired, varying the spaces between notes and the connections between them to create an expressive rhythmic flow.

When used continuously, the modern legato requires carefully planned fingering, since the same finger cannot be used on consecutive notes in any voice. To avoid 'running out of fingers' in long melodies, the organist must make frequent use of finger substitution, where fingers are exchanged on a key after it has been depressed to prepare for the following note or passage. The mastery of this technique is vital in the performance of music conceived for the sustained modern legato touch. To change fingers on a key, the shorter finger should either move, or find itself in position, under the longer one. The substitution should be made quickly, with as little movement as possible, to prepare the necessary finger immediately to depress the next key. A simple scale can be practised in many ways to gain experience in substituting fingers:

Substituting fingers on chords is also needed in places to create a smooth harmonic line. In this case each substitution takes place separately, as shown below:

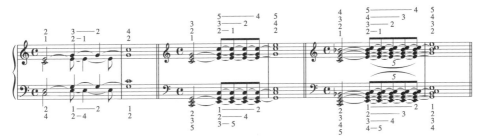

Another useful technique in achieving a fluid legato line is the glissando, where fingers slide from one key to another. Most commonly, the finger or thumb slides off a black key onto the white key directly above or below it. This relaxed sliding motion can greatly facilitate fingerings and should be practised by every finger to assure independence. For the thumb, the tip should be used on the black keys, moving to or from the base of the thumb on the white keys. The following variation on a chromatic scale covers the necessary movements, with most fingers sliding both up and down from a black key:

Although the fingers generally do not slide from one white key to another in legato playing, in many places it is expedient for the thumb to do so. The technique involves a co-ordinated raising and lowering of the wrist to permit pivoting from one key to another using the base and tip of the thumb. In order to ascend with the left thumb and descend with the right, the base of the thumb is placed on the first white key, with the tip of the thumb over the next. By raising the wrist quickly, the movement from base to tip can be effected without breaking contact between the keys. For descending left-hand and ascending right-hand passages, the tip of the thumb is placed on the first key, with the wrist raised. A swift downward motion of the wrist will enable the organist to move from the tip to the base of the thumb smoothly. Again, a diatonic scale passage furnishes a good exercise for the thumb glissando:

In this way, independent melodic lines can be played by the thumbs alone, creeping skilfully along the keys while the fingers perform the other parts of a composition.

Pedalling

The organist's feet must become as skilful as the hands, and a primary consideration is learning to find the intervals on the pedalboard without looking at the feet. Touching the knees and heels provides a gauge for playing intervals between the two feet, and each foot must also be capable of playing seconds and thirds independently, requiring flexible ankles and secure positioning of the foot on each pedal. The various types of articulation discussed above should be practised using the toes of both feet so that the same flexibility of touch will be heard in melodic lines performed on the pedals. Written documents as well as the high benches and short pedal keys of many historical organs suggest that until the eighteenth century, the basic pedal technique was to play adjacent notes with the same toe and to alternate the toes of both feet in more figurative passages. (Heels were certainly used in special cases, since as early as 1511 Arnolt Schlick describes the performance of two parts by one foot.) The changing aesthetic towards a closer legato during the nineteenth century led to greater use of the heel in pedalling, although like the move towards modern fingerings, this was a gradual process. In his *Practical Organ-School* (1818), Johann Christian Rinck indicates two ways of pedalling scales, the old method, alternating the toes of both feet, and the newer method, using the toe and heel of the same foot. Most of his pedal exercises are still for alternate toes, however, and in some figurations he goes so far as to cross the toe of one foot over the other to avoid using the heel and toe of one foot (Rinck 1818/1870: 32–3).

To achieve the modern legato on the pedals, the techniques of substitution and glissando must be learned by the feet. The principles are the same as in the fingering examples, to use the smallest gestures possible and to perform these quickly. In toes-only pedalling, the substituting toe should be placed on the depressed pedal directly behind the other toe to liberate it for the next note to be played. When heels are used, it is generally best to keep them forward on the key, with the substituting toe placed slightly behind. Since pedal substitution is most frequently needed in lines with large intervals, practising this technique with scales is not very useful. The following exercise based on open fifths and fourths is more suitable:

In gliding from a black key to a white key, the toe should be placed at the edge closest to the white key to minimise the distance of the glissando. The chromatic exercise given above for the hands can be used to practise this with the feet. Glissandi with one foot between two black keys are also required in some repertoire; for this one slides on the toes, turning the heel in the direction of the slide to assist the motion.

The ear is always the most important arbiter in determining the best way to finger or pedal any given passage of organ music. The technical advice included here is meant merely as a guide to finding the most efficient and comfortable way of approaching the keyboard. Nevertheless, people and organs have their idiosyncrasies, and what works on one instrument with one organist may not be suitable in another context. Technical complexities of organ playing should not take precedence over musical considerations; precepts of fingering and pedalling need to be continually reassessed to ensure that they produce the type of sound desired by the organist.

Registration

A vital aspect of organ playing is the choice of timbres, controlled by registers, for different musical moods and textures. There are no easy generalisations to be made about registration, for it demands a thorough knowledge of historical instruments and treatises, an ear that is well attuned to instrumental colour, and a vivid musical imagination and sense of style. Facile statements that registration should 'bring out the musical structure' or 'suit the musical style' tell us little about a practical approach to this elusive art. The type of instrument and function for which the music was originally conceived provide some guideposts for the modern performer. Historical sources usually recommend specific combinations of stops for three general purposes which are musically interlinked: (1) to imitate other sounds, such as canaries, little bells or military trumpets; (2) to create a suitable mood for the mode, liturgical function or expressive content of the music; and (3) to 'orchestrate' the musical texture with sounds that blend well together and are well balanced dynamically.

The typical late medieval organ was a *Blockwerk*, literally a 'block' of sound that could not be separated. To obtain variety between the foundation sounds and the higher pitched mixtures, two general approaches were first adopted: to construct multiple keyboards, each controlling a specific type of sound, and to divide the windchest so that by means of a ventil the organist could control the flow of wind to various sets of pipes. These methods have continually been adopted in different styles of organ building, but the most significant way to isolate organ colour became the use of registers, or stops, to control the flow of wind to individual ranks of pipes. This was first introduced in Italy towards the end of the fifteenth century, allowing the individual sounds of the medieval *Blockwerk* to be mixed together at the organist's discretion. This chorus of principal sounds at octave and fifth pitches constitutes the basis of most styles of organ building, and until the nineteenth century the standard Italian organ design was a succession of separable principals to which were added one or two flutes.

During the renaissance, Flemish builders augmented the principal chorus with a variety of colourful flute and reed stops, usually introduced on secondary manual divisions. German composers made full use of these new possibilities to bring out plainsong or chorale melodies with distinctive organ timbres on multiple manuals and pedal. During the second half of the seventeenth century, the French developed registrational schemes for organs with from two to five keyboards and pedal. These combinations were intrinsically related to the textures adopted in organ music, where specific colours were featured on different manual divisions (see Chapter 12). The Spanish and English, on the other hand, exploited the new sounds on one keyboard by controlling different registers for the treble and for the bass. In this way, it was possible to isolate a melody performed on a reed or cornet sound from the foundation accompaniment played in the other half of the keyboard compass.

The gradual inclusion of flute and string stops into the principal chorus during the course of the eighteenth century led to the 'tutti' concept in registration, where the entire organ was employed as a musical entity, like a large orchestra. Rather than contrasting different colours in terraced dynamics and solo–accompaniment textures, the new aesthetic called for a smooth crescendo from the softest foundation stops to the full organ. The fundamental pitch was emphasised by the inclusion of more 8′ registers, while pneumatic devices enabled the organist to play using manual and suboctave couplers. Enclosed divisions of pipes permitted gradual dynamic progressions, and sudden contrasts of sound were effected by quick registrational changes, made possible by ventils and, later, by electric combination action. This romantic approach to organ sound makes different demands on the organist, requiring more frequent changes of timbre and the sensitive use of the swell pedal.

This general overview only hints at the many factors that influence an organist's choice of registration. National styles of composition and different aesthetics of organ sound are treated in much greater detail in the subsequent chapters of this book. But the most important advice concerning registration is often overlooked: since the organist rarely hears the instrument at the console the way it sounds in the room, it is necessary to listen while someone else plays to experience the organ in its acoustic. Only in this way can the performer determine which registrations are most effective and well-balanced. Listening from the audience's point of view can also inform the organist about the most suitable type and amount of articulation.

Practical concerns

Most teachers suggest that a solid keyboard technique be acquired on the clavichord, harpsichord or piano before a student begins to study the organ. Lemmens recommended that a young musician practise the piano for finger dexterity, and this view has been strongly established in organ curricula throughout the world, where prospective students must often pass a piano proficiency examination. Although it is highly desirable for beginning organ students to be familiar with other keyboard instruments, one should not forget that the approach to playing the keys of an organ, a wind instrument, is almost diametrically opposed to that of the piano, a percussion instrument. Organists must focus on releasing the keys to create breathing space in the musical line, whereas pianists are more concerned with attacking the keys, using varying degrees of arm and body weight to produce different types of tone.

Great strength is not usually needed to depress the keys of an organ, but some pressure must be continually expended to keep the key depressed for the duration of the note. The maintenance of this small, albeit constant, pressure presents the danger of repetitive strain injury for organists who are not fully relaxed when playing. This can be especially painful in the upper forearm and should be checked early to avoid complications that can require long periods of rest and even surgery. A good way to assess and control muscular stress in the arm when playing a given passage is to rate the amount of tension on a scale from 1 to 10. Then try to vary the tension by making the arm more and less tense when playing. Organists are often surprised when asked to become more tense, but this is a useful method for learning to control the exertion of the arm muscles. As Frederick Alexander and others have demonstrated, there is no point in 'trying to relax', because the very act of trying creates another sort of tension which can be as detrimental as that which one sought to eradicate in the first place. Awareness of one's body while playing is an important step towards using it effectively and without injury. Many types of physical therapy can be helpful to organists, including the Alexander Technique, as well as more ancient techniques of creating harmony between mind and body, such as yoga and t'ai chi.

Stravinsky's criticism of the organ, mentioned in the Preface, was that 'the monster never breathes'. To sound musical and human, organists must give the illusion of breathing, by using sensitive articulations and shaping melodic phrases. Singing in a choir or playing a wind, brass or stringed instrument can help to develop a keen ear for melody that can then be transferred to organ playing. Most importantly, organists should listen frequently to vocal repertoire and to music for other instruments so that they are familiar with different combinations of timbre and ways of projecting musical ideas to an audience.

Although one usually feels more virtuous the longer one works, it is best to practise in short frequent sessions instead of protracted ones at longer intervals. This is a real problem for organists, who rarely have an instrument that is readily accessible to them. But short breaks during the course of a practice session will help to keep the mind and body alert. It is also possible to reinforce organ practice with work at home on the clavichord, harpsichord or piano, or indeed by 'thinking through' a piece without playing any keyboard at all.

To make the quickest progress in learning new techniques and repertoire, one must be creative when practising, rather than mindlessly repeating pieces over and over again. Slow practice is invaluable in training the body to perform accurately, in a relaxed position with enough time to prepare each note properly. Once you feel comfortable at a slow speed, the tempo can be gradually increased so that the feeling of ease and security are preserved as the hands and feet move faster. The danger of playing slowly is that it demands intense and continuous concentration on details, else the mind may start to wander and sloppiness creep in. To prevent this, slow practice should be employed in short but frequent doses throughout a practice session.

When tackling a new piece, it is best to divide the music into short sections and to focus on each of these individually for a while rather than playing through an entire work repeatedly. This helps to understand the structure of the piece and how the sections relate to each other. It also permits you to isolate the most difficult passages so that you can concentrate on these when you are fresh and your mind is most ready to learn. Learning a piece backwards is a good way to focus on individual sections. With this technique, you begin by studying the last part of a piece and then proceed backwards by section to the opening. Since the conclusion of a work generally includes some degree of recapitulation, knowing the end can be of assistance in learning the beginning. Practising backwards also offers a psychological advantage when you perform the piece from the beginning, since you are always playing into the music you know best.

The process of dividing a musical work into small sections for practice also helps to analyse its structure and to determine its salient features, which should be brought out in performance. Is the piece based on a pre-existing melody, and if so, how are the melodic contours enhanced by the figuration and harmony? The performer needs to prioritise aspects of the musical structure to emphasise in performance so that the guiding gestures of a piece are conveyed clearly to the listener, with a balance between fore-, middle- and background elements.

In contrapuntal music, the independence of parts should be reflected in your practice routines. It is best to take the music apart so that each individual line is learned first, played with the same fingering or pedalling that will be used when everything is put together. One can then separate the music played by each hand and pedal, later combining the two hands alone and each hand with pedal, and finally putting all the parts back together.

To gain technical assurance in difficult passagework, try varying the rhythms systematically. A seemingly endless sequence of semiquavers is learned more thoroughly if it is broken down into smaller groups and practised in rhythmic units: first, as an alternation of 'long–short' rhythms, then reversed as 'short–long', then 'long–short–short–short', and finally its reversal, 'short–short–short–long'. The hand should be relaxed on the long notes, and you should not begin to play the short notes until the fingers are prepared to move quickly and without interruption to the next long note.

To ensure that the articulation in one hand or pedal does not suffer when all the parts are united, practise with a mute manual or pedal, so that as you perform the full texture, your ear will be drawn only to the voice that is played where stops are drawn. This is a good way to develop listening skills so that you are able to hear all voices clearly. Singing one voice while playing the others is another method for learning contrapuntal music and refining the ear. And for the very ambitious, try playing a melody on another instrument while accompanying yourself with the pedals of the organ! (The north German composer Nicolaus Bruhns is said to have done this while playing the violin.) The more creative you are in finding ways to challenge yourself while practising, the more successful will be your quest to learn and perform the organ repertoire. The goal must surely be to achieve the sort of facility and freedom exhibited by J. S. Bach, the master organist who enabled each instrument to 'play itself'.

8 A survey of historical performance practices

Kimberly Marshall

In my opinion, there are faults in our way of writing music, which correspond to the way in which
we write our language. That is, we write things differently from the way in which we execute them;
which means that foreigners play our music less well than we play theirs.

(François Couperin 1717: 39)

The notation of music is at best an approximation of the timbre, quality
and placement of sounds in time. Musicians universally rely upon aural
traditions to fill in notational gaps, and this is especially true in keyboard
training, which usually takes place in individual lessons where the teacher
instructs the pupil through verbal descriptions and practical demonstrations. Traditions of interpretation are passed from generation to generation through this personal contact where ambiguities arising from the
descriptions can be clarified by the demonstrations. Over time, changing
musical aesthetics are reflected in changing approaches to interpretation,
so that the performance traditions for earlier musics are gradually transformed. This is especially true for the organ's vast repertoire, which spans
a wide chronological and geographical spectrum with many variations in
musical style and organ building. To perform this music convincingly
today, it may be helpful to assess relevant information preserved in historical organs, treatises on keyboard technique, and sources of music. This
chapter presents a selective historical overview of fingering, ornamentation and rhythmic alteration as practised in the performance of organ
music until the time of Bach.

Sixteenth-century German sources

The first written sources to describe aspects of organ-playing technique
date from the sixteenth century, when instrumental music was developing
independently of vocal forms and printing enabled experts to disseminate
their teaching through practical tutors. The earliest of these for organists
was published in Mainz in 1511 by Arnolt Schlick. Entitled *Spiegel der
Orgelmacher und Organisten*, the treatise deals with such pragmatic issues
as constructing a smooth responsive action and voicing pipes well. His
infrequent remarks on performance concern the organist's position at the
instrument and provide guidelines on registration. The proper bench

height ensures a relaxed position of the hands and feet so that the top manual of a two-manual organ is at the height of the organist's 'stomach and belt' and so that the feet 'hang or hover' over the pedals (Schlick 1511: ciii v; 1980: 49). If the bench is too low, the organist must lift the feet off the pedals, which does not permit 'scales or running passages in the contra-bass'. Schlick stresses the importance of finding 'a seemly average size' for the pedal keys, so that two parts can be played with one foot (Schlick 1511: cii v; 1980: 45). This suggests that German organists made full use of the pedal in the early sixteenth century, as confirmed in another place by Schlick, who reports that the pedal can take two or three voices to enable organists to realise fully the voice parts of polyphonic compositions (Schlick 1511: bii v; 1980: 29). Such sophisticated pedalling was required in at least one work by Schlick, his ten-part setting of the hymn *Ascendo ad Patrem meum*, where four of the voices are executed by the feet.

Hans Buchner's *Fundamentum* of c1520 is the earliest known treatise to describe fingering at the keyboard. His nine rules employ the second and fourth fingers for strong beats, using 2–3–4 in both hands for figuration involving the interval of a third, 2–3–2–3 for ascending passages in the right hand and descending passages in the left, and 4–3–2–3 for descending passages in the right hand and ascending ones in the left. Buchner's description of the execution of the mordent is unusual: the written note is played and held as the lower auxiliary is played and released. The third finger is predominantly used on notes with this ornament in the fingered arrangement of the hymn *Quem terra pontus* that is appended to the treatise. The suggested fingerings are impossible if one tries to hold the keys for their full notated value, but an interesting characterisation of the three voice parts results from releasing the notes as soon as they become awkward to hold. The use of the same finger in succession for notes in the top voice suggests the use of a structured legato to bring out the cantus firmus. The middle voice of the composition is shared between right and left hands, creating a more open articulation, while there are large breaks between the notes of the bass. When he cautions organists to hold notes according to their notated values, Buchner is probably proscribing a haphazard approach to articulation, so this statement does not necessarily contradict the early releases required by his systematic fingerings.

Sixteenth-century Spanish treatises

After mid-century, there was a proliferation of music publication in Spain, including the detailed treatise of Santa María referred to in the previous chapter. Santa María is the only Spanish author to discuss position at the keyboard, and he recommends holding the fingers higher than the hand, with the second, third and fourth fingers close together over the keys and the thumb dropped below and partially curved under the palm. The low wrist and contracted fingers of this position are shown in Netherlandish paintings of organists from the preceding century (Soderlund 1986: 22), so this way of holding the hand had a long history in performance before it was documented in print. Santa María advocates releasing each key before the next is depressed in order to produce a clear distinct sound (see above, p. 99), and he provides detailed fingerings to realise this articulation, according to the note values and the degree of ornamentation appropriate to them. A succession of semibreves or minims, requiring extensive ornamentation, should be executed by the principal fingers, the third finger of the right hand and the second or third finger of the left hand. Shorter notes do not allow time for using the same finger on successive keys: paired fingerings are best suited to passages of minims or crotchets, while patterns of three and four consecutive fingers permit the speed required in runs of consecutive quavers or semiquavers. The paired fingerings for crotchets that Santa María recommends are 3–4 for the right hand ascending, 3–2 for the right hand descending, 2–1 for the left hand ascending and 3–4 for the left hand descending. For semiquavers he advocates the use of 4–3–2–1 and 1–2–3–4 in both hands. Although Santa María does not stipulate that the fingers cross over the thumb, the low position of the thumb and its use in fast passagework suggest that this may have been the case. A Spanish contemporary, Venegas, is the earliest writer to describe the third finger crossing over the thumb, and this is shown in his scale fingerings for the right hand descending and the left hand ascending (Sachs/Ife 1981: 69). Bermudo's fingerings are exclusively in four-note groups, proceeding from the thumb to the fourth finger and vice versa, which Cabezón replicates for the left hand, while reiterating Santa María's paired fingerings for the right hand.

Santa María considers ornamentation to be an obligatory facet of keyboard interpretation, and he describes a great variety of embellishments which he divides into three categories, *redobles, quiebros* and *glosas*. The simple *redoble* can be likened to a turn,

and the reiterated *redoble* concludes with a trill on the upper auxiliary:

Santa María cautions that redobles should never be very long, 'for that would make the music ugly' (Santa María 1565: 47r; 1991: I, 123). The simple *quiebro* alternates the note with its upper or lower auxiliary,

while the reiterated *quiebro* is like a trill:

Hernando de Cabezón seems to favour the simple *quiebro* when he writes that *quiebros* should be played quickly, to accent the note written in the score (Sachs/Ife 1981: 67). Both the *redoble* and the reiterated *quiebro* may also begin before the beat on the upper auxiliary, a practice that was current when Santa María described it as 'very stylish'. All of these ornaments are played with the principal fingers on the main notes. Santa María concludes his discussion of ornaments with an extensive table of *glosas*, or divisions, with which to decorate all ascending and descending intervals. He stipulates that *glosas* are to be played only on semibreves, minims and less frequently on crotchets, and that all voices should be given an equal number of *glosas*, with imitating voices decorated identically, if possible (Santa María 1565: 58r; 1991: I, 157).

Three types of rhythmic alteration for playing with good style a group of four equal notes are discussed by Santa María. The first type creates a succession of 'long-short' patterns by lingering on the first note a bit longer than its notated value, shortening the second, lingering on the third and shortening the fourth. This is the way that passages of crotchets should be performed and it is the first of three ways for executing quavers. The second way to play groups of quavers is the reverse: shortening the first, lingering on the second, shortening the third and lingering on the fourth. Santa María considers this to be much more elegant than the first method. The third and final way to perform quavers is to hurry through three of them and linger on the fourth, grouping the notes in fours, 'as if three of the quavers were semiquavers and the fourth quaver were dotted'. The example of dotted notes is probably not meant to be taken too literally, since Santa María later cautions that the holding back and hurrying should not be excessive, but only in moderation (Santa María 1565: 45v–46r; 1991: I, 118–20). The author considers this type of alteration to be the most elegant of all, although there is ambiguity as to whether the long quaver falls on or off the beat. Certainly, it is more instinctive to lengthen the downbeat and shorten the upbeats, and this may have been what Santa María intended to describe (Sachs/Ife 1981: 32, note 6).

Italian sources of the late sixteenth and seventeenth centuries

The first writer to relate keyboard fingering to musical accentuation is Girolamo Diruta, who presented his treatise as a dialogue between himself as teacher and an aspiring keyboard player from Transylvania, hence its title, *Il Transilvano*. The first part of this work, published in 1593 and reprinted several times, contains discussions of notation, the musical scale, fingering and ornamentation, and thus is relevant to a consideration of performance practice. Diruta opens his remarks on organ playing by describing to his student the proper position at the instrument. The organist should sit in the middle of the keyboard and allow the arm to guide the hand, which should be level with the arm and shaped like a cup, with the fingers curved. This hand position is more natural than the one advocated by Santa María and became predominant in later styles of performance. Diruta's method of fingering is organised according to the rhythmic position of each note. Notes which fall on the beat are considered to be 'good', and they are played by the 'good' fingers, or the second and fourth fingers of each hand. When the first note of a scale is on the beat, it is played 2–3–4–3–4–3–4 by the right hand and 4–3–2–3–2–3–2 by the left. A 'bad' finger, either the thumb or fifth finger, begins a scale that starts off the beat. Descending scales on the beat are played 4–3–2–3–2–3–2 by the right hand; since Diruta considers the fourth finger of the left hand to be weaker than that of the right, he proposes the regular pairing of 2–3–2–3–2–3–2 for the left hand. He avoids using 2–1–2–1 in ascending passages by the left hand because this could place the thumb on a black key (Diruta 1593: 6r and 6v). Although the principle of 'good' fingers on 'good' notes might seem to create a 'hiccup' pattern of articulation emphasising the downbeat, this does not occur because in moving from the 'good' to the 'bad' finger of each pairing, the hand must shift position. This creates a surprisingly clear and even execution of the short notes in fast passages and should remind us that early fingering patterns do not dictate a specific type of phrasing. One would imagine that a similar approach would have been practised by Adriano Banchieri, a contemporary and admirer of Diruta, although the scale fingerings he proposes begin with the third finger, alternating with the second or fourth finger depending on the hand employed and the direction of the scale (Banchieri 1608: 62; 1982: 52). Banchieri does not make a 'good–bad' distinction with regard to metric placement, and the barring of the examples he gives suggests that the third finger of both hands was used on downbeats. Despite these differences, he seems to have had great respect for Diruta's method, and he contributed two of his own ricercars to *Il Transilvano*.

Diruta provides exercises for the student to gain familiarity in fingering stepwise scale passages and those with leaps, both on and off the beat, thereby requiring different fingerings. He advocates practising the hands separately, always keeping them light and relaxed (Diruta 1593: 8r and 8v).The exercises are followed by a discussion of two types of ornament, the *groppo* and the *tremolo*. *Groppi* are figures used to ornament long notes so that they connect gracefully. Diruta gives many examples to show how characteristic melodic formulas can be embellished with shorter notes. As its name implies, the *tremolo* is a trill, beginning on the main note and alternating with the upper auxiliary. The *tremoletto*, a short *tremolo*, is reported to have been employed by Claudio Merulo to decorate notes descending by step. It is composed of one or two alternations with the upper note, like Santa María's simple *quiebro*. Diruta recommends that *tremoli* be added at the beginning of a ricercar, canzona or other work, as well as in single lines played by one hand when the other hand has several parts. Banchieri recommends for *tremoli* the use of the third and fourth fingers of the right hand and the first and second of the left (Banchieri 1608: 63; 1982: 53). Diruta does not believe that the correlation between fingering and metric placement can always be applied to *tremoli*, and he gives the player guidelines to ensure that passages following *tremoli* are executed correctly (Diruta 1593: 9v–11v).

The ornaments used in Italian instrumental music imitate those heard in vocal music, and the main-note trills and melodic patterns of the *groppi* serve to enhance the lyricism of the musical line. The cultivation of a cantabile style is of paramount importance, and composers either left these crucial decisions entirely to the performer, in which case no embellishments were notated, or they wrote out the embellishments in mensural notation with the assumption that the performer would recognise the ornamental function of these notes and play them with the freedom of an improvised decoration. The intricate figures in Italian organ music are designed to elicit certain emotional responses from the listener, and the sensitive performer will express the underlying mood of the music by articulating its rhythmic gestures.

Diruta does not mention any type of rhythmic alteration to enliven the performance of keyboard music, although his discourse on registration shows his concern with evoking the moods associated with the musical modes (see the Appendix, pp. 316–18 below). It is nevertheless clear that a flexible approach to metre is required to enhance the expressive content of Italian music, especially in free forms such as the toccata. Frescobaldi recommends rhythmic freedom in several places, including the famous excerpt from the preface to his First Book of Toccatas (1616): 'This manner of playing must not be subject to a beat, as we see practised in modern madrigals, which however difficult, are facilitated by means of the beat, conducting it now slow, now rapid, and even suspending it in the air, according to their affetti, or sense of the words' (transl. Hammond 1983: 225). The changing keyboard figures in Italian toccatas are thus analogous to the emotions expressed in madrigals. Frescobaldi's keyboard intabulation of Arcadelt's madrigal *Ancidetemi pur*, included in his Second Book of Toccatas (1627), provides a concrete realisation of this tradition, illuminating the emotive language of abstract keyboard music.

Fingering and ornaments in early English keyboard music

There are no known treatises on organ performance from which to cull information about early English practices; however, fingerings are included in many sources of English keyboard music, dating from as early as 1530. These are very similar to the Spanish methods, where the third finger of the right hand alternates with the fourth and second fingers in ascending and descending scales, and the left hand pairs the thumb and second finger (although with 2 on the beat instead of 1) for ascending passages and the third and fourth for descending. Contemporary fingerings of music by such composers as John Bull and Orlando Gibbons are published in Lindley and Boxall c1992. Although often known collectively as the 'virginalists', English composers wrote much music for the organ, such as the In Nomine, Miserere and Felix namque settings based on sacred cantus firmi (see Chapter 13). Secular keyboard music was played on both plucked stringed instruments and chamber organs, requiring the player to change the performing style to suit the different types of sound and acoustical settings. Since much of the same music served for virginals and organs, the same fingering patterns were probably adopted on all keyboard instruments. Although there are no surviving descriptions of the hand position used by English organists, representations on the title pages of *Parthenia* and *Musicks Hand-maide* depict virginalists holding the wrist slightly higher than the hand and fingers, suggesting that Santa María's antiquated hand position had not been disseminated with his fingerings.

There are no contemporary instructions regarding the performance of ornaments in the early English repertoire, as indicated by either single or double strokes through the note stems. (For notes without stems, the strokes are placed above, below or through the note.) An ornament table in British Library Add. MS 31403, dating from c1680–1700 and attributed to the composer Edward Bevin, presents four ornaments, including the single stroke realised as an ascending third, and three compound symbols, two of which are variants on the double stroke (Ferguson 1975: 144–5). The usefulness of this information is undermined, however, by the late date of the source and the idiosyncratic nature of the compound ornaments, none of which appear in surviving keyboard music. The best approach to realising ornaments indicated by strokes is to determine a suitable decoration based on the context and the length of the note. Clues may be found in the ornaments from Spain and Italy: the *quiebro* works well on alternate notes using either upper or lower auxiliaries, and the *tremolo* provides punctuation at cadences. The twelve ornaments explained in Christopher Simpson's *The Division-Violist* of 1659 (reproduced in J. A. Sadie 1990: 427) might also provide ideas for realising the single and double strokes of the keyboard music, and further guidance may be gleaned from studying written-out ornaments in particular sources (see Hunter 1992 and Wulstan 1985: 125–55).

The influence of French embellishment practices was keenly felt in English music following Charles II's restoration of the monarchy in 1660. This is evident in the upper-note shakes of the ornament table attributed to Henry Purcell in the 'Instructions for beginners' included in some editions of his posthumous *Choice Collection of Lessons for the Harpsichord or Spinnet* (London 1696). There has been debate over the realisation of the English beat, which appears as a compound ornament resembling the *port de voix* with *pincé* that is ubiquitous in contemporary French music. Ferguson argues that the beat should be performed as a mordent, because the realisation appearing after the name 'beat' in the table is actually the compound ornament 'forefall and beat', whose label was omitted due to a printing error (Ferguson 1975: 149–52). However reasonable this hypothesis may seem, it is undermined by the inclusion in Nivers's ornament table of the *agrément*, an ornament similar to the compound beat, as well as by the infrequent appearance of the forefall and beat in Purcell's music.

Fingering, ornamentation and pedalling in German music: 1570–1700

The earliest publication of music in new German tablature, Elias Nikolaus Ammerbach's *Orgel oder Instrument Tabulatur* of 1571, opens with a short introduction that discusses fingering and ornamentation. Ammerbach was influenced by Venetian musical style, and his fingerings for the descending right hand (4–3–2–3–2) and left hand (2–3–2–3) are identical to those published slightly later by Diruta. He differs from Diruta in his recommendations for ascending passages, pairing 2–3 for the right hand and using the consecutive 4–3–2–1 for the left hand. The frequent turn figure is played 3–2–3–4 by the right hand, and surprisingly incorporates the thumb in the left hand fingering 2–3–2–1, occasionally causing the thumb to play a black key, a situation that does not seem to bother the author (Ammerbach 1571/1984: lxxxii–lxxxviii). Like his fingerings, Ammerbach's ornaments betray Italian influence, and he includes the same two types as Diruta. The *groppi* are sequential figurations with which to decorate the music, and the *tremoli* are ascending and descending mordents.

There are no extant tutors to provide insight into the performance of music by Sweelinck and his German students, Samuel Scheidt and Heinrich Scheidemann. Contemporary manuscript copies include fingerings, and these reflect aspects of both Spanish and Italian practice, with the paired fingerings for the right hand originating from the third finger as 3–4 ascending and 3–2 descending, and those for the left hand starting on the second finger as 2–1 ascending and 2–3 descending. Of special interest is the use of the second, third and fourth fingers in figuration spanning the interval of the third, so that the second and fourth fingers of both hands often appear on the beat. The fifth variation of Scheidt's *Ach du feiner Reiter* (*Tabulatura nova*, 1624) includes fingerings for repeated notes in both hands, alternating 3 with 2 in the right hand and 2 with 1 in the left hand, so that the principal finger plays on the beat.

In the third volume of his *Syntagma musicum* (1619), Michael Praetorius describes four types of ornament to be used in the new Italian style: (1) the *accentus*, different patterns for connecting two long notes at different intervals, (2) the *tremulo* and *tremoletto*, main-note trills that alternate the ornamented note with either its upper or lower auxiliary, (3) the *groppo*, a *tremulo* with the upper note concluding with a turn and (4) the *tirata*, a quick scale passage. Although these ornaments are discussed in a chapter on singing, Praetorius writes that the *tremuli* are called 'mordanten' by organists and that they sound better on the organ and plucked instruments than in the voice. He likewise defines the *tirata* as a long, fast scalewise run up or down the keyboard, so it seems to have been conceived for an instrumental context. Praetorius acknowledges the help of Giulio Caccini and Giovanni Battista Bovicelli, whose *Regole Passaggi di Musica Madrigali* furnished some of the examples in *Syntagma musicum*. Similar Italianate ornaments are found in the writings of later German theorists, such as Johann Andreas Herbst (1653), Johann Crüger (1660) and Christoph Bernhard (c1660).

By the beginning of the eighteenth century, French musical practices, including the use of the French *agréments*, were taken up by some German composers of organ music. J. C. F. Fischer provided a table for the French ornaments he adopted in his *Musicalisches Blumenbüschlein* of 1696, and Johann Gottfried Walther gave similar examples of trills and mordents in his *Praecepta der musicalischen Composition* of 1708. The transition from Italianate decoration, which continued to feature in German music, to French-based *agréments* was not universal or clearly defined, and this poses a problem in performing the music of Buxtehude and his contemporaries (see Neenan 1987). One finds written-out trills starting on the main note in the organ music of Buxtehude, yet many of the manuscript sources include French ornament symbols. Since most of these were copied much later than the music was composed, the *agréments* probably reflect the performance style of the copyist rather than that of Buxtehude. The difference between the Italian and French approaches is represented in extant copies of Nicolaus Bruhns's chorale fantasia *Nun komm' der Heiden Heiland*. Walther's copy contains only the Italianate ornamentation of the original, while in others based on a copy by Agricola, the musical text is overladen with French *agréments* (see Radulescu 1993). These sources reflect different traditions of ornamentation that probably co-existed in eighteenth-century Germany, given the amount of cultural interchange in the Hanseatic cities and the propensity of German musicians to incorporate diverse aspects of foreign musical styles. There are therefore no easy answers for the modern performer, who should assess the context of each ornament to determine how most effectively to render it.

Other ambiguities in the performance of German baroque music concern the transcription of the original tablature notation, where horizontal rows of letters indicate the notes in each part, into mensural notation, where notes are positioned on staves. Tablature was used by German organists well into the eighteenth century, and it sometimes contains information about the division of the music between the hands that may be lost in modern staff notation. Because the different octaves are indicated by special signs that are easily left out or misread, confusion can arise concerning the correct octave placement of some notes. Finally, although each voice part occupies a continuous horizontal row in tablature, the use of pedal is not usually indicated, so that this decision was left to the performer. (This is also the case with organ music that was notated in staff notation, since the usual format was on two staves only.) Whenever possible, facsimiles of the original sources should be consulted to help organists evaluate the decisions made by modern editors in transcribing the music.

French classical style

The Sun King Louis XIV, who reigned from 1661 until his death in 1715, was a great patron of the arts, and during this time many organists published their works, often including instructions for registration, tables explaining the symbols for ornaments, and additional information about how to perform the music stylishly. French composers delighted in the rich sounds of their instruments, as shown in titles such as Récit de Cromorne, Basse de Trompette, and Tierce en taille (see Chapter 12). In this codified repertoire, the mood, rhythmic flow and shape of the melodic lines were conceived according to standard registrational schemes, and the close link between music and timbre must be realised to achieve a convincing interpretation. More general aspects of French musical style had great influence throughout Europe. The French system of *agréments*, small symbols in the score indicating the type and placement of ornaments, was avidly taken up by composers from other countries, including J. S. Bach. Predominant among these embellishments was the trill, known in French as *cadence* or *tremblement*, which was distinctive in beginning on the upper auxiliary rather than upon the note to be ornamented. The French trill puts dissonance on the beat, as opposed to the Italian *trillo*, exemplified in the music of Frescobaldi, where the ornament begins on the main note.

Guillaume-Gabriel Nivers provides one of the most detailed prefaces in his *Livre d'Orgue* of 1665. He advocates paired fingerings for the right hand originating from the third finger (3–4 ascending and 3–2 descending) and for the left hand (2–1 ascending and 3–4 descending). These same fingerings are reiterated in Monsieur de Saint-Lambert's treatise, *Les Principes du Clavecin* (1702), as well as in the influential *Art de toucher le clavecin* of François Couperin (1717), where only right-hand scales are given. Although these are methods for harpsichord playing, the remarks on fingering are relevant to organists since they represent a general approach to the keyboard that would have been taught to beginners. The metric values of the fingering examples in all three sources are ambiguous, and there does not appear to have been a correlation between 'strong' fingers and 'strong' beats in the French systems. Couperin acknowledges the complexity of the subject when he writes: 'The manner of fingering does much for good playing; but, as it would require a volume filled with remarks and varied passages to illustrate what I think and what I make my pupils practise, I will give only a general idea here' (Couperin 1717: 10). His remarks provide a bridge between earlier and later approaches, particularly in his advocacy of legato playing and the use of finger substitution in stepwise passages of ornamented slurred notes:

In addition to paired fingerings for scales in the right hand, he gives alternative fingerings for scales with several sharps or flats, and he also includes special fingerings to accommodate specific difficult passages in his music. In the preface to his *Pièces de Clavecin* (1724) Jean Philippe Rameau advises passing the thumb underneath the other fingers to execute extended running passages, a method that he considers to be 'excellent, especially when there are sharps and flats to play' (Rameau 1724: 5; 1979: 18). This is an important document for the use of thumb-under fingerings in France at about the same time that J. S. Bach and others were introducing them in Germany, although most French classical organ music was composed prior to this time.

Nivers' table of ornaments is the earliest to be published, and it includes five types of embellishment that were to become standard in the French repertoire: the *cadence* beginning on the upper note; the *double cadence*, or trill with termination; the *coulade*, filling in the middle note of an open third; the *port de voix*, an appoggiatura coming from above or below the note; and the ascending *port de voix* with *pincé*, called 'agrément' by Nivers, a combined ornament where a lower appoggiatura leads into a mordent. (A similar combination for the English 'beat' is attributed to Henry Purcell in posthumous editions of his *Choice Collection of Lessons;* see above, p. 120.) The realisations of these ornaments does not make it clear whether they begin on the beat, although later French tables consistently show this to be the case, despite differences in the nomenclature and the variety of embellishments included. The table preceding Jean-Henri d'Anglebert's *Pièces de Clavecin* of 1689 was especially influential, since it was referred to by Saint-Lambert and copied by J. S. Bach. Some of the ornaments are more applicable to the harpsichord than the organ, but those in the opening group, shown in Example 8.1, are suitable for both instruments, and were frequently found in German sources.

Despite the schematic rendering of trills in such tables, Couperin makes clear that in performance they should begin more slowly than they end, with an imperceptible acceleration. For trills of any considerable length he recommends the following three parts: stress, or dwelling on the upper auxiliary, the repercussions of the trill, and the *point d'arrêt* or stopping point (Couperin 1717: 23–4). The mechanical rhythms of the realisations should therefore be rendered with appropriate flexibility and

Ex. 8.1 The opening of d'Anglebert's ornament table of 1689

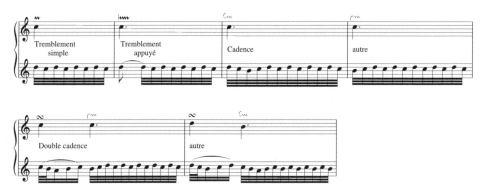

a sense for the context in which each ornament occurs. The number of alternations varies according to the context and duration of the note.

Nivers writes that the organist should imitate the nuances of the human voice, demarcating all the notes while subtly slurring some. To distinguish clearly each note in diminutions or in running scale passages, he advises the organist to lift each note quickly while playing the next note, but for the *ports de voix* and slurred passages, 'the fingers are not raised so promptly', creating an articulation 'between distinction and confusion' that 'partakes a bit of each' (Nivers 1665: preface, n.p.). These descriptions suggest that running passages were played with a structured or balanced legato, while slurs indicated a more overlapping touch. The frequency of paired fingerings and the limited use of finger substitution in Couperin's treatise suggest that he employed both structured and balanced legato, while Rameau seems to be describing the latter when he writes: 'the finger that has just pressed a note leaves it at the instant that its neighbour presses another; for raising one finger and pressing with another should be performed at the same instant' (Rameau 1724: 4; 1979: 17).

The pre-eminence of dancing at the French court exerted a strong effect on the rhythmic conception of instrumental music. André Raison makes clear that even when playing sacred music organists should observe the movement and character of the various dance metres, 'except that the beat should be a bit slower because of the sanctity of the place'. Couperin makes a distinction between *mesure*, or the number of beats in a bar, and *cadence*, or movement, the combination of tempo, accent and phrasing that creates the expression of a piece of music (Couperin 1717: 40). In order to convey French music convincingly, one must infuse the equal beats of the measure with *cadence*, the feeling intended by the composer. Such nuances of timing and accentuation are taught by example and cannot be captured in notation, leading to the problem stated by Couperin in the excerpt opening this chapter, 'that foreigners play our music less well than we play theirs'.

The types of rhythmic alteration employed by the French are generally referred to as *notes inégales. Lourer*, the most commonly employed, was used to enhance the performance of a melodic line moving by step in notes of equal value. Rather than playing the notes as written, one would make them unequal by lingering on the downbeat and passing more quickly through the upbeat. This is a natural way to define metre when playing the organ, and the uneveness should be subtle and spontaneous. The amount of inequality is determined by the character of the music, and it should be slightly varied so that it does not create a repetitive rhythmic pattern. The use of *inégal louré* is not appropriate in quick tempi, for passages marked *égal* or *marqué*, for disjunct melodies, for notes marked with dots, dashes or lines above them, or for repetitions of a single note.

When pairs of equal notes are marked with a slur and a dot, or in some cases only slurred, they should be performed 'short–long', or *coulé*. This rhythmic convention was widely used outside of France; it is described by Santa María and Frescobaldi, and is also known as the Lombardic rhythm or Scotch snap. It produces a distinct expressivity in melodic lines and was not commonly employed in French organ music as *inégal louré*. For citations from the many sources on rhythmic inequality, see Donington 1992: 452–63.

The third principal rhythmic alteration practised in French classical music is overdotting, *notes pointées* or *piquées*. It was used for works in the style of the French overture, where successions of dotted rhythms added majesty to the opening and closing sections. Such passages were rendered even more incisive in performance by lengthening the dotted notes and shortening the upbeat scale passages so that they were left as late as possible and executed very quickly. This type of performance may have originated with Lully's *Vingt-quatre violons du roi*, from which it was disseminated, along with French musical style, throughout Europe (see Donington 1992: 448–51). Overdotting can be an ideal way to enliven organ works in the French overture style.

Fingering and ornamentation in the organ music of J. S. Bach

Bach's works for organ are considered by many to be the apogee of writing for the instrument, so it is vital to search for performance conventions

Ex. 8.2 The 'Explanation of musical signs' provided by J. S. Bach for his son Wilhelm Friedemann

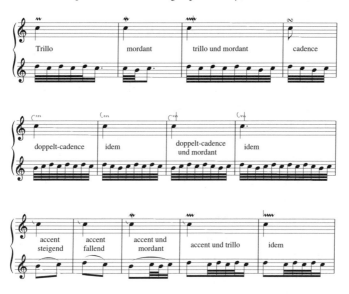

pertaining to his music. His compositions incorporate aspects from various national schools, notably the Italian and French, which suggests his acquaintance with these styles of performance, but it is difficult to apply any system of fingering, ornamentation or rhythmic alteration too rigidly because Bach's music is a unique and complex synthesis that defies easy categorisation. The composer wrote instructions concerning fingering and ornamentation in a notebook that he compiled for his son Wilhelm Friedemann in 1720. The fingering is found in two short pieces, entitled *Applicatio* and *Praeambulum*, where the movement progresses in quavers, with mainly conjunct melodies in the former and disjunct arpeggiation in the latter. The paired fingerings that Bach indicates for both hands in the C major *Applicatio* seem rather old-fashioned when compared to reports of Bach's playing, attributing to him 'the new mode of fingering' in which the thumb was made a principal finger (David and Mendel 1945: 309). But in the G minor *Praeambulum*, where there is a greater frequency of black keys, the thumb is indicated before the second finger plays a black key, suggesting the use of the thumb-under technique. This is admittedly very little evidence upon which to assess Bach's keyboard fingerings, but it demonstrates the co-existence of old and new systems depending on the requirements of the music. C. P. E. Bach describes both approaches to fingering in his *Versuch* of 1753, and elements of both are found in a copy of the Prelude and Fugue in C major from the *Well-Tempered Clavier* II with fingerings by Johann Caspar

Vogler, one of Bach's oldest pupils. (This is published in Soderlund 1986: 127–9.)

The table of ornaments that Bach included in the *Clavier-Büchlein* for Wilhelm Friedemann, shown in Example 8.2, contains the most important French *agréments*, with some differences in nomenclature from standard French practice. (Facsimile reproductions of Bach's ornament table alongside that of Jean-Henri d'Anglebert are found in Ritchie and Stauffer 1992: 318.) The French *tremblement* is called *trillo* in Bach's table; the *pincé*, *mordant* (which should not be confused with the modern definition of this term); and the *cheute* or *port de voix*, *accent*. The salient features of these ornaments are the same, reflecting the influence of the French performance style on the music of Bach and his German contemporaries. Italianate embellishment that is written into the score by the composer is also found in some of Bach's organ works. As with the music of Frescobaldi, the performer must render the notated ornaments with spontaneity, so that they decorate rather than dominate the melodic line. The subtleties of the human voice provide an excellent model to the organist, who must beware losing the music's singing quality to achieve mechanical precision in executing the ornaments.

Postscript for modern organists

Concern with recreating the original conditions of musical performance is a relatively recent phenomenon with many potential dangers. Nuances of aural expression are even more difficult to convey in words than in notation, yet the historian of performance practices relies largely on written descriptions to determine how music was created by past interpreters. Ten minutes at the keyboard with any one of these would be far more illuminating than a surviving treatise or table of ornaments. Many of the historical sources that inform us about earlier practices raise more questions than they answer, and the preceding sketch is merely an attempt to identify some of the most important documents and to summarise their contents relating to performance at the organ. While this author is painfully aware of the lacunae in her essay, a more fundamental shortcoming would be the implication that one can learn to play the organ beautifully by assimilating the rules and methods described in early treatises. One is reminded of Forkel's warning after his attempt to capture in words the elements of Bach's keyboard technique: 'A person may, however, possess all these advantages, and yet be a very indifferent performer on the clavier, in the same manner as a man may have a very clear and fine pronunciation, and yet be a bad declaimer or orator' (David and

Mendel 1945: 308). Especially futile for the modern performer is the application of a performance style that is inappropriate to the organ being played, for example attempting to follow Couperin's instructions to harpsichordists on mammoth romantic organs, or using Lemmens's organ technique on a moderately-sized baroque instrument or replica. The bits of information distilled here are not meant as a recipe for performance, but rather as a compilation of cooking ideas from eminent chefs of the past. It is hoped that they might inspire, rather than constrict, the creativity of organists today.

9 Organ music and the liturgy

Edward Higginbottom

The organ and liturgy stand in close relationship. The construction of organs in the churches of Western Christendom, and their use in its liturgies, is the phenomenon to which is owed the existence of most of our organ literature. Our critical appreciation of organ music is deeply coloured by a knowledge of the context of its composition and performance, including inevitably the liturgical conditions which gave it purpose and shape. Without such knowledge some of the repertory can be unintelligible, and much of it less rich in significance.

There are obvious reasons why the organ was developed within the context of liturgical buildings and liturgical purpose. In the history of Western civilisation it was the only single instrument capable of providing an adequate level and diversity of sound in large and sometimes acoustically intractable buildings. This is still true today, if we except electro-acoustic options. To produce this mass of sound, it had the advantage of relative ease of operation though not of construction. Its place in ecclesiastical buildings was underwritten by scriptural authority, notably Psalm 150 with its reference to 'laudate eum in chordis et organo', whatever the significance of the vulgate term 'organo' is against the Hebrew original. As to its desirable effect on the faithful, Cardinal Bona had little doubt: 'the sound of the organ', he wrote in his *De divina psalmodia* (Paris, 1663), 'brings joy to the sorrowful soul, evokes the happiness of the heavenly city, rouses the lazy, refreshes the watchful, induces love in the just, and brings the sinner to repentance'.

In this account of the organ's relation to the liturgy a broad distinction has to be made between the Roman Catholic Church and the Reformed Churches. The musical needs arising in the Reformed liturgies were very different. Indeed there are parts of the Reformed Church, including the Calvinists, which refused altogether the use of the organ in divine office. The English Puritans were to take the same (destructive) view. They were of course an extreme sect of the English Reformed Church, and their views lasted only as long as the Commonwealth, from 1649 to 1660. Thereafter, organs were re-established as a desirable piece of furniture in the Anglican Church. The Roman Catholics themselves recognised environments where the organ was honoured in its absence, including the

Sistine Chapel and the Primatial Cathedral of Lyons (referred to in Benedict XIV's bull *Annus qui* of 1749). Charles Burney was to comment on the unembellished and organless liturgy of Lyons Cathedral as he passed through the city in 1770. And religious orders distinguished for the austere character of their monastic life and liturgical practice, such as the Carthusians, often dispensed with the organ in divine worship. But broadly speaking the Roman Catholic Church made extensive use of the instrument in its offices and sacraments, notably the Mass, as did the reformed Lutheran Church, enriching their liturgies, and therefore the organ literature, with music of all sorts. Thus, between the main historical division of the Western Church, the Roman Catholic and the Reformed or Protestant, there is not a distinction which accords to one a liturgical use of the organ and to the other none. Nor is the organ literature of one more extensive than the other. However, between the two main branches of Western Christendom we can point to a distinctive manner in which the organ was integrated into the liturgy, and it is this manner of integration, shaping the literature so decisively, that claims our attention.

It is best to view matters in their chronological order, and to start with the practices of the Roman Catholic Church, in whose ecclesiastical buildings organs began to appear from the tenth century onwards. To understand *how* the organ was used we have to wait for the earliest surviving examples of liturgical organ music, dating from the end of the fourteenth century. Importantly, a source of *c*1400 known as the Faenza Codex (of Italian provenance), contains the first extant settings for organ of the Kyrie and Gloria of the Mass. This is a good starting point to grasp the essential nature of organ music within the Roman Catholic liturgy. The source contains a number of short pieces for the Kyrie and Gloria which were clearly intended to alternate with voices. The nature of the alternation is made clear by the composition itself: the left hand carries a plainchant line (the setting *Cunctipotens genitor Deus*) against which a florid right-hand part provides an elaborate discantus. The portions of the plainchant quoted in the left hand indicate the exact extent of the organ's participation. In the second Kyrie–Gloria set the organ plays the following sections of the text (shown in bold), implying a sung rendition of the remainder:

> **Kyrie eleison.** Kyrie eleison. **Kyrie eleison.** Christe eleison. **Christe eleison.** Christe eleison. **Kyrie eleison.** Kyrie eleison. **Kyrie eleison.**
>
> [Intonation: Gloria in excelsis Deo]. **Et in terra pax hominibus bonae voluntatis.** Laudamus te. **Benedicimus te.** Adoramus te. **Glorificamus te.** Gratias agimus tibi propter magnam gloriam tuam. **Domine Deus, Rex caelestis, Deus Pater omnipotens.** Domine Fili, unigenite Jesu Christe. **Domine Deus, Agnus Dei, Filius Patris.** Qui tollis peccata mundi, miserere

nobis. **Qui tollis peccata mundi, suscipe deprecationem nostram.** Qui sedes ad dexteram Patris, miserere nobis. **Quoniam tu solus sanctus.** Tu solus Dominus. **Tu solus altissimus, Jesu Christe.** Cum sancto spiritu. **In gloria Dei Patris. Amen.**

This method of presenting a liturgical text is called 'alternatim', and to our certain knowledge it was employed as early as the fourteenth century, and continued until the early years of the twentieth. It is essential to understand that the practice was not one in which the organ provided preludes, interludes and postludes, leaving the liturgical text complete; rather it was a practice in which half the text was subsumed by the 'versets' played by the organist, and where therefore the organ was an essential partner in the complete presentation of the text. The usage was extended to all the major sung liturgical items, including the Ordinary of the Mass (but generally not the Credo – at least after the Counter-Reformation), items of the Proper (often the Gradual + Alleluia and invariably the Offertory), the canticles at Lauds and Vespers (Benedictus and Magnificat), the Te Deum at Matins, the hymns at these and sometimes at other offices as well, the psalm antiphons (and on feasts of the first class the psalms themselves), and responsorial chants. The manner in which the liturgical text was divided between organ and voices might often vary, but in strophic items (e.g. hymns and canticles) it followed the verse structure. For non-strophic items such as the Mass Ordinary, the division between organ and choir depended upon the manner in which the Kyriale (or the Graduale for the Proper) divided the texts. The ninefold Kyrie would always fall into so many sections, permitting five verses for the organ and four for the choir. The Gloria on the other hand saw a wide diversity of presentations, ranging from the twelve sections in the setting by Philip ap Rhys (*fl.* 1545–60) yielding six organ versets, to the twenty-four sections of the troped (i.e. extended with special textual additions) Gloria of Girolamo Cavazzoni's *Missa de beata virgine* (*Intabulatura d'organo, libro secondo,* 1543), giving twelve versets for the organ. In between comes the design encountered in the French classical school where the text is divided into eighteen sections, nine of which are taken by the organist (normally the same nine as in the Faenza example above). Arrangements for the Sanctus and Benedictus might be complicated by the role of the organ during the Prayer of Consecration and at the Elevation. A difference in approach is found between Roman sources (see Table 9.1 below) which prefer the organ to be played during the Elevation, and French sources (see Table 9.3 below) which expect the Benedictus to feature in the alternatim arrangements. Thus François Couperin's *Messe pour les couvents* (1690), following the Roman rite for monastic houses, contains an Elevation verset, whereas his *Messe pour les paroisses* (1690), in accordance with Parisian usage, has a Benedictus verset. This evidence simplifies a complex liturgical environment in which some French organ masses might contain both Benedictus and Elevation versets (de Grigny and Raison), and in which the Benedictus and Elevation could, as it were, be run together (the Benedictus was taken as a single unit in the alternatim scheme by this time). The situation appears more straightforward in seventeenth-century Italian sources, where a tradition of expressive Elevation toccatas responds to both the letter and spirit of the prescription of the *Caeremoniale episcoporum* (see below) for 'more serious and softer' music at this point in the Mass. The Elevation toccatas of Girolamo Frescobaldi (1583–1643) are distinguished examples in the genre.

At first sight this manner of presenting a liturgical text may appear peculiar, especially to the Protestant mind. What are we to make of only half a text? What benefit does the practice afford? Occasionally these basic questions are addressed in the official prescriptions of the practice. Its raison d'être, we are told, stemmed from the laudable wish to elaborate the liturgy. And its utility lay in allowing the community to worship without the fatigue of reciting liturgical texts in their entirety (thus the 1582 Dominican Ordinal envisages alternatim organ music 'ad levamen chori'). The ancient practice of singing psalms antiphonally responded to this need; the organ followed suit, displaying its capacity for musical elaboration: the Faenza Codex shows the organ pouring out an intricate right-hand discantus above a left-hand cantus firmus. In the same way as gothic architecture, stained glass, vestments and ceremony elaborated liturgy, the organ added its decorative voice. It was a voice which set up a dynamic spatial and stylistic relationship with the singers. It was also a partner which offered an economy of means compared with alternatim practices contrasting various vocal dispositions (such as polyphony against plainchant).

If it were only the surviving sources of liturgical organ music from which we were able to judge things, our understanding of alternatim practice would be imperfect, even misleading. Fortunately, we are not dependent on the music alone for our information: we have other sources, notably the ceremonials issued by the Church to regulate liturgical practice, including the participation of the organist. The earliest official text to prescribe the organist's role, though not the earliest authoritative text to mention in detail the practice, is the *Caeremoniale episcoporum*, the bishops' ceremonial, published in Rome in 1600. This, and many other official publications of the time (graduals, antiphoners, processionals) speak of the intention of the counter-reformers to bring order and good practice into the liturgical life of the Church. However, although it is the authoritative statement for the Roman (Tridentine) rite,

Table 9.1

Prescriptions of the *Caeremoniale episcoporum* (Rome, 1600)
concerning the use of the organ in the liturgy

Office / Mass	Liturgical item
Matins	('from the beginning'). 'from the Te Deum, as in Vespers'. (Deo gratias).
Lauds	'at the end of the psalms'. Hymn. Benedictus.
Vespers	(Procession). 'at the end of psalms'. Hymn. Magnificat. Deo gratias. (Procession).
Mass	(Procession as far as Introit). Kyrie. Gloria. 'at the end of the Epistle'. Offertory. Sanctus. Elevation. Agnus. Communion antiphon. 'at the end of Mass'. NOT PERMITTED: Credo. Benedictus.
Terce	Hymn. 'after any psalm'.
Compline	Nunc dimittis.
passim	Processions.

the bishops' ceremonial was by no means the only text of its sort. The religious orders also began to publish ceremonials, among them the Benedictines (including the important French reform of St Maur), Franciscans, Dominicans, Cistercians and Premonstratensians. A number of dioceses were also active in this field, particularly in France under the impulse of neo-Gallicanism. An analysis of these texts provides the best and certainly the most comprehensive view of alternatim practice. (For further reading, see Higginbottom 1976 and 1980, and Van Wye 1980.) Tables 9.1–9.3 summarise the prescriptions of three key sources, the 1600 *Caeremoniale episcoporum*, the *Caeremoniale divini officii, secundum ordinem fratrum BVM de monte Carmeli*, published in Rome in 1616 for the use of the Carmelite order, and the *Caeremoniale Parisiense* of 1662, published for use in the diocese of Paris. The tables record the liturgical items in which the organist's participation was prescribed. Items in brackets were included only on occasions of special solemnity. Otherwise, broadly speaking, the prescriptions applied to feasts of the first and second class, and down to double majors.

What view do these tables afford of alternatim practice? They reveal among other things that the extant repertory of liturgical organ music gives us only a partial insight into the practice. Where for instance is the extensive repertory we would expect for the canticles at Lauds (Benedictus) and Compline (Nunc dimittis)? Where are the seventeenth- and eighteenth-century settings of the Introit and Gradual + Alleluia of the Mass (though they exist in the literature of the fifteenth and sixteenth

Table 9.2

Prescriptions of the *Caeremoniale divini officii secundum ordinem fratrum B. Virginis Mariae de monte Carmeli* (Rome, 1616) concerning the use of the organ in the liturgy

Office / Mass	*Liturgical item*
Matins	all antiphons after psalms. Te Deum. Responsories.
Lauds	all antiphons after psalms. Benedictus + antiphon. Deo gratias.
Vespers	all antiphons after psalms. Magnificat + antiphon. Responsory. Deo gratias.
Mass	Introit. Kyrie. Gloria. Gradual (first Alleluia in Eastertide). Alleluia. Prose. Offertory to Preface. Sanctus. Benedictus to Pater noster. Agnus to Communion. Deo gratias. NOT PERMITTED: Credo.
Little hours	all antiphons after psalms.
Compline	all antiphons after psalms. Nunc dimittis + antiphon. Marian antiphon.
passim	Processions.
offices of the dead	NO ORGAN

Table 9.3

Prescriptions of the *Caeremoniale Parisiense* (Paris, 1662) concerning the use of the organ in the liturgy

Office / Mass	*Liturgical item*
Matins	Invitatory. Hymn. (3rd, 6th, 9th antiphons). (3rd, 6th) + 9th responsories. Te Deum.
Lauds	'as at Vespers'
Vespers	1st, 3rd, 5th antiphons. (5th psalm). Responsory. Hymn. Magnificat + antiphon. Benedicamus Domino.
Mass	Kyrie. Gloria. Alleluia. Prose. Offertory to preface. Sanctus. Benedictus to Pater noster. Agnus. during communion. Deo gratias. Domine salvum. NOT PERMITTED: Credo.
Terce	ORGAN
Compline	Hymn. Nunc dimittis + antiphon. Marian antiphon.
Station after Vespers	Responsory / Prose / Antiphon. Benedicamus Domino.
Benediction	ORGAN
passim	Processions.

centuries)? Where are the settings of the antiphons and responsories referred to in the ceremonials?

The Proper of the Mass offers an especially intriguing area of study when we attempt to relate extant musical examples to ecclesiastical prescription. For the Introit we possess a strikingly rich pre-1600 repertory (examples are found in the Buxheimer Orgelbuch *c*1470, Buchner's *Fundamentum c*1520, the Lublin Tablature, 1537–48, and the Leopolita Tablature *c*1580, this last source boasting all of forty-seven settings). However, following the appearance of the *Caeremoniale episcoporum*, and other seventeenth-century ceremonials, the picture becomes confused. Though the bishops' ceremonial is silent on the subject, and though Introit settings after 1600 are wanting, three important monastic ceremonials refer to alternatim Introits, including the Carmelite ceremonial analysed above in Table 9.2 (the other two texts are for German Benedictines and Recollects, respectively the *Caeremoniale Benedictinum . . . monasteriorum Germaniae*, Dillingen, 1641, and the *Caeremoniale ff. minorum recollect. almae nostrae provinciae Germaniae inferioris*, Brussels, 1675). Benedictine organists in German houses were permitted to play two versets, one replacing the psalm verse and the other for the repeat of the Introit after the 'Gloria Patri'. As for the instruction of the *Caeremoniale episcoporum* 'at the end of the Epistle', this conceals a diversity of usage, both before and after 1600. Table 9.4 gives an idea of practice prescribed by French ceremonials of the seventeenth and eighteenth centuries. When Frescobaldi includes a 'Canzon dopo la Pistola' in his *Fiori musicali*, it is likely that it substituted entirely for the Gradual. Adriano Banchieri (*Conclusioni*, 1609, and *L'organo suonarino*, 4/1638) mentions this practice, and also that of playing the repeat of the Alleluia after the verse.

The Sequence (Prose in French sources) was often played alternatim, following its strophic pattern. Among the extant musical sources, the French classical school furnishes a number of examples (see in particular Nivers, *2. livre d'orgue*, 1667). But far more numerous are the extant settings of the Offertory, pointing to the universal practice of providing musical cover for the extended liturgical ceremonies at this point in the Mass. English pre-Reformation examples, of which there are several, show a number of approaches to integrating the chant; all show the intonation taken by the cantor. Later in time, there is evidence to suggest that the Offertory verset was often free-standing, substituting for the whole of the Offertory chant. Indeed, its free-standing nature accounts for its frequent appearance in the extant literature. Even if this item were intoned, the organist was free to continue as he liked, at least when plainchant cantus-firmus settings were no longer the norm. In French

Table 9.4

Alternatim patterns for the Gradual and Alleluia as prescribed by a number of French ceremonials of the seventeenth and eighteenth centuries

Source	Gradual		Alleluia				
	R	V	Allel.	ii + jubilus	V	Allel.	jubilus
Ord. ... Praemonstratensis (1635)	O					O	
Caer. ...cong. S. Mauri ord. S. Benedicti (1645)	cc O						O
Caer. Paris. (1662)				O			O
Cér. des religieuses de ... Montmartre (1669)							O
Caer. ... ff. min. (1669)	cc O						
Rit. Cisterciense (1689)	O	C					O
Caer. monast. ord. S. Benedicti (1695)	O						O
Cer. de Toul	NO ORGAN						O
Ord. ... Praemonstratensis (1739)	O					O	
Cér. de S. Pierre de Remiremont (1750)	O		c		cc	O	?

Key: O = organ verset   R = respond
        c(c) = cantor(s)   V = verse
        C = choir   jubilus = melismatic flourish at end of alleluia
Note: absence of a symbol implies a sung performance

churches the custom of intoning the Offertory before the organist continued went on well into the nineteenth century, despite the protestations of Abbé Poisson (*Traité theorique et pratique du plain-chant*, Paris, 1750) and de La Fage (*Cours complet de plain-chant*, 1855–6) that it would be better to omit the intonation altogether if only two or three words of the chant were to be heard. The practice of taking the Offertory 'tout entier' is explicitly prescribed by the *Cérémonial monastique des religieuses de l'Abbaye Royale de Montmartre* (Paris, 1669) and the diocesan *Cérémonial du diocese de Besançon* (Besançon, 1682), and was no doubt envisaged by others. As for the Communion, among the practices sanctioned by the ceremonials organ music might be provided for the antiphon itself, following Roman usage, or during the distribution (preceding but excluding the antiphon), preferred in French seventeenth- and eighteenth-century sources, and presumably envisaged by Nicolas de Grigny's verset 'pour la communion' (*Premier livre d'orgue*, 1699).

When we consider these practices relating to the Proper of the Mass, it can easily be appreciated that the more an alternatim exchange is associated with liturgical chants appearing maybe only once a year (for a particular feast), the less likely it is that we shall find extant literature relating to it: organists naturally preferred to leave examples of their work with a broader application. This is true also of the office antiphons and responsories, items in which the organist was also clearly involved. For example, the *Caeremoniale Parisiense* (see Table 9.3 above) gives the following alternatim pattern for the Vespers responsory:

Intonation: cantors // R̷ to Repetendum: organ // Repetendum: choir // V̷: cantors // Repetendum: organ // 'Gloria Patri': cantors // R̷: choir

(NB Repetendum is the second portion of the respond)

From a reading of these and other analyses of ecclesiastical prescription, we get a better idea of what the extant repertory represents, and when it departs from the formulae established by the ecclesiastical sources, what may be the reasons. For instance, the organ masses of Girolamo Frescobaldi from the collection *Fiori musicali* contain an irregular number of versets for the Kyrie, as many as twelve for the Messa della Domenica, and none at all for the other parts of the Ordinary of the Mass (Gloria, Sanctus and Agnus). Ordinarily five versets are required for an alternatim Kyrie. The explanation for Frescobaldi's provision lies not in an unorthodox alternatim pattern, but more simply in the provision of versets showing a range of compositional procedures from which five might be chosen. Frescobaldi's omissions for the other items of the Ordinary are no more significant than François Couperin's omission of versets in his organ masses for the Gradual/Alleluia, Prose and Communion. It does not mean that none of these items was played by the organist: he would have supplied them as a matter of course, no doubt directed if not also inspired by the techniques exemplified in the versets to hand. Furthermore, when Clérambault publishes two organ suites (1710) without liturgical affiliation, it does not mean that they could not be used for the Magnificat (mode of antiphon permitting). And when Manuel Rodrigues Coelho publishes sets of four versets for the Benedictus and Magnificat when generally six are required (*Flores de musica*, 1620), he does not intend a new form of alternation, but proposes to demonstrate the musical techniques involved in incorporating the psalm tone successively in each of the four voices of the polyphonic texture.

Ecclesiastical prescription also tells us many other things about the practice: when the organist was expected to attend (according to the solemnity of the feast), how he was expected to tailor his music to the liturgy, when he was expected to play in a particularly devotional style, sometimes employing the plainchant as a cantus firmus on such occasions. When organ music is used in alternation with plainchant (in passing it is worth noting that references are to be found of alternatim practices involving various forms of vocal polyphony) it has to conform to a number of specific requirements. In the early days of the practice it was normal, indeed *de rigueur*, that the organ verset incorporated the plainchant itself, as a cantus firmus in textures of various degrees of polyphonic elaboration. As polyphonic styles yielded to freer concertante idioms, the cantus-firmus technique was retained (sometimes in response to ecclesiastical prescription) for the initial versets, or for versets of particular solemnity. At all times the organist had to respect the mode of the chant in use, a discipline which led to a codification of 'tones' appropriate to this or that mode, and to cadences which provided endings analogous to those of the replaced section of chant (Howell 1958). The collections of French classical organ music grouped according to 'ton d'église' reflect this requirement. These and other collections, sometimes called 'suites', are a pragmatic way of dealing with the organist's role, providing him with sets of versets appropriate not for this or that item in particular, but for any item in general, depending upon the mode, and barring reference to a specific plainchant (a particular mass setting or hymn, for example). The advantage of not tying down a set of versets to a particular item could indeed be a selling point: André Raison provides five organ masses in his first *Livre d'orgue* (1688), but by avoiding reference to specific plainchants not only does he make his masses polyvalent (having nevertheless to respect the mode of the alternatim plainchant), he also squeezes three Magnificat sets out of each mass (21 versets ÷ 3 = 7 allowing also for the Magnificat antiphon), yielding fifteen Magnificats in all.

In addition, the organist was expected to observe the timing of the liturgy: he could only elaborate when liturgical circumstances permitted, as (and notably) at the Offertory of the Mass. Here the large-scale offerings of the French classical school show what could be achieved in propitious circumstances. To comment adversely on the brevity of invention elsewhere in the French repertory, or in any other alternatim repertory, is to miss the point completely. Where, in the same repertory, we might expect to encounter large-scale pieces for before and after the services, none exists. Indeed, apart from the possibility of processional music, there is no evidence for the use of the organ in this context, and the concluding Deo gratias movements from the masses of the French school are as short as any other verset.

Behind the practice lay the art of improvisation. No organist was appointed to his task without being able to demonstrate fluency in improvisation. In the early years of the sixteenth century at St Mark's Venice, the tests for candidates comprised improvising a strict four-part fantasia on a given theme, the improvised treatment of another theme, passing the cantus prius successively through all four voices of the texture, and responding extempore and alternatim to the choir. Given the number of days when the organist had to attend, the number of services at which he played and the number of versets required at each, it is scarcely surprising that improvisatory skills were a sine qua non. (A calculation for Nicholas Lebègue, organist at the Parisian church of St Merry in the second half of the seventeenth century, brings his annual total of versets to c8,000.) What is surprising is the appearance of published (and indeed manuscript) collections of liturgical organ music. What was their purpose? Most likely to provide an exemplar for those wishing to learn the art, as well as a source for those whose inspiration might not be on the highest level. At the same time, the surviving music is but a minute fraction of what was improvised over the centuries in the context of alternatim practice, and in some respects it may be unrepresentative of the practice, inclined to greater complexity (for pedagogical and 'artistic' purposes) than the commonplaces of improvisation. Thus in 1690 François Couperin published his two organ masses to demonstrate to the world at large his compositional skills in the musical genre then best known to him. We may be grateful that he did not restrict himself to the dimensions of the organ masses contained in the Thierry MS, though these modest efforts may resemble much more closely the alternatim practice in Parisian churches of his time.

And what of the text? It is clear that in the era before the reforms and counter-reforms of the sixteenth century the notion of text in liturgy was different. Audibility was not a prerequisite. There are numerous examples of 'inaudible' texts in Latin church music, from Notre-Dame organum and melismatic plainchant to the dense early sixteenth-century counterpoint that Erasmus (among others) objected to. The work of the reformers in bringing the text to our attention by translating it, by laying it simply before us, and the work of the counter-reformers in excising melisma from plainchant (in the so-called Medici editions of the antiphoner and gradual) and calling for a more straightforward polyphonic style, speak of a quite different attitude from that displayed by the medieval and early renaissance mind. At the inception of alternatim practice, the text was seen not as revelation but as incantation. It was there, and profoundly there, even when not heard. Its manner of being conveyed by the organ fitted this outlook perfectly. The history of alternatim organ music from the seventeenth century betrays a change which in its way fails to recognise the pre-Reformation condition of alternatim practice. Thus when Pope Benedict XIV refers in his bull *Annus qui* of 1749 to the importance of instrumental music in the liturgy 'adding to the force of the text so that its significance penetrates the minds of the faithful, moving the latter to consider spiritual matters', and when in the same year the French theoretician Cousin de Contamine writes that 'the organist must strive to convey the text passed over in silence by the choir' (*Traité critique du plain-chant*, Paris, 1749), they are giving to the text a status it previously did not enjoy, and which, if it had, would not have sought alternatim organ music as a means of liturgical elaboration.

The difficulty of the 'omitted' text is regularly referred to in seventeenth- and eighteenth-century ceremonials. These sources often propose that the text taken by the organ should be recited 'intelligibili voce' (i.e. in a manner understood by those attending the service) during the organ verset. The phrase 'intelligibili voce' underlines the central purpose of the directive: not only to ensure the continuous presence of the liturgical text, but to make it audible and fully comprehensible to those attending divine worship. When the *Caeremoniale episcoporum* uses the phrase 'intelligibili voce', we cannot be sure whether its prescription applies to the Mass as well as to the offices. French sources tend to exempt the Mass, but they mention in greater detail another manner of presenting omitted office texts hinted at in the *Caeremoniale episcoporum*: that the texts might be *sung* 'along with the organ'. This proposal (we can find it incorporated in a group of Magnificat versets in Coelho's *Flores de musica*) undermines the very notion of alternatim organ music. There is little evidence that performances of organ versets with sung cantus firmi were widespread, notwithstanding the plausibility of the idea when cantus-firmus settings were the norm. What is much more likely is that the choir member appointed to declaim the 'omitted' text might have sung it on a reciting tone. The practice is referred to in at least two French ceremonials of the seventeenth century, and also by Nivers in his *Dissertation sur le chant gregorien* (Paris, 1683), who recommends pitches to be used for each of the church tones to avoid the worst of the harmonic confusion arising from the procedure.

The view of the organ as a provider of music against which a text was recited was eventually to bring about the end of the practice, a point reached in ecclesiastical legislation when Pope Pius X proscribed alternatim organ music in his *Motu proprio* of 1903. Nonetheless, the practice continued for a while, particularly in France, receiving its coup de grâce only as a result of the sweeping liturgical reforms of the Second Vatican Council (1962–5). Before then, Olivier Messiaen's *Messe de la Pentecôte*

(1951), following Tournemire's scheme (see below) offers no more than five movements standing in a loose liturgical relation to the Mass: 'Entrée', 'Offertoire', 'Consécration', 'Communion', 'Sortie'. What might be interpreted as Propers are nothing of the sort, but pieces of liturgically 'incidental' organ music.

If we define liturgical organ music strictly, as denoting music whose omission would lead to the loss of an integral and necessary part of the liturgical text or action, then we can see how the term suits alternatim practice but fits less well contexts in which liturgical texts are presented in their entirety. These are the contexts more commonly and eventually exclusively encountered in the liturgies of the Reformed Church, principally the Lutheran and Anglican. To these we now turn.

The German principalities were rich in fine organs at the time of the Reformation: a tradition of building on a grand scale was well established, and organ music was part and parcel of people's experience of the liturgy. If we except the doctrinal differences, much that appears in the reformed liturgy of the Lutheran Church has its roots firmly in the Roman Catholic practice. Even with respect to language, Latin continued to be used for certain items of the liturgy, such as the Gloria in excelsis and the Magnificat. In accordance with this traditional stance towards the liturgy, it is perhaps not so surprising to find cases of alternatim practice hanging over into the Lutheran. For instance Samuel Scheidt's *Tabulatura nova* (1624) contains examples of alternatim Magnificats and hymns, Heinrich Scheidemann (*c*1596–1663) and Matthias Weckmann (1621–74) have left us with examples of alternatim Magnificats, and J. S. Bach an alternatim Te Deum in its Lutheran translation *Herr Gott, dich loben wir* (BWV 725). However, there are definite limits to the interpretation of J. S. Bach's organ music in the light of alternatim practice: the oft-cited notion that Part III of the *Clavierübung* (1739) is an organ mass is entirely erroneous, confusing the presence of chorale-prelude settings of chants for the Kyrie and the Gloria (both items being retained in the Lutheran Mass) with alternatim workings. Indeed, apart from the Te Deum, nothing by Bach conforms inescapably to alternatim practice, and much is liturgical only in a looser sense: the sense in which chorale preludes clearly relate to liturgical sung items and (certainly in their manifestation in the *Orgelbüchlein*) might be played as preludes to a vocal rendition of the chorale within the Gottesdienst.

The general picture for Lutheran practice is varied, and complicated furthermore by the use in many churches of choirs and instrumentalists whose participation in the liturgy became a distinguishing feature of

German reformed practice. It has to be remembered that even in Roman Catholic contexts there were places and times when choirs took over the organ's role. The *Cérémonial de Toul* of 1700 tells us how, when the Ordinary was sung 'en musique' (i.e. in a polyphonic setting), the organist's role was reduced to playing preludes and interludes. In the Lutheran orbit, such might also be the organist's role. A description of a service at St Lorenz, Nuremberg in the late seventeenth century refers to the organist playing 'interludes' for the Kyrie, Gloria, Sanctus and Agnus. Likewise at Vespers, when the Magnificat was sung with vocal and instrumental forces, the need was removed for independent organ music, except perhaps as a prelude. When J. S. Bach wrote a 'Fuga sopra il Magnificat' (BWV 733), he was certainly not providing a liturgical item, though he might have been providing an extended prelude to it.

Within a varied and sometimes ill-defined picture in the Lutheran Church we can glimpse some irrefutable facts. The first is that alternatim practice continued for some time, and perhaps longer than we might imagine. In the early seventeenth century Michael Praetorius (*c*1571–1621) refers more than once to the advantages of alternatim organ/choir performances of his music. The existence of alternatim Magnificats by Scheidemann, Buxtehude, and others provides evidence for later in the century. And descriptions of Matins in Leipzig in the early eighteenth century include reference to an alternatim Te Deum (exemplified also in BWV 725).

The second is that chorale preludes were used to introduce the chorale melody to the congregation, and that these preludes may have been on an extensive scale, though when on the scale of the chorale preludes of Bach's *Clavierübung III*, given the didactic and recreational purpose of that collection, it is as likely that they were performed outside as inside a liturgical context. The extensive use of hymns in the Lutheran liturgy (at the Hauptgottesdienst – the main Sunday morning service with sermon and communion – as many as ten might be sung) meant that the duty of preluding before the hymn became the most significant of the organist's duties, analogous in this respect to the Roman Catholic's alternatim duties, and depending like them on a fluent improvisatory skill. There is no knowing what tolerance priests and congregations showed towards long and elaborate chorale preludes, such as Bach has left us. The arguments advanced in the seventeenth century for and against organ music in the Gottesdienst tell us only that practice might vary considerably. J. C. Voigt (*Gespräch von der Musik*, 1742) and J. Adlung (*Anleitung zur musikalischen Gelahrtheit*, 2/1783) pleaded that the preludes announcing the chorales be to the point, using always the chorale melody (Williams 1984: 22); so it is clear that some organists were self-indulgent. It is also difficult to determine for sure the status of chorale verses, though they may have been used as interludes between hymn verses if not as alternatim versets. It was also the practice to fill in certain moments of the service, as for instance between the hymn and the sermon, when a chorale 'Nachspiel' would have been in order, and before a cantata to cover the preparation of the musicians (including tuning!), here the organist choosing the key and chorale of the cantata. If in this area there is any development to note over the seventeenth to the nineteenth centuries, it is that the role of the organist as *accompanist* became increasingly important. In the early days of the Reform, chorales were sung unaccompanied and often unharmonised. As the organist took up the task of accompanying (and therefore also harmonising them), so his independent role became less important. To judge from Burney's report of a service in Bremen Cathedral in 1772 the tradition of unaccompanied singing survived in some places well on into the eighteenth century, but to judge also from the surviving literature, the art of preluding on the chorale fell well short of the accomplishment shown in the earlier part of the century.

The third fact to note is that the preludes, toccatas and fugues of the great Lutheran school of organists, Franz Tunder (1614–67), Vincent Lübeck (1654–1740), Georg Böhm (1661–1733), Nicolaus Bruhns (1665–97), Dieterich Buxtehude and of course J. S. Bach, may have belonged to extra-liturgical contexts as much as to liturgical ones. There is no evidence for their regular use as preludes and postludes to Hauptgottesdienst and Vespers until we get some way into the eighteenth century. J. A. Scheibe, perhaps from his experience of Hamburg practice, refers in 1745 (*Der critische Musikus*) to the fact that organists who played at the beginning and end of services had an opportunity to reveal their talents to the full. Such terms of reference strongly suggest the possibility of extended compositions in the free style (such as preludes and fugues). Earlier in the century, the descriptions we have of 'preluding' before the services at St Thomas Leipzig are extremely vague, and do not indicate the type of organ music used. The patchy evidence before this time allows us to say only that in certain places such may have been the practice, as it appears to have been at Danzig (where a surviving Order of Service of 1706 for the Catherinenkirche refers explicitly to organ music after the service). Lest it should be thought that this creates a crisis of context for an important part of the organ repertory, it should be remembered that public recitals, auditions and demonstrations were part of the musical culture of seventeenth- and eighteenth-century northern Europe.

The subject of Anglican organ music provides a footnote to the foregoing survey. James Clifford, in *The Divine Services and Anthems usually sung in His Majesties Chappell* (1663 and 1664) suggests that before the

Civil War voluntaries were played immediately before the first lesson at Matins and at Evensong. Edward Gibbons (organist at Exeter Cathedral before the Civil War) has left us 'A Prelude upon the Organ, as was then used before the Anthem' (Morehen 1995: 44). These and other references to the use of the organ at the Offertory of the Mass have nothing to do with organ music integral to the liturgy, i.e. without which the liturgy would be incomplete: the organ lent its voice in a purely optional and additional fashion, apart from the practice of 'giving out' psalm and hymn tunes (Burchell 1992). Here a tradition arose which has something in common with the Lutheran, though much more modest in scope, involving a decorated presentation of the congregation's melody prior to singing. In the eighteenth century this practice was extended to include short organ interludes between verses. Such music however scarcely counts as organ repertory, though the *Voluntary on the Old 100th* by Henry Purcell, which may have had a preludial function, shows how it might have been raised to an artistic level. The freely composed organ voluntary became in the eighteenth century the staple fare of English organ composition, and served a generalised need for 'incidental' organ music in the liturgy.

Little has been said about the organ literature of the nineteenth and twentieth centuries. We know that alternatim practices continued into the early years of the twentieth century in the Roman Catholic liturgy, but such practices were no longer at the heart of things. In the French school we remember not so much Justin for his *L'organiste à la messe . . . 11 messes: plainchant alternant avec l'orgue* (1870) as César Franck for his chorals (1890). The French were part of a wider tendency in the nineteenth century to give the organ a repertory belonging more to the concert than to the liturgy. If Mendelssohn's organ sonatas, Franck's chorals and Widor's symphonies might be heard in church, it was not the liturgy which had inspired them, nor the liturgy which had a particular use for them. Rather it was the instrument that brought them to life, and a belief that the organ had its place in the musical world at large alongside the piano, the string quartet and the symphony orchestra. The organ itself found a place in secular institutions, in the large public halls of Europe, affirming that strictly musical purposes were being served in writing for it. This change of focus continues into and through the twentieth century in the works of Marcel Dupré and Paul Hindemith, Louis Vierne and Max Reger, Jehan Alain and Kenneth Leighton. Much of this music might have a place in church services of both the Catholic and the Protestant persuasion, but only as para-liturgical offerings, filling in gaps in the liturgy, or preceding and then concluding a service. A closer affinity to the liturgy may be descried in the music of Charles Tournemire, whose *L'orgue mystique* (1927–32) takes us through the church's liturgical year, and shows a deep musical affiliation to plainchant. However, it is more in design and style that his music appears to be liturgical than in its precise role in the liturgy, where it serves, like so much other music, as fillers. In itself, the use of plainchant as melodic material is no guarantee of liturgical usefulness, as we may see from a work such as Maurice Duruflé's triptych on *Veni creator spiritus* (op. 4). And a deeply felt religious dimension, as in Messiaen's organ music, is no indicator of liturgical purpose, his music being essentially a matter for the concert hall rather than the church, or more precisely for the recital rather than the service.

A knowledge of liturgical context can lead to a wish to respect that context in the presentation of organ music in modern performance. Outside the domain of liturgical practice itself, various levels of liturgical reconstruction are possible, from alternatim organ masses performed with plainchant choir to German chorale preludes introducing performances of the chorale itself. Care is needed in any of these circumstances. For instance, the wholesale musical reconstruction of an organ mass raises as many problems as it apparently solves: the alternation of organ and voices is not a musical matter alone; it is a form of antiphony in which both parties enjoin in a ritualistic presentation of a sacramental text. In addition there are problems reconciling the stylistic juxtaposition of keyboard styles and plainchant (even taking into account relevant performing styles for the chant), problems that do not exist in the ritualistic context of divine worship. Still less obvious is the desirability of playing a whole organ mass from one end to the other without the intervening chants, as though it were some self-contained musical form. This practice does the music a grave disservice. For much of the repertory, at least that belonging to the seventeenth and eighteenth centuries, a better solution is to select a group of tonally related but stylistically varied versets from a mass, and present them as a surrogate suite. Thus, for the classical French repertory, six or seven versets from a Gloria setting would represent a viable 'concert' option, in line with Clérambault's formulation in his organ suites. To turn to the German Lutheran tradition, the manner of assembling collections of its organ music has little to do with performing contexts or intentions: J. S. Bach clearly did not intend the *Clavierübung III* to be played as some sort of unified whole, though from a compositional point of view there is an extraordinary degree of design, balance and coherence in the collection. Few players would imagine (and rightly) a chorale prelude to be somehow musically incomplete without a vocal performance of the chorale. Whether or not the repertory hinges closely on liturgical contexts, most contexts of modern performance suggest a necessary dissociation of organ music from the liturgy, apart perhaps for those pieces, dating largely from the fifteenth and sixteenth centuries, where the cantus firmus of the organ verset provides a plainchant line demanding completion in an alternatim pattern.

10 Italian organ music to Frescobaldi

Christopher Stembridge

Introduction

Frescobaldi is obviously central to any discussion of Italian organ music. What is sometimes forgotten is that, like J. S. Bach, he comes at the end of a great tradition – at least as far as Italy is concerned. His most important pupil and follower was Froberger. Through him, and indirectly through others such as Kerll, Frescobaldi was to exercise considerable influence on German keyboard music, not least on Bach himself.

The great age of Italian organ building was already in decline when Frescobaldi was born in 1583. The last large instrument to be built was that by Luca Blasi for St John Lateran in Rome in 1598. The new enormous basilica of St Peter's where Frescobaldi was to serve most of his lifetime never had an organ commensurate with its size, its importance or the stature of its organist. Most seventeenth-century Italian organs do not extend below 8′ C and have a range of four octaves (C/E–a^2 or c^3). Virtually all Frescobaldi's music can be played on such an instrument quite satisfactorily. This has given rise to the idea that the Italian organ was always a small instrument, especially since many such organs still exist and because the basic format remained unchanged for another two centuries. The bulk of this chapter will therefore attempt to explain the Italian scene up to Frescobaldi, relating its music not only to the large instruments that survive (e.g. San Petronio, Bologna, 1471; Arezzo Cathedral, 1534; San Giuseppe, Brescia, 1581; St John Lateran, Rome, 1598 – all of these based on 16′ or 24′ principali) but also smaller 6′ and 4′ organs.[1]

The beginnings

The earliest Italian source of organ music is the Faenza Codex of c1420. Like other organ music of the period, the pieces, which represent both sacred and secular forms, are composed for two voices, almost certainly intended to be played on organs in Pythagorean tuning (i.e. with perfect fifths and all but one or two major thirds virtually unusably wide). The music is written on two six-line staves. Like the English, the Italians preferred staff notation to letter or number tablature and were later to develop their own keyboard notation retaining the six-line stave for the right hand while adding first a seventh and later an eighth line to the left-hand stave in order to avoid adding leger-lines. This notation is normally called 'Italian keyboard tablature'. While it would appear to be closer to ordinary notation than to other types of tablature, the use of the word 'tablature' is justified by the fact that the system makes no attempt to demonstrate the integrity of the part-writing in polyphonic music – instead it merely informs the player which notes to play, while the division of the music between the upper and lower staves indicates quite clearly which notes are to be played by the right and left hand respectively. This system, with the left-hand stave growing to seven and then eight lines, remained in use even for printed music well into the seventeenth century. Example 10.1 shows part of a polyphonic verse from Frescobaldi's 1627 Second Book of Toccatas.

Unfortunately no organ music by the most famous fourteenth-century Italian organist-composer, Francesco Landini (*c*1325–97), is known to have survived. It is also particularly disappointing that no later fifteenth-century Italian organ music has come down to us, since all the evidence points to there having been a remarkable development. This is suggested not only by the stature of Marc'Antonio Cavazzoni's *Recerchari, motetti, canzoni . . . libro primo* of 1523, but also by the fact that some very grand organs had been built by 1500, notably that by Lorenzo da Prato for San Petronio, Bologna (1471) which still survives, as well as the well-documented instrument by Fra Urbano in St Mark's, Venice (1489).[2] Both these organs were based on a principale of 24'. Furthermore, the well-known requirements for candidates seeking employment as organist in St Mark's show that the standard of musician-ship amongst players was very high (see p. 140).

The development of the sixteenth-century organ

It would be interesting to know not only what sort of music was played in the late fifteenth century, but also how the transition was effected from the organ tuned in perfect fifths to the sixteenth-century preference for a mean-tone temperament with good major thirds, which is clearly required for all music from Cavazzoni to Frescobaldi. (Notice the Italian predilection for placing the major third on top of chords.) As early as 1468 the first known split keys for additional semitones were added to the organ of Cesena Cathedral (see Wraight and Stembridge 1994). It may be assumed that these were to provide G♯ in addition to A♭.[3]

Ex. 10.1 Frescobaldi, *Ave maris stella*, verse 4

(a) Facsimile of original edition of 1627
(end of verse 3 and start of verse 4)

(b) Transcription into modern keyboard score

(c) Performing edition

The co-existence of sacred and secular forms already noted in the Faenza Codex is a feature that is typical of published books of organ music throughout the sixteenth and well into the seventeenth century. Marc'Antonio Cavazzoni, his son Girolamo and Frescobaldi all produced books in which both hymns and secular songs, madrigals or dance movements provided the basis of organ compositions. Toccatas, unless specified 'da sonarsi all'Elevazione' (to be played during the consecration at Mass), and ricercars were neutral in this respect. Most Italian keyboard music of the period was designed to be played on any keyboard instrument and may work equally well on organ or harpsichord – much of it even on the clavichord as well. The organ was not confined to church use but, particularly in the case of smaller instruments, was employed in secular music-making. There was even a kind of organ designed for private use – the equivalent, in organ terms, of the clavichord. This was the small single or two-rank instrument with paper pipes. One of these is

Figure 10.1 Organ in the Palazzo Pubblico, Siena, built by Giovanni Piffero.

represented in the intarsia of the Duke of Urbino's studiolo (*c*1475). Another, made by Lorenzo da Pavia in 1494, has partially survived; this had a principale 6′ and an ottava (see Donati 1993: 277, n. 5). An organ clearly intended for both secular and liturgical use is the 4′ instrument by Giovanni Piffero still to be seen and heard in the Palazzo Pubblico (formerly the Curia) in Siena where it is positioned between the chapel and the great hall – Sala del Mappamondo (see Figure 10.1).

The sixteenth-century organ in Italy could be based on either C or F. Typical ranges were F–f³ or a³ without F♯, G♯ or g♯³ (i.e. a 6′ instrument) or the same an octave lower (FF–f^2) (cf. e.g. Santa Maria della Scala, Siena, G. Piffero, 1517, shown in Figure 5.4) or FF–a^2 (e.g. San Petronio, Bologna, Lorenzo da Prato, 1471, which has a 24′ principale effectively FFF–a^1). Smaller organs based on c (4′) might, like the 1519 instrument in the Palazzo Pubblico, Siena, have a range of c–a^3 (without c# or g#^{3}); larger (8′ or 16′) organs would normally have the same range extended by an octave (e.g. Arezzo Cathedral, Luca da Cortona, 1534: CC–a^2, without CC# or g#^{2}).

When assessing the capabilities of the larger instruments, today's organist should avoid making the mistake of assuming that the presence of only one keyboard, an octave of pedal pull-downs and a small number of stops (basically a principal-based ripieno and a flute) pose strict limitations. Given a 16′ or 24′ principale, a keyboard range of nearly five octaves, doubling or even trebling of the basic ranks in the treble range together with a shallow case designed to project the sound, the grandeur leaves little to be desired. As for variety, the range of keyboard makes it possible to use the principale, both on its own or in combination with other stops, at either 16′ or 8′ pitch. Similarly the ottava may be used at 8′ (as a smaller principale) or 4′ pitch. The XV (fifteenth) can be used as a 4′. The flauto in XV may be used on its own or in conjunction with any of these three. The fact that the upper harmonics are nearly always to be drawn separately obviously increases their usefulness and provides far more variety than a single mixture stop could do. Thus an organ with only seven stops will have between thirty and forty possible registrations.

Italian organ-stop nomenclature is quite easy to understand once the basics have been grasped. The ripieno is normally made up of a principale (open diapason) and an unbroken series of upper ranks, each of which can usually be drawn separately, unlike north European mixture stops. (Exceptions exist: Piffero tends to group XIX and XXVI, XXII and XXIX.) Note that the twelfth was not present in the Italian ripieno until the late baroque period. Given an 8′ principale the other stops would be:

Written	Italian term	English equivalent	Pitch
VIII	ottava	Octave	4′
XV	decimaquinta or quintadecima	Fifteenth	2′
XIX	decimanona	Nineteenth	$1\frac{1}{3}$′
XXII	vigesimaseconda	Twenty-Second	1′
XXVI	vigesimasesta	Twenty-Sixth	$\frac{2}{3}$′
XXIX	vigesimanona	Twenty-Ninth	$\frac{1}{2}$′
XXXIII	trigesimaterza	Thirty-Third	$\frac{1}{3}$′
XXXVI	trigesimasesta	Thirty-Sixth	$\frac{1}{4}$′

and so on.

Given a 16′ principale the VIII would be at 8′ pitch, the XV at 4′ pitch, etc. A 12′ principale means that the keyboard begins at FF. The relationship of the upper ranks to the principale remains the same, as also in the case of instruments based on 24′, 6′ or 4′ principale. The upper ranks (i.e. above XV) normally break back in the upper octaves; XXVI and above will break back twice.

The open flute ranks were not to be used in the ripieno but either singly or in conjunction with the principale, also in some compound registrations (see Antegnati's directions below). A small organ would normally have one flute stop pitched at an octave, a twelfth, or two octaves above the principale: flauto in VIII (flauto in ottava), flauto in XII (flauto in duodecima), flauto in XV (flauto in decimaquinta). Larger organs had two or even three flutes. Sometimes in later sixteenth-century organs the flauto in VIII and the principale were divided into treble and bass sections. Larger sixteenth-century instruments had two (occasionally three) pipes for each note in the treble of the principale, the VIII and sometimes the XV.

The tremulant (tremolo) was also a common feature of the earlier sixteenth century, for use mainly with the solo principale. Towards the end of the century it tended to be replaced by the fiffaro or voce umana, a second rank of principale pipes on a separate slide, for the treble half of the keyboard only, tuned slightly sharp to give a beating effect.

Advice concerning registration

L'arte organica by the organist and organ builder Costanzo Antegnati, published in Brescia in 1608, is an invaluable source of information about registration. This brief treatise is in the form of a dialogue between Antegnati and his son. In discussing various organs made by his illustrious family, he recommends certain combinations of stops; in most cases he also adds some useful comments. Since he reveals himself to be of a rather conservative nature – an image that is supported by his *stile antico* ricercars published the same year – we may with reason safely assume that his views reflect those typical of Italian organists of the second half of the sixteenth century. His instructions may be codified as follows:

1. Ripieno: Use for all Intonationi, introits, the beginning and end of Mass when a toccata should be played, using the pedals.
2. Mezzo-ripieno: **principale, VIII, flauto in VIII, XXIX, XXXIII** or, when there is no XXXIII on the organ (even if there is a XXIX) the quasi mezzo-ripieno: **principale, VIII, flauto in VIII, XXII, and XXVI.**
3. **principale, VIII and flauto in VIII.**

4. **principale and flauto in VIII**. This combination is good for all kinds of music and for accompanying motets.
5. **principale, VIII and flauto in XII**. This is very good for all kinds of things, but especially for canzonas and music with divisions.
6. **principale and flauto in XII**. For music with divisions and fast pieces like canzonas.
7. **principale and flauto in XV**. For music with divisions.
8. **principale, VIII and flauto in XV**. This is also very effective for music with divisions.
9. **VIII and flauto in VIII**. This is wonderful for music with divisions and for canzonas; very good for all kinds of things.
10. **principale solo**. Most delicate. I usually use this for playing during the consecration at Mass. Also for accompanying motets with few voices.
11. **flauto in VIII** solo.
12. **VIII solo**. This may be used on its own only in large [i.e. 12′ – FF compass] organs where it is like the principale of a small organ. Otherwise the **principale** and the **flauto in VIII** are the only stops used on their own.
13. **principale solo** with tremulant. This is only for playing adagio and without divisions.
14. **flauto in VIII** with tremulant. As for no. 13 above.
15. **VIII and flauto in VIII** with tremulant. As for nos. 13 & 14 above. [When Costanzo Antegnati's son interrupts the dialogue to say that he has heard canzonas with divisions played on this combination of stops (even with the tremulant) by worthy men, Costanzo replies that they must pardon his saying so, but they have no understanding or taste, because playing fast on this registration only creates confusion.]
16. **principale and fiffaro**. The fiffaro is often called voci umane and rightly so because of its sweet sound. It is used exclusively with the principale and without adding any other stops as otherwise everything would sound out of tune. This combination is for slow music played adagio and as legato as possible.

In addition, Antegnati mentions two stops on the Duomo Vecchio organ (i.e. the old cathedral in Brescia, still extant but rebuilt by Serassi) that are rarely found. The first is a second principale, also found at San Marco in Milan. This stop was divided so that the treble played on the keyboard, the bass only in the pedal. When used together with the flauto in VIII, the treble half of the keyboard played both stops together while the bass half had the flute on its own. If played one octave lower, the flute (4′ pitch) replied at the same pitch as the treble (8′ + 4′). It was therefore possible to play a dialogue that could be accompanied on the pedal.[4] Finally, Antegnati recommends changing registrations just as the music might pass from one style to another, returning at the end to the initial registration.

Other aspects of performance

Transposition and split keys

The co-existence during the sixteenth century of F-range and C-range organs suggests that transposition was common practice. Such a supposition is supported by the fact that Giovanni Gabrieli included transposed versions of his fairly simple *intonationi* alongside untransposed ones in his publication of 1593. He was presumably thereby helping the inexperienced organist to cope with an everyday problem.[5] The importance of mean-tone tuning has already been mentioned. (Costanzo Antegnati gives a method in *L'arte organica* which insists on good – if not perfect – major thirds; see Stembridge 1993.) Such a system restricted transposition to a certain extent. To solve this problem many Italian organs were provided with extra chromatic (split) keys throughout the sixteenth century and, particularly in the South and in Sicily, until the second half of the seventeenth century (see Wraight and Stembridge 1994). There were usually two extra keys in each of the middle octaves: a♭ and either d♭ or d♯. Clearly, the need for these extra keys was determined by the requirement to play at pitches suitable for singers and possibly other instruments. Some organs had as many as four extra chromatic keys to the octave. The development was taken to its extreme in the *arciorgano* designed by Nicola Vicentino and built by Vincenzo Colombo in 1561. This, similar in construction to Vicentino's *archicembalo*, has thirty-one notes to the octave. The fact that at least five such organs are known to have existed belies the notion that such an invention represented only the aspirations of the lunatic fringe (see Stembridge 1993: 55–7). The importance of truly consonant major thirds was and remains vital to sixteenth-century (and much seventeenth-century) Italian organ music.[6]

Very little extant organ music of the period strays beyond the confines of normal mean-tone tuning, i.e. it is very rare to find chromatic notes other than f♯, c♯, g♯, b♭ and e♭. Some seventeenth-century music does seem to make use of the fact that many organs did in fact have extra keys, notably the *Recercar con obligo del Basso come appare* in Frescobaldi's *Fiori Musicali* (Venice, 1635). Other instances are to be found in Banchieri and the Neapolitan school, especially in Giovanni Salvatore's book of 1641.

Pedals

While there is documentary evidence for virtuoso pedal playing at an early date in Italy, indications for the use of pedals in Italian organ music are rare (see Tagliavini 1992: 187). In a manuscript source dating from the first half of the sixteenth century, the player is told, in one piece, to play the lowest notes on the pedals (transcribed in Göllner 1982: 49). In the

1604 print of Annibale Padovano's *Toccate et ricercari d'organo* pedal notes are indicated by letters placed beneath the music system. Frescobaldi's directions for the *Toccata Quinta* and *Toccata Sesta* (1627 book) 'sopra i pedali, e senza' leave the door open for *manualiter* performance. The same kind of indication is given by Gregorio Strozzi, *Capricci da sonare cembali, et organi* (1687). Clearly pedals were often used to hold a pedal-point, leaving the left hand free to do more interesting things. On a large organ the pedal pull-downs would play at 16′ pitch while one might play at 8′ pitch on the manual. Contrabbassi, which were sometimes added as independent pedal stops, were pitched in unison with the principale. (Not until the eighteenth century was it normal for Italian organs based on an 8′ principale to have a 16′ contrabbasso playable on the pedals.) On a large organ this meant, when playing at 8′ pitch, that the pedal could effectively double the bass line at 16′ pitch – if it were not moving fast.

The modes
There is today an unfortunate tendency to disregard the importance of the modes. Through overuse of hindsight all modes tend to be perceived as simply either major or minor, albeit with some antiquated characteristics that they were soon to lose. In this one-ended view of progress a notable dimension of the music becomes lost. The Frescobaldi who wrote innovatory toccatas was the same Frescobaldi who composed sets of fantasias and ricercars in the twelve modes codified by Glareanus and Zarlino or who, in his last publication, the *Fiori musicali* (1635), adhered to the tradition of using only the third and fourth modes for elevation toccatas. We can appreciate the full significance and musical effect of innovatory modulations – not only in Neapolitan *stravaganze* but also in the much earlier *Recerchari* of Marc'Antonio Cavazzoni – or the extended voice-ranges (as in, for example, Giovanni Gabrieli's Ricercar del VIIº e VIIIº tono) only if we have some inkling of how the modes functioned. Virtually all polyphonic music, whether canzonas or ricercars, as well as most toccatas, is composed in a particular mode; this is of considerable help to the performer in understanding the character of a particular composition. Vocal music, sacred and secular alike, normally shows a very clear correlation between text and choice of mode. For a summary of the modes and their attributes, see the Appendix, pp. 316–18 below.

The repertoire by genres

The ricercar

In the first quarter of the sixteenth century, pieces composed in a relatively free style without a fixed number of voices are often labelled 'Ricercar', 'Recercada' or similar. These range from the small-scale compositions by Fogliano in the Castell'Arquato manuscript to the two big improvisatory 'Recerchari' in Marc'Antonio Cavazzoni's publication of 1523; these latter use the full range of a four-octave keyboard (F–f^3) and modulate to such an extent that all the available semitones in normal mean-tone tuning are required. The writing suggests that they were conceived primarily for a large organ and were therefore probably performed on a 12′ *ripieno* (FF–f^2). (They cannot be played on a four-octave C compass without being transposed.) Their elusive sense of form and extensive use of *passaggi* relate them to subsequent toccatas (see below). Marc'Antonio's son, Girolamo Cavazzoni, published his first book of Ricercars, Canzonas and Hymns in 1543. The four ricercars are the earliest keyboard pieces of the genre in strictly imitative style. They use several subjects, in succession rather than simultaneously, and introduce divisions well suited to the keyboard. Others, such as Jacob Buus, Andrea and Giovanni Gabrieli, composed monothematic ricercars, while in the South, Giovanni de Macque and his pupils Mayone and Trabaci based their ricercars on two, three and sometimes four subjects treated concurrently. Frescobaldi's *Fantasie* of 1608 fall into the same category just as much as his *Ricercari* of 1615.

Nearly all these pieces are written for four voices; the range of each of these is normally confined to the same extent (little more than an octave) that it would be in vocal music. The mode is usually implicit where it is not mentioned in the title. While the ricercars of the Neapolitan school and Frescobaldi are written predominantly in white notation, some of those of the Venetian school contain varying incidence of *tremoli*, trills and divisions. A comparison of Buus's *Recercar Primo* from his *Intabolatura* of 1549 with the simpler version in the part-books of his *Secondo Libro* of the same year throws light on keyboard performance, as shown in Example 10.2. A reassessment of Diruta's comments on embellishment in his *Transilvano* suggests that contrapuntal music of the period should be embellished at the keyboard considerably more than current performance practice would generally admit.[7]

While the north Italian ricercar after Luzzaschi is often of a rather improvisatory nature, evident in its somewhat loose structure (see especially Giovanni Gabrieli), a more rigorous approach came from the Low Countries. Of major importance are the twelve ricercars of Giovanni

Ex. 10.2 Buus, Recercar Primo

(a) Part books, 1549

(b) Intabolatura, 1549

(a) cont.

(b) cont.

(Jean) de Macque, a student of Philippe de Monte. These compositions contain very little material not based on one of their (normally three) subjects. Closest in style to these are Frescobaldi's *Fantasie*.

A cantus firmus such as the Re di Spagna or a hymn such as Ave maris stella was often used as the basis of a fantasia or ricercar by the Neapolitans (cf. Rodio, Mayone and Trabaci). Buus, Andrea Gabrieli, Macque and Frescobaldi sometimes used a subject in augmentation as a cantus firmus in their ricercars. Many hymns and versetti (e.g. in organ masses) are in effect miniature ricercars; the same divergent tendencies towards inclusion of written-out ornamentation (e.g. in Merulo) or not (e.g. Frescobaldi) apply.

The canzona

The earliest published Italian keyboard music was Andrea Antico's book of *Frottole* (1517). These are keyboard arrangements of fairly straightforward homophonic vocal compositions, mainly by Bartolomeo Tromboncino and Marchetto Cara. In Marc'Antonio Cavazzoni's 1523 book we find, alongside intabulations of motets, arrangements of chansons, including one of Josquin's *Plusieurs regretz*. Girolamo Cavazzoni

(1543) also used Josquin as well as Passereau chansons as models. The Italian practice of playing French chansons on four instruments led to original ensemble compositions being written in the same style. Claudio Merulo and Giovanni Gabrieli wrote such pieces which were then sometimes re-arranged for keyboard (cf. Merulo's 1592 book and Gabrieli's *La Spiritata* in Diruta's *Transilvano*). Andrea Gabrieli, like Merulo and others, wrote quite richly embellished keyboard versions of chansons (*Qui la dira, Orsus au coup, Petit Jacquet* etc.) but also 'Ricercari ariosi', a kind of hybrid form with rhythmic figuration of the canzona type used in an imitative polyphonic composition. Somewhat similar pieces by Rocco Rodio are entitled 'Ricercar', cf. also de Macque's *Ricercar V° tono*. The term 'fuga' was also used for such pieces (cf. Giovanni Gabrieli). De Macque, Mayone and Trabaci wrote canzonas often in two or more sections, usually thematically related. Frescobaldi further developed such forms in his second book of toccatas (1627) and *Fiori Musicali* (1635), adding as bridge passages extended cadences (cadenzas) in toccata style.

The capriccio

The word 'capriccio' was used as a generic term for keyboard pieces in the title of publications by Mayone and Trabaci. It was also used for compositions of a basically polyphonic nature, having much in common with the ricercar, fantasia and canzona, but usually treating one subject only. Outstanding examples include de Macque's *Capriccio sopra re fa mi sol* and Frescobaldi's 1624 set.

The Toccata

In order to establish the mode before a vocal work was sung, the church organist would play. As we know from the lutenist Dalza's 'tastar de corde', secular vocal or instrumental music was similarly introduced. Andrea Gabrieli's *Intonationi* are mini-toccatas intended to serve this purpose. Giovanni Gabrieli's set consists of pieces that are even shorter. The book in which Giovanni published all these *Intonationi* in 1593 also contains three of Andrea's toccatas.

Marc'Antonio's *Recerchari* discussed above are perhaps to all intents and purposes toccatas. The manuscript example which begins in mode III and finishes in mode I may well have been designed for liturgical use as a bridge between vocal items sung in these two modes. It is conceivable that the longer printed *Recerchari* were also used in this way by simply terminating at an intermediate cadence rather than playing from beginning to end – an approach sanctioned by Frescobaldi in the introduction to his books of toccatas a century later. The modulatory nature of Cavazzoni's pieces would seem to support this hypothesis. While these large-scale pieces, like some of Giovanni Gabrieli's toccatas (see especially that in mode I), appear to have been conceived for the *ripieno* of a large Renaissance organ, the intricate passagework of Claudio Merulo's toccatas suggest a smaller instrument – perhaps a 4′ organ or a harpsichord or even a combination of the two: claviorganum.[8] The texture of these works is often that of a solo part – reminiscent of virtuoso *passaggi* written for a solo instrument such as a cornet or a viol – which passes from one hand to the other, while the free hand provides accompanying chords in the nature of a continuo realisation. For contrast, Merulo introduces imitative polyphonic sections into his toccatas. That these should be played more slowly, with respect to the written note-values, than the free-style sections is suggested by the fact that a manuscript version has minims in such sections where the print has crochets (see Example 10.3). The same manuscript often omits such polyphonic sections entirely; this could, like Frescobaldi's suggested curtailing of his toccatas, be the result of an accepted tradition which treated compositions in a slightly cavalier fashion not so acceptable to later generations – on the other hand, these omissions might well reflect earlier versions of Merulo's toccatas, the polyphonic sections being perhaps added at a later stage. Comparison of two versions of the *Toccata Ottava* from Merulo's second book (Rome 1604), seen in Example 10.3, show how the composer developed *passaggi*, or perhaps simply provided more notes in the print reflecting what his students would have added when playing from the simpler manuscript version.

Merulo's printed toccatas (contained in the two books he prepared at the end of his life, published in 1598 and 1604) are ordered according to the modes, with two, sometimes three, pieces in each of the ten modes used in Venice. Although each of Frescobaldi's books (1615 and 1627) contains twelve toccatas, these are not ordered by mode, unlike the same composer's sets of *Fantasie* (1608) and *Ricercari* (1615). In his second book, Frescobaldi includes an embellished madrigal in place of a twelfth toccata; this, together with the comparison that he draws in his foreword between the 'modern madrigal' and the toccata – both requiring the same rhythmic freedom in performance – brings the toccata into the realm of vocally inspired keyboard music, alongside the ricercar and the canzona.

The significant juxtaposition of *madrigale passaggiato* and toccata in fact pre-dates Frescobaldi, since it is found in both of Ascanio Mayone's books of *Diversi Capricci* (Naples, 1603 and 1609). (Mayone organised each book to reflect a stylistic development from *stile antico* ricercars, some based on cantus firmi, through canzonas, madrigal and toccatas to exuberant virtuoso variations in the latest style.) Mayone's toccatas are well structured, often ending with a ricercar section. The *Toccata Seconda*

Ex. 10.3 Merulo, *Toccata Ottava*

(a) Manuscript version (Turin, Giordano II)
Comparing this with the 1604 print, this illustrates presumably an earlier stage. In the print there is a little more passagework; quaver passages (b. 40) are dotted or embellished. The note-values for the Ricercar section starting in b. 42 have been halved in the print.

(b) Published version of 1604

(1603 book), the most convincing of this 'prelude and fugue' type, makes considerable demands on the player and seems to require pedals. It is possible that Mayone sometimes had a non-keyboard instrument in mind when he wrote wide intervals and exotic scale passages: he is known to have been an accomplished player of the chromatic harp. (A ricercar in the second book is specifically designated for harp.)

Giovanni de Macque was perhaps the first keyboard composer to develop the *durezze e ligature* style – slow-moving sustained four-part writing with long-held dissonances, though Ercole Pasquini uses it too. One of the most striking pieces in this style is Trabaci's *Consonanze stravaganti* (1603). It occurs in Mayone, Banchieri and of course Frescobaldi. A favourite dissonance was the diminished fourth, which requires meantone temperament if it is to be distinguishable from a major third.

Frescobaldi's toccatas demonstrate his acquaintance with most of the music so far discussed, yet he developed his own particular style to the extent that it is easily recognisable. His *passaggi* seem to be more specific to the keyboard than those of Merulo. His expressive use of chromaticism and dissonance is more conservative than that of the Neapolitans. The logical mind of the great contrapuntist is never abandoned in the flights of fancy that enabled him to bring the toccata to perfection.

Recommended editions

Of the many facsimile editions now available, two are worth special mention because they are good reasonably priced reproductions of beautifully engraved editions of keyboard music made with the composers' collaboration. They are published by *Studio per edizioni scelte*, Florence:

> C. Merulo, *Toccate d'intavolatura d'organo* (Rome, 1598 and 1604, repr. in one volume, 1981)
> G. Frescobaldi, *Toccate . . . Libro Primo* (Rome, 1637, repr. 1978)
> G. Frescobaldi, *Toccate . . . Libro Secondo* (Rome, 1627, repr. 1978)

Experienced players should find it worth while becoming familiar with reading the Italian keyboard tablature (two extended staves). In the case of Merulo the only other available edition is Ricordi, which has modernised the beaming and often suppressed the information given in the source which indicates which hand should play what. In the case of Frescobaldi there are modern alternatives:

1. Suvini-Zerboni, the Opera Omnia, vols. 2 and 3
2. Zanibon (containing only the toccatas from these collections)

For Frescobaldi's other works

Fantasie, Canzoni, Orgelwerke I (Bärenreiter)
Capricci, Canzoni, Ricercari, Orgelwerke II (Bärenreiter)
Capricci, in open score with old clefs (Suvini-Zerboni)
Fiori Musicali (a) in open score with old clefs (De Santis, Rome)
     (b) in open score with modern clefs (Armelin, Padua)
     (c) two-stave reduction, Orgelwerke V (Bärenreiter)

Other music

Anthologies

Die italienische Orgelmusik am Anfang des Cinquecento, ed. K. Jeppesen (Hansen)
Faber Early Organ Series, vols 16–18, ed. J. Dalton (Faber)
Neapolitan Keyboard Composers, ed. R. Jackson (Corpus of Early Keyboard Music (CEKM 24)

Composers

A. Antico, *Frottole* (Doblinger)
G. Cavazzoni, *Orgelwerke* (2 vols., Schott)
M.-A. Cavazzoni, *Recerchari . . .*, publ. in Jeppesen (see above). New edition planned 1998 (Armelin, Padua)
G. Cavaccio, *Sudori musicali* (CEKM 43)
A. Gabrieli, *Orgelwerke* (5 vols., Bärenreiter)
A. Gabrieli, *3 Messe per organo* (Ricordi)
G. Gabrieli, *Composizioni per organo* (Ricordi)
G. de Macque, *Ricercari sui 12 toni* (Zanibon)
A. Mayone, *Diversi Capricci per sonare* (2 vols., Zanibon)
A. Padovano, *Toccate e Ricercari* (Zanibon, but also CEKM 34)
E. Pasquini, *Collected Keyboard Works* (CEKM 12)
T. Merula, *Composizioni per organo e cembalo* (Paideia / Bärenreiter)
C. Merulo, *Messe d'intavolatura d'organo* (CEKM 47, also Doblinger)
G. Salvatore, *Collected Keyboard Works* (CEKM 3)
G. M. Trabaci, *Composizioni per organo e cembalo* (2 vols., Paideia / Bärenreiter)

Further music of the period is available in other volumes of CEKM, including C. Antegnati (vol. 9, note-values halved), F. Bianciardi and C. Porta (41), O. Bariolla (46), Bertholdo (67), G. M. Cima (20), and Frescobaldi's works preserved in manuscripts (3 vols., 30).

For music after Frescobaldi see in particular the following (CEKM unless otherwise indicated): L. Battiferi (42), B. Pasquini (6 vols., 5), M. Rossi (Zanibon), A. Scarlatti (Paideia / Bärenreiter), D. Scarlatti (Bärenreiter), B. Storace (7), G. Strozzi (11) and D. Zipoli (Müller).

11 Iberian organ music before 1700

James Dalton

Introduction

Iberian organ music to *c*1700 is traditional, in that the principles of composition in the works of composers of the *siglo de oro*, such as Morales and Victoria, are essentially maintained in the various types of organ music through the seventeenth century. There is the lasting impression that, although ornamentation and registration are becoming increasingly elaborate, the musical motet style of *c*1500 provides the basic technical structure right up to Cabanilles; colour and elaboration are applied within this style rather than constituting a part of some new way of composing, as in French or German late seventeenth-century organ music. Iberian composers, however they may compare for progressiveness and even technical ability with their contemporaries in other European countries, show tremendous musical expressiveness and conviction in their works. It is conspicuous that composers of vocal music (e.g. Morales, Guerrero, Cebollas, Victoria) and those for organ described here are almost mutually exclusive. Organists did not always occupy the position of maestro de capilla: Cabezón was *musico de cámara y capilla* to Philip II, Aguilera's position in Huesca (Aragon) was designated *Portionarius et organis praeceptor*, while Correa de Arauxo and Cabanilles were organists in Seville and Valencia respectively. Most likely there were regional characteristics: Francisco Peraza, Diego del Castillo as well as Correa lived in Seville, while Aguilera, Jimenez and Bruna were active in Zaragoza, but because of the relatively small quantity of surviving music and instruments any definite conclusions could be misleading.

Organs

The scale of the Iberian organ before the eighteenth century was generally not very big, and the instrument can best be appreciated in the context of the music written for it. It is not unexpected to find that a good number of organ builders from the Netherlands were active in different parts of Spain in the sixteenth century, just as they were in France and Germany and other European countries. Organs in the cathedrals of Seville, Lérida and Barcelona were made by Netherlanders before 1550, and the Flemish organ builder Gilles Brebos built four organs for the huge conventual church at El Escorial between 1579 and 1585. Juan Brebos made organs for Toledo cathedral in 1592, and for the Alcazar in Madrid in 1590 and 1606. Although the introduction of stops such as Rohrflute and Quintadena, and particularly reeds – Chirimía (Schalmei), Orlos (Krumhorn), Dulzayna (Regal) – was a Flemish contribution to the Spanish organ, the main constituent of the instrument was its Principal chorus – Lleno – and this can be seen in instruments of all sizes, the extra stops in large organs being reeds and others for variety. An instrument from the mid-sixteenth century, made by Gaspar de Soto, is in the Capilla del Condestable of Burgos Cathedral and has the following specification:

Bass (C/E–c^1)

Flautado de 13 palmos	Principal 8′
Octava	Octave 4′
Quincena	Fifteenth 2′
Diez y novena	Nineteenth $1\frac{1}{3}$′
Tapadillo	Stopped Flute 4′
Lleno III	Mixture III

Treble (c$\sharp^1$–c^3)

Flautado de 13 palmos	Principal 8′
Octava	Octave 4′
Quincena	Fifteenth 2′
Docena	Twelfth $2\frac{2}{3}$′
Diez y setena	Seventeenth $1\frac{3}{5}$′
Flauta principal II	(?undulating) Principal II
Lleno III	Mixture III

Pedal 8′ notes with short keys (they are pull-downs); notes in the same order as short octave manual.

In Iberian organs generally the stops are divided at c^1/c$\sharp^1$; sometimes the two parts belong to the same stop, e.g. Flautado 13 in the Burgos specification, and sometimes they are of different stops, e.g. the Diez y novena (bass) and the Docena (treble) in the same organ. This arrangement enables different registrations to be used for bass and treble parts of the keyboard, making possible a solo registration in the right hand with accompaniment in the left, and vice versa. It is a feature well known from organs of other countries, notably England, the Netherlands and Italy, but one that has been turned to particular advantage by Spanish organ composers; throughout the seventeenth century particularly there is an incomparable wealth of pieces *de medio registro*, composed to exploit the registrational possibilities of the divided keyboard. The pedal board is likely to be limited to one octave, and the notes would be played by pressing studs or short keys. On small organs the notes would only be pull-downs attached to the lowest octave of the manual; larger organs may have a rank of independent pipes of 16′ pitch in addition to the coupler. In either case the function of the pedals would be limited to holding long notes (Contras). One look at an old Spanish pedal board is enough to eliminate any question of an elaborate independent part!

Here is a similar design from the early seventeenth century, at Garganta la Olla (Cáceres). This organ, which dates from about 1625, was originally in the Convent of Yuste. The horizontal Clarín is from *c*1700:

Bass (C/E–c^1)

Flautado	Principal 8′
8^a	Octave 4′
12^a	Twelfth 2$\frac{2}{3}$′
15^a	Fifteenth 2′
Lleno	Mixture
Cimbale	Cimbel
Trompeta real	Trumpet (vertical, 8′ in case)

Treble (c^1♯–c^3)

Flautado	Principal 8′
8^a	Octave 4′
12^a	Twelfth 2$\frac{2}{3}$′
15^a	Fifteenth 2′
Lleno	Mixture
Cimbal	Cimbel
Octavin	Octavin 1′
Tapadillo	Stopped Flute 4′
Corneta real	Cornet V
Clarín	Clarín (horizontal) 8′

Finally a rather more splendid design from later in the century, still however with one manual and essentially traditional: San Juan Bautista of Mondragón by Joseph de Echevarría, 'Maestro artifice de hacer órganos', with the assistance of Padre Maestro Joseph de Hechevarría 'de la Orden Seráfica de nuestro Padre San Francisco'. The contract is dated 20 November 1677:

> With these stops is made the plenum of a good organ, and said stops are very necessary.
>
> **Bass**
>
> | | |
> |---|---|
> | Flautado principal de 13 | Principal 8′ |
> | Octava | Octave 4′ |
> | Docena clara | Twelfth 2$\frac{2}{3}$′ |
> | Quincena | Fifteenth 2′ |

Decimanona	Nineteenth $1\frac{1}{3}'$
Compuestas de lleno	Mixture
Zimbala	Cimbel

Treble

Flautado principal de 13	Principal 8'
Octava	Octave 4'
Docena clara	Twelfth $2\frac{2}{3}'$
Quincena	Fifteenth 2'
Decimanona	Nineteenth $1\frac{1}{3}'$
Compuestas de lleno	Mixture
Zimbala	Cimbel

The stops outside the plenum of the organ:

Bass

Trompetas reales	Trumpet (vertical) 8'
Trompetas reales	Trumpet (vertical) 8'
Dulzainas	Regal 8'

Treble

Corneta real	Cornet
Trompetas reales	Trumpet 8'
Dulzainas	Regal 8'
Clarines	Clarín (horizontal) 8'

Additional stops because the church lacks sufficient echo:

Bass

Segundo flautado abierto	Second Principal (open) 8'
Sobre zimbala	High Cimbel
Nazarda mayor	Nazard

Treble

Segundo flautado abierto	Second Principal (open) 8'
Sobre zimbala	High Cimbel
Nazarda mayor	Nazard

And the following *juguetes alegres* [toy stops]:

Cascabeladas	little bells
Jugueros	moving figures in the case
Bordones de la Gaita Zamorana	bagpipe drones
Atabales	drums

A register of great brilliance will be the treble half-stop of *clarines*, a stop which has been built in no organ except in the organ which I have now made in the convent of San Diego de Alcalá de Henares (Eibar, 1659), and by its excellence it will be seen as great novelty. . . . The [pipes] will be placed in the main cornice like cannons, which will beautify all the façade of the organ.

In character, Iberian organs of the sixteenth and seventeenth centuries are gentle-sounding, their richness achieved by the variety of registers, rather than by force – Vente and Kok state that the 'smallest organs always have a full chorus of flautado stops . . . an interior trompeta real [vertical, inside the case] and for bigger instruments two horizontal half-stop reeds and a treble cornet, and so on' (Vente and Kok 1970: 142). As far as tonal impressions can be explained technically, various points in Iberian organ building are consistent with the sound produced by the 'vocal, gentle, fluework' (Andersen 1969: 157). Taking the renaissance organ in Evora cathedral (Vente and Flentrop 1970: 5), the wind pressure at 56 mm is low (it may well have been even lower originally), pipe scales are small, with e.g. c^1 on the Flautado de 12 palmos having a diameter of 48 mm, compared to c52 mm in Töpfer's 'normal scale'; the mouth width at 0.21 of circumference is smaller than the conventional 0.25, and the cut up is around one third of the width, more than a quarter, consequentially reducing the brightness of tone. The reeds also are quite 'free of any suggestion of heaviness' (Andersen 1969: 167). They are thin-tongued, and frequently horizontally laid out – Regals no less than Claríns – and can speak with precision and colour.

Sources of music

Printed sources

1. Juan Bermudo: *Declaración de instrumentos musicales* (1555)
   150 folios; 14 keyboard pieces
      facsimile ed. M. S. Kastner, Bärenreiter (1957)
2. Luis Venegas de Henestrosa: *Libro de Cifra nueva para tecla, harpa, y vihuela . . .* (1557)
   78 folios; 138 compositions, including more than 40 by Antonio de Cabezón
      modern edition in *Monumentos de la música española (MME)* 2, ed. H. Anglès (1944)
3. Tomás de Santa María: *Libro llamado Arte de tañer Fantasia, asi para Tecla como para Vihuela, y todo instrumeto . . .* (1565)
   two books 94 + 124 folios
      facsimile ed. D. Stevens, Gregg reprint (1972)
4. Antonio de Cabezón: *Obras de musica para tecla arpa y vihuela recopiladas y puestas en cifra por Hernando de Cabeçon su hijo* (1578)
   213 folios; 129 compositions, including *versos, fabordones*, Magnificats on each of the eight tones, Kyries, 12 *tientos*, many ornamented motets, *canciones* à 4, 5, 6, nine sets of *diferencias* (variations)
      modern edition in *MME* 27–9, ed. H. Anglès (1966)
5. Manuel Rodrigues Coelho: *Flores de Musica pera o instrumento de Tecla, & Harpa* (1620)

241 folios; 24 *tentos*, sets of *versos* for all the tones
>modern edition in *Portugaliae musica (PM)* 1 and 3, ed. M. S. Kastner (1959, 1961)

6. Francisco Correa de Arauxo: *Libro de Tientos y Discursos de Musica Practica, y Theorica de Organo, intitulado Facultad organica* . . . (1626)

1–12:   *Tientos* for complete (undivided) stops on tones I–XII

13–24: *Tientos* for complete stops on various tones; easier than nos. 1–12

25–51: *Tientos* for half stops (*medio registro*) (pieces with solo for treble or bass)

52–7:   *Tientos* à 5 – one undivided, two with two *tiples* (right-hand solos), three with two *baxones* (left-hand solos)

58–61: Pieces with demisemiquaver movement – two with one *tiple*, one with one *baxon*, one *Susana* (ornamented chanson)

62–5:   Pieces in triple time – two undivided, one with one *tiple*, one *Guárdame las vacas* (ornamented variations)

66:      *Gaybergier* (Crecquillon) – ornamented chanson

67–9:   Plainchant settings

>modern edition in *MME* 6 and 12, ed. M. S. Kastner (1948, 1952)

Manuscript sources

7. Coimbra M242
184 folios containing 230 compositions, including works by Antonio Carreira and Heliadorus de Paiva
>modern edition (partial, but including the *tentos* of Carreira) in *PM* 19, ed. M. S. Kastner (1969)

8. El Escorial LP29 (formerly MS 2186)
Seventeenth-century copy; 131 folios; 58 compositions, the majority of which are anonymous; a number by Diego de Torrijos, one *tiento* by Aguilera de Heredia, many *versos*

9. El Escorial LP30 (formerly MS 2187)
Seventeenth-century copy; 106 folios; 67 compositions, the main source for Aguilera and Jimenez, and includes several pieces by Bruna as well as the celebrated *Medio Registro alto* by Peraza.

10. Porto MM42 (formerly 1577)
Although located in Portugal, this MS contains Spanish compositions in *cifra* (number) notation. The most frequently named composers are Bartolomé de Olague and Andrés de Sola, while many of the pieces are anonymous. There are isolated works by Aguilera and Bruna.

11. Braga MS 964
a manuscript of 259 folios, compiled in the first part of the eighteenth century, including most of the known works of Pedro de Araujo. The collection includes a large proportion of Rodrigues Coelho's *Flores de Musica* published in 1620.
>modern edition (incomplete) in *PM* 25, ed. G. Doderer (1974) and 11 (ed. K. Speer (1967)

12. Madrid MSS 1357, 1358, 1359 and 1360

The four volumes of *Flores de música*, an enormous anthology of organ music compiled from 1706 to 1709 by Antonio Martín y Coll (?1660–?1740), a Franciscan friar, then organist of the monastery of San Francisco el Grande at Madrid. They run to more than 1,800 pages in total, and besides containing examples of the various styles of seventeenth-century Spanish organ music, include a large amount of secular music. Although the great majority of the pieces are unattributed in the manuscript, a considerable number have now been identified as the work of Aguilera, Bruna, Cabanilles, various Italian and French composers, and particularly of Andrés Lorente (1624–1703), organist of the monastery of San Diego at Alcalá de Henares and Martín y Coll's teacher. Lorente's contribution occupies the first 80 folios of the second volume of *Flores*, which are written in *cifra* tablature.

13. Barcelona EBc M729, 751
   199 folios and 432 pages respectively
   These are the main sources, along with El Escorial LP30 of compositions by Pablo Bruna.
      modern edition: see under Performing Editions.
14. Barcelona EBc M386
   360 pages; the manuscript, dated 1722, contains 98 compositions by Cabanilles, the copy made by a fervent admirer.
15. Barcelona EBc M387
   424 folios; dating from 1694–7, the manuscript consists of 500 works, almost entirely by Cabanilles.

Music

The main type of composition, *tiento* (Portuguese *tento*), or *obra*, based on polyphonic motet style, occurs through the sixteenth and seventeenth centuries while, fairly closely derived from it, come the *Tiento de medio registro*, *Tiento de falsas*, *Tiento de contras*, and the profusion of *versos* for Mass and particularly Office music. Hymn settings, based on plainchant cantus firmus, often appear, and from Bermudo (1555) to Cabanilles the 'Spanish' Pange lingua (a Mozarabic melody, occurring in a setting by the late fifteenth-century composer Johannes Urreda). There are, in addition to these, keyboard intabulations of chansons, already much practised by German composers of the fifteenth and sixteenth centuries, settings and transcriptions of *canciones* and dances in the late seventeenth century, which reflect current tastes in music, and occasional *passacalles* and *batalla* compositions.

As to notation, almost all pieces are written in open score, further indication of the traditional approach to composition. In Italy, for example, score notation was general until the early seventeenth century, but thereafter was employed only for contrapuntal pieces such as capric-

cios and canzonas, while for keyboard toccatas the two-stave system was
used; however, even the most flamboyant of the keyboard works by
Cabanilles are notated in score. Only in the books by Bermudo and Santa
María, which are primarily of musical instruction and explanation, are
the compositions printed in parts; in Santa María's case they are intended
as demonstrations of the technique of composing, while Bermudo
describes his short pieces as being written for organ. The first printed
music using *cifra* (number) notation, which is definitely a kind of
score, is the *Libro de cifra nueva* (1557) of Venegas. It includes works by
many composers, among them Cabezón, Mudarra, Palero, although there
is no mention of Venegas himself as a composer; he may have seen his
function as editor and arranger, acting as transcriber of pieces by
Janequin, Morales, Clemens non Papa etc.[1] Cabezón's *Obras*, published
by his son in 1578, also uses *cifra*, as does *Facultad Organica* of Correa de
Arauxo.

Correa's practical advice concerning registration applies to the *tientos
de medio registro*, described as a new type of composition, 'célebre inven-
ción' and much used in the kingdoms of Castille, although not known
elsewhere. He explains that there are four types: one with a solo for the
right hand accompanied by the left, and vice versa; and one with two parts
for the right hand accompanied by the left, and its reciprocal. Altogether
there are eighteen *de tiple* (R.H. solo), thirteen *de baxon* (L.H. solo), two
de dos tiples (R.H. à 2), and three *de dos baxones* (L.H. à 2). The one-
manual organ, with stops divided at $c^1/c\sharp^1$, lends itself to this technique of
composition. For registration of the solo parts, Correa relies largely on
the discretion and judgement of the organist. In the three *glosas* (variations) on the *Canto Lleno de La Immaculada Concepción*, no. 69, which is a
medio registro de tiple, he assigns the lower parts to the Flautado and for
the treble the Mixtura which seems best to the organist. This 'mixture'
means a combination of stops, not necessarily the Lleno register, as in his
prologo punto noveno Correa refers to the Mixtura de flautado and the
Mixtura de lleno. Furthermore, in describing the method of performance
of the pieces with two solo voices (*medio registro de dos tiples* or *dos
baxones*) he writes, in the note to No. 54 that when the solo parts are in the
treble they may be played on the Lleno, with the accompaniment on
Flautado; but when in the bass they may use Lleno or Trompetas, with the
treble accompanying parts again on Flautado, and adding for good
measure that the registration must not cause the parts to become confused so as to make the bass sound above the treble. Example 11.1, from
Tiento de 1° tono de mano derecha by Bruna, provides a clear demonstra-
tion of the system for a right-hand solo; it also shows, in bars 11, 19 and 22
the characteristic rhythmic feature of $3+3+2$ quavers in ¢ time,

Ex. 11.1 Bruna, *Tiento de I° tono de mano derecha*

noticeable throughout the seventeenth century in Spanish organ composition.

Most of the later seventeenth-century music is traditional in form and registrational means: *Tiento lleno, Tiento de Falsas* (meaning suspensions, equivalent to the Italian *ligature e durezze*), *Diferencias* etc. A type which is apparently new, although it had probably existed in improvisation for some time, is the *Tiento de Contras*, in which the notes of the pedal are used for long holding notes or pedal points, the stops being 16′ and 8′ Contras (open flue pipes). These provide the staple types of composition in Cabanilles, notwithstanding his striking harmonies and figurations. In the first volume of the collected edition by H. Anglés, which contains biographical information as well as detailed descriptions of sources of music and organs, the various types of *tiento* appear, fundamentally traditional, yet characteristically evolved. For example, the *Tiento (X) lleno 3° tono* is essentially ricercar-like in its opening section, although thematic intervals and figuration are individual; thereafter (bar 80) comes a section in triple metre using the main theme, with the final bars (127–37) back in **c** time, as shown in Example 11.2a, b and c respectively.

The opening of *Tiento de 6° tono de falsas (XIX)*, shown in Example

Ex. 11.2 Cabanilles, *Tiento lleno 3° tono*

11.3, demonstrates the start of a potentially eternal progression of suspensions, continuing as seems to be general in *falsas* pieces for slightly over 100 bars.

Also characteristic in this respect is the *Tiento de 1° tono de Contras (VI)* which lasts for well over 200 bars and alternates between duple and triple metre over sustained pedal notes – the opening D (see Example 11.4) lasts for 33 bars, and further sections use E, A, C, G, F and d, most of them more than once.

The *medio registro* type of arrangement is now described as *partido de mano derecha* (or *izquierda*) and makes use of the existing seventeenth-century apparatus for virtuosic and extended work: *Tiento de 3° tono.*

Ex. 11.3 Cabanilles, *Tiento de 6° tono de falsas*

Ex. 11.4 Cabanilles, *Tiento de 1° tono de Contras*

Partido de Mano Izquierda (XI) or *Tiento Partido de dos Tiples de 4° tono (XIV)* produces more than 200 bars in the normal mould, while *Tiento (XXI) de Batalla, partido de mano derecha* could be thought of as for the horizontal Clarín half-stop (from c#[1] upwards) provided for the Valencia Cathedral organ in 1693;[2] but this does not imply that *batalla* compositions in the seventeenth century were intended for the *lengüetería* – these bristling batteries of horizontal reeds flourished from 1700 onwards and were quite unknown to Correa, Jimenez, Bruna and Cabanilles himself, all of them *batalla* composers.

Performing editions (see also under Sources of music)

Anthologies

Liber Organi XI: *Orgelmusik des spanischen Barock*, ed. J. Wyly, Schott (1966)
includes pieces for Clarín from the Martín y Coll collection, and three pieces
by Josef Elías, a pupil of Cabanilles

Antología de Organistas clásicos siglos XVI–XVII, ed. L. Villalba Muñoz (1914),
rev. S. Rubio, UME (1971)
includes twenty-three short pieces by Tomás de Santa María, otherwise works
from El Escorial MSS with works by Peraza and Clavijo de Castillo, and ten by
Aguilera de Herédia

*Seventeenth-Century Spanish Organ Music from 'Huerto ameno de varias flores de
musica'* (2 vols.), ed. S. Fortino, Universal Edition (1986, 1987)
a score of works from the Martín y Coll collection, vol. 1 identified as
Cabanilles, Bruna, etc., vol. 2 anonymous

Composizioni Inedite dai 'Flores de Musica' di Antonio Martín y Coll, ed. C. Stella
and V. Vinay, Suvini Zerboni (1979)
20 pieces from the collection, including five by Andrés Lorente

Spanish Organ Masters after Antonio de Cabezón (Corpus of Early Keyboard
Music 14), ed. Willi Apel, American Institute of Musicology (1971)
particularly notable for the inclusion of almost all (seventeen) of Aguilera's
known compositions for organ

Faber Early Organ Series, vols. 4, 5 and 6, ed. J. Dalton, Faber Music (1987)
Vol. 4 includes music by the Portuguese composers, Antonio Carreira,
Heliadorus de Paiva and Rodrigues Coelho, as well as sixteenth-century
Spaniards; vol. 5 includes five substantial works by Aguilera and Correa, and
the majority of vol. 6 consists of compositions by Bruna and Cabanilles

Individual composers

Sebastián Aguilera de Herédia, *Obras para Organo*, ed. L. Siemens Hernandez,
Editorial Alpuerto (1977)
preferable to Corpus of Early Keyboard Music 14, although difficult to obtain

Obras Completas para Organo de Pablo Bruna, ed. J. Sagasta Galdos, Institución
'Fernando el Católico' Zaragoza (1979)
twenty-two *tientos* etc., three sets of *versos*, seven Pange lingua settings

J. Cabanilles, *Musici Organici Opera Omnia*, ed. H. Anglès, Barcelona, Biblioteca
Central, seccion de musica, 4, 8, 13, 17 (1927–56)

J. Jimenez, *Collected organ compositions*, ed. W. Apel (Corpus of Early Keyboard
Music 31), American Institute of Musicology (1975)

12 The French classical organ school

Edward Higginbottom

A survey of French organ music before 1800 is bound to recognise the unique flowering of the years 1660 to 1740. The repertory of this period is often referred to as 'classical', the term 'baroque' ill suiting, according to some commentators, the essential nature of its musical language. The corpus of extant music is large and includes music by well-known and versatile composers such as Guillaume-Gabriel Nivers (1632–1714), François Couperin (1668–1733) and Louis-Nicolas Clérambault (1676–1749). Others, such as Jacques Boyvin (1653–1706), André Raison (d. 1719) and Pierre Dumage (1674–1751), are known only for their organ music. The work of these composers merits pride of place in an account of French organ music of the seventeenth and eighteenth centuries.

The publications of the last forty years of the seventeenth century stand out as the central monument in the classical school (see Table 12.1). They emanate from the period in French history when Louis XIV outstripped all his European rivals in cultural endeavour. The beginning of his reign, from 1660, marks the coming of age of French baroque music. The Italian artists and musicians, imported by Cardinal Mazarin (1602–61) to boost the claims of Italian culture over French, left in the early 1660s, bereft of their patron. The more or less final manifestation of their struggle was the performance in Paris in 1662 of Cavalli's *Ercole amante*, an event noted for the success of the additional dance music by the young Jean-Baptiste Lully rather than Cavalli's score. The moment was ripe for a resurgence of national identity and pride in French art. In the musical domain Lully was the predominant voice in this process, aided by the privileges granted him by the King, and the institutions Louis XIV patronised. Some of the composers whose organ music we possess also basked in the King's patronage: Nivers, François Couperin, Nicolas Lebègue (1631–1702) and Louis Marchand (1669–1732) were all 'organistes du roi'. But the whole of Paris caught some glancing rays of his brilliance. The fashioning of the French classical style during this period made the city the equal of any in Europe for its organ music: the Court (Nivers, François Couperin, Lebègue, Louis Marchand), the metropolitan cathedral (Antoine

Table 12.1
Parisian organ publications 1660–1740

1660	F. Roberday	*Fugues et caprices*
1665	G.-G. Nivers	*Livre d'orgue contenant cent pieces de tous les tons*
1667	G.-G. Nivers	*2. livre d'orgue contenant la messe et les hymnes*
1675	G.-G. Nivers	*3. livre d'orgue des huits tons de l'eglise*
1676	N. Lebègue	*Les pièces d'orgue*
[1678]	N. Lebègue	*Second livre d'orgue . . . contenant des pièces . . . sur les huits tons . . . et la messe*
1682	N. Gigault	*Livre de musique* (2 vols.)
1685	N. Gigault	*Livre de musique . . . contenant plus de 180 pièces . . . plusieurs messes, quelques hymnes*
[1685]	N. Lebègue	*Troisieme livre d'orgue . . . contenant des grandes offertoires et des elevations; et tous les noëls les plus connus*
1688	A. Raison	*Livre d'orgue contenant cinq messes*
1689	J. H. d'Anglebert	*Pièces de clavecin . . . quelques fugues pour l'orgue . . . livre premier*
1690	J. Boyvin	*Premier livre d'orgue contenant les huit tons à l'usage ordinaire*
1690	F. Couperin	*Pièces d'orgue consistantes en deux messes*
1690	G. Jullien	*Premier livre d'orgue*
1699	N. de Grigny	*Premier livre d'orgue contenant une messe et les hymnes*
1700	J. Boyvin	*Second livre d'orgue contenant les huit tons à l'usage ordinaire*
1703	G. Corrette	*Messe du 8e ton pour l'orgue*
1706	Guilain	*Pieces d'orgue pour le Magnificat* [original edn lost, survives only in part in a later transcription]
1708	P. Dumage	*1er livre d'orgue contenant une suite du premier ton*
1710	L.-N. Clérambault	*Premier livre d'orgue contenant deux suites*
1712	C. Piroye	*Pièces choisies . . . tant pour l'orgue et le clavecin*
1714	A. Raison	*Second livre d'orgue*
1714	P. d'Andrieu	*Noëls, O Filii, chansons de Saint Jacques*
[1732]	L. Marchand	*Pièces choisies pour l'orgue*
[<1733]	J.-F. d'Andrieu	*Noëls, O Filii, chansons de Saint Jacques* [rev. edn of 1714]
1737	M. Corrette	*Premier livre d'orgue contenant quatre Magnificats*
n.d.	J.-F. d'Andrieu	*Premier livre de pièces d'orgue*
n.d.	L.-C. d'Aquin	*Nouveau livre de noëls pour l'orgue*
[c1740]	M. Corrette	*Nouveau livre de noëls*

Calvière, 1695–1755), the grand and fashionable churches of St Merry (Lebègue), St Gervais (François Couperin), St Sulpice (Nivers), St Nicolas-des-Champs (Gigault), the communities of religious, such as the Franciscans (Louis Marchand) or the community of the Abbey of Ste Geneviève (Raison), all played host to richly talented players. Not that the provincial cathedrals lacked their celebrities: Jacques Boyvin at Rouen, Nicholas de Grigny (1672–1703) at Rheims, Gilles Jullien (1653–1703) at Chartres, Dumage at the collegial church of St Quentin.

The moment was propitious for other reasons: in the first half of Louis XIV's reign the French economy flourished as never before; cathedrals and churches could afford magnificent instruments, publishers could reckon on a return, organists were well rewarded for their labours. These social, economic and political springs to the production of organ music are important to grasp: they explain why we possess relatively so much (and so much of value) from the period of Louis XIV's reign, and relatively so little from either before or after. And they explain why the music celebrates an art in the ascendancy, where new idioms are exploited with vigour and panache.

Table 12.1 lists all the publications of French organists over the period 1660 to 1740. It gives us a very clear idea of the composers who were most prolific. Nivers and Lebègue stand out. Moreover, the *Livres d'orgue* of these two are sizeable affairs, containing at least 50 pieces each, and sometimes as many as 100. They represent the most influential part of the repertory, setting models of compositional and improvisatory practice for their own generation as well as the succeeding. Roughly speaking the publications divide into collections of versets by *ton de l'église* and by liturgical item. In use they overlap, and the distinction is not as significant as it might appear. Where the collections are by *tons de l'église* the publication takes the form of groups of six to nine short pieces gathered by key in a sequence that almost always sees a Plein Jeu beginning and a Grand Jeu ending (see below for a discussion of these types), with a varied selection of more intimately registered pieces in between. The individual pieces are generally no more than a page or two long. Where the collections are organised around a liturgical item the organisation of individual pieces is not much different: each liturgical item will have its required number of versets in the appropriate key (*ton de l'église*), with occasionally the emergence of the relevant plainchant as a cantus firmus or as the basis of the melodic material of the verset. Without exception all this music provides for the alternatim practice of the day, discussed in detail in Chapter 9. Whilst Nivers and Lebègue are undeniably the most prolific composers of such music (with Boyvin not far behind), it is the next generation which brings their work to full maturity, notably François Couperin and de Grigny. In terms of invention and scale nothing surpasses the organ masses of François Couperin or the mass and hymns of de Grigny's *Livre d'orgue* of 1699. Clérambault's *Livre*, though extremely attractive, is much smaller in scope. And d'Aquin's noëls, though brilliant, have little of the depth of François Couperin and de Grigny. Against these publications a number of manuscript sources merit our attention, notably the collection of Louis Couperin's (*c*1626–61) organ pieces owned by Guy Oldham (Oldham 1960), the Louis Marchand manuscripts conserved in the Bibliothèque Municipale at Versailles (Dufourcq 1972: 122), and the Montreal *Livre d'orgue*, containing nearly 400 pieces of Parisian provenance from the second half of the seventeenth century (Gallat-Morin 1988).

One of the effects brought about by the music's liturgical role is its brevity: the music needed to be concise to fulfil its liturgical purpose. At the same time, even outside a liturgical context the French did not cultivate large-scale movements in the same way as their Italian and German contemporaries, and it is generally true that they made a virtue out of proceeding discretely from one musical event to another rather than organising these events into overarching architectural designs. In addition, the French were explicit in their view that music had an overriding purpose: to engender thoughts and feelings of an unambiguous and well-defined nature. They were not interested in music whose impact was general, and they had a horror of technical devices rigorously applied and obviously stated, as well as a horror of the overstated. In pursuing their principal objective, and recalling Le Cerf de la Viéville's dictum that 'La science de la Musique . . . n'est autre chose que la science d'émouvoir vivement et à propos' (1706; see Le Cerf de la Viéville 1725: iv, 60), French composers lavished care and attention on individual musical gesture, on a languishing *port de voix* here, a graceful melodic inflection there, an animated dotted figure a bar later. The moment, exquisitely shaped, was as important as the architecture of the whole. These concerns played upon the French organ repertory. In one very obvious respect Gigault could mark in several pieces in his 1685 publication the point at which versets might end earlier than the final bar, without fearing damage to the structure of the verset. But more significantly, the French organist invariably sought to encapsulate a mood in the clearest terms by observing a musical code of gesture and effect. And their work was judged on the effectiveness of the portrait drawn as much as on the ingenuity and craft revealed. This was colourful and evocative music, and in making it the French organists were greatly aided in their task by the instruments they played.

The French classical organ was like no other. As exemplified by the instrument completed in 1687 by A. Thierry for St Louis-des-Invalides, Paris, it displays several unique characteristics: an almost endless supply of solo effects in its Bourdons and Flûtes, colourful and dominating reeds, and a principal chorus noted for its depth and warmth rather than its transparency and brilliance.

St Louis-des-Invalides, Paris, A. Thierry (1679–87)

Grand Orgue (C–c³)		Positif (C–c³)	
Montre	16′	Montre	8′
Bourdon	16′	Bourdon	8′
Montre	8′	Prestant	4′
Bourdon	8′	Flûte	4′
Prestant	4′	Nasard	$2\frac{2}{3}$′
Flûte	4′	Doublette	2′
Grosse Tierce	$3\frac{1}{5}$′	Tierce	$1\frac{3}{5}$′
Nasard	$2\frac{2}{3}$′	Larigot	$1\frac{1}{3}$′
Doublette	2′	Fourniture	III
Quarte de Nasard	2′	Cymbale	II
Tierce	$1\frac{3}{5}$′	Cromorne	8′
Fourniture	V	Voix humaine	8′
Cymbale	IV		
Cornet	V	**Echo** (c¹–c³)	
Trompette	8′	Bourdon	8′
Clairon	4′	Flûte	4′
Voix humaine	8′	Nasard	$2\frac{2}{3}$′
		Quarte	2′
Récit (c¹–c³)		Tierce	$1\frac{3}{5}$′
Cornet	V	Cymbale	II
Trompette	8′	Cromorne	8′

Pédale (AA–f)	
Flûte	8′
Trompette	8′

The instrument was imposing both in size and in sound, matching the dimension of instruments belonging to the great German organ-building schools of the same period. Four manual divisions (Grand Orgue, Positif, Récit and Echo) were a commonplace in the larger churches and the cathedrals of the kingdom. But the Pedal was not part of the lavish provision: it contained often only two or three 8′ stops (Trompette, Bourdon and/or Flûte). Significantly, until the second part of the eighteenth century, the 16′ stops (Bourdons, Montres and Bombardes) were found on the manual divisions, not the Pedal. The Pedal had only a minor role to play in the music written for the French organ. The Récit and Echo divisions were short compass. The Cornet (a five-rank stop sounding 8′, 4′, $2\frac{2}{3}$′, 2′ and $1\frac{3}{5}$′)

was ubiquitous, appearing as an upper-compass register on the Grand Orgue, Récit and Echo (though some Echos had a separately drawn Jeu de Tierce), and as a composite sonority (i.e. separately drawn stops of the same pitches, known as the Jeu de Tierce) on the Grand Orgue and Positif. The Jeu de Tierce ran from top to bottom of the manual compass. The Cornet and Jeu de Tierce derived their special timbre from the 'Sesquialtera' colouring of the twelfth and seventeenth ranks, as well as from their wide scaling.

The guiding principle in French organ design was the provision of a large and varied palette of registrations. So many and so important did these registrations become that composers often referred to them in considerable detail in the prefaces to their publications. These so-called 'Mélanges des jeux' draw attention to the unusual sensitivity of the French organist towards colour: the performance of French organ music was nothing if not a careful and judicious setting forth of the various registration possibilities of the instrument.

The attributes and roles of the registrations are best considered in the context of an examination of the compositional genres with which they are associated. The linking of musical genre to registration, not unknown in other schools of course, is in the French case taken to the point where the two are inseparable. We need to distinguish the following main compositional types in the French classical tradition: Plein Jeu, Grand Jeu, Fugue, Duo, Trio, Récit, Dialogue and Fond d'orgue. The Plein Jeu, Grand Jeu and Fond d'orgue are terms which plainly describe a registration scheme. In other genres, registration schemes may either be prescribed in the title of the piece, as for instance 'Duo sur les Tierces' and 'Récit de Cromorne en Taille', or understood from the many references in the Mélanges des jeux. Thus when a composer failed to specify a registrational scheme, the player knew what was intended from the musical genre, and would not traduce the idiom by playing on an inappropriate registration.

Plein Jeu

Plein Jeu refers to the registration scheme employing the principal chorus of the Grand Orgue (sometimes 'Grand Plein Jeu') and/or the Positif ('Petit Plein Jeu'). It was good practice to couple the Positif to the Grand Orgue. The Plein Jeu runs from the lowest sounding pitch of the chorus (a Montre 16′ on a large instrument) to the highest (the Fourniture and Cymbale, together comprising a mixture combination of seven or more ranks). The tonal quality of the individual stops is crucial: the principal

Figure 12.1 At the church of St Ouen in Rouen, France, the Flemish builder Crespin Carlier built, in 1630, the organ whose case survives today. The introduction of the south Brabant school of organ building to France in the early seventeenth century, encouraged by the composer Jehan Titelouze, was profoundly influential in the development of the French classical organ. The case establishes a preference in France for a traditional structure of Grand Orgue and Postif de Dos, with the pipes in each arranged in single stories. The small Récit, Echo or occasional Bombarde divisions were not expressed in the layout of the main façade. The case now contains a large and well-preserved instrument of 1890 by the great nineteenth-century French builder Aristide Cavaillé-Coll.

ranks are relatively wide-scaled, as are the mixture ranks. This gives to the French Plein Jeu its characteristic breadth and warmth (allowing also the stopped ranks, the Bourdons, to blend easily when drawn with the principal foundations). The arrangement of the breaks in the Fourniture and Cymbale, dropping back earlier than in (for instance) north German instruments, produced distinctive effects in each register: in the bass, unusual strength and clarity; in the middle register, weight; and in the treble, particular richness, as the breaking ranks doubled and redoubled the independent ranks of the chorus and lower ranks of the mixtures. The registration was all about weight and fullness, and it gave rise to a compositional style that strove for the same effect: a full-voiced (four or five parts), loosely-knit polyphonic texture, not fugal but showing nevertheless its genesis in the fantasia style of the late renaissance, not least through its alla breve notation. The registration is conceived with a continuous mass of sound in view, where clarity of line is not a prerequisite. Indeed, independent lines above g^2 tended to become submerged in the overlapping upperwork of lower voices. When fugal textures were encountered the player turned to other registrations (see below).

The Plein Jeu was without exception the piece which opened a liturgical item, and it often incorporated as a cantus firmus the plainchant which it replaced. This might be the complete melody of a hymn, or the opening Kyrie of the Mass. Here the Pedal Trompette 8′ was drawn, and the chant played as an extra voice in the texture, sometimes in the bass register, more often in the tenor voice, the left hand providing the bass part. Just as (at the time) the plainchant was sung in slow even notes, so its incorporation in the Plein Jeu proceeded on the lines of long equal notes, highlighted by this distinctive timbre. Thus, not only was the mode of the chant announced, but specific reference was made to the melody of the chant to be taken up by the congregation.

Grand Jeu

The Grand Jeu stands at the other end of the registration spectrum: the flue chorus gives way to the reeds. The practice of combining reeds and the principal chorus in a grand tutti effect was altogether alien to the French classical tradition (and difficult to achieve on French winding). Where the Plein Jeu aimed at weight and plenitude, the Grand Jeu embodied brilliance and panache. The reeds of the French classical organ are of three distinctive types: the Trompettes (including the 4′ Clairon) with full-length resonators; the lighter Cromorne, with half-length; and the plaintive Voix Humaine, having a quarter or less. The first two types are employed in the Grand Jeu, the Trompettes, with their vivid attack and massy volume, dominating the texture. Where they weaken and become less reliable in the treble, the Cornet stop was drawn to compensate. Thus the Grand Jeu normally comprised Trompette and Clairon (8' and 4'), Cromorne and Cornet and Jeu de Tierce registers. A foundation stop or two (not 16' unless there was a 16' reed) was commonly added to stabilise the reeds.

Just as the Grand Jeu sounded totally distinctive from the Plein Jeu, so did its associated musical style: the genre is noted for its vigorous and declamatory manner; fanfare figures abound, and the registration allows for brilliant exchanges between manuals (sometimes moving back and forth every bar) or between right and left hand, in dialogue fashion. It was possible for the exchanges to be conducted over three or even four manuals, employing the Récit Trompette or Cornet as a third participant, and the Echo as a fourth. The 'Offertoire sur les Grands Jeux' of de Grigny (see extract in Example 12.1) shows this manner, as well as the general brio of the Grand Jeu style.

Appropriately enough, the Grand Jeu was placed at the end of an alternatim sequence, and its use at the Offertory of the Mass was de rigueur. The Offertoires of Nivers, de Grigny, Couperin, Marchand and others are the pièces de résistance of the French classical tradition, written on a large scale (liturgical ceremony at this point requiring between five and ten minutes), displaying the highest levels of brilliance, power and resource. The organist naturally turned to the Grand Jeu at this moment because it offered the most varied and exciting timbral display of any.

Fugue

In between the Plein Jeu and the Grand Jeu are found a number of genres having more intimate registrations and styles. They tend to follow a particular order within the context of a suite or a liturgical item, and the first of them is often the Fugue. The French were not keen on demonstrations of technical accomplishment in their Fugues, and to make comparison with Bach in this respect is futile; the French Fugue is a modest display of contrapuntal craft. But what it lacked in craft it made up for in personality: subjects were eloquent, often vocal in character, and set in a manner which threw their appearances into expressive relief. The music is discourse rather than technique. The organist played the Fugue not on the principal chorus, which lacked voice-leading clarity (and also the personal touch), but on the reeds, the Trompettes of the Grand Orgue for the

Ex. 12.1 De Grigny, Offertoire sur les Grands Jeux

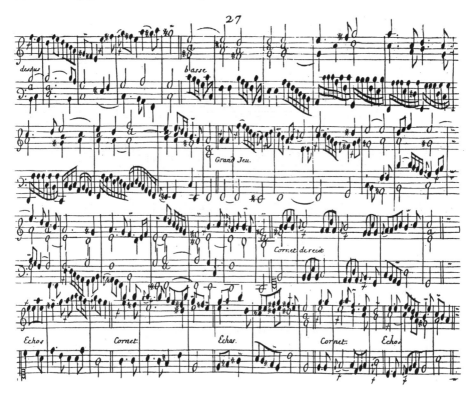

Fugue grave, the Cromorne of the Positif for the Fugue gai. Surprisingly, drawn by themselves (with the steadying influence of a principal rank or Bourdon), the reeds could be played in a quite intimate style. Sometimes for four-part textures, reeds and a Jeu de Tierce could be drawn on separate manuals for left and right hands; still more kaleidoscopic effects across three divisions might be achieved for the Quatuor with the addition of the 8′ Pedal Flûte.

Duo, Trio

The Duo and Trio are precisely that: movements in two- and three-part textures, the Duo in a loosely contrapuntal style with motives passed from one hand to the other, the Trio more like a trio sonata, with the left-hand functioning as a continuo bass. François Couperin's 'Dialogue en trio du Cornet et de la Tierce' (from the Gloria of the *Messe pour les Paroisses*) provides an example of this type with each upper voice differentiated by the registration scheme, and the Pedal (eventually) providing the bass

Ex. 12.2 Clérambault, Trio (*Suite du premier ton*)

line. However, Couperin's verset (a veritable 'Trio à trois claviers') is more elaborate than most in the genre. More commonly the upper voices share a right-hand registration, and (in line with the French manner of treating the Italian trio idiom) the second part tends to shadow the first, providing harmonic depth and perspective rather than an independent contour. In these cases (the 'Trio à Deux Dessus'), the registration scheme sets off the dessus parts against the bass, perhaps Cromorne 8′ in the right hand and a Jeu de Tierce in the left, as so elegantly displayed in Clérambault's Trio from his *Suite du premier ton* (see Example 12.2); equally, the scheme could be reversed, with a reed in the left hand and the Jeu de Nasard or de Tierce in the right.

These schemes gave the Trio a very personal tone, not unlike the effect achieved in a diversely registered Fugue. They were part and parcel of a genre which emphasised 'le gracieux'. The schemes for the Duo tended to reflect a more boisterous musical language. Duos were commonly marked 'gai' or 'vite', and revelled in vigorous rhythms and dashing fingerwork. Nothing suited this more than the Jeu de Tierce combinations of the Grand Orgue and Positif (as Couperin prescribes in his 'Duo sur les Tierces' from the Gloria of his *Messe pour les Paroisses*) which on a large instrument might include for the left hand the Grosse Tierce ($3\frac{1}{5}'$) of the Grand Orgue (built up from the 16' Bourdon). Alternatively the left hand might be played on the Grand Orgue Trompette or Positif Cromorne.

Récit

The Jeu de Tierce or Cornet may be counted the soul of the French classical organ. Whilst it played an essential role in the Grand Jeu, bolstering the trebles of the reeds and lending body and luminosity to the texture as a whole, it was more especially prized for its capability as a solo colour, being the chief registration option for the numerous Récits of the French school. Here the solo hand took on the eloquence of the human voice, the musical gestures derived from the vocal idioms of opera and motet, by turns declamatory and lyrical, richly invested with expressive ornaments (notably the *port de voix* and *tremblement appuyé*). In a word, the Récit sings. It also incorporated decorative figuration, for the Jeu de Tierce was valued for its quicksilver mobility. François Couperin gathers these various qualities together in the celebrated 'Tierce en Taille' from the Gloria of his *Messe pour les Paroisses*, in which the récit line appears in the tenor voice (the taille) surrounded by the gentle haze of Bourdons and Flûtes of the jeu doux. Dumage exemplifies the same features in his equally expressive 'Tierce en Taille' from his *1er livre d'orgue* (see Example 12.3).

When the Cromorne is featured en taille, the style is even more vocal (mélanges often refer to 'a singing style' in connection with the Cromorne). And the Voix Humaine, drawn for the most intimate essays in the Récit style, and always supported by a Bourdon 8', comes closer still to the voice. When the Positif is used for these solo lines, it makes good use of its position: at the back of the player, hanging over the gallery rail, in intimate relationship with the listener (see Fig. 5.8, p. 68 above).

A different and distinctive type of Récit is the Basse de Trompette or Cromorne, in which the pungency of the reeds in the bass register is put to a quite different musical use: pieces in this genre are vigorous, full of bold melodic contours and heroic gestures.

Dialogue

When the solo line of the Récit moved from one hand to another, or from one registration to another, the term 'Dialogue' was often used, denoting

Ex. 12.3 Dumage, Tierce en Taille (*Suite du premier ton*)

the conversational aspect of the composition. The Dialogues of the
French school are as many and as various as the simpler Récits. They
range from the Basse et Dessus type (where right and left hand exchange
the solo line), to the Récit en Dialogue (where the conversation is between
two timbres, often Cornet and Cromorne) to the 'Récit en Dialogue avec
Echo' (requiring a fourth manual). These pieces show just how aware
composers were of the individual character of each solo timbre, crafting
the solo line to produce the best effect on the jeu assigned to it. The
Dialogues are among the most idiomatic pieces in a highly idiomatic
school of organ composition.

Fond d'orgue

The most luxuriant mélange of the French school is the fond d'orgue,
drawing on the foundation stops, both Montres and Bourdons, sometimes coupling Positif to Grand Orgue. The effect comes close to the
fiffaro registration used in the Italian school for Elevation versets: it is
deeply harmonious, serving impeccably the *durezze e ligature* style of the
music written for it. Louis Marchand has left us a sublime example of the
type in his Fond d'orgue in E minor from the Versailles MS. At a less inten-

sively expressive level, the combination is used to create the jeu doux or accompanying mélange (as in Example 12.3).

Although space precludes an account of late eighteenth-century French organ music (Claude Balbastre is its leading figure), we cannot pass over in silence the accomplishments of earlier composers. Five publications stand as beacons in an otherwise nearly deserted landscape in the centuries preceding the classical school: three anthologies of anonymous organ music from the presses of the Parisian publisher Attaingnant, all appearing in the year 1531, and nearly one hundred years later, in 1623, a collection of hymns by Jehan Titelouze (organist of Rouen Cathedral), followed in 1626 by his Magnificat versets. The Attaingnant prints are in effect the first extant examples of French keyboard music. Two volumes comprise organ masses and versets for the Te Deum and Magnificat, the third, motet and chanson intabulations. The Titelouze collections serve only the offices, but with such a display of craft that they stand beside the work of Scheidt and Sweelinck in the field of early seventeenth-century contrapuntal writing for the organ. This highly conservative and impressive style is glimpsed only briefly in the shreds and patches of extant literature between 1626 and 1660. Music by Charles Racquet (conserved by Mersenne in his *Harmonie universelle*, 1636–7), by Jean-Henri d'Anglebert (*Pièces de clavecin*, 1689 – containing organ fugues from the early 1660s), and by Roberday shows the polyphonic idiom still in good voice. At the hinge of the new age stands the music of Louis Couperin, miraculously preserved in manuscript. His extraordinary achievement provides us with the key to understanding how the old polyphonic style of Titelouze, Racquet and Roberday was transformed into the dazzling variety of genres of the classical school.

Recommended editions

Authoritative complete editions of the organ music of Louis and François Couperin are published by L'Oiseau Lyre, and of de Grigny by Heugel. Of the *Archives des maîtres de l'orgue des XVIe, XVIIe et XVIIIe siècles* (ed. A. Guilmant and A. Pirro), which appeared at the beginning of the century, and which contain a great many of the authors of the classical school, Titelouze included, many have been re-issued under the Kalmus and the Schott imprints. Nivers has been published by Bornemann, Schola Cantorum and Heugel (the three *Livres* respectively), Boyvin's two *Livres* by les Editions Ouvrières, and Clérambault's single *Livre* by Schola Cantorum. For an anthology of music from the period, see vols 7–9 of the

13 English organ music to *c*1700

Geoffrey Cox

Pre-Reformation organ music

No English organ music from before 1500 has survived. There are a few earlier instances that are sometimes cited, but they can all be discounted for one reason or another. The pieces in the Robertsbridge Codex, which date from about 1320, are probably of French or Italian origin, despite the fact that they have been preserved in England (Caldwell 1973: 1–9). The Buxheimer Orgelbuch, compiled in Germany about 1470, includes transcriptions of some sacred and secular vocal pieces by John Dunstable, but these are only intabulations by a German organist and not original keyboard settings by Dunstable. One other piece sometimes thought to be an early example of English organ music is an anonymous Felix namque copied about 1420 (Dart 1954: 201; Caldwell 1973: 14), but this is more likely to be a simple piece of vocal discant.

It is not until the first half of the sixteenth century that a large corpus of genuine English organ music is to be found. In this pre-Reformation period in England, most of the organ music is strictly liturgical in function, being designed for performance at specific points during the Mass and Office. The pre-Reformation period can be said to extend up to the accession of Elizabeth I in 1558, for, despite the introduction of the first Book of Common Prayer in 1549, the Latin rite was fully restored in the reign of Mary (1553–8). The main two composers around the middle of the century were John Redford (*c*1486–1547) and Thomas Preston (active in the 1540s and 50s), who were followed by Thomas Tallis (*c*1505–85) and William Blitheman (died 1591), most of whose liturgical organ music probably dates from the reign of Mary.

Liturgical organ music used plainsong as its basis, being intended for performance at points in the liturgy in place of the sung chant. During the Mass, for instance, the chants of both the Ordinary and the Proper could be set for the organ. The only complete English organ setting of the Mass Ordinary that survives is one by Philip ap Rhys, and even this omits the Credo. A few other isolated mass movements by other composers survive, such as the Agnus Dei by John Redford shown in Example 13.1, in which the chant is given out in long notes in the right hand. As Redford sets only the portion of the chant normally sung for the first and third petitions, it

Ex. 13.1 Redford, Agnus Dei

can be assumed that his setting, like so many others of the period, was intended for *alternatim* performance with sung portions of the original chant (see Chapter 9).

The Proper of the Mass (Introit, Gradual, Alleluia, Offertory, etc.) seems to have been set more often for the organ, and organ settings of the Marian offertory *Felix namque* appear to have been especially popular. Redford's younger contemporary, Thomas Preston, who was active in the reign of Queen Mary, wrote at least eight organ settings of this chant, in which only the opening word 'Felix' was normally sung, leaving the remainder of the chant to be incorporated into the organ setting.

As well as in the Mass, the organ was heard at the daily Offices at Matins, Lauds, Vespers and Compline. For these, organ music included settings of the canticles (Te Deum, Magnificat, etc.) hymns (Ecce tempus, Veni redemptor, Iste confessor, etc.) and antiphons (Lucem tuam, Gloria tibi Trinitas, etc.). In the hymns, it appears that the organ must have performed alternate verses only, the others being sung. Hymn, canticle and mass versets are generally short, in keeping with their *alternatim* function.

Not all English keyboard music before the Reformation was based on plainchant. From the first half of the sixteenth century there also survive dance pieces by Hugh Aston and others, an anonymous *Uppon la mi re*, and other pieces that appear to be freely composed. Some non-liturgical works are to be found in the Mulliner Book, a valuable source of pre-Reformation organ music compiled by Thomas Mulliner, Almoner of St Paul's Cathedral. As this volume was not completed until about 1570 or later, it is difficult in the case of some of its contents to say whether they date from before or after the accession of Elizabeth. One such piece in Mulliner's collection is the one entitled *Voluntary* by Richard Allwood. This is the earliest known piece using this title, which has remained an

English peculiarity to this day. Originally it seems to have denoted a type of organ music not based on plainchant, but on any freely composed theme or 'point'.

Another interesting title attached to several pieces in the Mulliner Book and afterwards is 'In nomine'. Almost all of the works bearing this title are based on the chant Gloria tibi Trinitas, and the practice of using the title 'In nomine' appears to stem from the popularity of the In nomine Domini section of Taverner's *Missa Gloria tibi Trinitas*, where the chant appears as the cantus firmus. Surviving mid-sixteenth-century instrumental transcriptions of this section of Taverner's mass include two for strings and two for keyboard, one of the latter being in the Mulliner Book. Subsequent settings of the chant retained the title 'In nomine', even when they were not derived directly from Taverner's mass. The peculiar tradition of writing such works extended well into the seventeenth century, for example with works by John Bull (c1562/63–1628), who wrote all of his In nomine settings in England before he departed for the Netherlands in 1613. Indeed, the tradition of the In nomine probably belongs more to the period following the Reformation than to the period before it. It is significant that no pieces titled 'In nomine' can be dated with certainty before 1558.

English organ music from the Reformation to the Restoration

With the accession of Elizabeth in 1558, the Latin rite was again suppressed, and a further revision of the Prayer Book was authorised with an Act of Uniformity in 1559. Thus the old liturgy in which the organ had played such an integral part disappeared, and the function of organ music in the English church changed. In the early years of the seventeenth century, the organ was often heard in the Chapel Royal playing an 'offertorye' during the Communion service, but it also developed entirely new roles. One composition by Edward Gibbons of Exeter, dated 1611, is described as 'A Prelude upon ye Organ, as was then usuall before ye Anthem', from which it would appear that organ music was customary before the anthem at Morning and Evening Prayer. There is also evidence to suggest that the practice of playing a voluntary between the psalms and the first lesson at these services dates from this period (see Morehen 1995).

The most important outcome of these new uses of the organ was that composers were encouraged to write organ music that was not based on plainchant. Lacking a fully developed English tradition in this field, it seems likely that English composers at the time looked to foreign models, particularly from Italy and Spain. Antonio de Cabezón, the greatest Spanish keyboard composer of his day, spent more than a year in England in 1554–5 in his capacity as court organist to Philip II of Spain, and his *tientos* (some of which were published in 1557 and 1578) were possibly models for the fancies and voluntaries of William Byrd (*c*1543–1623) and others. Whatever the case, the freely imitative forms in England entered a period of tremendous growth, and the resulting compositions were known variously as fancies, verses and voluntaries – terms that were largely interchangeable.

Thomas Morley described the fantasy as a piece in which 'a musician taketh a point at his pleasure and wresteth and turneth it as he list' (*A Plaine and Easie Introduction to Practicall Musicke*, 1597). The 'point' need not necessarily be original or even the composer's own, for some fantasias are reworkings of vocal pieces or of string fantasias. Furthermore, each fantasia need not be based on a single point throughout; most of those by Orlando Gibbons (1583–1625), for example, take several points and treat them imitatively in turn. Some fantasias by Byrd and others fall into several contrasted sections which include dance-like passages and brilliant toccata writing, as well as purely contrapuntal sections. It is often difficult to decide which of these pieces were written for use on church organs and which were more appropriate for the virginals or perhaps the domestic chamber organ.

One form certainly intended for the organ was the Fancy or Voluntary for Double Organ, the earliest surviving example of which appears to be a piece by Orlando Gibbons (see Example 13.2). 'Double' in this context refers simply to an organ of two manuals – 'Great' and 'Chair'. The terms 'ten' and 'base' are used to distinguish between the two in Benjamin Cosyn's virginal book, which is the only surviving source for Gibbons' piece. The left hand is given a series of intermittent solos on the Great Organ while the right hand plays continuously on the Chair Organ, although both hands play on the Great at the end. It is doubtful, however, that Gibbons intended this particular work to be played in this way: the clumsy arrangement of the manual changes towards the end has forced different editors to adopt various solutions, and the assigning of left-hand solos throughout the work does not always suit the musical texture. It is significant that Cosyn also attempted to arrange the piece following this one in his manuscript as a double-organ piece, but abandoned the attempt after twelve bars. It seems likely that the style of using left-hand solos on a louder registration could have been suggested to English composers (or arrangers, in the case of Cosyn) by the *medio registro* (divided stop) pieces of Francisco Correa de Arauxo, published in Spain in 1626. Gibbons could hardly have known these pieces before his death in

Ex. 13.2 O. Gibbons, Fantasia (arranged for Double Organ by Cosyn)

1625, but Cosyn (who lived until 1652 or later) could conceivably have arranged Gibbons' piece in imitation of the Spanish models.

Leaving aside this peculiar Gibbons/Cosyn arrangement, some genuine pre-Restoration double-organ voluntaries by John Lugge (d. *c*1647) and Richard Portman (d. *c*1655) have survived. Lugge wrote three such works, all using left-hand solos as in Cosyn's arrangement of Gibbons, while the latter part of Portman's Verse for Double Organ reflects the influence of the French *dialogue de deux chœurs* style, in which both hands alternate simultaneously between the two manuals (see Example 13.3).

As well as freely imitative pieces, composers continued to write settings of plainsong (including the In nomine), though the increasing tendency after the Reformation was to set the plainsong melodies in long unembellished notes against highly figurative accompanying parts. Many of these pieces give the impression more of being exercises in compositional technique than of fulfilling a liturgical function, and like most keyboard music of the period they are as likely to have been played on the harpsichord as on the organ. Among the earliest examples after the accession of Elizabeth are two settings of Felix namque by Tallis, dated 1562 and 1564. Blitheman's pupil John Bull, together with Thomas Tomkins (1572–1656), continued the tradition of writing plainsong settings right up to the time of the Commonwealth, after which it was discontinued.

Settings of other pre-existing melodies also became popular – notably

Ex. 13.3 Portman, Verse for Double Organ

those on the hexachord (Ut re mi fa sol la). Here the techniques were similar to those employed in plainsong settings, and some pieces – especially those by Bull – display remarkable rhythmic complexity. In one of Byrd's settings of *Ut re mee fa sol la*, part of the song 'Will you walk the woods so wild' is introduced in the third variation against the rising and falling six-note scale (C–A). This piece is also an early example of a keyboard duet, for in the only surviving copy (in the hand of Tomkins) the notes of the hexachord are written out separately at the end of the piece with a direction for 'the playne song Briefes to be played by a Second person'. Later keyboard duets dating from the period include *A Verse for two to play on one virginall or organs* by Nicholas Carleton (d. 1630), which is actually an In nomine setting, and *A Fancy for two to play* by Tomkins. In addition to the above-mentioned forms, composers produced sets of variations, grounds, and dance movements for keyboard. All of this music was probably intended for the virginal, although some of it could also have been played on domestic chamber organs.

Of the English organist-composers who left England and worked abroad, John Bull deserves special mention for his contribution to the keyboard repertory, although much of his music lies just outside the mainstream of the English tradition. Many of his fantasias probably date from after 1613, when he settled in the Netherlands, as also do his two settings of the Salve Regina, which was not normally set by English composers on account of its Catholic text. Bull's keyboard settings of the Dutch carols 'Een Kindeken is ons geboren' and 'Laet ons met herten reijne' are notable for their simplicity and charm, as well as interesting for the few registration instructions (not for English organs) that the latter contains.

Very little is known about the practice of registration in English organ music up to this time. English church organs were only of modest size, with no mixtures and no reeds. Thomas Dallam's well-known organ for Worcester Cathedral in 1613 may be taken as typical of its period, and here the highest-pitched stop on the chair organ was the 'two & Twentieth (or squeelers) of mettal' which would have sounded at 1-foot pitch:

> The specification of Thomas Dallam's organ for Worcester Cathedral in 1613, incorporating details given by Nathaniel Tomkins in a letter to John Sayer dated 22 May 1665 (Oxford, Bodleian Library, Add. MS C.304a, f. 141)

Great Organ

Two open diapasons of metall. CC fa ut a pipe 10 foot long.	[8′ and 8′]
Two principals of metal (octave to ye diapasons) (all in sight)	[4′ and 4′]
Two small principals or 15ths of metal	[2′ and 2′]
One twelfth of metall	$[2\frac{2}{3}']$
One recorder of metall, a stopt pipe	[8′]

Chaire Organ

One principal of mettal (a five foot pipe in front)	[4′]
One (stopt) diapason of wood	[8′]
One flute of wood (unison to ye principal)	[4′]
One small principal or fifteenth of mettal	[2′]
One two & twentieth (or squeelers) of metal	[1′]

None of the early Dallam 'double organs' have survived, but the Gloucester Cathedral organ, with its cases by Robert Dallam and his son-in-law Thomas Harris, is representative of instruments of this type (see Figure 13.1). Pedal 'pull-downs' operating the lowest manual notes may have been known in some places (for example at Jesus College, Cambridge, in 1635) but the evidence for this is scanty, and certainly no independent pedal stops were provided. Other fascinating problems for the modern performer include the question of pitch (see Chapter 4, also Caldwell 1970 and Clark 1974), and the interpretation of the contemporary ornament signs (see Chapter 8, also Le Huray 1981 and Hunter 1992).

Restoration organ music

Throughout the period following the Reformation, the use of organs in worship had been regarded by many as a superstitious and popish practice. Puritan opposition had mounted steadily until two ordinances issued by Parliament in 1644 finally called for their destruction. Very few church or cathedral organs were left standing during the Commonwealth,

Figure 13.1 The small two-manual pedal-less organs associated with the English choral service in the seventeenth century have all been removed, but here at Gloucester Cathedral the double case survives with its original decorated front pipes. The smaller Chaire case was probably built by Robert Dallam in 1639-41 and exhibits craftsmanship of exceptional quality. The main or Great case, erected by Dallam's son-in-law Thomas Harris in 1666, follows a more confident classical design, but its coarser workmanship reflects the urgency of the period immediately following the restoration of the monarchy in 1660. The instrument inside the case has been altered frequently as fashions in liturgy have changed. In the nineteenth century it was a typical work from the factory of Henry Willis, for much of the twentieth century it has been known as a large romantic instrument by Harrison & Harrison. In 1971 it was rebuilt on neo-classical lines (but with electric action) by Hill, Norman and Beard in consultation with the organ expert Ralph Downes.

and it was not until the restoration of the monarchy in 1660 that they were heard again. The demand for new organs at this time must have been great, and several builders who had worked abroad now introduced new ideas into English organ building. As early as around 1661 Robert Dallam, who had spent the years of the Commonwealth in France, recommended the inclusion of mixtures and reeds in his proposed organ for New College, Oxford. These stops and other new ones such as the cornet were also found on the organs of Bernard Smith and Renatus Harris, the two builders who dominated the English scene for the remainder of the century. Harris had spent his early years in France, while Smith appears to have worked in Holland before settling in England. The organ built by Smith for Christ Church Cathedral, Oxford, in 1680 is fairly typical of the period:

Christ Church Cathedral, Oxford, B. Smith (1680)

Great Organ (GG–c^3)		Choir Organ (GG–c^3)	
Open diapason	8′	Stopped diapason	8′
Stopped diapason	8′	Principal	4′
Principal	4′	Flute	4′
Twelfth	$2\frac{2}{3}$′	Fifteenth	2′
Fifteenth	2′		
Tierce	$1\frac{3}{5}$′		
Sesquialtera	III		
Cornet (c#^{1})	IV		
Trumpet	8′		

English organ music also took a new direction at this time. The main organist/composers in the early years following the Restoration were Matthew Locke (*c*1622–77) and Christopher Gibbons (1615–76), to whom may be added the less significant names of Benjamin Rogers (1614–98), Albertus Bryne (*c*1621–*c*70) and John Hingston (d. 1683). The organ works of John Blow (1649–1708) and Henry Purcell (1659–95) represent the most important contributions to the English repertory of the late seventeenth century.

Most organ works of the Restoration period were simply called 'voluntary' or 'verse', titles that had been familiar also before the Commonwealth. Several styles were represented, however, and these now displayed the characteristics of the early baroque. The Commonwealth and Puritan opposition in general had seriously retarded the growth of English organ music by the middle of the century, and developments abroad – especially in Italy – had left it far behind. Not surprisingly, therefore, continental influences played a large part in bringing English organ music up to date after the Restoration.

One of the most significant influences came through the keyboard music of Girolamo Frescobaldi (1583–1643) and his school. In a published essay of 1672, Matthew Locke named Frescobaldi and his south German follower J. J. Froberger (*c*1616–67) as two of the most worthy keyboard composers, and there is abundant evidence not only that organ music by Italian and south German composers was known in England during the second half of the seventeenth century, but also that it influenced the work of English composers. Froberger himself visited England as early as 1651 or 1652, and a number of foreign organists working in England after the Restoration could also have helped to introduce new styles (Cox 1989: 21–34). Frescobaldi's organ works were obviously known to Blow, who boldly 'incorporated' parts of several of them into works of his own.

Although English pieces rarely copied the overall forms of the Italian or south German organ canzona, ricercar or toccata, they frequently employed styles that derived from them. Blow's *Chromatic Voluntary* in D minor, for instance, clearly shows the style of the contemporary ricercar, although decorated and enlivened according to contemporary English taste. Compared with earlier English organ music, the Restoration voluntary and verse tended towards monothematicism, with fewer imitative sections and the sections becoming increasingly differentiated in style. The second section of Purcell's Voluntary in G for instance, is written in canzona style, while the first section uses the characteristic *durezze e ligature* (dissonances and ties) style deriving from Frescobaldi (see Example 13.4).

One result of the development of English organs at this period was an increased interest in types of organ music employing specific registrations. Voluntaries for double organ continued the pre-Commonwealth tradition, but introduced new features such as solos for the right hand, and dialogue between the two manuals, which appear to derive from French models. Two Voluntaries for Double Organ in D minor, one by Purcell and the other anonymous (edited in *Early English Organ Music*, vol. 2, ed. R. Langley 1986), are among the finest English works of the period. The earliest English cornet voluntaries, written by Blow, appear to have been intended for single-manual organs with a cornet half-stop in the treble, perhaps deriving from Spanish or Belgian models (Cox 1983: 4–17). The writing for the right-hand cornet solos is generally very florid, while the left hand plays on the accompanying stops which sound in the lower manual compass up to c^1, as can be seen in Example 13.5, from Blow's Cornet Voluntary in A minor. This work uses two parts on the cornet stop towards the end, as do some Belgian and French works, but Blow's works for cornet stop are remote from the *récit de cornet* style. The

Ex. 13.4 Purcell, Voluntary in G

earliest English trumpet voluntaries in the latter half of the seventeenth
century were written in a crude style, possibly in imitation of ceremonial
ensemble music for trumpets and drums, and remotely related to the
Iberian *battalla* (Cox 1995: 30–45).

Although French influence in English organ music at this time was
minimal in the general sense, it was very strong with regard to the style of
ornamentation. This may be attributable to the fact that a large quantity
of French harpsichord music had found its way into English sources by
the middle of the seventeenth century (Caldwell 1973: 151–2, 164).
Although the signs and names of the English ornaments differed from the
French, it is clear that the style of ornamentation used in English organ
music after the Restoration (Ferguson 1975: 148–52) was based on French
practice.

Blow's death in 1708 marks the end of the Restoration period in
English organ music. After this, a standard two-movement form became
widely used in which an introductory slow chordal movement (usually
designated 'diapasons' or 'full organ') was followed by a quick movement
in Italian concerto style, often merely in two parts and exploiting such
solo stops as the trumpet or cornet. Late baroque style, stemming from
the sonatas and concertos of Corelli and others, had found its way to the
English organ loft, and the superficiality of the fast movements in voluntaries gave rise to much contemporary criticism. Some blamed the play-

Ex. 13.5 Blow, Cornet Voluntary in A minor

houses, or 'Synagogues of Satan' for the light-hearted and wanton airs
that greeted eighteenth-century ears in church. Arthur Bedford in his
Great Abuse of Musick (1711) lamented the decline of fugal writing and
the lack of dissonances in works by the most modern composers.
'Discords', he claimed, 'are like some sharp Sawces, which whet the
Appetite, and make the Meat relish the better ... This Art hath languish'd
since the Death of Dr Blow.' The transition to the new style of the eighteenth century is evident in the works of William Croft (1678–1727),
Philip Hart (*c*1676–1749) and John Reading (1677–1764), and it is but a
short step from these to the more familiar eighteenth-century works of
Stanley, Greene and Boyce.

Recommended editions

Anthologies

Alte Englische Orgelmeister/Old English Organ Masters, Liber Organi 10,
    ed. G. Phillips (Schott, 1958)
*Early English Organ Music: An anthology from Tudor and Stuart times in
    two volumes*, ed. R. Langley (Oxford University Press, 1986)
English Organ Music: An Anthology from Four Centuries in Ten Volumes,
    ed. R. Langley, vols. 1–2 (Novello, 1987–88)

Faber Early Organ Series: European Organ Music of the Sixteenth &
Seventeenth Centuries, vols. 1–3: England, ed. G. Cox (Faber Music,
1986)
Old English Organ Music for Manuals, 6 vols., ed. C. H. Trevor (Oxford
University Press, 1966–72)

Pre-Reformation

Early Tudor Organ Music I: Music for the Office, Early English Church
Music 6, ed. J. Caldwell (Stainer & Bell, 1966)
Early Tudor Organ Music II: Music for the Mass, Early English Church
Music 10, ed. D. Stevens (Stainer & Bell, 1969)
The Mulliner Book, Musica Britannica 1, ed. D. Stevens (2nd edition,
Stainer & Bell, 1954)
Tudor Keyboard Music c.1520–1580, Musica Britannica 66, ed. J. Caldwell
(Stainer & Bell, 1995)

Reformation to the Restoration

Altenglische Duette / For Two to Play, ed. F. Goebels (Bärenreiter, 1973)
John Bull, *Keyboard Music: I*, Musica Britannica 14, ed. J. Steele and F.
Cameron (2nd edition, Stainer & Bell, 1967)
William Byrd, Tallis to Wesley 8, ed. P. Ledger (Hinrichsen, 1968)
William Byrd, *Keyboard Music: I and II*, Musica Britannica 27 and 28, ed.
A. Brown (Stainer & Bell, 1969 and 1971)
Benjamin Cosyn, *Three Voluntaries*, Early Organ Music 14, ed. J. Steele
(Novello, 1959)
Orlando Gibbons, *Tallis to Wesley* 9, ed. G. Phillips (Hinrichsen, 1957)
Orlando Gibbons, *Keyboard Music*, Musica Britannica 20, ed. G. Hendrie
(2nd edition, Stainer & Bell, 1967)
John Lugge, *Three Voluntaries for Double Organ*, ed. S. Jeans and J. Steele
(Novello, 1956)
Thomas Tomkins, *Keyboard Music*, Musica Britannica 5, ed. S. Tuttle (2nd
edition, Stainer & Bell, 1964)

Post-Restoration

John Blow, *Thirty Voluntaries and Verses for the Organ*, ed. W. Shaw (2nd
edition, Schott, 1972)
John Blow, *Complete Organ Music*, Musica Britannica 69, ed. B. Cooper
(Stainer & Bell, 1996)
Christopher Gibbons, *Keyboard Compositions*, Corpus of Early Keyboard
Music 18, ed. C. Rayner, rev. J. Caldwell (Hänssler/AMC, 1989)
Matthew Locke, *Seven Pieces from 'Melothesia' (1673) for Organ or
Harpsichord*, Tallis to Wesley 6, ed. G. Phillips (Hinrichsen, 1957)

Matthew Locke, *Organ Voluntaries*, ed. T. Dart (2nd edition, Stainer & Bell, 1968)

Matthew Locke, *Melothesia (1673)*, ed. C. Hogwood (Oxford University Press, 1987)

Henry Purcell, *Organ Works*, ed. H. McLean (2nd edition, Novello, 1967)

Benjamin Rogers, *Voluntary for the Organ*, Early Organ Music 11, ed. S. Jeans (Novello, 1962)

14 Catholic Germany and Austria 1648–c1800

Patrick Russill

In 1648 the devastating Thirty Years War was ended by the Peace of Westphalia. Though this left some Catholic areas in essentially Lutheran north and central Germany (and southern Protestant areas too, like Nuremberg and Württemberg, including Stuttgart) it was in the south that the Catholic heartlands lay. From Baden in the south-west, they ran through parts of Swabia (including the publishing centre of Augsburg) and Bavaria (Munich pre-eminent) with the large bishoprics of Passau and Salzburg leading to the expanses of the Austrian Empire in which Vienna and Prague were the major centres. These areas had always looked south of the Alps for trade and culture. After the War, with the revival of Catholic Counter-Reformation confidence, Italian baroque art-forms were eagerly adopted, while the desire of many German princelings for monarchical splendour, in the style of Louis XIV, made their courts increasingly receptive to French taste also. The raising of the Turkish siege of Vienna in 1683 and ensuing victories reinforced both the prestige of the imperial Viennese court and the mood of religious triumph in Austria and her supporting German principalities. This was reflected in the many powerful monasteries, such as Melk, Weingarten and Ottobeuren, rebuilt in the first half of the eighteenth century in a dazzling conjunction of princely and celestial glory – artistically, the climax of a process of original re-interpretation of forms invented in Italy and France (the organ at Melk is shown in Figure 14.1).

A similar process of stylistic absorption and re-interpretation characterises the south German keyboard school (though its curve of achievement follows a somewhat different trajectory). Acting as a creative bridge between traditions, it produced beautiful, distinctive work – too little known today – and importantly influenced the development of European keyboard music generally. The Viennese court provided the focal point for a generation who vigorously developed forms inherited from Italy and whose music was widely disseminated – Johann Jacob Froberger (1616–67) above all, also Alessandro Poglietti (d. 1683) and Johann Kaspar Kerll (1627–93). Georg Muffat (1653–1704) and Johann Caspar Ferdinand Fischer (c1662–1746) integrated a new range of cosmopolitan idioms with southern Catholic tradition. Late baroque and

Figure 14.1 The organ in the abbey at Melk, Austria, built by G. Sonnholz in 1731-2. In Catholic southern Germany and Austria the spatial separation of departments elaborated as a musical principle in Hamburg and the north was interpreted, instead, as a matter of architectural style. Instruments were frequently divided on either side of a window (or indeed windows), requiring a detached keydesk or console for the player.

rococo features were absorbed by Muffat's son, Gottlieb (1690–1770), and Johann Ernst Eberlin (1702–62). But ironically, as German baroque architecture reached its apogee in the mid-eighteenth century, with stunning organs to match, more vapid styles were infiltrating organ galleries, leaving composers like Joseph Seger (1716–82) of Prague and Johann Georg Albrechtsberger (1736–1809) holding out doggedly against the erosion of compositional ideals and functional integrity.

Instrument and style

The symbiotic relationship between a characteristic organ type and an idiomatic repertoire – highly sophisticated in baroque France, northern Germany and even England, for example, and fundamental to all baroque organ schools – appears much looser in Catholic Germany and Austria. Yet this was a crucial factor assisting the international currency of much south German music in the seventeenth and eighteenth centuries, in contrast to other more idiosyncratic repertories.

That southern Catholic composers traditionally favoured a spectrum of one-manual textures, and a range of forms, transferable between organ and strung keyboard instruments is due not to instrumental deficiences – far from it – but to an essentially 'open' attitude to the keyboard family. (Only the sustained pedal-point and *durezze* idioms were exclusive to the organ.) So the relationship between organ and style depended not on specific timbres matched to specific idioms, but rather on fundamental, unidiosyncratic virtues: a vibrant, sustained chordal sound neither obscuring, nor troubled by, busy figuration above or below; a promptness of attack and equality of balance as effective in tight-knit, voluble counterpoint as in more fractured textures; transparency in vocal-style polyphony. Such simple virtues – also found in other European organ types, though speaking in very different accents – are embodied with a brilliant, relaxed boldness by many south German baroque instruments, large and small.

Much of this repertoire can be delivered in as authentic (if gently spoken) a vernacular by the little 1693 choir organ (by Paulus Prescher of Nördlingen) in the monastery of Mönchsdeggingen, Swabia (Fischer and Wohnhaas 1982: 176) –

Manual: $8.4.4.2.1\frac{1}{2}.1$
Pedal: permanently coupled (16′ added 1757)

– as by the thrillingly restored 1634 Putz/1708 Egedacher organ in Schlägl Abbey, Upper Austria:

Hauptwerk (C/E–c^3)		Unterpositiv (C/E–c^3)	
[upper manual]		[lower manual]	
Principal	8′	Copln	8′
Copl	8′	Principal	4′
Octav	4′	Flauta	4′
Spitzfletten	4′	Octav	2′
Quint	3′	Quint	1$\frac{1}{2}$′
Superoctav	2′	Cymbalum	III
Mixtur	VII–X		
Cymbel	II		
Pusaundl	8′	**Pedal** (C/E–b♭)	
		Principal	16′
		Octav	8′
Tremulant (for the whole organ)		Octav	4′
		Mixtur	V
		Grosspusaun	16′
		Octavpusaun	8′

Minus the luxury of the manual 8′ reed and the pedal 16′ reed, this is the sort of scheme, typical of moderate to large churches throughout the seventeenth century, for which Poglietti mapped out a comprehensive exploration of registrational possibilities in his *Compendium* of 1676 (see Faber Early Organ Series 15, p. vi). He includes various permutations at 8′ alone (sometimes including tremulant), (16) 8.8, (16) 8.8.4, (16) 8.4.4 and (16) 8.8.4.2$\frac{2}{3}$, registrations of 4.4.2, 4′ or even 2′ alone, 'open' registrations of 8.8.2$\frac{2}{3}$, 8.2 and 8.4.4.1$\frac{1}{3}$ as well as plenums with doubled pitches – hardly prescription, rather encouragement to be imaginative and varied.

Liturgical verset collections

The south German organ is rooted in liturgical alternatim practice (see Chapter 9). If its harvest appears meagre in scope compared with the liturgical riches of France or Protestant Germany, it is still highly characteristic. Only a small amount of music specifically for the Mass survives,[1] but virtually every notable composer (Froberger and Georg Muffat excepted) produced sets of tiny versets for the Office, with remarkable consistency of approach, from Sebastian Scherer (1631–1712) in 1664 to Albrechtsberger a century later.

Kerll's *Modulatio Organica* (1686), a collection of Magnificat versets in each of the eight church tones (see Appendix, pp. 316–18 below), was intended and regarded as a model both in function and in technique. Each

Ex. 14.1 Kerll, Magnificat Secundi Toni

tone, topped and tailed by brief Italianate *intonazioni*, is provided with five fughettas (in many later collections, six or more), none usually longer than fifteen bars. They seem to distil the limitations of the tradition: no specified manual changes or alternation; no manual solos; no specified linkage of idiom and registration; a range of idioms largely conditioned by neatly laid-out, hand-comfortable counterpoint; the pedals (if indicated at all) restricted almost entirely to Italian-style pedal-points. They also seem unappealingly stunted, with little exploitation of the chant (in later collections, usually none at all, thus making them liturgically all-purpose) and no strong devotional response to the text.

However, a different perspective is gained if versets from the best collections – the *Modulatio* itself, the *Octi-Tonium Novum Organicum* (1696) of Franz Xaver Murschhauser (1663–1738), a pupil of Kerll at St Stephen's Cathedral, Vienna, Gottlieb Muffat's *72 Versetl samt 12 Toccaten* (1726), Fischer's *Blumen-Strauss* (1732 or earlier) or Eberlin's *65 Vor-und Nachspiele* (manuscript *c*1740) – are even only partially restored to a liturgical context. Interleaved with the proper chant and registered according to Poglietti's advice, these little contrapuntal cat's-cradles, woven from pithy motivic invention, form witty and elegantly proportioned liturgical units. The sparkling Magnificat fugues of Johann Pachelbel (1653–1706), parts of whose training and output are intimately linked to Catholic organ culture, seem far closer to this tradition than to his own Protestant heritage.[2] This succinct fugal technique became an integral part of south German compositional study: the playful counterpoint of Kerll's Magnificat Secundi Toni (see Example 14.1) resonates as strongly in Haydn's and Mozart's string quartet development sections and racy finales as in the *manualiter* preludes of Bach's *Clavierübung III* and 'Kirnberger' collection (BWV 696–9, 701, 703–4).

Free forms in the mid-seventeenth century

The traditional debt to Italy of keyboard music in southern Germany and Austria was given a fresh aspect by Froberger's dynamic transplantation of Frescobaldi's techniques and intensity north of the Alps, following his studies with the Roman master between 1637 and 1640 or 1641. His imperial presentation autographs, of 1649 and 1656 for Ferdinand III (reigned 1637–57) and a smaller volume for the newly crowned Leopold I (reigned 1658–1705) around 1658, develop the familiar Frescobaldian toccata and contrapuntal templates (alongside 'French' harpsichord suites and a Netherlandish variation-set) not just with Germanic concern for structure and thematic organisation, but with concern also for poetic content.

Froberger is most boldly Roman in the Bernini-esque gestures of the two toccatas *alla levatione* of the 1649 book (FbWV 105 and 106)[3] and Toccata V of 1656 (FbWV 111) in the same style. More thoroughly Germanic re-interpretations of this *durezze e ligature* style come from his followers: Kerll's Toccata IV subsumes chromaticisms and dissonances within a shifting contrapuntal texture, while Pachelbel left two examples of outstanding delicacy, the 'Fantasias' in E♭ and G minor, one melodic in impulse, the other harmonic.

Froberger is essentially a contrapuntal thinker, even in his multi-sectional toccatas (Butt 1995: 183–8). The long, sustained pedal-point is just not part of his musical character – unlike Frescobaldi or his sturdy acolyte at Ulm, Scherer, or even Kerll or Pachelbel. In a development significant for the later north German praeludium, Froberger uses unpredictably embellished chordal rhetoric, not as an expressive end in itself, but to generate tension which is then released in a series of contrapuntal sections related by thematic transformation. The first two toccatas (FbWV 101 and 102) of 1649 are particularly fine, especially the second – perfectly balanced formally and possessing a stirring, cumulative chromatic intensity.

As for Froberger's strict contrapuntal works, a Bach-dominated historical hindsight (Buelow 1985: 161) does not do justice to the music itself – the steely, accelerating vigour of Canzona II of 1649 (FbVW 302), the nobly single-minded working-out of subject and counter-subject of Ricercar I of 1658 (FbVW 401) or the consistently high order of keyboard polyphony and thematic transformation throughout the ricercars and capriccios of 1656 (FbVW 407–12 and 507–12). Amongst these are such splendid things as the swirling chromatic slippages in Capriccio II (FbVW 508), the pathetic grandeur of Ricercar I (FbVW 407) – given in an extended variant by François Roberday in his *Fugues et caprices* (1660), the earliest publication of the French baroque organ – and the poignant Ricercar V (FbVW 411).[4]

Froberger undoubtedly confirmed south German keyboard music on its cosmopolitan course. His travels point towards other routes of his influence, north and west, in his own day. As well as visiting Brussels and Cromwellian London, he forged close contacts with the north German Matthias Weckmann in Dresden (see p. 226), and with Louis Couperin, Roberday and leading *clavecinistes* in Paris. Thirty years after his death, the appearance of large printed anthologies and manuscript copies as well (Silbiger 1993)[5] testify to his renewed significance for a musical Europe by then avidly debating issues of national style and stylistic synthesis.

His younger colleagues Kerll (who had also studied in Rome, with Carissimi and possibly with Frescobaldi) and Poglietti (whose recorded career is exclusively Viennese) also exercised international influence through manuscript copies and prints, even into the eighteenth century. Kerll's canzonas are entertaining *jeux d'esprit*, quite unlike Froberger's in aim and technique. His toccatas (more fantastical and less architectural than Froberger's) and Poglietti's twelve ricercars,[6] though at opposite ends of the formal spectrum, highlight two important issues affecting performance of much of this repertoire.

First, the music often places a high premium on the player piercing through the patina of the notation – whether it be the seemingly unrelieved virtuosity of the toccatas or the apparently calm polyphonic flow of the ricercars – to search out the affect of the moment, distinguishing between stasis and mobility, finding lyricism in the midst of virtuosity and rhetoric in counterpoint, in order to convey an eventful narrative.

Secondly, the accepted inter-changeability of instruments, particularly in toccata, contrapuntal and ostinato forms, often demands decisive interpretation in apparently non-committal notational areas. Kerll's Toccata V *tutta de salti* appears particularly suitable for harpsichord, while Toccata VI *per li pedali* is obviously for organ. But other toccatas positively invite performance on either. According to instrument: should full chords be plain, broken or embellished? Should tied notes be restruck or notes of the same pitch tied? Should ornaments be retained or added? On the organ: where should there be manual changes? When (rather than whether) should the pedals be added for cadential reinforcement and pedal-points (including implied ones)? How might Kerll have handled these issues in playing Toccata VII (see Example 14.2) on the great 1642 Freundt organ, which he must surely have known, in Klosterneuburg Abbey, just outside Vienna?

Uniquely luxurious for the period (Williams 1966: 68, 71), Klosterneuburg canonised characteristics typical of substantial organs of the region for 150 years to come: a shimmering, dominating *Hauptwerk*, a complete but often uncoupleable Pedal department, secondary manuals

Ex. 14.2 Kerll, Toccata VII

for colouristic contrast rather than as a complement to the tutti, a huge variety of 8′ and 4′ colours and an absence of mutations:

[Haupt]Werk (C/E–c³) [middle manual]		Rückpositiv (C/E–c³) [bottom manual]	
Principal	8′	Nachthorn gedackt	8′
Principal flöten	8′	Principal	4′
Copl	8′	Spitzflöten	4′
Quintadena	8′	Klein Copl	4′
Octav	4′	Octav	2′
Octav Copl	4′	Superoctav	1′
Offene flöten	4′	Cimbl scharf	II
Dulcian (flue)	4′	Krumbhorn	8′
Quint	3′		
Superoctav	2′		
Mixtur	XII–XIV	**Pedal** (C/E–b♭)	
Cimbl gross	II		
Dulcian	16′	Portun Principal	16′
Pusaun	8′	Subbass	16′
		Octav	8′
		Choralflöten	8′
Brustwerk (C/E–c³) [top manual]		Superoctav	4′
		Mixtur	VII–VIII
		Rauschwerk	III
Coplflöten	4′	Grosspusaun	16′
Superoctav	2′	Octav Pusaun	8′
Spitzflöten	2′		
Regal	8′		
Tremulant		Rp/Hw	

The late seventeenth century

In the last quarter of the seventeenth century, as new French fashions and Italianate styles met at the south German cultural crossroads, one volume of keyboard music stands out: Georg Muffat's *Apparatus musico-organis-ticus* published in 1690, the year he moved from Salzburg Cathedral to the court of the Bishop of Passau. Proud of his studies with Lully in Paris and Pasquini in Rome (where he had also been part of Corelli's circle), Muffat openly advertised his cosmopolitan zeal.[7] The twelve toccatas of the *Apparatus* combine acquired styles – Corellian concerto and sonata, Lullian overture, Pasquinian keyboard style – with his inherited south German tradition, in sectionalised, varied, balanced designs: an original and ambitious concept. The best are grand creations – in an entirely different league from the modest, though attractive toccatas of Johann Speth's contemporary *Ars magna* (1693) – and are worthy Catholic counterparts to Buxtehude's praeludia (see Radulescu 1980).

Toccata VI enshrines an individualistic tribute to the expressive rhetoric of Frescobaldi's elevation toccatas. Nos. VIII, IX, X and XI display even greater subtlety of stylistic fusion, suggesting a range of timbres and textures spreading across regional boundaries: the adaptation of French and Italian orchestral idioms, mixed with *durezze e ligature* style, for the openings of nos. VIII, X (Example 14.3) and XI (Example 14.4) brings the German *plenum* and Italian *ripieno* within hailing distance of the French *Grand jeu* and *Plein jeu* conventions.

Ideal the Schlägl and Klosterneuburg organs may be for the *Apparatus*, but the music almost appeals for the inspired eclecticism of south German instruments of the mid-eighteenth century, or for the Frenchified organs of Andreas Silbermann in Muffat's childhood Alsace (itself a region of mixed culture) at Marmoutier (1709) and Ebersmünster (1728) – never more so than at the end of Toccata III from which de Grigny 'borrowed' some bars for the *Point d'orgue* of his 1699 *Livre d'orgue*.

The *Apparatus* has two important period companions, the first being the seven capriccios and two ricercars of Nicolaus Adam Strungk (1640–1700). Though his major appointments were in Hamburg and Saxony, these works, written while he was in Vienna and Italy in the mid-1680s, are cast from the strict, open-score Catholic mould, deploying double and triple counterpoint of surprising scale, ingenuity and vigour. Outstanding are a lyrical Capriccio *sopra il Corale Ich dank dir schon*, dated 1684, and an austere ricercar on the death of his mother written in Venice in 1685.[8]

Ex. 14.3 Georg Muffat, Toccata X

Ex. 14.4 Georg Muffat, Toccata XI

The second is a forerunner of Bach's '48', the *Ariadne musica* (1702) by the Francophile Kapellmeister of the Baden court, J. C. F. Fischer (see Walter 1990). Its twenty tiny preludes and fugues, in most of the major and minor keys, consistently present the prelude–fugue coupling (perhaps for the first time) as a balanced, complementary diptych. Pedal indications and the inclusion of five seasonal chorale ricercars point to a liturgical intent, perhaps as a more 'modern' counterpart to his equally fastidious, but more traditional verset collection *Blumen-Strauss*. The refined organisation and warmth of his motivically patterned textures make it no surprise that C. P. E. Bach included this stylish, mature composer with Strungk amongst the south German masters (headed by Froberger, Kerll and Pachelbel) who had a formative influence on his father (David and Mendel 1945: 278).

Ostinato forms

Despite Buxtehude's two ciaconas and passacaglia, 'keyboard ostinato pieces were cultivated mainly in Italy and South Germany, not in the north' (Snyder 1987: 236). Though the southern works may be texturally slighter and formally more loose-limbed than Buxtehude's, they are delectable and varied (see Kee 1988). Kerll's Passacaglia, possibly the earliest German example, treats its simple, descending four-bar bass with a sophistication accommodating both continuity and contrast (best registered simply, like most of this repertory, to avoid over-emphasising the ostinato unit). Muffat however uses double-bars and repeat signs to sectionalise his two examples in the *Apparatus:* a winsome Ciacona in G major and a spacious Passacaglia in G minor, which punctuates Italianate variations with a grand eight-bar progression, served up *en rondeau* every sixth statement.

This southern repertory often cunningly exploits the idiomatic diversity the ostinato form invites. While Pachelbel's chamber music-like Ciacona in D minor demands pedals – which need not rule out performance on a domestic instrument – his little-played F major and wonderful F minor ciaconas both effectively thwart exclusive identification with just one instrument. Harpsichordists rightly do not hesitate to play Muffat's two ostinato works from the *Apparatus musico-organisticus.* Similarly, organists should have no compunction in appropriating Fischer's delicate Chaconne in G and expansive Passacaglia in D minor, the final works in his harpsichord collections, *Musicalisches Blumen-Büschlein* (1696) and *Musicalischer Parnassus* (1738 or earlier): they inhabit just the same textural territory.

The eighteenth century

Georg Muffat's evident Viennese court ambitions (he formally presented the *Apparatus* to Emperor Leopold I) were fulfilled by his son, Gottlieb, who served as court organist 1717–63. Appraisal of this significant composer is sorely hampered by the lack of a complete edition. Though his harpsichord suites (raided by Handel) and liturgical versets are available, only a few of his large-scale organ works have been published. There are hidden riches here. The contrapuntal works – including thirty-two ricercars and nineteen canzonas, which even in their open-score layout (like Bach's *Art of Fugue)* perpetuate the strict traditions of the previous century – are strong, thematically distinguished and without the stiffness

Ex. 14.5 Gottlieb Muffat, Capriccio XV 'desperato'

of his famous teacher, Johann Fux. Comparison of his twenty-four toccatas and capriccios (an original coupling) with the more bullish, extrovert toccatas of his father is fascinating: Gottlieb tends to introspection and retrospection, delving far back into the old Italianate toccata tradition (he made his own copies of Froberger's works) but also exploiting French *clavecin* ornamentation and up-to-date instrumental idioms. Perhaps the atmosphere of the court of Emperor Karl VI (reigned 1711–40), with its curious adoption of Spanish court formalities, played some part in Gottlieb's highly personal mixture of archaic austerity and delicate emotional sensibility, as in the Toccatas and Capriccios nos. X–XII and the Capriccio XV 'desperato' (see Example 14.5).

Such moodiness contrasts with the vibrant new churches of the late German baroque and the glamorous new organs sited amidst their exuberant stucco-work and swirling frescoes. Key aspects of the period include: the airy disposition of cases around a west window, stunningly so at Weingarten Abbey (Gabler, 1737–50, shown in Figure 5.11); the innovation of free-standing, reversed consoles, giving players a commanding view of the liturgical action; the glorious *rapprochement* between the south German *plenum* and the reeds and mutations of the classical French organ as at the abbeys of Ottobeuren (Riepp's Trinity organ, 1761–6), Amorbach (Stumm brothers, 1774–82) and Neresheim (Holzhay, 1792–7) (Williams 1966: 79–84).

A generous, moderately-sized instrument would still typically possess two or three mixtures on the *Hauptwerk*, no mutations and a reed frequently only in the pedal, but also now various strings at 8′ and even 4′ (often double-ranked), undulants and flutes of various pitches, construction and scaling. Balthasar Freiwiss's 1752–4 organ in the former abbey of Irsee, Swabia, is a lovely example (Fischer and Wohnhaas 1982: 122):

Haubt-Manuale (C–c³)		Brust-Positive-Manuale (C–c³)	
Subprincipal (stopped, wood)	16′	Flautta dolce	8′
Principal	8′	Coppl	8′
Copl	8′	Principal	4′
Quintadena	8′	Fugara	4′
Solicinal	8′	Fletten gedeckht	4′
Viola de Gamba (2 ranks)	8′	Viola (2 ranks)	4′
Octav	4′	Super-Octav	2′
Flötten offen	4′	Mixtur	V
Spiz-Fletten	4′		
Rohr-Fletten	4′	**Pedal** (C–f)	
Sesquialtera	II	Principal-Bass	16′
Mixtur	VI	Sub-Bass gedeckt	16′
Cymbalum	IV	Octav-Bass (wood)	8′
		Violon-Bass (2 ranks)	8′
		Quint	6′
Bp/Hm		Hohlflautten	4′
		Cornet	V
		Fagott	8′

The rococo affective elements and late baroque contrapuntal energy of the *IX Toccate e Fughe* (1747) by the Salzburg Kapellmeister Eberlin are finely judged for the sonorities of the period instrument – the brilliant but internally complex *plenum*, the treble emphasis of the various flutes and strings, the lyric foundational warmth of combined stops of widely diverse scaling – as mediated by both a rich, plaster-vaulted acoustic and an expressive unequal temperament: hence the riskily extended sequences (for example, Toccatas I and III and Fugue VI), the high proportion of two and three-part writing in four-voice fugues, compensating rhythmic drive (as in the double Fugue II), chromatic incident (at high speed in Fugue III) and gentle dissonance (above all in the sensuous, syncopated *durezze e ligature* Toccata VI, whose immediate progenitor is Gottlieb Muffat's Capriccio XII).

By this time serious organ composition was already being undermined by the taste for lighter styles and for naïve programmatic and colouristic effects, famously peddled by Vogler and Knecht later in the century. Even a liturgical verset collection can throw up astounding moments: the *Sturm und Drang* of the Praeludium Tertium from *Certamen Aonium* (1733) by the monk-organist of Asbach Abbey Carlmann Kolb (1703–65) veers dizzily between wild rococo ecstasy and eccentric sensationalism.

Seger by contrast maintains a more old-fashioned, generally sober style, in the orderly textural tradition of Fischer (who was probably also of

Bohemian origins), as in his *8 Toccaten und Fugen,* published post-humously in 1793.[9] The picture of an energetic school in Prague, headed by Seger and his pupils, including Brixi, Kopriva and Kuchar, is blurred somewhat by problems of attribution and reliability of sources.

Educated at the abbeys of Klosterneuburg and Melk, Albrechtsberger was perhaps the last composer formed by the baroque south German organ tradition. His *Octo toni ecclesiastici,* probably written while he was organist at Melk, 1759–65, is in the classic south German alternatim verset format, but with each tone rounded off by a full-scale fugue: those for tones III, IV and V are outstanding. Both Mozart (in appreciations of Albrechtsberger and Eberlin) and Haydn (in sending Beethoven to Albrechtsberger in 1794–5) openly acknowledged the vital, unpedantic counterpoint of the south German tradition as an essential ingredient in the synthesis that was the mature Viennese classical style.

While Albrechtsberger's later preludial and fugal works, from his time at St Stephen's Cathedral, Vienna, illustrate a tradition becalmed, his Organ Concerto (1762) reminds us that those same changes in musical styles and tastes that eroded the solo role of the organ in church promoted its *concertante* role, in Masses and instrumental works by Mozart, Michael and Joseph Haydn, Brixi and Vanhal amongst others. It is ironically indicative of general decline that the finest solo organ works of the south German late eighteenth century, Mozart's Fantasias K 594 and K 608, have nothing to do with the regional organ gallery traditions: written for a 'mechanical' (i.e. machine) organ, they were neither inspired by nor intended for a conventional instrument, nor even conceived to be played by human hands.

Recommended editions

The indefatigable Rudolf Walter has edited the verset collections of Kerll, Murschauser, Fischer, Kolb, and Albrechtsberger, Muffat's *Apparatus* and Eberlin's *IX Toccate e Fughe* for Alfred Coppenrath of Altötting and Eberlin's *65 Vor- und Nachspiele* for Doblinger. However, for the complete Kerll and for Muffat's *Apparatus* the editions of John O'Donnell and Michael Radulescu respectively for Doblinger should be preferred. Werra's 1901 edition of Fischer's complete keyboard works (Breitkopf) remains desirable. Gottlieb Muffat's *72 Versetl* are edited by Walter Upmeyer (Bärenreiter), while other selected works of his come from Kistner & Siegel's *Die Orgel,* Series II (nos. 8, 10, 13 and 16) edited by F. W. Riedel, as do Poglietti's *12 Ricerari* (nos. 5 and 6). Seger's *8 Toccaten und Fugen* are published in the same house's *Organum* series (no. 22).

Impecunious students will give thanks for the single-volume Dover reprint of the Adler edition of Froberger's organ works (and also for Dover's Pachelbel volume) but they should not use it without at least consulting Siegbert Rampe's new four-volume complete edition (Bärenreiter, still in progress) and Silbiger's 1993 article.

15 The north German organ school

Geoffrey Webber

When J. S. Bach applied for the post of organist at the Jakobikirche in Hamburg in 1720 he had hoped to inherit one of the most famous organs in north Germany (see Figure 15.1). Like many of the finest organs of the period it was an instrument that had been enlarged several times over, most recently by the most famous of all north German builders, Arp Schnitger. Earlier builders including members of the Scherer family had contributed to the fifty-three-stop instrument of three manuals and pedals recorded by Michael Praetorius (Praetorius 1619/1985: 168),[1] and in 1635 Gottfried Fritzsche had added a fourth manual and new *Rückpositiv*. Schnitger, who had just completed an enormous instrument for the nearby Nikolaikirche (four manuals, with sixty-seven stops including a 32′ Posaune as well as a 32′ Principal for the case), completely replaced all the workings of the organ, keeping most of the flue pipework but adding a new set of fourteen reed stops. Bach made no secret of his admiration for the north German organs he encountered, and had the greatest respect for particular celebrated combinations of player and instrument, notably Johann Reincken at the Katharinenkirche in Hamburg, Georg Böhm at the Johanniskirche in Lüneburg, and Dieterich Buxtehude at the Marienkirche in Lübeck.

Recently it has once again become possible to experience something of the overwhelming power and beauty of one of these large north German instruments that Bach knew. The organ at the Jakobikirche in Hamburg survived the Second World War by being temporarily dismantled, and in 1993, exactly 300 years after Schnitger finished his work on the instrument, Jürgen Ahrend rebuilt the organ in its Schnitger form, having already benefited from the experience of restoring other notable Schnitger instruments in the Netherlands and Germany. An organ such as this reflects the full spectrum of the surviving music of the north German organ school, encompassing both the colossal effects and extreme delicacy suggested by the surviving repertoire. The specification of the organ as restored by Ahrend is shown below.

Figure 15.1 The organ in the Jacobikirche, Hamburg, Germany, rebuilt by Arp Schnitger in 1690–3. After various changes and upheavals this instrument has been restored close to its original state by Jürgen Ahrend (1993). The survival of this and other such instruments is central to our understanding of north German music of the seventeenth century. The main case holds a large chorus at 16′ pitch; the *Rückpositiv* is at 8′ pitch, and the 32′ pedal is divided in towers on either side. The case is a modern replica of the one destroyed in 1944 and the prospect pipes are by Ahrend.

Hamburg, Jakobikirche
Scherer, Fritzsche, Schnitger, Lehner; restored 1993 by Ahrend

Werk (C/E–c³)

Principal	16′
Quintadehn	16′
Octava	8′
Spitzflöht	8′
Viola di Gamba	8′
Octava	4′
Rohrflöht	4′
Flachflöht	2′
Super Octav	2′
Rauschpfeiff	II
Mixtur	VI–VIII
Trommet	16′

Oberpositiv (C/E–c³)

Principal	8′
Rohrflöht	8′
Holtzflöht	8′
Spitzflöht	4′
Octava	4′
Nasat	3′
Octava	2′
Gemshorn	2′
Scharff	IV–VI
Cimbel	III
Trommet	8′
Vox humana	8′
Trommet	4′

Rückpositiv (C,D,E–c³)

Principal	8′
Gedackt	8′
Quintadehna	8′
Octava	4′
Blockflöht	4′
Querpfeiff	2′
Octava	2′
Sexquialtera	II
Scharff	VI–VIII
Siffloit	$1\frac{1}{2}$′
Dulcian	16′
Bahrpfeiffe	8′
Trommet	8′

Brustpositiv (C/E–c³)

Principal	8′
Octav	4′
Hollflöht	4′
Waldtflöht	4′
Sexqualtera	II
Scharff	IV–VI
Dulcian	8′
Trechter Regal	8′

Pedal (C,D–d¹⁾)

Principal	32′
Octava	16′
Subbaß	16′
Octava	8′
Octava	4′
Nachthorn	2′
Rauschpfeiff	III
Mixture	VI–VIII
Posaune	32′
Posaune	16′
Dulcian	16′
Trommet	8′
Trommet	4′
Cornet	2′

2 Tremulants
Cimbelstern
Trommel
Couplers BP/W, OP/W

Certain features stand out from this specification as characteristic of Schnitger's work and that of other north German builders of the period: the large number of reeds of different types, the relatively small number of mutation stops (though including the high Siffloit), the substantial mixtures, and the well-stocked Pedal and *Rückpositiv* departments, crucial for conveying chorale melodies. It is notable that even with a pedal department of fourteen stops, no room was found for a pedal 8' flute. This is probably because the main solo timbres on the *Rückpositiv* are so powerful that only the 8' Octava provides sufficient support. Other typically north German sounds include the Quintadena stops, often found at 16', 8' and 4' pitches on the same organ, the short-length reeds, the narrow-scale Sexquialtera and the 2' pedal solo stops – the bright Cornet (a single reed stop) and the wide-scaled Nachthorn. Toy stops were also included in many instruments, the Trommel (drum) effect being created by placing two low-pitched pipes next to each other so that the sound from their mouths creates a heavy beating. The similarly large instrument in the Marienkirche in Stralsund (shown in Figure 5.6) also contains a bird-stop: a high-pitched pipe placed in water.

The principal duty of the north German organist of the seventeenth century was to play chorales and chants in conjunction with the choir and/or congregation, either preluding beforehand, or providing verses on the organ alone, or even improvising flourishes between each line of a sung verse.[2] The art was essentially one of improvisation, but the surviving written-down examples of the forms give us some impression of the styles of playing employed by the organists week by week. In alternatim settings of the same chorale (or chant) by different composers the number of verses provided often differs, suggesting that either the particular tradition of performance varied very widely, or perhaps alternatively that the compositions were written down not for specific liturgical use but rather just as examples of the art for purely artistic or didactic reasons.

The earliest sources of music from the north German organ school date from around the turn of the seventeenth century, and contain mostly chorale and chant settings for alternatim performance with choir or congregation (see Chapter 9). Most of the repertoire in the main sources, such as the Celle and Visby Tablatures, is anonymous, but the first major figure to emerge is Hieronymus Praetorius, organist of the Jakobikirche in Hamburg at a time when the fifty-three-stop instrument was in use. The style of this period has rightly been called monumental; four- and five-part textures are built around a slow-moving cantus firmus, the harmony enriched with many passing notes. However, lighter textures are also to be found, along with flamboyant cadential flourishes

Ex. 15.1 H. Praetorius, Magnificat (tone vi)

for the right hand. Example 15.1 shows the conclusion of the Magnificat on the Sixth Tone.

During the late sixteenth and early seventeenth centuries close links existed between organ builders in Germany and the Netherlands, and the fame of the Dutch builders was such that some German churches even commissioned Dutch organs to be built and shipped to Germany. A parallel line of influence was evident in organ playing and composition, for in the person of Jan Pieterszoon Sweelinck the Netherlands boasted an organist who matched the reputation of the organs themselves. Although Sweelinck's finest compositions are arguably his fantasias, it was his work in the field of cantus firmus elaboration that was to have the most significant effect on contemporary German composers. Several Germans studied with Sweelinck, a fact that is neatly exemplified in a surviving variation set on the chorale *Allein Gott in der Höh sei Ehr* which contains verses composed by his pupils Andreas Düben, Peter Hasse and Gottfried (brother of Samuel) Scheidt.[3] But the finest German composers to benefit from study in Amsterdam were Jacob Praetorius (son of Hieronymus) and Heinrich Scheidemann from Hamburg, and Samuel Scheidt from Halle. If the music of Hieronymus Praetorius and his contemporaries reflects an already flourishing school of organ playing at the turn of the seventeenth century, the work of this Sweelinck-influenced trio marked the beginnings of the great period of north German organ music that lasted throughout the seventeenth century.

The principal achievement of the Sweelinck-influenced organists and their contemporaries was to expand the north German style through the use of a wider range of textures from the two-part *bicinium* upwards, the development of more varied figurative passagework, and the use of echo techniques involving up to three manuals. Along with this development of particular textures and styles came the crystallisation of particular stop combinations, some universal and others peculiar to individual players and instruments. The surviving indications of particular registrations found in the introduction to Samuel Scheidt's *Tabulatura nova* (1624) and other sources such as the Lüneburg tablatures illustrate the care with which the organists made use of the huge range of possibilities available on the German instruments. One example is reported as having been a favourite of Jacob Praetorius (who was organist of the Petrikirche in Hamburg), and indicates a specific playing style in which the cantus firmus is elaborated simultaneously on the manual and the Pedal:[4]

Oberwerk:	Trumpet 8′, Zink 8′, Nasard 3′, Gemshorn 2′, Hohlflute 4′
Rückpositiv:	Principal 8′, Octave 4′
Pedal:	Principal-Bass 24′, Posaune 16′, Trumpet 8′, Trumpet 4′, Cornet 2′

A specific registration such as this, which could scarcely be copied on instruments outside the north German sphere, nevertheless serves to demonstrate the reed-dominated combinations employed in cantus firmus performance, and also reveals that although the solo line was normally presented on the *Rückpositiv*, nearest the congregation, this was not always the case. For the modern player, the most important matter to solve when performing the chorale works of this period is the allocation of the appropriate pitch and division to the cantus firmus part. Scheidt's instructions are essential in this regard, revealing, for example, the common practice of playing the cantus firmus on the pedals at 4′ pitch. Another specific technique, uniquely north German, consisted of giving extra weight to the cantus firmus line by playing it simultaneously on the manuals (in the tenor voice) and in the upper of two pedal parts.[5]

The large cantus firmus repertoire of music by Jacob Praetorius, Scheidemann and Scheidt is a vivid testimony to the organ playing skills for which these composers were renowned in their lifetimes. Much of their music reflects an approach to organ playing which stemmed largely from the application of pre-conceived devices and figures which were common material amongst organists of the time, analogous to the addition of diminutions and ornamental figures recommended by the singing treatises of the period. At times the continuous repetition of particular melodic patterns or echo passages seems over-zealous to the modern ear, but the rewards are rich for those who seek out the finest music of this repertoire. Scheidt's often vocally inspired counterpoint brings great beauty to many of his chorale and chant versets, and masterpieces such as his six-verse setting of the communion chorale *Jesus Christus, unser Heiland* show to good advantage the highly ordered and consistent manner in which he manipulated the standard organ textures employed by Sweelinck. By contrast, the chorale settings by Jacob Praetorius and Scheidemann betray a greater freedom of style. A composition such as the seven-verse setting of *Vater unser im Himmelreich* by Praetorius contains a multitude of idioms, together with a sense of adventure that allows him to write a chromatic passage in verse 3 that could only be played on instruments with extra notes providing sub-semitones (see Vogel 1986a: 240). The chief vehicle for this improvisatory mode of performance was the so-called chorale fantasia. As the name suggests, the organist elaborated upon a melody in a free manner, changing style and presentation of the melody in a continuous movement of considerable length. Although it is tempting to think that such enormous works in this genre could not possibly have been intended for liturgical use, it is clear from the contemporary accounts that organists were indeed minded at times to improvise on a chorale for up to a quarter of an hour or more, at the risk of incurring the wrath of the clergy (see Webber 1992). Playing continuously for this length of time demanded the use of contrasting registrations, normally achieved by the alternation of manuals with echo effects, but one source specifically calls for changes of stops within the work itself, a practice that is mentioned in a report on the playing of Jacob Praetorius (Davidsson 1991: 49). Only a fragment survives of a chorale fantasia by Praetorius, the beginning of a setting of *Durch Adams Fall ist ganz verderbt*, but this is enough to show that three manuals and pedals were required, the chief melody line sounding on the *Rückpositiv*, the echos on the *Oberwerk*, and the accompanying harmony played on the *Brustwerk*. Example 15.2 demonstrates this alternation between *Rückpositiv* and *Oberwerk* in a passage containing characteristically fluid rhythms.

Scheidemann's large and impressive surviving output contains both extended chorale fantasias, such as *Ein feste Burg* and *Wir glauben all an einen Gott*, and, at the other end of the spectrum, single-verse chorale settings which stand at the beginning of the tradition of the simple chorale prelude that gathered pace towards the end of the seventeenth century. In this particular format the melody is presented as a delicately embellished cantus firmus in the soprano voice, set against lower voices that preimitate each line of the melody in turn, as in *Nun bitten wir den heiligen Geist*. Finally, Scheidemann's output also contains a number of arrangements of vocal works by Lassus, Hassler and others, a result of the demand

Ex. 15.2 J. Praetorius, *Durch Adams Fall ist ganz verdebt*

made on organists to perform motets liturgically as solo organ pieces on occasions when no choir was present.

The next generation of north German composers, principally Matthias Weckmann and Franz Tunder, continued to cultivate the two main forms of chorale verset and chorale fantasia. Matthias Weckmann's surviving compositions mark the final outpouring of the Sweelinck/Scheidt style of patterned figuration, made at times even more intense through the use of strict canon. Hans Davidsson has proposed that the monumental cycles on *Es ist das Heil uns kommen her* and *O lux beata Trinitas* were composed to fulfil unusually grand metaphysical conceptions, a possibility that is suggested not least by the fact that Weckmann composed a total of six verses on the three-verse hymn *O lux beata Trinitas* (Davidsson 1991: 123–60). Weckmann also developed even further the rich textures and flamboyant cadences of the Hamburg tradition, as seen in the concluding section of the fantasia that comprises the sixth verse of *Es ist das Heil uns kommen her*, in which the texture becomes seven-part (with double pedalling), culminating in the final chord which stretches from the top note of the manuals to the bottom of the pedals (c^3 to C). Tunder's chorale music is scarcely less spectacular, and although his surviving output suggests a marked preference for the chorale fantasia style, one of his best compositions is a three-verse setting of *Jesus Christus unser Heiland*, notable in particular for the opening pedal flourish (probably the earliest surviving example of an opening pedal solo in an organ work, seen here as a logical grafting of the manual technique of

Ex. 15.3 Tunder, *Jesus Christus unser Heiland*

introducing the first note of a chorale with a run of semiquavers) and for the appearance at the conclusion of the piece, shown in Example 15.3, of the secondary leading-note (i.e. rising by semitone to the fifth as well as the octave of the chord), techniques that were both to be more fully exploited by Dieterich Buxtehude.

Chorale settings that survive from the last quarter of the seventeenth century indicate a rise in popularity of the simple chorale prelude,[6] a development that coincided with the beginning of the gradual decline in the use of alternatim versets. The great master of this generation is, of course, Dieterich Buxtehude, who in 1668 succeeded Tunder at the Marienkirche in Lübeck, one of the tallest and most gracefully proportioned churches of the Hanseatic cities, which housed two three-manual organs, a large west-end instrument with fifty-two stops and a smaller instrument in a side chapel (Snyder 1987: 78–87). The most conservative of Buxtehude's settings are those in the format of chorale versets, continuing the tradition of Scheidemann and Weckmann (though avoiding the scale of Weckmann's larger cycles), but Buxtehude's individual voice is arguably heard more clearly in the freedom of the fantasias and in the more intimate surroundings of the chorale prelude. Moreover, Buxtehude seems to have experimented with novel approaches, as seen in his settings of the chants of the Magnificat and Te Deum, where aspects of the verset, fantasia and even praeludium traditions are combined in unusual ways, and in his use of a chorale for the composition of a keyboard suite. One of his most attractive chorale works to display a wide

Ex. 15.4 Buxtehude, *Wie schön leuchtet der Morgenstern*

variety of approaches is his setting of the Epiphany chorale *Wie schön leuchtet der Morgenstern*. The composition comprises three different sections in triple time (6/4, 6/8, 12/8, probably implying a gradual increase in tempo) broken up by a single passage in common time which concludes with a free cadential section, similar to connecting passages in the contemporary praeludium. Stylistically there are both conservative and modern elements, the former evident in the demisemiquaver flourishes and echos, the latter in the modern harmonic sequences and gigue-like idiom adopted in the concluding sections, reflecting the cross-over of sacred and secular styles seen in the chorale suite. At the opening of the work Buxtehude leaves the characteristic rising fifth of the chorale melody clearly audible before introducing a lilting pastorale idiom in the upper voices, as shown in Example 15.4.

In the short chorale preludes Buxtehude embellishes the chorale melodies with rhetorical yet subtle decorations, underpinned by carefully chosen dissonances in the accompanying voices, serving to enhance the expression inherent in the chorale melodies themselves without ever overpowering them. Amongst the more poignant settings of penitential chorales, that of *Ach Herr, mich armen Sünder* (the melody of which is familiar today to the words 'O sacred head sore wounded') is one of the finest examples. It is notable at the outset that Buxtehude chooses to keep the first phrase of the chorale completely without elaboration, making the rhetorical entry of the second phrase, beginning a fourth higher than the

Ex. 15.5 Buxtehude, *Ach Herr, mich armen Sünder*

melody itself and entering after a rest, all the more effective (see Example 15.5).

Buxtehude's contemporaries such as Vincent Lübeck, Johann Reincken and Nicolaus Bruhns also produced fine works based on chorales and chants, with Reincken's colossal fantasia on *An Wasserflüssen Babylon* being one of the last great peaks of this genre, and the old scheme of chorale versets discovered a new lease of life in the guise of the chorale partita, of which the Lüneburg organist Georg Böhm left several examples. Like Buxtehude's chorale suite these represent a meeting of secular and sacred keyboard idioms. Some, like *Ach wie nichtig, ach wie flüchtig*, were probably intended for the harpsichord (as is suggested by the use of broken-chord figuration and a low AA), but others may have been intended for the organ as they call for the use of pedals. Böhm also set chorale verses in a more traditional manner, and showed further innovation in one of his settings of *Vater unser im Himmelreich* in which he introduced prominent Italian and French features, the former seen in the pedal part in continuous quavers (based on the Italian repeated-note string style), and the latter in the florid ornamentation of the embellished chorale line.

During the first half of the seventeenth century organ playing unrelated to liturgical melodies seems to have had a relatively low priority, particularly as the contemporary service books often expressly forbade the playing of organ music that had no relation to a sacred text, but the principal genre employed by the generation of Scheidemann and Jacob

Praetorius was the praeambulum or praeludium. The style was generally restrained and the length of works often brief, consisting of either a single section in homophonic style, or a homophonic section leading into an imitative one, in the same way that several chorale works of the period developed from a homophonic to a more imitative style. If such pieces were used in services it was probably to set the key for sung items such as concertato motets. A few more substantial free works do survive from the first half of the century, but these have a greater affinity with sixteenth-century forms such as the fantasia than with the emerging praeludium, or take the form of extended abstract works using idioms more familiar from the chorale tradition, such as Scheidemann's Toccata in G which opens in the manner of a chorale setting with a semiquaver run leading to a held note.

The expansion of the praeludium form around the middle of the century came about through substantial structural and stylistic develop-ments that originated both within the north German school itself and outside. The indigenous transformation consisted of the gradual disin-tegration of the uniform and continuous textures of the earlier part of the century through the increasing use of rests and rhetorical chordal ges-tures, a feature no doubt connected with the large reverberation times found in the spacious north German churches, producing a more varied and virtuosic idiom. This is first seen in the music of minor composers such as Jacob Bölsche and Christian Flor, and also in the praeludia by Franz Tunder. The external influence at this time was that of contempo-rary Italian keyboard music, which both modified the structural basis of the praeludium and provided new stylistic elements as well. The crucial Italian genre in this respect was the variation canzona. A number of such works were composed by German organists around the middle of the century, notably Scheidemann, Tunder and the Copenhagen organist Martin Radeck. The vital ingredients are the use of duple- and triple-time sections based on the same theme, and in Radeck's work, the use of an improvisatory connecting passage between two sections in an expressive chordal idiom derived from the Italian style of *durezze e ligature* (dis-sonances and ties).[7] The amalgamation of the praeludium and variation canzona can be seen to emerge in the surviving compositions of Weckmann – a transitional stage that is reflected in the assorted terminol-ogy employed in the sources: Fantasia, Fuga and Praeambulum. Weckmann is known to have had a great interest in Italian music, and during his time at the Dresden Court he came into contact with many Italian musicians and struck up a friendship with the visiting south German pupil of Frescobaldi, Johann Froberger. Weckmann's indebted-ness to Froberger is clear from his toccatas and canzonas for manuals only (probably intended more for the harpsichord than organ). Two crucial new features appear in Weckmann's free works for organ with pedals: first, the use of several fugal sections after the manner of the variation canzona in conjunction with free improvisatory passages, and second, the use of specific stylistic idioms originating in the organ music of Frescobaldi, including the rapid ascending scale followed by a large downward leap, snapped rhythms and written-out trills that gradually increase in speed.

The great age of the north German praeludium in the final two decades of the seventeenth century was dominated by Buxtehude.[8] His extensive surviving output of praeludia shows a constantly changing approach to the genre, with few fixed designs beyond the basic alternation of free and related fugal sections. As well as developing further the kind of improvisatory free writing seen in Tunder's praeludia (particularly in his cultivation of the pedals), Buxtehude made his own many of the Frescobaldian idioms seen in Weckmann's works. He also adopted additional styles from the same south European tradition, such as the fugato style based on brief upbeat themes in duple or triple time (as can be seen in the 'Presto' section of the Praeludium in E major, BuxWV 141). In particular, Buxtehude showed great initiative in seeking out new types of fugal theme from the Italian and south German schools, injecting a far wider variety of themes than was part of the earlier praeludium style. As well as providing a multitude of canzona-based themes he also embraced the traditions of the chromatic ricercar and fugal gigue, as can be seen in one his finest works, the Praeludium in E minor (BuxWV 142). Buxtehude also showed himself alive to more contemporary Italian styles such as the string writing of Corelli, seen both in his adoption of string-like themes and figuration, and in the use of tonally oriented sequences. An apparent innovation on Buxtehude's part can be seen in his incorporation of an ostinato bass, seen most effectively in his Praeludium in C major (BuxWV 137) and Praeludium in G minor (BuxWV 148). In addition to the praeludia with pedals and three separate ostinato works, we also have an assortment of works by Buxtehude for manuals only, either in full praeludium form or shorter works entitled Canzona, Canzonetta or simply Fuga (as in the case of the popular gigue-like fugue, BuxWV 174). A few works are entitled Toccata, the implications of which are clearly shown in the Toccata in D minor (with pedals, BuxWV 155) by a particularly substantial quantity of keyboard figuration (as also seen in Johann Reincken's Toccata in G for manuals only), here including examples of the *stile brisé* and demisemiquaver arpeggio figuration. This remarkable work also contains a fugal section using triple counterpoint and a notably sublime example of the connecting passage in *durezze e*

Ex. 15.6 Buxtehude, Toccata in D minor

ligature style, introduced here by a typically north German flourish and carefully paced through a gradual increase in harmonic dissonance leading to the final $\frac{9-8}{7-6}$ double suspension before the final cadence (see Example 15.6).

Whilst the late seventeenth-century praeludium was dominated by the figure of Buxtehude, several fine compositions can be found in the surviving output of Bruhns, Böhm and Lübeck. Nicolaus Bruhns, a pupil of Buxtehude who died in his early thirties, was an outstanding violinist as well as organist, a feature that is evident in the string-like figurations of his great Praeludium in E minor (Butt 1995: 207–9). Further imaginative touches are evident in the fugal sections of this work. The first juxtaposes elements of the ricercar and canzona traditions in an unusual manner: although other composers, including Buxtehude, had mingled the two traditions in a single theme, combining the thematic outline of a chromatic ricercar with the repeated-note quavers of a canzona (as in the Praeludium in G minor BuxWV 148), Bruhns chose instead to juxtapose the two, preserving the subject *quasi* ricercar and the counter-subject *quasi* canzona (see Example 15.7a). The second fugue subject involves a melodic shape derived from Italian vocal music, an unexpected rest (again similar to a vocal tradition, this time the dramatic sigh or *suspiratio*) and the hemiola rhythm (see Example 15.7b).

Lübeck's Praeludium in E major is one of most exuberant and melodious works in the repertoire, and contains the same successful balance of north German and Italian styles that occurs in Buxtehude's finest works.

Ex. 15.7 Bruhns, Praeludium in E minor

The manuscript source of this praeludium contains a rare indication of registration in this genre: the fugato section in semiquavers (in a similar style to many passages in Buxtehude's works) is marked 'Rückpositiv scharff'. Although the large-scale effects found in the free sections of the praeludia of Buxtehude and his contemporaries were clearly designed for the *organo pleno* registration (which, according to Mattheson, did not include reeds in the manuals), the stop combinations that were employed for the fugal sections are less easy to determine. One particular possibility which relates clearly to the organs of the period is the use of consort registrations in imitation of contemporary instrumental ensembles, recommended by Michael Praetorius. Here, similar stops are combined at different pitches, such as the same type of reed, quintadena, flute or principal stops at combinations of 16′, 8′ and 4′ pitches (Vogel 1986b: 32–4).

In the early eighteenth century the north German organ school soon began to decline. A growing reliance on lengthy vapid passagework seems to have been a particular problem, especially in those works which were cast in the increasingly popular bipartite prelude and fugue structure, but equally there was an apparent lack of organists of the calibre found in the previous generation. Good composers were indeed to be found, but as in the case of the leading Hamburg composers Reinhard Keiser and Georg Philipp Telemann, they were more inclined to put their energy into secular musical activities, in opera or instrumental music, than into organ and church music. The legacy of the north German organ school, however, can be found in the organ music of J. S. Bach, who despite failing to secure the post of organist at the Jakobikirche – it went to an organist who made a large financial donation to the church – absorbed the essential elements of the style into his own music, and also continued the quest to enrich the German tradition with ingredients from contemporary French and Italian music.

Recommended editions

Volumes 10–12 of the Faber Early Organ Series (ed. Glahn and Elmer) present a varied selection from the entire north German organ school from Hieronymus Praetorius to Böhm. The complete cycle of Magnificats by Praetorius is available in an edition of the Visby (Petri) Tablature by Jeffery Kite-Powell (Heinrichshofen's Verlag) and separately in Corpus of Early Keyboard Music 4, ed. C. Rayner. Sweelinck's keyboard music is cheaply accessible in a single volume from Dover, though a more modern scholarly edition exists in the *Opera Omnia* (Alfons Annegarn, ed. Leonhardt). Scheidt's complete *Tabulatura nova* is currently being published by Harald Vogel for Breitkopf, but is already available complete in earlier editions including the *Denkmäler deutscher Tonkunst*, vol. 1 (revised in 1958 by H. Moser), and a healthy selection is available in a single volume from Peters (ed. H. Keller). Two of the most prominent editors of the repertoire in recent years have been Werner Breig, working for Bärenreiter, and Klaus Beckmann, for Breitkopf. From Breig comes a three-volume set of Scheidemann (with G. Fock), and the chorale works of Jacob Praetorius and Matthias Weckmann. Beckmann has edited the complete works of Tunder, Bruhns, Böhm, Lübeck and Reincken, as well as of many lesser composers, and provided two important anthologies of chorale works and free works by various authors. The free organ works of Weckmann have been edited both by Hans Davidsson (Gehrmans Musikförlag) and S. Rampe (Bärenreiter).

It is an unfortunate fact that most of the surviving sources of the north German school are of central German rather than north German origin, and the approach of many editors has been to accept them as partially corrupt and try to restore what may have been the original composer's intentions – a task as hazardous as it is noble. For this reason players are encouraged to study different editions of a single composer where they are available, as in the case of the two recent editions of the music of Bruhns, by Beckmann and M. Radulescu (Doblinger). The problem is particularly acute concerning Buxtehude. Hedar's edition for Hansen aims to reproduce the sources as they stand, and should be used with caution. Beckmann (Breitkopf) and Christoph Albrecht (Bärenreiter) offer differing solutions, and both should ideally be consulted. (Beckmann's revised edition of 1995–7 is much to be preferred to his pioneering 1971 edition, which lacks a critical commentary alongside the music.)

16 The organ music of J. S. Bach

David Yearsley

Johann Sebastian Bach spent almost his entire life in a small region of
central Germany whose boundaries are marked by the town of his birth,
Eisenach in Thuringia, and the place of his death, the Saxon city of
Leipzig, which lies only one hundred miles to the east. Unlike his famous
contemporary Handel, who was also born in the region, Bach did not
venture beyond this relatively confined area save for two years spent as a
chorister in the north German city of Lüneburg, and occasional trips to
the important musical centres of Lübeck, Hamburg, Dresden and Berlin.
But Bach's music stands in counterpoint to the provinciality of his biog-
raphy; his organ works encompass an unprecedented range of diverse
traditions, demonstrating a mastery of the organ art that flourished in his
native Thuringia, a fluency in the flamboyant language of north German
organ playing of the preceding generation, and a profound knowledge of
French and Italian idioms, the dominant national styles of the eighteenth
century. Bach transformed and synthesised techniques and styles ranging
from the *stile antico* of renaissance polyphony to the most up-to-date
thrills of Italian orchestral writing.

According to C. P. E. Bach his father had been exposed to a wide range
of music from an early age: he had studied the music of 'some old and
good Frenchmen', Italian and south German composers of the seventeenth century including Girolamo Frescobaldi, Johann Pachelbel,
Johann Jakob Froberger, Johann Caspar Kerll, Nicolaus Adam Strungk,
and the most important north German organists of the period –
Dieterich Buxtehude, Johann Adam Reincken, Nicolaus Bruhns, and
Georg Böhm (David and Mendel 1966: 278). Bach received his initial keyboard training from his brother Johann Christoph, with whom he went to
live after being orphaned at the age of ten. Johann Christoph had been a
student of Pachelbel, one of the most important influences on the organ
music of central Germany, and Bach became acquainted with a wide
variety of keyboard music through his brother's collection of manuscripts. As the famous anecdote about his copying of a forbidden manuscript by moonlight suggests, the young Bach was an avid copyist and
Johann Christoph's collection of keyboard music provided his introduction to far-flung styles.

The Lutheran chorale and its elaboration formed the foundation of the central German tradition of organ composition that Bach would have learned from his older brother, and the earliest surviving examples of Bach's music are pieces of this type. These early chorale settings are to be found in the so-called Neumeister chorales, a collection of music from the inner Bach circle brought to light again in 1985. The Neumeister chorales are written in the conservative central German style prevalent around 1700, and some of the pieces in the collection may even date as far back as Bach's studies with his brother. Although the settings are essentially central German in orientation, Bach moves beyond the conservative harmonic and formal parameters of his native tradition by introducing elements of the more extrovert North German style, as, for example, in the setting of *Herr Gott nun schleuss den Himmel auf* BWV 1092, where rhetorical chordal treatment of the chorale melody alternates with quick improvisatory flourishes which reach their apotheosis in a free, improvisatory peroration expressive of the central theme of the chorale text, the unlocking of heaven. The Neumeister chorales reflect the young Bach's exposure to the instruments and compositional styles of both north and central Germany, early signs perhaps of his ability to draw on various idioms.

It was as a chorister at the Michaeliskirche in Lüneburg (c1700–2) that Bach gained first-hand knowledge of the compositional methods and performance techniques of the north German organ tradition. The famous organist Georg Böhm played regularly in the city's main church, the Johanniskirche, which housed a large instrument originally built by Hendrik Niehof from 1551 to 1553 and rebuilt by Friederich Stellwagen a century later. The variation types found in Bach's partitas on chorale melodies (BWV 766–8), which probably date from 1705–6, show the influence of Böhm. From Lüneburg Bach made excursions to the nearby city of Hamburg to hear one of the great organists of the day, Johann Adam Reincken. Bach first heard the large organs of Hamburg during his formative years as an organist, and the instruments made a lasting impression on him. According to his student J. F. Agricola, Bach greatly admired Reincken's organ in the Katharinenkirche, an instrument very different from those found in Thuringia. Agricola relates that Bach 'could not praise [the organ] enough' for its plentiful and distinctive reeds, sixteen spread out over its four manuals (Adlung 1768: 187). The organ had a massive *plenum* on the *Hauptwerk* crowned by a ten-rank mixture and a plentiful Pedal division of some seventeen stops including a Principal 32′ and Posaune 32′. This instrument and that at the Jakobikirche (see Chapter 15 and Figure 15.1) possessed the qualities emphasised in surviving accounts of Bach's organ aesthetic: both had

large, strong Pedal divisions – Bach was especially impressed by the 32′
stops at the Katharinenkirche – which provided the instruments with
sufficient gravity (a concept better connoted by the German word
Gravität); each had a powerful principal chorus capped by strong mixtures and a profusion of reed stops, such as the colourful Dulcians and
Regals, and the powerful 16′ Trompette on the *Hauptwerk* of both organs.
Bach spent his professional career playing organs very different from
those in the great northern churches, but the sound of these instruments
remained with him.

By the beginning of the eighteenth century the layout of most
Thuringian instruments no longer followed the so-called *Werkprinzip*
which continued to dominate in north German organs such as those in
Hamburg. Central German organs generally lacked a *Rückpositiv* and
housed all divisions within one deep case. In Thuringian organs the pedal
was placed not in side towers, as was the practice in the north, but on a
chest behind the main case. In order to compensate for the acoustical
problems inherent in its placement, the pedal had to be large and capable
of producing a strong, heavy sound. Thuringian organs were in general
less brilliant than their northern counterparts and had far fewer reeds,
with a much greater percentage of soft flue stops, particularly strings. The
instrument that Bach played as organist of St Blasius' church in
Mühlhausen was rebuilt in 1708–9 by J. F. Wender according to Bach's
directions and exhibits only some of these Thuringian features. The
organ had a *Rückpositiv*, a legacy of the seveteenth century (the instrument was originally built in 1687–91), but was characteristically
Thuringian in its concentration on subdued flue stops, such as the customary Viola di Gamba on the *Hauptwerk*, and the group of colour stops
(Gedackt 8′, Quintatön 8′, Salicional 4′) on the *Rückpositiv*. Among the
twenty-seven manual stops on the Mühlhausen organ there was only one
reed. The tonal scheme of this instrument is indicative of the central
German desire for stops appropriate to expressive chorale settings such as
those of the Neumeister set. The Mühlhausen organ also had a considerable pedal division of nine stops ranging from 32′ to 1′.

In the winter of 1705–6 Bach left his first post as organist in the town of
Arnstadt and journeyed to Lübeck, where he heard Buxtehude display his
mastery of the north German organ art. Buxtehude's flamboyant style
may have had an immediate influence on Bach's music for when he
returned to Arnstadt, having extended his four-week leave into four
months, the church council found much to complain about in his organ
playing. The hymn accompaniments BWV 715, 722 and 732, with their
severe chromaticism and improvisatory flourishes interpolated between
the lines of the chorale, may be the pieces for which Bach received a

reprimand from the council, unhappy with his 'curious' playing which included 'many strange tones' (David and Mendel 1966: 52).

Some of the more important lessons Bach learned from Buxtehude and his contemporaries are to be heard in Bach's youthful mastery of the large-scale praeludium, the centrepiece of the north German tradition. Like its northern models, the Praeludium in E major BWV 566 (the piece is also transmitted in a version in C major; see Williams 1980, I: 222) is laid out in sections, beginning with a typically northern introduction in improvisatory style. The opening section is bold and gestural, with exuberant figuration, organ points, pedal solo and sustained chords which venture into keys more remote than those explored by Buxtehude. This opening gambit is followed by a lengthy fugue treating a repeated-note subject similar in affect to those found in many northern praeludia. After an improvisatory interlude in the *stylus phantasticus* (a contemporary term for music written in a free style; see Snyder 1987: 248–57), Bach returns to the same fugue subject, now altering it from duple to triple time, and overlaying the counterpoint with virtuosic passagework as the piece careers towards its final cadence. Although less grandiose, the Praeludium in A minor BWV 551 follows more closely the five-part structure found in a number of Buxtehude's praeludia: opening and concluding sections in an improvisatory style surround two fugues which enclose a central free section. The great Passacaglia in C minor BWV 582 also traces its origins to the north, although it far surpasses any of its models in length, motivic variation and dramatic scope. After twenty-one passes through the lengthy passacagalia theme which produce a full-scale piece totalling some 168 bars, a massive fugue breaks out; Bach uses the passacaglia bass-line as the fugue subject and adds in two countersubjects, pursuing the contrapuntal permutations of these themes for more than 100 bars. The formal plan here marks a reversal of the strategy seen in Buxtehude's praeludia of having the passacaglia follow the fugue. The chorale fantasia on *Wie schön leuchtet der Morgenstern* BWV 739, composed at Arnstadt in 1705 or 1706, likewise borrows heavily from the north German tradition in its use of manual changes and sectional treatment of the lines of the cantus firmus.

As C. P. E. Bach noted, Bach also looked south for models, both to Italy and to France (see Williams 1984: 91–102). The Canzona BWV 588 and the Pastorale BWV 590, both of which forsake independent pedal (only the drones of the opening movement of BWV 590 require the use of the pedal), have much in common with the Italian composers and late seventeenth-century south Germans such as Kerll. The five-part writing of the central section of the *Pièce d'Orgue* BWV 572 reflects French influence with its interlocking suspensions, a harmonic idiom derived from the

French Plein Jeu which Bach learned by copying the organ books of 'old French masters', such as Nicolas de Grigny.

In 1708 Bach became court organist to the Duke of Weimar and it is here that he produced most of his organ music. The ducal chapel was a tall, narrow building with the organ placed high above the altar in the third gallery and recessed from the balustrade. Just below the third gallery was a special roof which could be closed in order to make a private organ practice studio. The Duke himself took great pleasure in Bach's playing, encouraging his court organist 'to try every possible artistry in his treatment of the organ' (David and Mendel 1966: 218). The precise makeup of the Weimar organ during Bach's tenure is not known, although it is clear that the instrument displayed some of the prominent features of contemporary central German organ building. It was a modest instrument (twenty-three stops, two manuals and pedal) of suitable size for a ducal chapel. The organ was crowded below the roof of the chapel and, in contrast to the vertical aspect of northern instruments, was spread out horizontally in one case with no *Rückpositiv* (Williams 1984: 124–5). By comparison with the rest of the organ, the pedal division, which was placed behind the main case, was rather large, and even included a 32' Gross Untersatz, along with the Violone 16' and Posaune 16', both of which are nearly ubiquitous in Thuringian organs of the early eighteenth century. The predominance of 8' flues (three on the *Hauptwerk*, and four on the *Positiv*) and the inclusion of 4' colour stops (the Quintadena on the *Hauptwerk*, and the Klein Gedact on the *Positiv*) allowed for an array of subdued combinations. Gentler but less brilliant than the northern organs, the instrument had only one manual reed, a Trompete 8' on the *Positiv*. Characteristic, too, is the Glockenspiel, a row of bells hanging from the outside of the case generally just above the keyboards and played from the top half of the *Hauptwerk* keyboard.

Early versions of the first seventeen of the so-called Great Eighteen Organ Chorales (BWV 651–7) date from Bach's Weimar years, and show the continued influence of Buxtehude, Böhm and Pachelbel on his development as an organ composer. The chorales employ a wide variety of textures and cantus firmus techniques, and demand a level of technical accomplishment far surpassing that of the contemporary organ repertoire. In contrast to these generally retrospective large-scale settings stand the exquisite miniatures of the *Orgelbüchlein*, the first of Bach's unique contributions to the history of organ genres. Probably written between the years 1713 and 1716, the *Orgelbüchlein* chorales demonstrate Bach's command of motivic and harmonic expression within finely wrought contrapuntal textures, in several cases including strict canonic writing. With its subtle variation of colours and distant placement high above the congregation, the Weimar organ would have been ideally suited to the expressive chorales of the *Orgelbüchlein*. On the title-page of the collection Bach articulates his overriding concern with the importance of obbligato pedal in organ pedagogy and chorale composition.

The concentration of musical material found in the *Orgelbüchlein* complements the other great development of Bach's Weimar years, his adoption of compositional techniques learned from Antonio Vivaldi. Copies of Vivaldi's concertos had been brought back to Weimar by the young Duke Johann Ernst in 1713, and from these pieces Bach learned the essential tools that he would use for the expansion and transformation of seventeenth-century genres into large-scale forms. Bach transcribed three of Vivaldi's concertos (BWV 593, 594, 596) for organ with obbligato pedal, along with several others for manuals alone, making careful study in the process of Vivaldi's hard-driving motivic energy, his use of extended circle-of-fifths harmonic sequences, and the formal organising principles based on the alternation of tutti and solo sections. Vivaldian ritornello structure, in which the opening theme (the ritornello) returns in different keys during the course of the piece, provides the often lengthy movements of Bach's later Weimar works with clearly marked formal articulation and a unifying narrative logic.

With such powerful conceptual tools Bach moved away from the multi-sectional layout of the northern praeludium towards the paradigmatic prelude and fugue pair found in his later works. The Toccata and Fugue in D minor BWV 538, the so-called 'Dorian', was probably composed during the Weimar years, and the Toccata clearly reflects Bach's exposure to Vivaldi's music, with its concerto form and indicated manual changes for the 'tutti' ritornellos and the 'solo' episodes. The Toccata in C BWV 564 witnesses the importation of Vivaldian orchestral writing into a genre once reserved for the improvisatory conceits of the north German style. The piece begins with virtuosic manual figures derived from the northern idiom; these exhortations give way to a demanding pedal solo which leads directly into a furious concerto-like movement of an Italianate cast. The Prelude in G major BWV 541 can also be seen as an integration of northern elements and Vivaldian techniques: the piece opens with solo passagework vaguely reminiscent of the north German style, but this figuration runs unbroken into an exuberant movement in simple ritornello form. The expansive Toccata in F BWV 540 begins as an organ point toccata, a favoured genre of Johann Pachelbel and other south German composers, but Bach takes the genre far beyond the range of his predecessors, as he lets loose a pair of canonic voices which chase each other above a sustained pedal note until the drone launches into a lengthy pedal solo built on the opening thematic material. The canonic voices have another go-round, and a second pedal solo leads right into a full-blown ritornello movement of unsurpassed energy, this truly modern music bursting out of the more 'traditional' generic limits of the opening.

The formal cohesion of these pieces contrasts with the irregular texture of the Prelude in A minor BWV 543, whose improvisatory freedom recalls the *stylus phantasticus* of Bach's northern precursors. The motoric fugue that follows owes much to the instrumental music of Reincken, as does the lively Fugue in G minor BWV 542, which may be associated with Bach's visit to Hamburg in 1720 to audition for the post of organist at the Jacobikirche. After a two-hour concert given by Bach at the Katharinenkirche, the ninety-seven-year-old Reincken proclaimed that the traditions of the north German organ art were not dead, but 'lived on' in Bach (David and Mendel 1966: 304). That Bach was an innovator would have been clear to the aged Reincken, but his comment expresses the equally important point that the lineaments of the north German tradition continued to be evident in Bach's music throughout his career, even after the transformations made possible through those lessons learnt from Vivaldi.

The compilation and composition of the six Trio Sonatas BWV 525–30 date from Bach's years at Leipzig, where he served as Director of Music from 1723 until his death in 1750. The set was assembled around 1727 and at least two of the movements – and most likely several more – are transcriptions of Bach's own chamber works. Bach had studied more modest trio textures in French organ music and had explored the organ trio already in the Weimar versions of two chorales from the Great Eighteen, the trios on *Allein Gott in der Höh' sei Ehr* BWV 664a and *Herr Jesu Christ, dich zu uns wend* BWV 655. But the six Trio Sonatas mark yet another of Bach's singular contributions to organ composition in their more highly profiled continuo bass-lines, idiomatic manual writing, and use of ritornello structures. Bach's trios went far beyond the rather more staid and generally shorter genre represented by his French models, and have no antecedents in the modest three-part chorales of Buxtehude and Pachelbel. The Trio Sonatas soon became a benchmark of technical control as they require the organist to manage three independent, and often very demanding, lines divided between two manuals and pedal.

Even while discharging his duties as Director of Music in Leipzig, Bach continued to pursue an active career as recitalist and as organ expert, examining and inaugurating a number of new organs (see Dähnert 1986). An excellent example of contemporary trends in central German organ building during Bach's mature years survives in the Schlosskirche at Altenburg, about thirty miles south of Leipzig (see Figure 16.1). The

Figure 16.1 The organ at Altenburg, Germany, built by Tobias Heinrich Gottfried Trost in 1735–9. This is one of two surviving instruments associated with the Bach family and installed in castle chapels (the other being the Herbst organ of 1732 at Lahm-in-Itzgrund). Both have only two manuals, but are developed with considerable emphasis on *Gravität*, incorporating massive choruses and 32′ pedal stops. In addition a wide choice of solo registers, including semi-imitative string ranks, allows for a new approach to colour and texture anticipating the *galant*. The Altenburg organ was approved by J.S. Bach on completion.

organ was built from 1735 to 1739 by Tobias Heinrich Gottfried Trost, and in September 1738 (or 1739) Bach examined the organ, approving its sound construction and remarking on the great beauty of each stop. The instrument has no *Rückpositiv*, and its forty-five stops are divided between two manuals and pedal in one long case.

Schlosskirche, Altenburg, Trost, 1735–39, II/46 (Dähnert 1980: 22)

Hauptwerk (C–c³)		Oberwerk (C–c³)	
Groß Quintadena	16′	Geigen-Principal	8′
Flaute travers	16′	Quintadena	8′
Principal	8′	Vugara	8′
Bordun	8′	Lieblich Gedackt	8′
Rohr-Flöte	8′	Hohl-Flöte	8′
Spitz-Flöte	8′	Gemshorn	4′
Viola di Gamba	8′	Flaute douce	4′
Octava	4′	Naßat	3′
Klein-Gedackt	4′	Octava	2′
Quinta	3′	Wald-Flöte	2′
Super Octava	2′	Super Octava	1′
Block-Flöte	2′	Cornett	V
Sesquialtera	II	Mixtur	IV–V
Mixtura	VI–IX	Vox humana	8′
Trompete	8′		
Glockenspiel (c¹)			

Pedal (C–c¹)	
Principalbaß	16′
Violonbaß	16′
Subbaß	16′
Octavbaß	8′
Posaunenbaß	32′
Posaunenbaß	16′
Posaunenbaß	8′
(Transmissions from Hw:)	
Quintadenbaß	16′
Bordunbaß	8′
Flaute traversenbaß	16′
Octavbaß	4′
Mixturbaß	VI–VII

Ow–Hw
Hw–Pedal
Tremulant (both manuals)
Tremulant to Vox humana (connected to Vox humana stopknob)

The most remarkable aspect of this characteristically Thuringian disposition is the profusion of 8′ string and flute stops in addition to the principals, all of which allow for an inexhaustible range of highly nuanced registrational possibilities, ideal for trios and expressive chorales. There are a total of only two reeds on the manuals: the Trompete on the *Hauptwerk* and the Vox humana on the *Oberwerk*. The Altenburg instrument possesses a substantial *plenum* which is darker and less brilliant than those of north German organs. The abundance of eight-foot stops and the inclusion of thirds in the Mixtures – a common feature in Thuringian organs – allows for *plena* which render with great clarity the dense polyphony of Bach's Preludes and Fugues, specifically written for *organo pleno*. Thuringian organs of the period bear a much closer resemblance to the symphonic organs of the nineteenth century both in the preponderance of 8′ foundation stops and in the horizontal layout of the organ. But lest empirical observations on the sound quality of these instruments lead to conclusions about the true 'Bach organ', one should remember Bach's praise of the very different Hamburg organs (see Dähnert 1970). Bach was apparently less lavish in his praise for the more famous organs of Gottfried Silbermann; although he found no major faults in these instruments, he criticised them for having mixtures that were 'all too weak', and questioned Silbermann's unwillingness to build new stops, presumably meaning the colourful string stops found on many Thuringian organs such as those by Trost (Williams 1984: 118). Bach's praise for aspects of north and central German organ building is embodied in the large organ of three manuals and fifty-three stops in the Wenzelskirche in Naumburg built by Silbermann's student Zacharias Hildebrandt in 1743–6. Bach, who may have been responsible for Hildebrandt obtaining this important contract, examined and approved the instrument in 1746. The Naumburg organ has a powerful *Rückpositiv* (Hildebrandt used the old case), strong reeds that add considerable force to the large *plena* (without thirds in the mixtures), a massive pedal and a variety of string stops (see Dähnert 1970). Hildebrandt's ability to draw on influences taken from Silbermann, Hamburg and contemporary trends in Thuringian organ building parallels Bach's own genius for synthesising disparate styles.

Wenzelskirche, Naumburg, Hildebrandt, 1743–6, III/53 (Dähnert 1962: 93–5; 192)

Hauptwerk (C,D–c³)		Oberwerk (C,D–c³)	
Principal	16′	Burdun	16′
Quintadehn	16′	Principal	8′
Octav	8′	Hollflött	8′
Spillflött	8′	Praestant	4′
Gedackt	8′	Gemshorn	4′
Octav	4′	Quinta	3′

Hauptwerk		Oberwerk	
Spillflött	4'	Octav	2'
Quinta	3'	Tertia	$1\frac{3}{5}'$
Weit Pfeiffe	2'	Waldflött	2'
Octav	2'	Quinta	$1\frac{1}{3}'$
Sex quintaltra	II	Süfflött	1'
Cornet	IV	Scharff	V
Mixtur	VIII	Vox humana	8'
Bombart	16'	Unda maris	8'
Trompet	8'		

Rückpositiv (C,D–c³)		Pedal (C,D–d¹)	
Principal	8'	Principal	16'
Quintadehn	8'	Violon	16'
Rohrflött	8'	Subbaß	16'
Violdigamba	8'	Octav	8'
Praestant	4'	Violon	8'
Rohrflött	4'	Octav	4'
Fugara	4'	Nachthorn	2'
Nassat	3'	Mixtur	VII
Octav	2'	Posaune	32'
Rausch Pfeiffe	II	Posaune	16'
Cimbel	V	Trompett	8'
Fagott	16'	Clarin	4'

Tremulant (Rp)
Wind coupler

The Preludes and Fugues composed by Bach during his Leipzig years exemplify his mature organ art at its most cerebral, highly controlled yet thrilling. Whereas Bach's early praeludia are filled with a discursive harmonic daring derived from the improvisatory style of the north German organists, the chromatic and contrapuntal explorations of the late pieces take place within a highly wrought and thoroughly thought-out framework; although these mature works are often exuberant there is nothing of the spontaneous here. All of the late preludes use ritornello technique to erect expansive formal structures, from the detailed motivic fabric of the buoyant Prelude in C BWV 547 to the labyrinthine architecture of the Prelude in E minor BWV 548. The fugues too demonstrate a range of formal approaches. In the Fugue in C BWV 547 Bach subjects the bar-long theme to an astounding array of procedures (inversion, augmentation, and inversion with augmentation) in formulating a truly compelling contrapuntal argument. The angular chromaticism of the subject of the great 'Wedge' Fugue in E minor BWV 548 is itself singular, but it is Bach's formal strategy which maps Vivaldian ritornello techniques onto a *da capo* aria form that marks another of his unique contributions to the history of organ composition.

Figure 16.2 Within a few years of returning to his native Saxony from journeymanship in France, the young Gottfried Silbermann was given the contract to build his masterpiece for the Cathedral at Freiberg, Germany. The instrument, completed in 1714, survives with few alterations and was known to J.S. Bach. It exhibits a confident synthesis of local and imported traditions, the most notable of the outside influences being French. The case, incorporating the whole instrument in one homogeneous unit and doing away with the obstruction caused by the old *Rückpositiv*, was designed by the organist, Elias Lindner.

The experiments in form and style evident in the 'Wedge' Fugue parallel the ageing Bach's attempt to produce encyclopedias of musical knowledge. This effort is embodied in the first of the three printed collections of organ music that Bach produced in his last decade, the third part of the *Clavierübung* (Keyboard Practice), published in 1739. This magisterial compendium consists of a total of twenty-one chorale settings (BWV 669–89) and four duets (BWV 802–5) framed by the Prelude and Fugue in Eb BWV 552. The Prelude is itself a synthesis of several national styles; it is a French Overture in Italian ritornello form, with the episodes constructed from an intellectual double fugue. The collection traverses the history of organ music, from the archaic polyphony of the *Kyrie* BWV 669–71, and the retrospective double-pedal setting of *Aus tiefer Not* BWV 686, to the modern Italianate trio on *Allein Gott in der Höh' sei Ehr* BWV 676, and the mixture of extreme chromaticism with *galant* touches in *Vater unser im Himmelreich* BWV 682. Following each of the nine large-scale chorale preludes Bach includes shorter *manualiter* settings that constitute a thorough summation of the small forms first explored in the Neumeister set. The collection closes with the monumental Fugue in Eb (BWV 552) which is in three sections, with the opening *stile antico* subject returning in both subsequent fugues.

The encyclopedic ambitions of the *Clavierübung III* contrast with the aim of the so-called 'Schübler' chorales BWV 645–50, published in the last two years of Bach's life. The set is made up almost entirely of arrangements of movements from Bach's own cantatas; by no means easy to play, the Schübler chorales are, however, less demanding technically than the *Clavierübung III* and may reflect a desire on Bach's part to produce a more popular collection. The Canonic Variations on *Vom Himmel hoch* BWV 769 published in 1748, comprise another chapter in the Bach encyclopedia of strict contrapuntal techniques, the project that dominates his last years. But the variations are much more than an artificial exercise in canonic writing, as Bach adapts the antiquated device of canon to the progressive musical style of the mid-eighteenth century. The collection marks Bach's attempt to synthesise fashionable music with counterpoint, transforming both in the process. Bach's late works crystallise the overarching theme of his organ music, demonstrating as they do his unique genius for taking from the old in his pursuit of the new.

Editions

The most authoritative and thoroughly researched edition of Bach's organ works is the *Neue Bach-Ausgabe*, published by Bärenreiter, whose well-presented volumes mark the pinnacle of scholarly achievement. There is one caveat, however: the editorial decision to regularise the beaming in many instances obscures what are often helpful notational hints as to how to divide passagework between the two hands, an issue that arises frequently in the early free works. Nor does the *NBA* include many pieces that have recently come off the 'spurious' list and are now considered genuine works of J. S. Bach. The place to find these pieces is the first edition of the complete works of J. S. Bach produced in the nineteenth century by the *Bach Gesellschaft*, which, in its entirety, is available only in research libraries. Fortunately, Dover has reprinted several cheap and practical volumes from the *Bach Gesellschaft*, which only occasionally offer readings that differ from those of the *NBA*. The Dover books provide an affordable and compact way to assemble a large collection of Bach organ music, although the print is rather small and in the volume of chorale preludes tenor and alto clefs crop up quite frequently, a frustration for many, but good practice nonetheless. The first complete edition of Bach's organ works, edited by Friedrich Griepenkerl for Peters, is still available, as is a cheaper Kalmus reprint of it. Although the more expensive *NBA* is to be recommended, the Peters is a good edition of considerable historical importance and offers some alternative readings based on now-lost sources. Questions as to which of Bach's keyboard pieces belong to the organ repertory are partially addressed by Heinz Lohmann, who edited the complete edition of Bach's organ music for Breitkopf & Härtel. This edition includes many pieces generally played now only on stringed-keyboard instruments, for example some of the *manualiter* concerto transcriptions. The Novello, Schirmer (ed. Albert Schweitzer) and Bornemann (ed. Marcel Dupré) complete sets present highly edited texts and are to be avoided as playing editions.

17 German organ music after 1800

Graham Barber

In 1845, Félix Danjou, the director of the French firm of organ builders Daublaine-Callinet, writing in the first edition of his magazine *Revue de la musique réligieuse, populaire et classique*, commented on the state of German organ composition:

> In Germany, not a step has been taken since Seb. Bach: the compositions of Adolphe Hesse and of Rinck always belong to the legato fugal style which Bach used exclusively in his works. Without doubt there is more freedom, less constraint, from the standpoint of the use of the legato style, in the compositions of Seb. Bach than is to be seen in the works of modern German composers. (quoted in Kooiman 1995: 57)

Danjou's generalisations on the music of the Thuringian Christian Heinrich Rinck (1770–1846) and the Silesian Adolf Friedrich Hesse (1809–1863), composers who might be said to have laid the foundations for nineteenth-century German organ music, while having an element of truth, are one-sided and not entirely accurate – for example, both composers wrote in equal measure in the legato fugal style and in the free variation manner. If organ music had failed to maintain the lofty standards of J. S. Bach, one has to look at least a hundred years earlier and to forces external to music for the causes of decline. Movements in philosophy and the arts such as *Aufklärung* (Enlightenment) and *Empfindsamkeit* (sensibility) had challenged accepted norms and traditions.[1] The Church lost its centrality in society, and had to compete with man's growing belief in his own self-sufficiency, as well as with a rise in nationalistic fervour. At the same time the demise of the Holy Roman Empire contributed to the impoverishment of the Church and its functions. Georg Feder neatly sums up the combined effect of all this on the early nineteenth-century German (Protestant) church music scene: 'congregational singing that dragged along laboriously; an impoverished liturgy in which music fulfilled a role of questionable value; organ music and organ playing which either cultivated a *galant*, pianistic style or was stiff and pompous; cantatas of slight musical value and choral music that was sentimental or bombastic' (Blume 1975: 376).

Certainly, in German organ music of the first part of the nineteenth century, works of real stature are rare, though there are many carefully crafted compositions which serve well their function as *Gebrauchsmusik*.[2] Rinck, who was born at Elgersburg, in Thuringia, was a pupil of Johann Christian Kittel (1732–1809), who himself was a pupil of J. S. Bach in Leipzig. For most of his working life Rinck was Stadtkantor and Hoforganist at Darmstadt in the Grand Duchy of Hesse-Darmstadt (see Donat 1933). In Part 6 of his *Praktische Orgelschule* Op. 55 (1819–21) he expresses the hope 'that I have not completely failed in my intention to promote a sense of the seriousness of the Church Style, so that beginners at the organ can profit'. Rinck's suggested specification for a two-manual and pedal instrument already shows reliance on the 8′ register as the main sound ideal:

I.Man:	16.8.8.8.8(or 4).4.4.3.2.2.IV.8
II.Man:	8.8.4.4.2.III
Ped:	16.8.8.4

Wolfgang Stockmeier comments thus on Rinck's style in the Foreword to his edition of Rinck's Flute Concerto Op. 55: 'two features in particular stand out: on the one hand the strong interdependence of the Baroque polyphony, and on the other, the pursuit of "modernity" in the manner of Haydn and Mozart'. Rinck undoubtedly shows an assured grasp of the gestural resources of classical concerto form, as well as a fluent technique of melodic extension. The texture is dominated by the top line, and is pianistic in manner, with Alberti basses accompanying the solo lines. As was customary at the time, the pedals merely emphasise the harmonic direction and add textural intensification, as with the double basses in the orchestra.[3] There is certainly much to enjoy, in contrast to the earnestness of Rinck's sacred works. In a later work, the 'Introduction with Four Easy Variations and Finale on a Theme of Corelli' Op. 108, Rinck takes as his model the classical Viennese pianoforte variation. After the Introduction he prefaces each section with an indication of tone colour: Thema: Andante. *Mit sanften Stimmen*; Variation 1: Andante. *Mit Prinzipal und Gedackt 8 Fuss*; Variation 2: Andante con moto. *Mit starken Stimmen*; Variation 3: Andante. *Für 2 Klaviere* (Dolce); Variation 4: Minore. Largo. *Mit starken Stimmen*; Finale: Allegro moderato. *Für volle Orgel*. Towards the end of the Finale Rinck marks a sudden change – Adagio. *Mit Gedackt und Gamba 8 Fuss* – as the music surprisingly modulates from D major (the dominant of the home key) to E♭ major (see Example 17.1). This betrays evidence of the romantic impulse which occasionally surfaces in Rinck's works.

   Rinck never quite shook off the shadow of the academic, serious style – indeed, he positively cultivated it. His *œuvre* is heterogenous, exhibiting baroque features of figuration and sequential treatment, early classical

Ex. 17.1 Rinck, Finale from 'Introduction with Four Easy Variations and Finale on a Theme of Corelli'

galant elements, and traces of romantic yearning. Hesse on the other hand – a generation younger – is clearly a child of the romantic period. He was born in Breslau (present-day Wrocław) and studied with Friedrich Wilhelm Berner (1780–1827), a great-grandpupil of J. S. Bach. Later he had lessons with Rinck at Darmstadt, before being appointed organist of the Bernhardinerkirche in Breslau. There, in 1831, he inherited an organ built by Adam Horatius Casparini dating from 1705–9, which had just been completely rebuilt by Hartig.

Bernhardinerkirche, Breslau, 1831, A. H. Casparini, rebuilt Hartig

Hauptwerk		Oberwerk	
Quintatön	16′	Principal	8′
Quintatön	8′	Flaut amabile	8′
Principal	8′	Salicet	8′
Flaut major	8′	Octave	4′
Spitzflöte	8′	Flaut minor	4′
Gemshorn	4′	Quinta	$2\frac{2}{3}$′
Doppelflöte	4′	Doppelflöte	8′
Superoctave	2′	Mixtur	IV
Mixtur	V	Cymbel	II
Cymbel	II	Oboe	8′
Trompete	8′		

Pedal	
Majorbass	32′
Principal	16′
Subbass	16′

Pedal (continued)

Violon	16′
Major-Quint	12′
Violon	8′
Quintatön	8′
Superoctave	4′
Trompete	8′

Manualkoppel
Pedalkoppel

Hesse altered the organ during his tenure, replacing the Spitzflöte 8′, Quintatön 8′ and Gemshorn 4′ on the *Hauptwerk* with Portunal 8′, Bourdon 16′ and Gamba 8′ respectively, and adding a Posaune 32′ to the Pedal.[4] Hesse's music is finely wrought and begins to make greater technical demands on the player. His Variations on an Original Theme Op. 34 are elegant and refined, while the Fantasie in F minor Op. 57 No. 1 is a free-form piece alternating rhetorical, expressive and contrapuntal elements in an organic construction. Hesse's Introduction to Graun's *Tod Jesu* Op. 84 deserves more detailed commentary. It begins in a solemn E♭ minor marked *Volles Werk* and proceeds to exploit the power of the instrument in massive chords separated by rhetorical pauses. A chromatically conceived five-voiced fugue unfolds in strict manner before being subjected to a series of tortuous modulations, finally arriving at a *stretto* above a dominant pedal, before a statement of the chorale *O Haupt voll Blut und Wunden*. The melody is marked to be played on the *Hauptwerk* on an 8′ stop together with Trompete 8′, and accompanied on Flaut and Salicet 8′, with Pedal Subbass 16′ and Flautbass 8′. This is an impressive piece with no real precedents. In its subjective internalisation of the Passion theme, it demonstrates how the organ could be fully integrated into the mainstream of romanticism. After the Napoleonic Wars, liturgical reform led to the reinstatement of the Protestant chorale which assumed an increasingly central role in the development of German organ music. However, instead of being a pure, objective phenomenon as in the past, it became the vehicle for fantasy, emotion and mystic vision.

As in the baroque period, two types of composition evolved in parallel: the short, liturgical work, usually styled *Choralvorspiel* and suitable for the Divine Service, and the long, complex *Choralfantasie*, for church or concert use. In addition, composers saw the creative possibilities of incorporating the chorale into the organ sonata.[5] Four of the six sonatas by Felix Mendelssohn-Bartholdy have chorale elements, though in each case the chorale has a different function. In Sonata 1 (first movement), the chorale *Was mein Gott will gescheh' allzeit* is a distant continuum of sound, which acts to calm and eventually subdue the *Sturm und Drang* substance of the main musical discourse; *Aus tiefer Not* underpins the central *minore* section of the first movement of Sonata 3; Sonata 5 is prefaced by a simple unadorned chorale; Sonata 6 is a fully developed set of variations on *Vater unser im Himmelreich*, with a fugue based on the opening motif – only the concluding Andante is unconnected with the chorale.

Mendelssohn's organ sonatas continued to exercise an influence over organ composers for the rest of the century. Tracing the legacy of chorale sonatas alone one can find examples in the works of Jan Albert van Eyken, Gustav Merkel, Christian Fink and Josef Labor; echoes are even heard as late as Camillo Schumann (1874–1946). The model is usually Mendelssohn's Sonata 1 first movement, with the second subject function given to the chorale. In this role, the plain, unadorned chorale melody, possessing 'values rooted in historic uniqueness' (Hilgemann and Kinder 1978: 32) is used as an agent to 'dissolve the conflicts between nature and the spiritual' (*ibid.*). There is a direct parallel in the works of the most important Catholic composer for the organ, Josef Rheinberger (1839–1901), whose twenty sonatas are a pivotal achievement. The nineteenth-century repertoire based on Gregorian cantus firmus material is largely ephemeral, consisting of simple versets, preludes and postludes on the main hymns and antiphons. However, in his *Pastoral-Sonate* (No. 3) Op. 88 in G major (1875) Rheinberger uses the eighth Psalm Tone as a formal device in exactly the same way as in Lutheran chorale sonatas – in the last movement it functions as a second subject in the manner of Mendelssohn's Sonata 1, being heard in both ethereal and triumphant guise. In his Sonata No. 4 Op. 98 in A minor (1876) he uses the ninth Psalm Tone, the so-called *Tonus Peregrinus*, which again functions as a second subject (in the first movement) and, metamorphosed in the manner of Liszt, as final peroration in the concluding *Fuga cromatica*. Max Reger (1873–1916) in his Sonata in D minor Op. 60 of 1901, while not using the chorale in a structural way, introduces *Vom Himmel hoch, da komm ich her* with the indication 'sehr lichte Registrierung' as a palliative to the emotional turmoil of the second movement, *Invokation*.

The same romantic concept of triumph over adversity governs the development of the chorale fantasia. Arising out of chorale settings in the baroque period, it acquired new programmatic connotations, notably in the hands of the composer and organ building theorist Johann Gottlob Töpfer, whose three essays of 1859 in the form – which he styles *Concert-Fantasie* – evolve continuously in a highly subjective manner. They are the vehicle for considerable technical display, with demanding manual and pedal semiquaver figuration. Both *Jesu meine Freude* and *Was mein Gott will, das g'scheh' allzeit* end with a full-scale fugue, the subject derived from the chorale melody. The latter, with its clear, tripartite form is in effect a chorale sonata. Töpfer's mastery lies in his strong counterpoint, his refined instinct for registral effect, and his fully integrated, rhetorical style. He undoubtedly drew inspiration from the music of Franz Liszt whose three major works for organ, the Fantasy and Fugue on the chorale *Ad nos, ad salutarem undam* (1850), Prelude and Fugue on *B-A-C-H* (1855/1870) and Variations on *Weinen, Klagen, Sorgen, Zagen* (1863), while standing at the opposite pole to Mendelssohn, had an equally powerful influence. Liszt's predilection for the mystical, and his daring experiments with both harmony and form left no composer of the second half of the nineteenth century untouched. *Ad nos* contains in extended and exaggerated guise all the gestural resources of the the chorale fantasia. *Weinen, Klagen*, while essentially a passacaglia presaging Reger's own towering examples, also has the chorale *Was Gott tut, das ist wohl getan* at the end to resolve the conflict inherent in the chromatic, ostinato theme.[6]

Heinrich Reimann (1850–1906) took the form of chorale fantasia a stage further in his *Wie schön leuchtet der Morgenstern* Op. 25 (1895), when he underlaid successive statements of the chorale theme with the verses of the chorale text, thereby bringing the correlation between verbal sentiment and musical commentary into sharp focus. As organist of the newly dedicated Kaiser-Wilhelm-Gedächtniskirche he became a potent force in the musical life of Berlin, founding a Bach Society and holding regular weekly concerts to promote the Thomaskantor's works. Among his students was Karl Straube (1873–1950), who was to become exceedingly influential in the German organ music scene. *Wie schön* is a cleverly constructed piece which functions as a template for Reger's own works. Reimann shows a strong grasp of Tristanesque harmony as well as a sure contrapuntal instinct. The instrument he had in mind was the large, contemporary organ, of which the firms Walcker, Sauer and Steinmeyer were the leading exponents, stating in the Preface that the Walze (the twelve-stage crescendo pedal which became *de rigueur* on the late Romantic organ) was indispensable to the performance of the work.

The chorale fantasia reaches its zenith in the seven chorale fantasias of Max Reger, written 1898–1900. The difference between Reger and his predecessors is that his works are longer, more complex, more demanding technically and written in that explosively charged style of emotional extremes which characterises all his music. As an example, *Straf' mich nicht in deinem Zorn* (1899) is typical, though it does not have the usual *Schlussfuge*. The text is a free paraphrase of the penitential Psalm 6. The chorale statements are framed and interspersed by freely composed material and the pulse of the music alternately races and slows down in

response to the evocative text. The extrovert style of writing makes pro-
digious technical demands on the player, as Reger himself was only too
well aware. Writing to Georg Stolz he admitted 'it is a miserably difficult
piece of music! It couldn't have turned out any easier simply because of
my inclination towards the mystical' (Hase-Koehler 1928: 91). After
Reger, Sigfrid Karg-Elert, Heinrich Kaminski and Karl Hoyer added their
own distinctive voices to the chorale fantasia. Reger, however, for his part
had exhausted the form and did not return to it again.[7] The *Choralvorspiel*
evolved slowly through the nineteenth century in parallel with the
Choral-Fantasie. It has often been considered that such works were of
little value, and it is true that they sometimes became routine and formu-
laic. However, these small-scale pieces form an important commentary
on the development of the extended concert works.[8]

Despite wide-ranging historical movements and trends in twentieth-
century music – neo-classicism, expressionism, modernism and so on –
the organ music of Max Reger continued to dominate the development of
German organ music. Moreover, it showed remarkable resilience, many
works being completely remodelled by Karl Straube on neo-baroque
lines, and transmitted in this manner through new editions to a whole
generation of performers (see Röhring 1974: 21–29). This process of
'purification', which was in keeping with the *Zeitgeist*, related precisely to
the *Orgelbewegung* ('Organ Reform Movement') with its emphasis on
clear, classical tone and its rejection of exaggeration and excess. Reger's
pupils continued to emulate their master's style while reacting subtly to
new ideals of sound and substance. Joseph Haas wrote free-form works in
the spirit of Reger's Sonata Op. 60 and Suite Op. 92, contributing a Sonata
in C minor Op. 12 (1907), dedicated to Reger, and two Suites in A♭ major
Op. 20 (1908) and A major Op. 25 (1909). The Variations on an Original
Theme Op. 31 (1910) are mainly reflective in character (see Example
17.2) and eschew the temptation of a tempestuous fugal finale in favour of
a sustained crescendo over a dominant pedal point.

    Haas's harmonic style, while complex and intense, is somewhat less
eliptical than his master's. The texture has the transparency of Reger's
middle to late works, and the thematic language tends towards the aphor-
istic. Haas's Ten Chorale Preludes for Organ Op. 3 (1904–5) are directly
modelled on his teacher's 52 Easy Chorale Preludes Op. 67. Karl Hasse
studied with Reger and Felix Mottl in Munich. His Suite in E minor Op. 10
(1913) is in four movements – Improvisation, Larghetto, Capriccio and
Ciacona. The Larghetto (see Example 17.3) shows how completely Hasse
had absorbed Reger's technique of tonal obfuscation within the functional harmonic system.

Ex. 17.2 Haas, Theme from 'Variations on an Original Theme'

Whereas Haas and Hasse remained wedded to the Reger style, Karl Hoyer was able to break free of the mould and forge an individual voice (see Hilmes 1996). While his Introduction, Variations and Fugue on the Chorale *Jerusalem, du hochgebaute Stadt* Op. 3 (1913) is a fully fledged chorale fantasia in the style of his teacher, his *Memento Mori!* Op. 22 (1922), four pieces on the subject of death entitled *Trauerzug, Totenklage, Totentanz* and *Verklärung*, inhabits a completely different sound world in which the predominant influence is Gustav Mahler. Clearly Hoyer had stepped back from the brink of atonality to pursue further the symphonic development of tonal themes.[9] Sigfrid Karg-Elert, though not formally a pupil of Reger, being only four years his junior, nevertheless came under his spell. While he borrows features from Reger in such works as his

Ex. 17.3 Hasse, Larghetto (Suite in E minor)

Symphonic Chorale *Jesu, meine Freude* Op. 87 No. 2 and in his *66 Choral-Improvisationen* Op. 65, the similarities are only surface deep. Karg-Elert does not belong to the Beethoven/Brahms tradition as Reger does: he is a musical chameleon, turning effortlessly from Grieg-influenced folk-song to experimental expressionism, from colouristic impressionism to the neo-baroque. Only occasionally does Karg-Elert consciously strive towards an organic process of composition, as in his Symphony for Organ

Op. 143 (1930) (see Barber 1989: 769–71). More typically he gains inspiration from external sources, as in his remarkable *Seven Pastels from the Lake of Constance* of 1921.

While Reger's pupils and others continued to explore the margins of tonality, new trends and fashions in music had unshakeably asserted themselves. In terms of organ music, neo-classicism rather than serial composition became the dominant force, and in this context Paul Hindemith (1895–1963) is a seminal figure. Despite a contribution of just three sonatas and two concertos, he epitomises the change in emphasis from the *organ as rhetorical machine* to the *organ as chamber instrument*. That is not to say that he was immune to the Reger influence – on the contrary, he considered it a key element in his musical development, stating that 'I owe thanks to Reger more than Bach'. However, in place of the profusion of notes, the unrelieved texture, the white heat of passion one finds an economy of gesture, transparency and coolness. These characteristics were in keeping with the wind of change which had affected the design of organs under the influence of the *Orgelbewegung*. The fact that both Sonata I (1937) and Sonata II (1937) end quietly is indicative of the new aesthetic. Although not a composer of religious music, Hindemith influenced several church musicians directly as Professor of Composition at the Hochschule für Musik in Berlin, where among his pupils were Hans Friedrich Micheelsen and Harald Genzmer. The next generation of composers, who were more directly under the spell of serialism, also benefited from the clear sonorities of the Organ Reform Movement. Wolfgang Stockmeier (b. 1931) has combined *inter alia* dodecaphonic procedures with traditional forms, notably in a series of ten sonatas, of which Sonata V (1976/7) is representative (see Example 17.4).

Since World War II Germany has been the crucible for much *avant-garde* activity, and the presence of György Ligeti in Hamburg, Mauricio Kagel in Cologne and Arvo Pärt in Berlin has exercised a powerful influence on composers of the younger generation. Despite this, the unbroken thread of liturgical organ composition has remained essentially within the conservative Lutheran chorale tradition.[10] As in previous periods, composers have written in large forms – though moving away from the chorale fantasy in favour of the baroque-style chorale partita and chorale concerto – as well as cultivating the short chorale prelude. Significant contributions have also been made in the twentieth century to music based on Gregorian themes.[11]

A survey such as this can only give a flavour of the richness of the nineteenth- and twentieth-century German repertory for organ. Certain pivotal figures inevitably dominate the period: Mendelssohn, Liszt

Ex. 17.4 Stockmeier, 1st movement of Sonata V

Abläufe
Lebhaft

(Hungarian by birth, but living and working in Weimar from 1848) and Reger. In the twentieth century there have been many important organist-composers, though, with the exception of Hindemith, few have occupied a position in the mainstream of Western musical development. The last sixty years have seen a huge upsurge in compositional activity which Adam Adrio attributes to the effect of the *Orgelbewegung* (Blume 1975: 483–95). Certainly, new sound ideals, rooted at least notionally in the past, inspired composers to begin to write in a style that was more relevant to the modern age. Restoration of old, that is, pre-nineteenth-century organs became a priority and has remained so. At the twilight of the twentieth century the situation has come full circle, with the vast organs of the late romantic period, once condemned as bombastic, decadent and irrelevant, being systematically restored to their original condition.

Editions

There are several works in modern editions by Rinck and Hesse. A selection of Rinck's works are in: J. C. H. Rinck, *Selected Works*, ed. Hofmann, 1993, Kassel (Bärenreiter) and of Hesse's works in: Adolph Hesse, *Organ Works*, ed. Stockmeier, 1975, Wolfenbüttel (Möseler). There are two complete editions of Mendelssohn's works: in five volumes, ed. Little, 1989, London (Novello); and in two volumes ed. Albrecht, 1993, Kassel (Bärenreiter). Similarly there are two complete editions of Liszt's works: ed. Margittay, 1970, Budapest/London (Editio Musica Budapest/ Boosey & Hawkes); ed. M. Haselböck, 1985, Vienna (Universal). The most authoritative edition of the works of Brahms (see Pascall 1995) is: ed. Bozarth, 1988, Munich (Henle). The complete sonatas of Rheinberger (reproduction of the original editions) are available ed. Bretschneider, 1991, St. Augustin (Dr. J. Butz Musikverlag) and the complete sonatas of Gustav Merkel, ed. Depenheuer, 1991, St. Augustin (Dr. J. Butz Musikverlag). Selected organ works by Töpfer are available ed. Busch, 1977, Bonn (Rob. Forberg Musikverlag); also Reimann's *Fantasy on the Chorale Wie schön leuchtet der Morgenstern*, ed. Dorfmüller, 1977, Bonn (Rob. Forberg Musikverlag). The complete works of Max Reger, Volumes I–VII, are available ed. Weyer, Wiesbaden (Breitkopf), after the Reger Collected Edition, ed. Klotz. Karg-Elert's works (see Gerlach 1984) are available from various publishers including Leuckart, Breitkopf, Möseler, Novello. The Symphony in F♯ minor Op. 143 is published by Peters edition (ed. Hartmann). There are several collected volumes of indicative material: *The Mendelssohn School*, a collection of organ music by students and colleagues, ed. Leupold, 1979, New York (McAfee); *Leipziger Orgelmusik des 19. Jahrhunderts*, ed. Gurgel, 1995, Wiesbaden (Breitkopf); *Chorale Preludes by Pupils of Reger*, ed. Busch, 1991, Mainz (Schott). Publishing houses specialising in lesser-known repertoire from the nineteenth century are Möseler (Wolfenbüttel), Rob. Forberg Musikverlag (Bonn), Dr. J. Butz Musikverlag (St. Augustin), and Musikverlag Alfred Coppenrath (Altötting). Publishers of the main composers of the twentieth century are as follows: Ahrens (Schott, Willy Müller – Süddeutscher Musikverlag), Bornefeld (Bärenreiter, Universal), Burkhard (Bärenreiter, Schott), David (Peters), Distler (Bärenreiter), Genzmer (Peters), Heiller (Doblinger), Hindemith (Schott), Höller

(Schott, Leuckart), Kaminski (Universal, Bärenreiter), Micheelsen (Bärenreiter), Pepping (Schott), Ramin (Peters), Raphael (Breitkopf), Reda (Bärenreiter), Schmidt (Universal, Leuckart, Weinberger, Doblinger), Schroeder (Schott), Stockmeier (Möseler, Kistner & Siegel).

18 French and Belgian organ music after 1800

Gerard Brooks

The symphonic tradition in French organ music that was to find its first real expression in the works of César Franck had its roots in the period that followed the French Revolution of 1789.

This so-called 'post-classical' era has often been criticised as a time when musical quality fell sharply after the glories of the 'Grand Siècle', but there were important cultural reasons for the changes in public taste that many organists felt obliged to follow. Furthermore, one must distinguish between the music that composers published (often very light in character) and their reputations as performers and improvisers.

The 'Terror' that followed the revolution, when thousands were executed or arrested as 'enemies of the Revolution' also marked the secularisation of the Church: her assets were seized and services abolished, leaving organists (and organ builders) without a livelihood. The churches themselves were used as storerooms, barracks or stables and many organs were sold or destroyed. Stories abound of organists trying to save their instruments by playing patriotic songs, thus following a musical trend that was to reflect the political and military mood of the time. The foundation of the Conservatoire in 1795 and the increasing interest in opera heralded a musical liberation that would mark a decline in solemn church music. Napoleon was not slow to appreciate the power of music as a propaganda tool, asking composers to write music that would glorify his armies: this was the era of 'battle' pieces that were by no means confined to the orchestra. One of the leading organist-composers of the day was Jacques-Marie Beauvarlet-Charpentier (1766–1834), whose 'Victoire de l'Armée d'Italie ou Bataille de Montenotte' (1796) contains all the expected elements (as well as the inevitable dedication to 'Citizen Bonaparte!'): sunrise, reveille, assembling of the troops, departure for battle and so on. To our ears, these sound like precursors of silent film music, and on the large Clicquot organs (such as that in St Sulpice, Paris) the effect would have been sensational. Claude Balbastre (1727–99), writer of a famous set of variations on the Marseillaise, was another composer who had to adapt to changing musical taste of the day.

The beginning of the nineteenth century marked some important musical developments: in 1802, Napoleon installed instrumentalists at

Ex. 18.1 Fessy, *Offertoire*

the Royal Chapel of the Tuileries – gone were the grand motets in favour of music much more in the style of Haydn's masses, with important parts for soloists; in 1803, the Prix de Rome was created to encourage composers; and in 1805, the Concert Spirituel (a series of sacred and instrumental music started in 1725) was reinstated. The musical style of the time took its lead from the opera – melodies in thirds, staccato bass notes with off-beat chords for example – and it was perhaps inevitable that the organ would follow: the subtleties of the Tierce en taille and the Plein Jeu of the previous era disappeared in favour of a simpler, more pianistic style, with short repeated melodic phrases, interrupted cadences followed by codas and so on, as illustrated by Example 18.1, from the *Offertoire* by Alexandre-Charles Fessy.

One of the most successful organists of the time, Nicolas Sejan (1745–1819) is also credited with being one of the founders of the French piano school. This is not to say that more conservative forms were completely absent – fugues, which had always been an established feature of French organ music were still being written, but much more popular with the public was the variation style that found voice in the Noëls and in pieces inspired by the Te Deum, especially the text Judex Crederis. This was an extended fantasy rather like the 'battle' pieces, but depicting the human condition before and after the final judgement of the Last Trump: thunder effects, diminished chords and fanfares were liberally used to dramatic effect. (Thunder effects were achieved by putting a plank across the bottom octave of the pedal and pushing down as required: it is worth noting that the organ builder Cavaillé-Coll included a thunder-effect lever ('tonnerre') throughout the nineteenth century, which produced much the same effect.) It was a matter of some honour that organists of the day improvised their own 'Judex Crederis', so unfortunately few were ever written down; one that survives (by the otherwise serious-minded

Ex. 18.2 Boëly, *Judex Crederis*

composer Alexandre-Pierre-François Boëly) gives an idea of the style (see Example 18.2).

Guillaume Lasceux (1740–1831) also wrote down his own *Judex Crederis* but much more important to our understanding of organ playing of the time is his *Essai théorique et pratique sur l'art de l'orgue* (1809) in which he gives a useful account of performance practice and registrations used by organists of his day: these show that while eighteenth-century sonorities were still used, the practice of drawing foundation stops with reeds – often thought to have started with Franck – was already established.

The sketchiness of some of Lasceux's music also suggests that good organists were both adept at and used to elaborating given material, indicating that the standard of playing was higher than some of the printed music might suggest. Although the compositions of Charles-Alexander Fessy (1804–56) and Louis-James-Alfred Lefébure-Wely (1817–69) reflect the public desire for simple and accessible music, both were highly accomplished performers – Saint-Saëns praised Lefébure-Wely's improvisations in particular. Both were pupils of François Benoist (1794–1878) who became professor of organ at the newly reorganised Paris Conservatoire in 1819 and was an important figure in the evolution of the traditional French organ school (along with Louis Niedermeyer, who founded his 'Ecole de Musique religieuse et classique' in 1853). Benoist was an early winner of the Prix de Rome, and also taught César Franck, Saint-Saëns and Bizet.

While spectacular elements of storm and battle pieces would continue to find echoes in later French organ music, the musical roots of Franck, Guilmant and later Vierne and Widor are to be found in those who held more firmly to the traditional if less appreciated values of harmony and

Ex. 18.3 Boëly, Fantasia and Fugue in B♭

counterpoint: in particular, Franck's teacher Benoist, Alexandre-Pierre-Francois Boëly (1785–1858) and the Belgian Jacques-Nicolas Lemmens (1823–81). Boëly especially was admired by the minority who deplored the current trends in church music, and he stands out as one who, for the most part, refused to give in to the demands of contemporary taste. He was one of the first French composers to give a prominent part to the pedals, and one of the few who revered and regularly played the works of J. S. Bach (something that was to be his undoing, for in 1851 he was sacked from his post at St Gervais for playing music that was deemed too serious). His abilities as a piano composer are evident in his organ music, in which lyrical melodies and use of sonata form sit happily alongside his more contrapuntal works. Of particular note are his Toccata in B minor and the Fantaisie and Fugue in B♭ major (see Example 18.3).

The opposition that Boëly faced in his church situation reflects the secularisation of his time. The decline in polyphonic music meant that the organs of Clicquot were less appropriate to what was being played: the contemporary critic Ortigue noted that the public considered 'the waltz and opera overture the perfect Introit and Offertory . . . this was the price the organ had paid for attempting to imitate the orchestra' (Gorenstein 1993). Many of the old instruments had been destroyed or damaged in the Revolution, and the general trend adopted by builders such as Daublaine-Callinet was towards a more orchestral style of instrument: the suppression of high mixtures in favour of powerful foundation tone and sonorous reeds. A new style of organ was certainly born at this time, but this in itself was not responsible for the change in musical taste – rather builders responded to the mood of the day. One name was to dominate the entire nineteenth century, that of Aristide Cavaillé-Coll.

Aristide Cavaillé-Coll (1811–99)

Cavaillé-Coll's reputation was launched by the organ he built in 1841 for the abbey of St Denis near Paris, which signalled the beginning of the symphonic style of organ building in France. Although this new movement meant that the character of many old organs was lost for ever when Cavaillé-Coll rebuilt them (a fate that overtook Cavaillé-Coll's own instruments in the twentieth century), few were in a playable state, and as the most advanced and able builder of his generation, Cavaillé-Coll produced organs that were to stand as masterpieces in their own right. In 1932, Widor summed it up: 'Our school owes its creation – I say it without reservation – to the special, magical sound of these instruments' (quoted in preface to Widor and Schweitzer's Bach editions).

Cavaillé-Coll was only twenty-two years old when he was awarded the important contract at St Denis in 1833 (see Figure 18.1), defeating several important organ builders of the day, including the Englishman John Abbey. The delay of nine years in completing the organ offers an intriguing insight into Cavaillé-Coll's early development: the original plan to rebuild the Clicquot/Lefèvre instrument of five manuals with seventy-one stops, including cornets, mutations and twenty-two reeds together with various theatrical effects, was different from the plan of 1841, which incorporated many of the new devices that he had learned from other builders and traditions: improved reservoir bellows, Barker's pneumatic lever, Abbey's venetian shutters for the swell, composition pedals and full manual compasses. A talented engineer, he refined all these elements and made them serve his purposes.

St Denis, Paris, Cavaillé-Coll, 1841

Grand Orgue (C–f³, second manual)		Positif (C–f³, first manual)	
Montre (from 2nd oct.)	32′	Bourdon	16′
Montre	16′	Bourdon	8′
Bourdon	16′	Salicional	8′
Montre	8′	Flûte	8′
Bourdon	8′	Prestant	4′
Viole	8′	Flûte	4′
Flûte traversière	8′	Prestant	4′
Prestant	4′	Doublette	2′
Flûte traversière	4′	Flageolet	2′

Figure 18.1 The case of the Cavaillé-Coll organ in St Denis. Cavaillé-Coll won the contract in 1833 with a five-manual scheme along essentially classical lines, but with the incorporation of a few of the theatrical effects popular in the early 1800s. By the time the instrument was completed in 1841 a more romantic note was apparent with the reduction of mutations and the introduction of strings and overblowing harmonic stops. The use of Barker's pneumatic lever, as refined by Cavaillé-Coll, permitted the employment of varied wind pressures and enabled the builder to multiply the number of chests. It was the forerunner of a whole series of large and increasingly sophisticated organs from this most influential of nineteenth-century builders.

Grand Orgue (continued)

Nasard ou Quinte	$2\frac{2}{3}'$
Doublette	$2'$
Grande Fourniture	IV
Petite Fourniture	IV
Grande Cymbale	IV
Petite Cymbale	IV
Cornet à Pavillon	V
Trompette	$8'$
Trompette	$8'$
Basson	$8'$ (bass)
Cor Anglais	$8'$ (treble)
Clairon	$4'$

Récit (C–f^3, third manual)

Bourdon	$8'$
Flûte	$8'$
Flûte	$4'$
Quinte	$2\frac{2}{3}'$
Octavin	$2'$
Trompette	$8'$
Voix Humaine	$8'$
Clairon	$4'$

Pédale (FF–f, i.e. 16$'$ stops effectively 24$'$)

Flûte ouverte	$32'$ (from CC)
Flûte	$16'$
Flûte	$8'$
Nasard	$5\frac{1}{3}'$
Flûte	$4'$
Basse-contre	$16'$
Bombarde	$16'$
Basson	$8'$
Trompette	$8'$
Trompette	$8'$
Clairon	$4'$
Clairon	$4'$

Positif (continued)

Tierce	$1\frac{3}{5}'$
Fourniture	IV
Cymbale	IV
Trompette	$8'$
Cor d'Harmonie	$8'$
Hautboy	$8'$
Cromorne	$8'$
Clairon	$4'$
Tremblant	

Bombarde (C–f^3, played from the second manual)

Bourdon	$16'$
Bourdon	$8'$
Flûte	$8'$
Prestant	$4'$
Nasard ou Quinte	$2\frac{2}{3}'$
Doublette	$2'$
Cornet	VII
Bombarde	$16'$
Trompette	$8'$
Trompette	$8'$
Clairon	$4'$
Clairon	$4'$

Combination pedals and accessories:
Swell pedal
Récit/Grand Orgue
Bombarde on Grand Orgue
Grand Orgue on/off
Positif/Grand Orgue fonds
Positif/Grand Orgue reeds treble
Positif/Grand Orgue reeds bass
manuals to pedal
sub-octave to all manuals

Although St Denis contained overblowing 'harmonic' stops and strident strings, the specification is still a compromise between the old and the new; Cavaillé-Coll was soon building instruments of a more balanced, 'orchestral' nature. A comparison with the famous organ he built at the church of St Clotilde in 1859 (where Franck was appointed Organist) shows how far behind he left the organ of St Denis:

St Clotilde, Paris, Cavaillé-Coll, 1859

Grand Orgue (C–f³, first manual)		Positif (C–f³, second manual)	
Montre	16′	Bourdon	16′
Bourdon	16′	Montre	8′
Montre	8′	Flûte harmonique	8′
Flûte Harmonique	8′	Bourdon	8′
Gambe	8′	Gambe	8′
Bourdon	8′	Salicional	8′
Prestant	4′	Prestant	4′
*Octave	4′	*Quinte	$2\frac{2}{3}$′
*Quinte	$2\frac{2}{3}$′	*Doublette	2′
*Doublette	2′	*Clarinette	8′
*Plein Jeu	VI	*Trompette	8′
*Bombarde	16′	*Clairon	4′
*Trompette	8′		
*Clairon	4′		

Récit (C–f³, third manual)		Pédale (C–d¹)	
Flûte harmonique	8′	Soubasse	32′
Bourdon	8′	Contrebasse	16′
Viole de gambe	8′	Flûte	8′
Voix celeste	8′	Octave	4′
Basson-hautbois	8′	*Basson	16′
Voix humaine	8′	*Bombarde	16′
*Flûte octaviante	4′	*Trompette	8′
*Octavin	2′	*Clairon	4′
*Trompette harmonique	8′		
*Clairon	4′		

(starred stops are controlled by the 'anches' pedals)
Couplers:
Tirasse Grand Orgue (Great to pedal)
Tirasse Positif
Tirasse Récit
Grand Orgue sur machine (Grand Orgue on)
Copula Positif sur Grand Orgue
Copula Récit sur Positif
Octaves Graves Grand Orgue (Grand Orgue sub-octave)
Octave Graves Positif

Octave Graves Récit
Anches Pédale
Anches Grand Orgue
Anches Positif
Anches Récit
Tremblant Récit (Récit tremulant)
Expression Récit (swell pedal)

Here we see characteristics of the more mature Cavaillé-Coll style: a Positif that is effectively a second Grand Orgue (which has particular significance when interpreting romantic French music on English organs with their much gentler Choir departments), and the generous provision of varied foundation tone. The Pedal department on these organs was voiced with particular care to give it sonority and independence, despite the apparent lack of 16′ flue stops; even relatively small instruments have reeds and flues at 16′, 8′ and 4′ pitch, all designed to have a robust tone and to speak promptly (again, this has implications when playing French repertoire on organs with gentler Pedal flue departments). The manuals are in a different order from the English system (which can pose problems where quick or complex changes between Positif and Récit are indicated):

	France	*England/America*
Top	Récit	Swell
	Positif	Great
Bottom	Grand orgue	Choir

The only exception to this is when the Positif is in a case behind the player's back; it is then playable from the lowest manual, for mechanical reasons. Cavaillé-Coll made considerable use of the Barker lever (named after its inventor, Charles Barker), a pneumatic device which assisted the key action – particularly on larger instruments – and also enabled him to experiment with different wind pressures for certain stops. It also enabled him to construct double chests for the manual departments, enabling the reeds and mixtures to be brought on separately from the foundation stops with a series of combination pedals; in addition, the Grand Orgue has its own combination pedal, all of which enables the player to achieve a crescendo from *pp* to full organ without having to change manuals or take his hands away from the keyboard. (To achieve this all the stops are drawn, but the combination pedals remain in the unhitched position; the player plays on the Grand Orgue manual with the Récit coupled through with the box shut. He then progressively hitches down the pedals that add the Positif/Grand Orgue coupler, the Grand Orgue itself, and then the reeds of the various departments in turn.) The 'Jeux de Combinaison' that are brought on by the 'anches' pedals can be pre-set in any desired

Figure 18.2 Layout of combination pedals at St Ouen, Rouen (Cavaillé-Coll, 1890), explained in Table 18.1, opposite.

combination of reeds and upperwork. This system (invented before the days of adjustable pistons), together with the unique sound of the Cavaillé-Coll organ, has exercised an influence that cannot be over-estimated on all French organ composers of the romantic period and beyond (see Figure 18.2 and Table 18.1).

Franck and Lemmens

While minor composers were quite able to dazzle their listeners with thunderous effects on the new style of organ that Cavaillé-Coll began to build in the 1840s, it took a new generation of composers to exploit the true value of his symphonic instruments. The two most influential early figures of the nineteenth-century French organ school were not French at all but Belgian. César Franck (1822–90) was born in Liège and moved to Paris in 1835, taking up his famous appointment as organist at St Clotilde in 1859 and at the Paris Conservatoire as Professor of Organ in 1872, succeeding Benoist. Franck developed relatively late as a composer, having spent his earlier years teaching and performing. His preference for orchestral and chamber music (rather than the more popular form of opera) kept him from being a mainstream composer, but it also meant that he was familiar with the symphonic poems of Liszt. These had a decided influence on his music, including the organ works (particularly the *Grande Pièce Symphonique*). Liszt's mastery of thematic transforma-

Table 18.1

Combination Pedals at St Ouen, Rouen

From left to right

Pedal Couplers	GO/Ped Pos/Ped Rec/Ped
Reeds or 'Jeux de Combinaison'	Ped Bombarde Positif Récit
Sub-octave couplers	GO Rec/GO
Swell Pedal	
Couplers to GO	GO/GO Pos/GO R/GO B/GO
Sub-octave coupler	R/R
Tremulant	R
Coupler	Pos/R (sic)
Super-octave coupler	R/R
Coupler	B/R

tion is constantly echoed in Franck's music: Franck's device of increasing the interval of a simple phrase, thereby creating a sense of yearning, is an integral feature of his style, seen here in the *Prélude, Fugue et Variation* (Example 18.4).

He wrote only a dozen major works for the organ: the *Six Pièces* of 1860–2 (admired by Liszt, who heard Franck play them in 1866), which include the *Prélude, Fugue et Variation* and the *Grande Pièce Symphonique*; the *Trois Pièces* of 1878; and the *Trois Chorals* (his best known organ pieces), completed just before his death in 1890. Franck's organ music, with its powerful chromatic harmony serving emotionally charged melodic themes, owes much to his spiritual nature, somehow fusing together a sacred vision with a secular style that is not far from Wagner, and which was to be further developed in the music of his pupil Louis Vierne.

Jacques-Nicolas Lemmens (1823–81) was appointed Professor of Organ at the Brussels Conservatoire in 1849, and created a considerable impression with his playing in Paris in the 1850s. Both men were fervent advocates of Bach (Lemmens was a pupil of the German organist Adolf Hesse, who could claim a teacher–pupil relationship that led directly back to Bach), but while Franck is said to have played with a good deal of rubato (particularly in his own works), Lemmens's style was more

Ex. 18.4 Franck, theme from *Prélude, Fugue et Variation*

serious: 'purity, elegance and clarity' (Archbold and Peterson 1995: 51) were the words that contemporary critics used to describe his playing (words that would later be applied to his pupil Guilmant). Benoist spoke of his 'calm and religious grandeur and strictness of style which suited God's temple so well . . . In these days it is a virtue to stay faithful to the . . . true art of the organ' – a veiled criticism of the popular style of the day adopted by Lefébure-Wely and others (although Lefébure-Wely was just as quick to compliment Lemmens on his playing). While Franck's teaching at the Conservatoire had more to do with musical interpretation and improvisation than technique, Lemmens's principal contribution to the history of the French organ school was an organ method, his *Ecole d'orgue* (1862), in which he advocated a legato style of playing that required a sure and supple technique: toes and heels in the pedal, finger substitution, surreptitious sliding from note to note, subtle tying of notes together in the manuals and so on. Lemmens is also remembered as the teacher of Guilmant and Widor.

The organ symphony: Guilmant, Widor, Vierne and Dupré

Several influential organist-composers emerged in the 1860s and 1870s in Paris: Saint-Saëns at La Madeleine, Gigout at St Augustine, Guilmant at La Trinité and Widor at St Sulpice. Camille Saint-Saëns (1835–1921) as a pupil of Benoist was very much a traditionalist with a knowledge and love of his musical heritage, and this is reflected in his organ music; he resisted many of Cavaillé-Coll's proposed changes to the Clicquot organ at St Merry (where he was appointed in 1858), and encouraged his pupils at the Niedermeyer School to study Bach as a preparation for their own composition. Gigout, best known for his Toccata in B minor and the *Grand Chœur Dialogué*, also wrote pieces in quieter style using Gregorian themes. It is however to Félix-Alexandre Guilmant (1837–1911) and Charles-Marie Widor (1844–1937) that we owe the creation of the so-called 'organ symphony' ('suite' better describes the nature of these multi-movement works). Both men came from organist families, were taught by Lemmens and acknowledged their debt to the instruments of Cavaillé-Coll. (Widor even went so far as to say that the Cavaillé-Coll organ was the perfect Bach organ – a view that would not find favour today.) They both had a lasting effect on their generation of pupils, and although both were rigorous in their academic approach to organ study, their musical characters were different. Widor was a visionary, wanting to take the musical language of the organ to new heights: 'the modern organ is essentially symphonic; the new instrument needs a new language, a different ideal from that of textbook polyphony'. Guilmant, on the other hand, looked more to the masters of the past, knowledge of whom enabled him to achieve an elegance in his compositions which made up for a slight lack of originality. Although Guilmant was the more wordly of the two, well travelled as a performer, he confined his writing to the organ, whereas Widor's organ music only accounts for about 10 per cent of his output.

Guilmant's organ music is divided into concert music (including eight symphonies), and the comprehensive sets of liturgical music for use in services. His concert music is vigorous in style, combining a lightness of touch with a keen ear for popular taste, often creating exciting music from modest themes. The wit and good humour found in Guilmant is also found in Widor, but there is a heightened sense of drama, achieved through marked use of contrasting timbres together with a vigorous use of rhythm, from dramatic pause to the use of staccato (in which a note is halved in value, following the teaching of Lemmens) – notably in his famous Toccata from the Fifth Symphony. Widor wrote ten organ symphonies, the last two being in a different style: *Symphonie Gothique* (1895) and *Symphonie Romane* (1900) are both based on plainsong themes and share an intensely spiritual and timeless quality. More than any other composer, Widor succeeded in marrying together the different divisions (reeds, strings and flues) of the Cavaillé-Coll organ into a single huge 'orchestra' without sacrificing its nobleness of character. Louis Vierne (1870–1937) judged Guilmant to 'know the organ best', but Widor he considered 'the greatest French organist'.

Vierne was a pupil of both Franck and Widor and, as assistant to Guilmant at the Conservatoire, had an important influence as a teacher. Although Vierne's music has all the qualities he learned from Widor and Franck – lyrical themes and a strong sense of architecture among them – there is an added dimension of powerful chromatic harmony; moreover, there is an overwhelming sense that the sadnesses of Vierne's personal life were projected through his music in a way not found in Widor or Guilmant, resulting in music that is at times joyful, at times restless and tormented, particularly towards the end of his life, as seen at the outset of his Sixth Symphony (Example 18.5).

As well as six symphonies, Vierne composed sets of *Pièces en Style Libre* and *Pièces de Fantaisie*, which are often descriptive in character ('Sur le

Ex. 18.5 Vierne, 1st movement of Symphony No. 6

Rhin', 'Fantômes', 'Carillon de Westminster'). Vierne was not alone in writing descriptive music: the new century saw the emergence of a new school of organ composition in France influenced by the success of Debussy's impressionist music; this 'colourist' school produced descriptive works often based around visual impressions: Ermend Bonnal's *Paysage Euskariens* is one of the best examples.

Although there were many highly accomplished organist-composers in the early part of the nineteenth century – among them Joseph Bonnet (1884–1944) and the short-lived Auguste Barié (1883–1915) – the most important figure and the man who was to renew the language of the symphonic organ was Marcel Dupré (1886–1971), who succeeded Widor at St Sulpice in 1934. Dupré was hailed all over the world as a performer and improviser, and had an immense influence through his many pupils. His style is unashamedly virtuosic (the Three Preludes and Fugues of 1920 were at first deemed unplayable), combining a sparkling dexterity in early works with an increasing harmonic intellectualism later on; above all, he had an absolute mastery of form and counterpoint. He often used Gregorian themes, notably in his *Symphonie-Passion* (1924). *Le chemin de la croix* (1932), which depicts the stations of the cross, is a brilliant if austere series of tone pictures. His Second Symphony (1929) is a landmark of original twentieth-century symphonic style. Dupré was also very active as an editor, producing his own editions of most of the standard organ repertoire. A near contemporary and fellow symphonist was the

Belgian organist and teacher Joseph Jongen (1873–1953), best remembered for his *Sonata Eroica* (1930).

Tournemire, Alain and Messiaen

If Dupré was the natural successor to the symphonic school of Widor, then Charles Tournemire (1870–1939), a pupil of Franck (and his eventual successor at St Clotilde), dominated the liturgical movement in early twentieth-century French organ music. His *L'Orgue Mystique* (a set of fifty-one Catholic 'Offices' each comprising five movements) used plainchant in a new way combining symphonic and liturgical traditions, but in the grand variation style of Beethoven rather than that of Widor. With its freedom of ebb and flow, the spirit of improvisation – of which Tournemire was a master – is never far from this music.

The mysticism of Tournemire is also found in the music of Jehan Alain (1911–40), whose career was cut short by the Second World War. Alain's highly original style, combining a limpid freshness with a passionate joy and sense of commitment, has no basis in any particular school, and although rhythm plays a fundamental role (as in his most famous piece *Litanies*), the music demands to be freed from any sense of metronomic confinement, just as the formal titles Alain used (Prelude and Fugue, Variations etc.) are treated with considerable freedom. His greatest work, *Trois Danses*, originally intended for orchestra, is intense music that seeks to reflect the human conditions of joy, grief and struggle ('Joies', 'Deuils', 'Luttes'). While Tournemire and Dupré remained faithful to the symphonic ideal of the Cavaillé-Coll organ, Alain sought new colours that sprang from his love of the classical organ of the past. Olivier Messiaen (1908–92) was also able to draw on sonorities resulting from a new style of organ building that reacted against Cavaillé-Coll and his followers and returned to the ideals of the eighteenth century (often by attempting to adapt existing symphonic instruments, with predictably poor results).

Like Alain, Messiaen created his own distinctive style outside of the symphonic tradition, exploiting even further the atmospheric, static qualities of which only the organ is capable: this is well illustrated in his early work *Le Banquet Céleste* (1928) and in *L'Ascension* (1933). Messiaen's music makes much use of religious imagery, often through the use of specific texts. His treatment of harmony as a decoration rather than as a means of progression is matched by his unusual treatment of form, in which a theme often grows out of development (rather than the other way round); this 'development–exposition' is seen in *La Nativité du Seigneur*, in which Messiaen also first used rhythmic motifs developed from Indian models. A third important element is his system of 'modes of limited transposition', a series of scales that form the basis for composition (rather as the twelve-tone row did for Schoenberg). The imitative use of birdsong in later works – *Messe de la Pentecôte* (1950) and *Livre d'Orgue* (1951) among them – makes peculiarly effective use of the high-pitched mutation stops of the contemporary organ.

Two other important composers of the twentieth century were Tournemire's prolific successor Jean Langlais (1907–91) and Maurice Duruflé (1903–85). Langlais's dramatic and colourful use of religious and poetic themes found particular voice in relatively short works such as his *Trois Paraphrases Gregoriens* (1934); in later years he also experimented with more contemporary techniques. Duruflé's subtle registrations, impressionistic style and distinctive use of Gregorian themes owes much to his teachers Tournemire and Vierne. He produced just a handful of masterly pieces, among them the *Suite* (1934). Mention should also be made of the Belgian Flor Peeters (1903–86), whose works combine both French and Flemish characteristics with an appealing use of modal harmony.

After a period of reaction against the symphonic organ, the late twentieth century has seen a re-evaluation of the symphonic instruments of Cavaillé-Coll and his followers alongside the organs of the classical age; this, together with the construction of historical copies as well as the sympathetic restoration of existing instruments, has led to a greater respect for the romantic style of organ building and related composition, assuring its place as an indispensable part of the French organ tradition.

Editions

All of the principal composers are published by the French publishing houses Durand, Leduc, Lemoine and Hamelle. There are also American editions of Vierne and Widor by Kalmus (which are photocopies of the original French edition) of Franck by Dover (a copy of the Durand landscape edition) and a new edition of Widor by AR Editions (ed. Near). Langlais is published by Leduc, Bornemann and Combre, Tournemire by Heugel. The complete works of Boëly may be found in Bornemann. Of the minor composers, some of Lefébure-Wely's music is published by Harmonia-Uitgave and Oxford University Press, and that of Fessy and Beauvarlet-Charpentier by Chanvrelin.

19 British organ music after 1800

Andrew McCrea

In 1812, A. F. C. Kollmann, the German-born theorist and organist at the Royal German Chapel, St James's Palace, summarised the state of organ music in Britain as follows:

> Though very fine compositions for the organ have been published by Mr. S. Wesley, and by other able masters, they are still for manual keys only, and the use of obligato [sic] pedals is not yet promoted by them. But a true idea of the latter begins now to become pretty general, by increasing circulation of Sebastian Bach's Organ Trios, and of other works for the Organ, published by Messrs. S. Wesley and Horn. (Kollmann 1812: 15)

Kollmann's expression of confidence in Bachian textures as models for the future development of a British organ repertoire is not surprising given his profound interest in his countryman's music. He found it remarkable, however, that despite London's importance as 'the most opulent city on the face of the globe', there was not a single instrument equal to the organs of Germany and the Netherlands, and that even some of the most populous and richest churches in England lacked an organ. He further lamented the general inadequacy of an organist's remuneration and concluded that organ playing as a 'particular study' was not encouraged as on the continent (Kollmann 1812: 21).

Kollmann's thirty-year residency in London notwithstanding, the typical British organ must have remained ineffectual in his opinion when compared with the continental giants at Haarlem, Weingarten and Hamburg (Michaeliskirche), and the *laissez-faire* attitudes to the art of organ playing perplexing. The extant 1764 John Byfield organ at St Mary's, Rotherhithe (restored by Noel Mander in 1959; see Figure 5.9, p. 69) provides an excellent opportunity to see what Kollmann knew as a large indigenous organ around the time of his arrival, an instrument fully commensurate with the full and solo-stop voluntaries of Stanley, Boyce, Walond and their imitators then in circulation. However, things were not at a standstill at the time Kollmann was writing. The extant 1821 Henry Lincoln organ built for St John's Chapel, Bedford Row, London (now at Thaxted Parish Church, Essex) shows – as the only largely unaltered organ from the opening of the nineteenth century – a stop-list similar to those of its forebears but with some innovatory shifts. Although not enough to satisfy a European viewpoint, it did however demonstrate a change in musical sensibilities. Its additional unison pedal pipes, fortification of 8′ Open Diapason tone, and shift away from the mounted Cornet stop – used previously for movements which, according to William Crotch's contemporaneous comment, were 'vulgar, trifling and ridiculous' – reflected orchestrally inspired concerns for strength and timbral cohesion (Thistlethwaite 1990: 3–48).

Thaxted Parish Church, Essex, Henry Lincoln, 1821

Great Organ (FF,GG–f^3)

Open Diapason Front	8′
Open Diapason (C)	8′
Stopped Diapason	8′
Principal	4′
Twelfth	$2\frac{2}{3}$′
Fifteenth	2′
Sesquialtra (FF–b)	IV
Cornet (c^1–f^3)	IV–III
Mixture	II
Trumpet	8′

Choir Organ (FF,GG–f^3)

Dulciana (FF–e grooved)	8′
Stopped Diapason	8′
Principal	4′
Flute	4′
Fifteenth	2′
Bassoon	8′

Swell Organ (e–f^3)

Open Diapason	8′
Stopped Diapason	8′
Principal	4′
Cremona	8′
Hautboy	8′
Trumpet	8′

Pedals (FF–c)

Pedal pipes	8′ [open wood pipes]

Swell/Great
Great/Pedal
Choir/Pedal

Nevertheless, Kollmann did acknowledge the skills of 'numerous able performers'. Though unnamed, William Russell (1777–1813) would presumably have ranked in his estimation as one of them. As a naturalised subject, Kollmann must have been familiar with a professional like Russell: perhaps a not untypical British 'jobbing' musician whose eclectic way of life – not confined to one 'particular study' – was reflected in the scope and proficiency of the music he wrote. Russell held a number of church appointments, eventually becoming the organist at St Anne's, Limehouse in 1798 and (from 1801) at the Foundling Hospital. He followed his teacher Samuel Arnold in mixing sacred and secular employment by becoming composer and pianist to Sadler's Wells Theatre and Covent Garden.

Samuel Wesley (1766–1837), a friend and colleague, lauded Russell's abilities as an organist and highlighted his commanding powers as an improviser and accompanist. Commenting on the two sets of *Twelve Voluntaries, for the Organ or Piano Forte* (1805 and 1812), he found them to be 'distinguished by Richness, Elegance and Variety', and the fugues to be the product of successful study.[1] The substantial instruments (with pull-down pedals) at both Limehouse and the Foundling Hospital, together with Russell's youthful immersion in the concert and theatrical mainstream, assured the maintenance of his wide musical palette. The eighth Voluntary from the first set provides an interesting bridge from the eighteenth to the nineteenth centuries: a dignified Diapason movement and a fugue surround a decorous Andantino for Hautboy and Cremona stops. These stops are twice combined and supported by pedal to form a trio texture (see Example 19.1). A separate stave for pedal was used by Russell in the second set.

The first appearance of published organ music by Samuel Wesley, the Op. 6 *Voluntaries*, occurred between 1805 and 1808.[2] Following soon after Russell's first set, nine voluntaries were published separately during this period and three more appeared between 1814 and 1817, the whole set being reissued together as *Twelve Voluntaries* (1819). The composer's attempt to encapsulate many varied moods within this traditional genre speaks of his broad interests and searching imagination. These multi-sectional works, together with the *Duett for the Organ* of 1812, explore the full extent of the organ of the period: slow and expressive movements for the Diapasons, occasional trumpet tunes, cantabile movements for Swell stops, and fugues for Full Organ (with or without the Trumpet) in the spirited Handelian manner or in a graver, more archaic style.

Wesley's taste for fluid changes of dynamic – approaching the suppleness of contemporary pianoforte writing – is clearly to be seen in the deft manual changes and use of the swell box in the first and second movements of Voluntary No. 5, and his sense of grave splendour – presumably helped by his familiarity with the European sacred vocal music

Ex. 19.1 Russell, 2nd movement 'Andantino' of Voluntary No. 8 (Set 1)

performed at the Portuguese Embassy Chapel – can be heard in the C minor 'Prelude' and 'Fugue' which stand as No. 3. Voluntary No. 9 in G minor/major, and the later No. 10 in F major (1814) are both multi-sectional but nonetheless coherent pieces ending in energetic fugues, and No. 11 in A major is a grandiose prelude followed by a fugue whose tonal excursions presage the chromatic writing of his son, Samuel Sebastian Wesley, in his Introduction and Fugue [in C♯ minor] (published in 1836, rev. 1869).

Wesley's contribution to the British organ concerto should not be overlooked.[3] The last flowering of a genre closely associated with Handel and his performances of oratorios, Wesley followed his brother Charles's lead (he composed fourteen concertos between 1775 and 1780) with five concertos, of which only the second and third survive intact. The second in D major (or possibly the first in B♭?) was performed at the first performance of Haydn's *Creation* under Salomon. It was a popular work and received a considerable number of performances and alterations over the years, including the addition of Bach's D major Fugue from Book I of the '48' in 1809.

This Concerto – once more with the Bach Fugue – made a further appearance in 1810 at Covent Garden during a performance of *The Messiah*, and a similar arrangement of Bach's E♭ Prelude BWV 552i by Wesley's colleague Vincent Novello (1781–1861), for the former to play at the Hanover Square Rooms in 1812, continued the fashion for orchestrating such works. Wesley's introductory duet to Bach's 'St Anne' Fugue BWV 552ii, performed at the benefit concert for William Russell's wife and children in 1814, is a good example of the period's sense of freedom in reinventing repertoire, Wesley's indefatigable advocacy of Bach's music and the ways in which the shortcomings of the British organ were circumvented (see Example 19.2).[4]

Thomas Adams (1785–1858) was renowned as both a performer and a composer. Although he was revered as a virtuoso player of transcriptions and as an extempore player, his published music for organ – apart from a handful of pieces which exude the concert platform quite plainly – is often extremely learned in character. The *Six Fugues for the Organ or Piano Forte* (1820) demonstrate Adams's knowledge of strict, book-learnt fugal writing in preference to older, scantier imitative counterpoint. The involved textures, dense and often awkward, imply the use of pedal pull-downs as a helping 'third' hand, and the various subjects delineate quite different moods in each case: the Handelian repeated idea of the third, the solid *stile antico* of the fourth in F minor, and the lyrical grazioso theme of the sixth in E major. Fugal writing became a central feature of his later works, for example the *Six Organ Pieces* (1825) dedicated to Thomas Attwood (1765–1838; composer, Organist of St Paul's Cathedral, friend of Felix Mendelssohn-Bartholdy and dedicatee of the latter's *Preludes and Fugues* Op. 37), as did Mozartian expressiveness in slower movements. The 'Pastorale' of the second Organ Piece notates the pedal part on a separate stave.

Keen to achieve a new status for an instrument increasingly seen as inadequate, the organ building and organ playing progressives gradually formulated their plans for larger and timbrally richer instruments. Although inspired by renowned continental organs, such plans usually showed their clear derivation from older home-grown instruments. The dissemination of J. S. Bach's organ works, and their adoption as models of all that was laudable in writing for the organ (the earlier efforts of Samuel Wesley and his so-called 'Sebastian Squad' coming to fruition with Mendelssohn's performances of Bach in England in the 1830s and 40s), also contributed to the mood for change. Their importance as a catalyst for the recalibration of organ technique and compositional aspirations cannot be underestimated. Travel abroad played its part too. The London critic Edward Holmes visited Dresden in 1827 and heard the famous

Ex. 19.2 S. Wesley, 'Introduction to Bach's "St Anne" Fugue'

Johann Schneider play Bach (fugues from the '48'). His first-hand opportunity to sample the capacity of the Silbermann organ to realise the polyphonic wholesomeness of Bach's music and observe Schneider's pedal technique was something that Samuel Wesley's generation had been denied. Holmes remained in control of his enthusiasm however. Wishing to preserve national identity, he asked if there existed a mechanic able to unite this foreign magnificence with the 'sweet *cathedral* [Holmes' italics] quality of tone for which those [organs] of the Temple, Westminster Abbey, &c. are noted' (Holmes 1828: 193). Builders like William Hill and Frederick Davison were eventually in a position to make real Holmes's vision: practical men whose domestication of continental organs really meant surpassing them in 'purity, power, and grandeur of tone' (Hill's words in his *Circular*, 1841), whilst defending what the preface to *Hamilton's Catechism* called 'the superiority of make and voicing of the pipes in the English organs' (Warren 1842: iv).

The British organ world of the second half of the nineteenth century was thus a changed place, and it displayed its metamorphosis in several ways: through organs based on continental principles (often termed the 'German System': C rather than FF or GG manual and pedal compasses (Thistlethwaite 1990: 181–214), coherent choruses augmented by additional colourstops, and equal temperament); through the availability of German and French organ music (overtly didactic in the case of Rinck's *Practical Organ School*, edited by Samuel Wesley and W. T. Best, amongst others); through works of more general inspiration to the British by Mendelssohn, Hesse, Merkel and later Rheinberger; and through the practitioners (composers for the organ were invariably organists) for whom *obbligato* pedal playing was the norm.

Samuel Sebastian Wesley's organ playing was considered to be 'similar to Mendelssohn's, and . . . distinguished by its classical purity' (*The Musical World* 18, 1843: 311) but, as the heir to his father and Adams (under whose influence he came in the 1830s), he was every inch the culmination of indigenous trends as well as an important link to the future. Eccentric in his retention of GG compass though involved in the design of new organs, and vehement in his opposition to the introduction of equal temperament despite the often acute chromaticism of his music, he possessed a creative and high-principled musicianship – an inspiration to his contemporaries and the next generation – which ultimately outweighed the idiosyncrasies.

Wesley was unparalleled as an extempore player, his published music often, as it were, 'photographing' the wayward part-playing, virtuosity and spontaneous shift from idea to idea. The two sets of *Three Pieces for a Chamber Organ* (1842) evince his spontaneity and search for an expressiveness (as in the Larghetto in F♯ minor from the second set) that the organ had hitherto not shown at the hands of his father or Adams. A young Hubert Parry heard Wesley improvise in 1865 and his report helps us recapture the robust counterpoint and note-spinning which would inevitably have had Bachian connotations:

> He began the accompaniment in crotchets alone, and then gradually worked into quavers, then triplets and lastly semiquavers. It was quite marvellous. The powerful old subject came stalking in right and left with the running accompaniment entwined with it – all in the style of old Bach.
>
> (Graves 1926: I, 56–7)

Despite the republication of Wesley's works with alterations for new C compass organs, it was left to the new entrepreneurs of the organ, Henry Smart (1813–79), W. T. Best (1826–97), and a host of others working in the aftermath of Mendelssohn's visits to England, including Edmund Chipp, Edward J. Hopkins and Sir Frederick Gore Ouseley, to explore new frontiers. Through their music they codified technique, implied good taste and thereby allowed the reconstituted instrument to come of age. For 'particular study', the lack of which Kollmann had earlier regretted, the College of Organists (from 1893 the Royal College of Organists) was founded in 1864.

Smart's music was, like Wesley's, born of improvisation. His biographer, William Spark (the organist, and with Smart, the designer of the new Leeds Town Hall organ by Gray & Davison), said of his improvisation on 'God Save the Queen' at the opening of the Leeds organ in 1859 that it had:

> the cunning hand of my old master, Dr. Samuel Sebastian Wesley; the subtle craft of Professor Haupt, in Berlin; the brilliant fancy of Lefébure Wely; the graceful melodies of Edward John Hopkins; [and] the thoughtful imagery of Alexandre Guilmant. The variations did not include the customary scale and arpeggio passages, but all were in due form and proportion – imitative, brilliant, diatonic, chromatic, canonic, choral, and fugal.   (Spark 1881: 209)

Leeds Town Hall, Gray & Davison, 1859

Great Organ (C–c⁴)

FRONT GREAT		BACK GREAT	
Double Diapason, metal	16′	Bourdon	16′
Open Diapason	8′	Flute à Pavillon	8′
Spitz Gamba	8′	Viola	8′
Stopped Diapason	8′	Flute Harmonic	8′
Octave	4′	Quint	$5\frac{1}{3}'$
Wald Flöte	4′	Octave	4′
Twelfth	$2\frac{2}{3}'$	Flute Octaviante	4′
Fifteenth	2′	Piccolo Harmonic	2′
Quint Mixture	IV	Cymbal	III
Tierce Mixture	V	Furniture	IV

Great Organ (continued)

FRONT GREAT		BACK GREAT	
Trumpet	8′	Contra Trombone	16′
Clarion	4′	Trombone	8′
		Trumpet Harmonic	8′
		Tenor Trombone	4′

Swell Organ (C–c⁴)		**Choir Organ** (C–c⁴)	
Bourdon	16′	Sub Dulciana	16′
Open Diapason	8′	Open Diapason	8′
Stopped Diapason, bass		Stopped Diapason, bass,	
and treble	8′	C–B	8′
Keraulophon	8′	Rohr Flute, metal (c)	8′
Harmonic Flute	8′	Salcional	8′
Octave	4′	Viol de Gamba (c)	8′
Gemshorn	4′	Octave	4′
Wood Flute	4′	Suabe Flute	4′
Twelfth	2⅔′	Flute Harmonic	4′
Fifteenth	2′	Twelfth	2⅔′
Piccolo	2′	Fifteenth	2′
Sesquialtra	IV	Ottavino, wood	2′
Mixture	III	Dulciana Mixture	V
Contra Fagotto	16′	Euphone, free reed	16′
Trumpet	8′	Trumpet	8′
Cornopean	8′	Clarion	4′
Oboe	8′		
Vox Humana	8′		
Clarion	4′		

Echo Organ (C–c⁴)ᵃ		**Pedal Organ** (C–f¹)	
Bourdon	16′	Sub-Bass, open metal	32′
Dulciana	8′	Contra Bourdon, wood	32′
Lieblich Gedact, wood	8′	Open Diapason, wood	16′
Flute Traverso, wood	4′	Open Diapason, metal	16′
Flute d'Amour	4′	Violin, wood	16′
Dulciana Mixture	IV	Bourdon, wood	16′
Carillons (f–c⁴)		Quint, open wood	10⅔′
		Octave	8′
Orchestral Solo Organ (C–c⁴)		Violoncello	8′
Bourdon	8′	Twelfth	5⅓′
Concert Flute Harmonic	8′	Fifteenth	4′
Piccolo Harmonic	4′	Mixture	IV
Ottavino Harmonic	2′	Contra Bombard, free reed	32′
Clarinet	8′	Bombard	16′
Oboe	8′	Fagotto	16′
Cor Anglais and Bassoon	8′	Clarion	8′
Tromba	8′		
Ophicleide	8′		

Orchestral Solo Organ (continued)

By mechanical combination:

Clarinet and Flute, in octaves

Oboe and Flute, in octaves

Clarinet and Bassoon, in octaves

Clarinet and Oboe, in octaves

Oboe and Bassoon, in octaves

Flute, Clarinet and Bassoon, in double octaves

Flute, Oboe and Bassoon, in double octaves

Solo to Great	Swell pedals to Swell and Solo
Great to Solo	Tremulant to Echo
Solo Super Octave	Tremulant to Swell (by pedal)
Solo Sub Octave	Ventil to Back Great
Swell to Great	Pedal to couple Back Great to Swell
Swell to Great, Super Octave	Crescendo and diminuendo pedals
Swell to Great, Sub Octave	Wind couplers to composition
Swell to Choir	pedals
Choir to Great	
Great to Pedal	
Swell to Pedal	
Choir to Pedal	
Solo to Pedal	
Echo to Solo	
Echo to Choir	
Full Pedal Organ	

4 adjustable composition pedals, each with an index for setting to desired combination of stops

a The Echo Organ was part of the original scheme but was not added until 1865.

Smart was the master of short mood pieces. Not combined in the sense of the Mendelssohn Sonatas Op. 65, nor really imitating Bachian movements, Smart's numerous preludes, postludes, marches, andantes, interludes (with mood indications to distinguish each piece) were written for every occasion with simple, easily remembered forms.[5] The layout of the Allegro maestoso from the Fantasia with Choral (*A Series of Organ Pieces in Various Styles,* No. 3) shows Smart to be completely at home with the modern Pedal organ at the second appearance of the strong ritornello theme, shown in Example 19.3.

The legacy left by Smart's contemporary William Thomas Best is centred more on his transcriptions,[6] his organ methods and his edition of Bach's organ works (commenced in 1885), than his own pieces for organ. His Sonatas in G major and D minor, and a miscellany of concert pieces

Ex. 19.3 Smart, Fantasia with Choral

do, however, epitomise his position as a concert organist: their unabstruse structures, technically demanding writing and inventive use of organ timbre were to have a lasting effect on original organ repertoire for concert use. They may be little known today but the management of the organ was substantially redefined by Best in these pieces (as it was in his arrangements). S. S. Wesley might have been praised for his pedalling but Best was a thoroughbred of a new generation, a generation with technique learnt at the cutting edge of choral accompaniment, arranging, and concert hall entertainment. Technologically the organ changed rapidly (pneumatic assistance and action, expanding tonal resources and a plethora of registrational aids) but the high technical standards nurtured by Best and his imitators aided their professional adaptation and survival.

Debates about the relative merits of transcriptions and original repertoire appeared at regular intervals. Sir Walter Parratt (1841–1924; organist of St George's Chapel (1882), Master of the Queen's Music (1893), and influential organ teacher), whilst acknowledging Best's performing skills, thought transcriptions to be anachronistic examples of 'misapplied skill', left over from a time with little original organ music, and moreover lamented the less-than-enthusiastic reception for works by prominent living composers; he includes Best with Sir Frederick Bridge, Edouard Silas, Francis Gladstone, Sir Alexander Mackenzie, Sir C. Hubert Parry and Sir Charles V. Stanford (Parratt 1892: 107). However, arrangements did popularise large tracts of often inaccessible repertoire, and showy concert divertissements, despite high-minded ideals, clearly had their aesthetic and secular role to play (see Clark 1994: 126–36). Town halls, concert halls and eventually cinemas saw the benefits of a now unrepeatable acceptance of the organ and its music in the public's collective imagination. Distinctions blurred, and it comes as no surprise to read an advertisement for Paxton's *The Organ Loft* from the 1920s which claims to be 'a series of 12 organ volumes [mostly original music] suitable for church, recital or cinema'. Calling for a better understanding of concert repertoire in a lecture to the Royal College of Organists in 1910, the blind organist Alfred Hollins urged more concert repertoire in order 'to bring out the capabilities of a modern concert organ to its fullest extent'. With numerous others (including Hollins, Purcell J. Mansfield, William Wolstenholme and William Faulkes), Edwin Lemare (1865–1934) and later Percy Whitlock (1903–46), as inheritors of the W. T. Best tradition, did just that with their concert overtures, sonatas, suites, scherzos, toccatas and innumerable characteristic pieces.

Lemare's Symphony Op. 35 and Sonata No. 1 Op. 95 show, as does Whitlock's Sonata in C minor, a broad orchestral sweep in which quasi-orchestral sonorities and differentiated moods take precedence over thematic processes. Although Whitlock's harmonic language is more chromatically charged, the Lemare and Whitlock Sonatas parallel one another in many respects: an agitated animato opening movement (prefaced by a graver introduction), a slow lyrical second movement, a cunning scherzo (see Example 19.4; Lemare uses his favourite sforzando off-beat chords), and an accumulative finale.

A large number of Lemare's characteristic pieces explore a variety of techniques. His well-known Andantino in D♭ – later adapted as the song 'Moonlight and Roses' – uses a favourite device where the thumb is required to play on the manual below the rest of the hand. Lemare's *Summer Sketches* Op. 73 also shows his advanced harmonic thinking and a conception of organ sonority – rather redolent of some of Karg-Elert's atmospheric pieces – undoubtedly developed through the production of his revered Wagner transcriptions.

The preference of Parratt's 'classicists' for form and compositional erudition over mood and virtuosity was the most significant difference with the concert composers (Grace 1926–7). Traditional genres – the prelude/fantasia/toccata and fugue, the chorale prelude and fantasia (including works based on plainsong), and the ostinato work – were all employed to 'advance' music *and* convey a lineage from the past, albeit an imported Germanic past. Stanford's early Prelude and Fugue in E minor for instance,[7] said to have been composed during his studies in Leipzig (Grace 1926–7: 1/2, 44), encapsulates a new 'symphonic' fluency and spontaneity which many of his older contemporaries were unable to

Ex. 19.4 Lemare, Scherzo from Sonata No. 1

III Swell (Celeste, Lieb 8', Viol d'Orchestre & Trem.)
II Great (Wald Flöte 8') - III
I Choir (Soft 8' & 4') - III
Pedal (Bourdon, Open Wood 16' & soft 8') - III

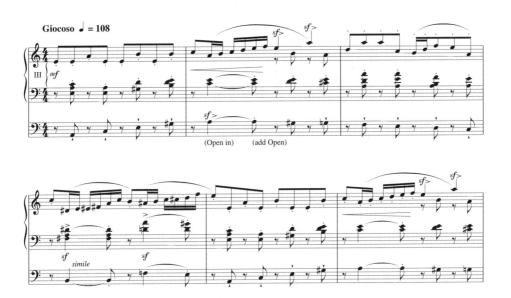

achieve in their formularistic schemes (see Example 19.5, showing the openings of (a) the Prelude and (b) the Fugue).

The effortless lyricism of the Prelude (the theme is constantly 're-orchestrated' against a *moto perpetuo* semiquaver figure) and the more solid and thematically reminiscent Fugue testify to a creativity in writing for the organ which came to full fruition in the better-known Fantasia and Toccata in D minor Op. 57. Here adventurous harmonies, Brahmsian melodiousness, and wit meet in thrilling proportions. By contrast, Parry's free works, the Fantasia and Fugue in G major and the Toccata and Fugue in G 'The Wanderer', with Reger-like fantasy and Brahmsian rhythmical skill, have much of the 'Bach reborn' feeling about them.

With the *Sixteen Preludes* 'Founded on Melodies from the English and Scottish Psalters' by Charles Wood and Parry's two sets of *Chorale Preludes*, the chorale prelude also became a firm fixture in composers' thinking for organ. A result of an increasing awareness on the part of organists of examples by Bach, and an increased appreciation of hymnody, these preludes were quite apart from the introductions and interludes to metrical psalm tunes of previous generations and played a joint role in both church service and recital. Harold Darke with his *Three Chorale Preludes* and Ralph Vaughan Williams in his *Three Preludes*

Ex. 19.5 Stanford, Prelude and Fugue in E minor

(a)

(b)

Founded on Welsh Hymn Tunes confirmed the genre. Parry's *Chorale Fantasias* and the pieces based on plainsong by Sir Edward Bairstow, *Prelude on 'Vexilla Regis'* and *Toccata-Prelude on 'Pange Lingua'*, are some of the most powerful expositions on liturgical melodies in the British repertoire.

The sonata, and with it the ethos of presenting and developing themes, occupied many composing for organ at the turn of the century. More than for Smart's generation or the concert composer-organists, it was the authority of the form and the transformation processes it encouraged which were of importance. The Sonata in C♯ minor Op. 5 by Basil Harwood, from 1886, is redolent of Rheinberger – not particularly surprising given the popularity of the latter in Britain – in its textures and structure, particularly in the fugal third movement, and in its inclusion of a plainsong melody as extra-thematic material. Harwood's allusion to orchestral sonorities is essentially an organist looking outwards rather than an orchestral composer looking inwards. The Sonata in G major Op. 28 by Sir Edward Elgar is a unique case of the latter; the language, rhetoric and pacing are thoroughly orchestral throughout, so much so that detailed echoes of it in the music of others are hard to find. The five Sonatas by Stanford (published between 1917 and 1921) and Bairstow's Sonata in E♭ also contributed further interpretations of the genre.

Of those writing for the organ in the years between the Wars, it was Herbert Howells who remained unparalleled. A skilled organist and, crucially, a composer whose horizons extended well beyond the organ loft, he was able to synthesise many elements towards a highly personal but profoundly idiomatic organ style. Again, as with S. S. Wesley, many traits were born of improvisation: the supple and rapid shifts in dynamic (available with the symphonic organs of Willis, Hill and Harrison), the expansion of a single seed-like idea over long periods, and the ability to encapsulate – in the sense of a tone poem – an atmospheric 'programme'. Filled with the contours of Elizabethan polyphony, but at times French in its impressionistic harmonies, or bitingly twentieth-century in its use of dissonance, Howells's home-grown music has captured the imaginations of countless British organists. His *Psalm Preludes*, in two sets, and the *Six Pieces* convey the feeling of large pieces but in microcosm, as do the aptly-named *Three Rhapsodies*. Example 19.6 is taken from the first Rhapsody's crescendo where the D♭ tonality is grandly asserted in glutinous but shifting chords; the texture could not be thicker, the 'tenor' right foot in the pedal binding the tutti together.

Curiosity about other cultures has always remained deeply rooted in the British psyche. Like Gauntlett and Smart in the 1840s and 50s (through their adopted builders), a few individuals from the 1930s

Ex. 19.6 Howells, Rhapsody No. 1

onwards – in particular the organist Ralph Downes – transmitted 'classi-cal' organ building principles to Britain (see Chapter 6). Ultimately it was not so much the German *Orgelbewegung* instrument which established itself as *de rigueur* but an eclectic, all-purpose instrument whose sonor-ities – more often than not a Dutch/German principal chorus with French reedwork – were grafted onto the existing format. The obverse of changes a century before, it gave sound precedence over technology; a return to mechanical action and a more uncompromising policy on classical organ-building (as with Maurice Forsyth-Grant) did not come about until the 1960s and 1970s. The eclectic style can be seen in the following specification of the Walker organ of 1952 designed by Downes for Brompton Oratory:

London, Brompton Oratory, J. W. Walker & Sons, 1952

Great Organ (C–a^3)		Choir Organ (C–a^3)	
Quintadena	16′	Gedackt	8′
Principal	8′	Principal	4′
Rohrflöte	8′	Rohrflöte	4′

Great Organ (continued)		**Choir Organ** (continued)	
Octave	4′	Octave	2′
Gemshorn	4′	Waldflöte	2′
Quint	$2\frac{2}{3}$′	Larigot	$1\frac{1}{3}$′
Superoctave	2′	Sesquialtera	II
Tertian	II	Scharf	IV
Mixture	IV–V	Cromorne	8′
Trumpet	8′	Tremulant	

Swell Organ (C–a³)		**Pedal Organ** (C–g¹)	
Baarpyp	8′	Principal	16′
Quintadena	8′	Sub Bass	16′
Viola	8′	Quintflöte	$10\frac{2}{3}$′
Celeste	8′	Octave	8′
Principal	4′	Gedackt	8′
Gedacktflöte	4′	Rohrquint	$5\frac{1}{3}$′
Nazard	$2\frac{2}{3}$′	Octave	4′
Octave	2′	Nachthorn	2′
Gemshorn	2′	Mixture	IV
Tierce	$1\frac{3}{5}$′	Bombarde	16′
Mixture	IV	Trumpet	8′
Cymbel	III	Trumpet	2′
Echo Trumpet	8′		
Vox Humana	8′		
Tremulant			

Great Sub Octave
Choir to Pedal
Great to Pedal
Swell to Pedal
Swell to Great
Swell to Choir
Choir to Great

Great and Pedal Combinations Coupled

In tandem with post-war developments in organ building, British composers for the organ responded with works which not only reflected the compositional mainstream (quartal harmony, free chromatic counterpoint, serial techniques, rhythmic experimentation etc.) but were distilled from the keenly voiced timbres classical voicing brought (e.g. characteristic reed and mutation stops, strong mixtures and 'terraced' choruses), but were clothed in genres which reunited the organ with its pre-romantic past. The organ has hardly been at the forefront of musical change in Britain, but the degree to which composers for it either took a clear internationalist stance during this period,[8] or sought, whilst still adapting to external currents in some way, to connect themselves with a more home-grown outlook, now provides a useful differentiation when looking back on the immediate past.

Belonging to the first group, Peter Racine Fricker made his mark during the 1950s and 60s with works inspired by the classical organ's contrapuntal clarity and coruscatory power. His *Ricercare* Op. 40, written for the Schnitger organ at Zwolle (The Netherlands), centres on the thematic expansion (in a duet, trio and fantasy-recitative) of a germinal motive. Fricker's granite-like 'emancipated' harmonies in the *Ricercare* reappear in the *Praeludium* Op. 60. The gestural spelling-out of chords and the linear trio sections in the latter piece demonstrate his preoccupation with intervals and their ability, as building blocks, to expand or contract into melodic lines or chords respectively.

The 1960s brought a number of experimental compositions for the organ. Born of a desire to be connected with the continental *avant-garde*, and making distinct departures from established neo-classical 'modern' styles, they now appear somewhat solitary works in their avoidance of traditional organ textures and techniques; for the most part they remain unknown. Peter Maxwell Davies ends his carol cycle *O Magnum Mysterium* with one such work, the *Fantasia on O Magnum Mysterium*, in which he unites his early fascinations with serial and medieval techniques. With the manual and pedals freed from traditional roles, the intricate interlocking of melodic lines and chords (three- to five- part chords are frequently used in the pedal) – all originating in the plainsong fragment – draws the listener into an inner world of varying densities. Nicholas Maw in his *Essay* and Hugh Wood in his *Capriccio* Op. 8 both employ serialist principles to generate the material and diffuse it (like Davies) across a wide area of pitch-space. Wood's use of glittering figuration with fluctuating metre and lyrical melody in *Capriccio* has something of Messiaen about it. John Lambert similarly disperses his thoughts across a wide 'pitch-canvas' in the *Organ Mass*; contrapuntal or chordal, the finely-chiselled webs of sound are here synonymous with the colours of the neo-classical organ. Each of these works, even if highly organised, furthered a cause, that of liberating pitch, timbre and rhythm from well-established routines. As an antidote to such organised and 'constructed' music, aleatoric principles have seen little impact. *Games* by Paul Patterson, one of the few works to employ aleatoricism, isolates (in any order the player wishes) musical elements so as to concentrate on each one separately.

Sebastian Forbes has provided a small but individual contribution to the organ repertoire with works which revel in the pointillist character of the neo-classical organ. Concerned with kaleidoscopic figuration and uncompromising contrasts, the Sonata, *Haec Dies* and *Capriccio* all delight in linear or chordal patterns which change articulation, speed, and registration. The Sonata, first performed in 1969 on the Flentrop organ at the Queen Elizabeth Hall, London, has a clear sense of sonata-form symmetry and, with its fragmentary opening presented with subtle variations in speed, is reminiscent of Tippett's ground-breaking Piano Sonata No. 2 of 1962.

A less acerbic (and therefore more accessible) stance since the 1960s has come from those composers who have appeared to remain on acceptable stylistic territory, and thus in tune with established traditions. Incorporating 'modernisms' but, through the frequency of their publications, establishing their own *lingua franca*, they have provided a body of music which is informed by the sounds and forms of neo-classicism but equally suitable for instruments built in other traditions. Kenneth Leighton, William Mathias and John McCabe in their early published works for organ (e.g. Prelude, Scherzo and Passacaglia Op. 41, Partita Op. 19 and Sinfonia Op. 6 respectively) might all show their working familiarity with the sound-world of Hindemith or Bartók, but they refuse to deny a pragmatism from closer to home. Leighton's composition is notably abstract but passionate in its lyrical working-out of minute motivic ideas in each movement, and the Partita by Mathias is stylish in its evocation of the baroque suite. Through their accessible writing and considerable involvement with church music, they have become the epitome of British modernity. Malcolm Williamson, in his Symphony, also attempted to balance strict compositional procedures (a chromatic chant-like melody is used as a series, contour, mode, and 'rhythmic regulator') with varied and familiar styles; a strong visionary element has been frequently present in his music.

Giles Swayne, Judith Weir and Francis Pott emerged as organ composers during the 1980s. Pott's monumental *Christus: Passion Symphony in Five Movements* is a programmatic work with evocative, rather expressionistic mood changes cast in predominantly chromatic and contrapuntal music, and Swayne's minimalistic *Riff-Raff* taps into a major contemporary current. The duet repertoire has been augmented by two British works in recent times: Leighton's *Martyrs*, based on the Scottish Psalter melody, and the mesmeric *Kyoto* by a pupil of Leighton, Stephen Oliver.

Editions

Helpful in providing an accessible picture of early nineteenth-century British repertoire, Novello's recent *English Organ Music* series (ed. R. Langley, 1988) – particularly vols. 6–10 – and the same editor's editions of William Russell and Samuel Wesley (Oxford University Press, 1980 and

1981 respectively) give useful cross-sections of organ styles and genres. Much of Samuel Wesley's music, along with that of many other nineteenth-century British composers, remains unavailable in modern editions, though his *Duett for the Organ* is available from Novello. For the twentieth-century repertoire, the following list indicates the publishers of the principal composers mentioned in the chapter: Ascherberg, Hopwood & Crew (Lambert), Augener (Bairstow, Howells, Stanford), Boosey & Hawkes (Maw), Novello (Darke, Elgar, Howells, Leighton, Lemare, McCabe, Oliver, Parry, Swayne, Williamson, H. Wood), Oxford University Press (Bairstow, Forbes, Fricker, Mathias, Whitlock), Schott (Fricker, Harwood, Lemare, Maxwell Davies), Stainer & Bell (Stanford, Vaughan Williams, C. Wood), UMP (Pott) and Josef Weinberger (Patterson). Some major composers have been granted retrospective albums of representative works (e.g. Novello's Parry Albums) or reissues of significant works (e.g. Whitlock's Sonata by Basil Ramsey in association with the Whitlock Trust).

20 North American organ music after 1800

Douglas Reed

The early nineteenth century

In her major study of American organ building, Orpha Ochse notes that 'the early nineteenth-century American organ was an instrument without a repertoire' (Ochse 1975: 111ff.). Although various method books included examples of original organ compositions, improvisation was a mainstay of church organists well into the nineteenth century. Nineteenth-century organ builders inherited traditions of eighteenth-century organ building in the English and German styles. David Tannenberg's last organ, built in 1804 for Christ Lutheran Church, York, Pennsylvania, shows his German heritage (Armstrong 1967: 110). An early three-manual instrument by William Goodrich of Boston for the First Presbyterian Church, New Orleans, Louisiana (1815–20) shows English influence (Owen 1979: 425):

Great: 8.8.4.2$\frac{2}{3}$.2.III (bass).IV (treble)
Swell: 8.8.4.8.8
Choir: 8.8.4.8

The roots of eclecticism, the juxtaposition and reconciliation of diverse elements, run deep in American society. The mixture of various national traditions, fascination with technical complexity, innovation and experimentation ('tinkering') were natural parts of an organ culture separated from the regional traditions of Europe. For example, William Goodrich owned a copy of Dom Bédos's *L'Art du Facteur d'Orgues*. With regard to organ building traditions in New England, Owen points out that 'the teachers were American and the subject matter was English, but the textbook was French' (Owen 1979: 45).

By mid-century, American-born musicians had written and published a repertoire of literature and instruction books (Owen 1979: 109ff.; Owen 1975–91). *American Church Organ Voluntaries*, published in 1856 by A. N. Johnson, was the first anthology of organ music compiled and published by an American-born composer. The volume includes original compositions by the editor and European composers, indications for the proper use of the printed selections for opening and closing voluntaries, sample organ stop lists, and instructions on the proper use of the stops.

Ex. 20.1 Johnson, Voluntary No. 1

Johnson begins the anthology with simple diatonic music arranged in short, repetitive phrases (see Example 20.1). He gradually introduces imitation and chromaticism, manual indications, dynamics, use of the swell, specific stop indications and the use of organ pedals.

Like Johnson's *Voluntaries*, much early nineteenth-century American printed repertoire was simple and predictable, attributes which made the music practical for keyboard players of less than advanced skills, for limited instruments of whatever style, and for congregations distrustful of 'display'.

The secular use of the organ expanded by mid-century with the construction of concert halls with organs. Like the church organ, the concert organ often accompanied vocal music. However, it was in the concert hall that music like *The Thunderstorm* by Thomas Ryder (1836–87) could flourish (Owen 1975–91, vol. IV). Ryder's detailed instructions for slowly pulling and pushing stops while sustaining several adjacent notes (a 'cluster' in late twentieth-century terminology) show a type of invention not to be heard again in American organ composition until the 1970s (see Example 20.2).

The later nineteenth century

By 1846, Boston had numerous three-manual church organs (Ochse 1975: 115), and by 1853 the city had its first four-manual concert organ, built by E. & G. G. Hook (Owen 1979: 447). Although the stop-list of the 1864 E. & G. G. Hook in Mechanics' Hall, Worcester, Massachusetts is conservative compared with the larger Boston Music Hall organ built in 1863 by the German Walcker company (Owen 1979: 459ff), the Worcester organ still plays in its original location as restored in 1982 (Edwards 1992: 205).

Mechanics' Hall, Worcester, Massachusetts
E. & G. G. Hook, Opus 334, 1864

Great (C–a³)		Swell (C–a³)	
Open Diapason	16′	Bourdon	16′
Open Diapason	8′	Open Diapason	8′

Ex. 20.2 Ryder, *The Thunderstorm*

"While holding the Pedals, quickly shut off swell stops, draw Gt to Swell coupler, then hold the notes
as below on the Great manual and slowly draw the designated stop, then push back slowly.
N.B. Be sure to hold the keys before drawing the stops."

"Draw Sw. St. Diap. then
shut off again."

"Draw Sw. St. Diap. then add Sw. Op. Diap;
then shut off Op. Diap. followed by St. Diap."

"Gt C. D. C♯ together"

"Ped."   "Leave Ped:"

"Draw Gt Op. Diap. half out and back."

"Draw Gt Op. Diap. clear out and
back, two or three times, before
going to next measure."

"While holding Ped: quickly
draw full organ, without
coupling pedals to keys"

"Draw full Ped:"

Great (continued)		**Swell** (continued)	
Viola Da Gamba	8′	Stopped Diapason	8′
Stopped Diapason	8′	Viol d'Amour	8′
Claribella	8′	Principal	4′
Principal	4′	Flute Octaviante	4′
Flute Harmonique	4′	Violin	4′
Twelfth	$2\frac{2}{3}$′	Twelfth	$2\frac{2}{3}$′
Fifteenth	2′	Fifteenth	2′
Mixture	III	Mixture	V
Trumpet	16′	Trumpet	16′
Trumpet	8′	Cornopean	8′
Clarion	4′	Oboe	8′
		Clarion	4′
		Vox Humana	8′

Solo (C–a^3)

Philomela	8'
Salicional	8'
Hohl Pfeife	4'
Picolo	2'
Tuba	8'
Corno Inglese	8'

Pedale (C–f^1)

Open Diapason	16'
Violone	16'
Bourdon	16'
Violoncello	8'
Quinte	$10\frac{3}{4}'$ [sic]
Flute	8'
Posaune	16'

Choir (C–a^3)

Aeolina & Bourdon	16'
Open Diapason	8'
Melodia	8'
Dulciana	8'
Keraulophon	8'
Flauto Traverso	4'
Violin	4'
Picolo	2'
Mixture	III
Clarinet	8'

Mechanical Registers

Swell to Great Coupler
Swell to Choir Coupler
Choir to Great Coupler
Solo to Great Coupler
Choir to Solo Coupler
Great to Pedale Coupler
Choir to Pedale Coupler
Choir to Pedale Coupler
  (super octaves)
Solo to Pedale Coupler
Swell to Pedale Coupler
Tremulant ('Swell')
Bellows signal
Pedale Check
Ventil (for Open Diapason in
  Pedale)
Ventil (for Quinte, Flute, and
  Posaune in Pedale)

Combination Pedals

Great Manual Forte
Great Manual Piano
Swell Manual Forte
Swell Manual Piano
Choir Manual Forte
Choir Manual Piano
(Pedale) operates on Open
  Diapason, Quinte, Flute
  and Posaune, and
  with the aid of Ventils,
  allows various
  combinations.
Couplers Forte
Couplers Piano
'Great to Pedale' Coupler

Balanced Swell Pedal, with
  double action

Like many of their contemporaries, John Knowles Paine (1839–1906) and Dudley Buck (1839–1909) studied in both America and Germany. Paine's early works, performed and published as early as 1861, present a dramatically different picture of organ composition and repertoire from *American Church Organ Voluntaries* (1856). Marked by fluent if predictable contrapuntal writing, Paine's various sets of 'concert' variations require an advanced manual and pedal technique. Buck's *The Last Rose of Summer* (Op. 59, publ. 1877) employs imitation, species counterpoint

32 FT WIDE.
40FT HIGH. 21 FT DEEP

Centennial Organ,
──── BUILT BY ────
E. & G. C. HOOK & HASTINGS,
Boston, Mass.

4 MANUALS.
32 FT PEDALE

Figure 20.1 The organ built by Hook & Hastings of Boston for the Centennial Exhibition in
Philadelphia (1876). It was provided with walkways and staircases, and there were glass panels
in the sides of some of the wind-chests so that the public could inspect the mechanism. There
were four keyboards and forty-one stops, including a two-stop Solo Organ.

and canon to generate a concise and dramatic form (see Example 20.3 for
the opening of the Introduction).

Variations II, IV and VII call for high levels of virtuosity in the manual
and pedal departments. Articulation marks throughout the piece show
the composer's regard for the possibilities of contemporary mechanical
actions. The introduction, statement of the theme and penultimate
(minor) variation call for subtle or complex stop changes which beg for
an adjustable electrical combination action, the development of which
was but a few years away.

Ex. 20.3 Buck, Introduction from *The Last Rose of Summer*

Charles Ives (1874–1954) composed the familiar *Variations on 'America'* in 1891. Irreverent humour, daring key changes and polytonal additions dating from 1894 distinguish the work, the high point of a genre of later nineteenth-century American compositions based on familiar hymn, folk and patriotic tunes (Arnold 1984 I: 272). The Mechanics' Hall Hook organ is an ideal medium for the performance of this repertoire. Hilborne Roosevelt (1849–86), who had used electricity in an American organ action as early as 1869, had become the most highly respected and innovative American builder by the 1880s. His organ for the 1876 Philadelphia Centennial Exposition (Figure 20.1) employed adjustable combination action, electric key action and electric motors to supply the wind (Ochse 1975: 267–8; for the organ at Great Barrington, Mass. of 1883, see Figure 5.15). The Farrand & Votey company, who bought the Roosevelt patents, built two instruments for Chicago's 1893 Columbian Exposition, the larger of which was purchased by the University of Michigan (Wilkes 1995: 1). This organ, like the entire Exposition, featured state-of-the-art use of electricity.

The early twentieth century

Composers whose careers bridged the turn of the century include George Chadwick (1854–1931), Arthur Foote (1853–1937) and Horatio Parker (1853–1919). Parker's *Canon in the Fifth*, Op. 68 No. 1 and *Revery*, Op. 66 No. 2 show imaginative command of contrapuntal and chromatic musical language. In the 1910s and 20s, many cities built municipal organs, sources of entertainment, education and civic pride for many people. Often predating the establishment of community orchestras, municipal organs were ideally suited to transcriptions of orchestral, vocal and piano music. Related developments included the unit organ, promoted by Robert Hope Jones, and the theatre organ, perfected by the Wurlitzer company.

Transcriptions and improvised music for silent films did not constitute the entire repertoire of the orchestral organists, however. Joseph Clokey (1890–1960), one of the leading composers of original music for the orchestral organ, wrote several suites which provide a hint of the folksy, popular spirit of much repertoire of this period. His *Fireside Fancies* Op. 29, include the following musical vignettes: A Cheerful Fire; The Wind In The Chimney; Grandfather's Wooden Leg (Humoresque); Grandmother, Knitting; The Cat (She purrs, meows, takes a sip of milk, and goes to sleep.); Old Aunty Chloe; The Kettle Boils.

In the 1890s, Ernest M. Skinner (1866–1960) began work with the Hutchings organ factory of Boston, a firm well known for its use of electric actions. Skinner, whose work demonstrated the highest artistic ideals, became the most successful and respected American organ builder of the early twentieth century. He invented numerous organ stops (Erzähler, Kleine Erzähler, French Horn, English Horn, Dulcet II, Corno di Bassetto, Heckelphone, Flauto Mirabilis, Flute Triangulaire, and others) which suited the art of the orchestral transcription, contemporary organ literature and contemporary worship patterns. Key concepts were beauty (as perceived by musicians of the time), mystery and unfocused sound. True to the American spirit of reconciliation of contrasting points of view, Skinner sought an all-purpose organ which could convincingly play literally any music including the masterworks of J. S. Bach.

Skinner built major instruments for churches and educational institutions across the United States. His art reached its zenith in three large organs built in 1928: University of Chicago (Rockefeller Memorial Chapel); University of Michigan (Hill Auditorium); and Princeton University Chapel. Of these three, the Hill Auditorium organ was uniquely situated in an ideal placement where it spoke directly into a resonant 5,000-seat hall. In Skinner's words, 'The acoustics are magnificent. The organ is of the first magnitude which, together with the acoustical advantages, presents the realization of an ideal rarely found' (Skinner 1981: 188). A two-page advertisement in *The Diapason* magazine proclaimed that the 'Renaissance of Mixtures' reached 'a culmination' in the Hill Auditorium organ (Holden 1985: 127).

University of Michigan, Hill Auditorium
E. M. Skinner, 1928
All manual compasses: C–c^4
Pedal Compass: C–g^1

Great Organ (61 notes)		Swell Organ (73 notes)***		Choir Organ (73 notes)***	
Violone	32'	Dulciana	16'	Contra Gamba	16'
Diapason	16'	Bourdon	16'	Diapason	8'
Bourdon	16'	Diapason	8'	Concert Flute	8'
Diapason	8'	Clarabella	8'	Gamba	8'
Diapason	8'	Rohrflöte	8'	Dulcet II	8'

**Diapason	8'	Viol d'Orchestre	8'	Dulciana	8'
Stopped Diapason	8'	Voix Celeste	8'	Kleine Erzähler	8'
**Claribel Flute	8'	Echo Dulcet	8'	Gemshorn	4'
Erzähler	8'	*String Organ	8'	Flute	4'
*String Organ VI	8'	Flauto Dolce	8'	Nazard	$2\frac{2}{3}'$
Quint	$5\frac{1}{3}'$	Flute Celeste	8'	Piccolo	2'
Octave	4'	Octave	4'	Tierce	$1\frac{3}{5}'$
Principal	4'	Flute Triangulaire	4'	Septieme	$1\frac{1}{7}'$
Flute	4'	Unda Maris II	4'	*String Mixture	
Tenth	$3\frac{1}{5}'$	Flautino	2'	Heckelphone (Solo)	16'
Twelfth	$2\frac{2}{3}'$	Mixture V	2'	Bassoon	16'
Fifteenth	2'	Cornet V	8'	French Horn (Solo)	8'
Mixture V	2'	*String Mixture		English Horn	8'
Harmonics IV	$1\frac{3}{5}'$	Posaune	16'+	Harmonica	8'
*String Mixture	IV 8'	Trumpet	8'+	Heckelphone (Solo)	8'
Trombone	16'	Cornopean	8'+	Bassoon	8'
**Orchestral Trumpet	8'+	Clarion	4'+	Clarinet	8'
Tromba	8'+	Oboe	8'	Celesta	
Clarion	4'+	Vox Humana	8'	Harp	
Celesta		Tremolo		Tremolo	
Harp					
Piano	8'				
Piano	4'				

Solo Organ (73 notes)***

Stentorphone	8'
Flauto Mirabilis	8'
Gamba	8'
*String Organ VI	8'
Octave	4'
Orchestral Flute	4'
*String Mixture IV	
Contra Tuba	16'+
Tuba Mirabilis	8'+
Tuba	8'+
Clarion	4'+
Heckelphone	16'
Heckelphone	8'
Corno di Bassetto	8'
French Horn	8'
Orchestral Oboe	8'
Chimes	
Tremolo	

Echo

Gedeckt	8'
Muted Viol	8'
Unda Maris	8'
Vox Humana	8'

* In separate box, floating
** Enclosed
+ Heavy wind
*** In expression boxes

Pedal Organ (32 notes)

Diapason	32'
Violone	32'
Diapason	16'
Diapason (bearded)	16'
Diapason (Gt)	16'
Violone	16'
Gamba (Ch)	16'
Dulciana (Sw)	16
Bourdon	16'
Echo Lieblich (Sw)	16'
Quint	$10\frac{2}{3}'$
Principal	8'
Octave	8'
Gedeckt	8'
Still Gedeckt (Sw)	8'
Cello	8'
Twelfth	$5\frac{1}{3}'$
Flute	4'
Tierce	$3\frac{1}{5}'$
Septieme	$2\frac{2}{7}'$
Mixture IV	2'
Bombarde	32'+
Ophicleide	16'+
Posaune (Sw)	16'
Bassoon (Ch)	16'
Quint Trombone (Gt)	$10\frac{2}{3}'$
Tromba	8'+
Clarion	4'+
Bass Drum	
Tympani [roll]	
Piano	16'
Piano	8'
Chimes	

A generation of major American composers born around the turn of the century wrote a small amount of organ repertoire: Virgil Thomson (1896–1989), Aaron Copland (1900–90), Roy Harris (1898–1979), Harry Partsch (1901–74), Walter Piston (1894–1976), Roger Sessions (1896–1985), Wallingford Riegger (1885–1961), Douglas Moore (1893–1969), Quincy Porter (1897–1966), Henry Cowell (1897–1965). The most significant item of this repertoire is Copland's Symphony for Organ and Orchestra, commissioned by Nadia Boulanger for her American concert tour in 1925 (Kratzenstein 1980: 183).

Unlike his contemporaries, Leo Sowerby (1895–1968) wrote a large repertoire of organ music (Crociata 1995: 53). His early works are idiomatically related to the sounds of the contemporary organ epitomised by the work of E. M. Skinner. *Requiescat in Pace* (1920) is a highly motivic, concise statement in honour of those who perished in World War I. It calls for dynamic extremes (*ppp* to *fff*), a wash of delicate orchestral colour, a variety of string tone at 16′, 8′ and 4′ pitch, chimes, and celesta. The musical effect depends on seamless, gradual crescendos and diminuendos which demand the availability of numerous combination pistons and multiple swell boxes. Quick successions of unusual combinations (e.g. Dulcet 8′ + Picc. 2′ and Voix Celeste, Vox Humana, Flautino 2′, Trem.) presuppose the availability of adjustable combination pistons and unaggressive upperwork (see Example 20.4).

Sowerby's Canadian contemporary Healey Willan (1880–1968), born in England, left a number of organ works including the massive Introduction, Passacaglia, and Fugue (1916), a major landmark in Canadian organ literature.

By the 1920s, a few leading American organists were calling for alternatives to orchestral organ sound and for a return to clearer ensembles for the performance of Bach and other early music (see Owen 1986). The demise of the orchestral organ and its literature, beginning in the 1930s, coincided with the rise of historically oriented performance. Consisting primarily of historic repertoire, Alexandre Guilmant's recital series for the 1904 St Louis World's Fair anticipated what would become the primary focus of performance repertoire by mid-century (Kroeger 1904). Elements which contributed to the development of historically oriented music making and organ building reform included: (1) rising standards of music education at the growing number of university music schools and conservatories throughout the United States and Canada, (2) increased availability of historic manuscripts and printed music, (3) improved electronic communication including radio broadcasts which began in the 1920s and (4) concerts and teaching by visiting European organists (Guilmant, 1903; Bonnet, 1917; Dupré, 1921).

Ex. 20.4 Sowerby, *Requiescat in Pace*

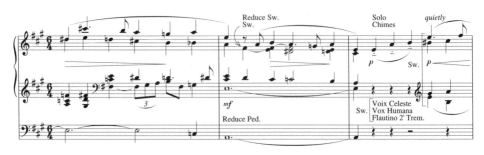

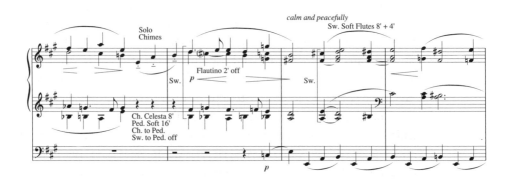

The *Method of Organ Playing* by Harold Gleason (1892–1980), former professor of organ at the Eastman School of Music of the University of Rochester, New York, illustrates the early emphasis on an historic and scholarly approach to music making on the organ. The *Method* incorporated much early music, information about historic instruments and performance practices, and contemporary repertoire in its many editions from the mid-1930s onwards.

In 1927 Ernest Skinner invited G. Donald Harrison of the English Willis firm to join his company. The 'Renaissance of Mixtures' for the Michigan organ was only a hint of the revolution at hand. Under Harrison's direction, the American Classic Organ as built by the Aeolian–Skinner company reached early maturity in less than a decade (Callahan 1990). Harrison created an all-purpose instrument with a decidedly French accent which would perform all historic and contemporary music in a convincing if not precisely authentic manner. The stoplist of the Aeolian–Skinner organ built for Strong Auditorium, University of Rochester is a prime example of the American Classic style as it had developed by 1937 (Ochse 1975: 383).

Strong Auditorium, University of Rochester
Aeolian–Skinner (G. Donald Harrison), 1937

Great: $16.8.8.8.8.4.4.2\frac{2}{3}.2.2.IV.IV.III$
Rück-Positiv: $8.8.4.4.2\frac{2}{3}.2.1\frac{3}{5}.1\frac{1}{3}.1.IV.III.8$
Swell: $16.8.8.8.8.4.4.4.2\frac{2}{3}.2.IV.IV.16.8.8.4$
Choir: $16.8.8.8.8.4.2\frac{2}{3}.2.1\frac{3}{5}.8.Chimes$
Solo: 8.8.4
Pedal: 16.16.16.16.16.16.8.8.8.8.8.4.4.III.II.16.8.8.4

American-born Walter Holtkamp, Sr. was the most radical, independent, and innovative reformer of the period. Also dedicated to a practical,
all-purpose organ for the historic and contemporary repertoire,
Holtkamp focused on a sound which would illuminate contrapuntal
musical styles. With his insistence on the placement of architecturally
arranged pipework near the player within the acoustical environment of
the room, Holtkamp made an enduring stamp on the course of American organ reform (Ferguson 1979). His organ for Crouse Auditorium,
Syracuse University (1950) remains one of his most striking visual
designs (see Figure 5.16). The last organ completed by the senior
Holtkamp shows a typical three-manual design which the Holtkamp
company continued to build under the leadership of Walter Holtkamp, Jr.

St. John's Abbey, Collegeville, Minnesota
Holtkamp Organ, 1961

Gt: $16.8.8.8.4.4.2.1\frac{2}{3}.IV.III.8.$
Sw: $8.8.8.8.4.4.2.1.II\ (Sesq.).IV.16.8.4$
Pos: $8.4.4.2\frac{2}{3}.2.2.1\frac{3}{5}.III.8$
Ped: $16.16.16.10\frac{2}{3}.8.8.4.4.IV.32.16.8.4.$

The later twentieth century

After World War II, a more comprehensive American organ reform movement, tied to the demand for the 'right' sound for historic repertoire,
rediscovered and applied a number of historic elements (e.g. mechanical
key action, encasement) largely ignored by the reformers of previous
decades (Pape 1978: 26). European organs by Flentrop, Rieger, and von
Beckerath installed in churches in the United States and Canada strongly
influenced American organ building in the 1960s (Fesperman 1982).
Recordings of European and American instruments and American literature on various aspects of the historic organ fuelled the organ reform
movement (see Blanton 1957, 1965; Fesperman 1962).

In 1963, the Canadian Casavant company installed its first mechanical action organ built since the turn of the century in Wolfville, Nova Scotia. Since then, numerous Canadian achievements include an instrument in the French classical style for McGill University in 1981 (Mackey 1981) and a mean-tone organ for the University of Toronto (1991), both built by Helmut Wolff (Edwards 1992). Bengt Hambraeus (b. 1928), who led the development of avant-garde organ composition in Sweden in the late 1950s before moving to Canada, wrote a *Livre d'orgue* (1980–1) for the inauguration of the McGill University organ.

In the early decades of the twentieth century several major European composers moved to the United States where they wrote a few solo organ works or ensemble works calling for organ: Paul Hindemith (1895–1963), Darius Milhaud (1892–1974), Arnold Schoenberg (1874–1951), and Edgard Varèse (1883–1965). Leading American-born composers who have written organ music in various neo-classical and neo-romantic styles include Samuel Barber (1910–81), Ross Lee Finney (b. 1906), Alan Hovhaness (b. 1911), Vincent Persichetti (1915–87), and Ned Rorem (b. 1923). Most of this repertoire is tied to electro-pneumatic instruments such as those built by Aeolian–Skinner and Holtkamp.

In the 1970s a Contemporary Organ Music Workshop at Hartt College of Music highlighted the work of a new generation of American composers whose approach to the organ ranged from conservative to radically experimental (Kratzenstein 1980: 188ff). Among these more progressive composers are William Albright (b. 1944), William Bolcom (b. 1938), Sydney Hodkinson (Canadian, b. 1934), and Daniel Pinkham (b. 1923).

Since 1970 two important strands characterise leading contemporary American organ building: (1) an eclectic approach (the attempt to reconcile various national styles, tuning systems, case designs, action types), best exemplified in the work of Charles Fisk and John Brombaugh, and (2) the refinement of a single style (especially north German and Dutch), epitomised by the work of George Taylor and John Boody. During the 1980s and 90s, several other American builders (Bedient, Brombaugh, Fisk, Rosales, Wolff and others) built instruments in specific styles (e.g. early Spanish, north German mean-tone, Cavaillé-Coll, early Italian, French classical) in an attempt to better illuminate the historic organ repertoire.

The Westfield Center for Early Keyboard Studies, in co-operation with Arizona State University, sponsored a 1992 symposium, 'The Historical Organ in America', in celebration of the inauguration of the new Paul Fritts organ at the University. A companion document by the same name (Edwards 1992) demonstrates two important facets of leading American organ building craft in the late twentieth century: (1) the attention to specific details of historic organ building practice as guides for current practice, and (2) the sharing of information among colleagues. The symposium included the premiere of *Arizona Visions: A Concerto for Organ and Cassette Tape with an Audience Handout of Computer Generated Graphics* by Robert Bates.

Since 1965, William Albright has emerged as the most significant and innovative composer in North America who has written a large repertoire for the organ (Reed 1976; Reed 1993). Several of Albright's early solo organ works relate to the large 1928 E. M. Skinner organ at the University of Michigan, rebuilt by the Aeolian–Skinner company in 1955 (Wilkes 1995: 21ff). The composer's detailed registrations for *Juba, Pneuma, Organbook I,* and *Organbook II* call for a vast sound-scape ranging from a nearly inaudible pianissimo to the loudest fortissimo. The final movement of *Organbook II* expands the sound of the organ through the medium of electronic tape. Many of Ernest Skinner's subtle, orchestral colours including Harp, Chimes, and Celesta, which survive in the minimally altered Swell, Choir, Solo and Echo divisions, play important roles in all of these early works.

Albright's *Organbook I* (1967), a major landmark of twentieth-century American organ literature, includes four movements: 'Benediction', 'Melisma', 'Fanfare', and 'Recessional'. Although the piece can be successfully performed on smaller, classically oriented instruments, the original concept of 'Benediction' calls for many subtle 8′ colours, numerous combination pistons, and remote sounds. The spatially notated rhythmic structure evolves from slowly paced events at the beginning to the eventual climax with quick, evenly pulsed chords (Example 20.5). An underlying tonal structure (V–I in E) contributes to the musical organisation of the work (Hantz 1973).

Melisma, basically a single line which grows in range and density, explores a variety of flute colours on four manuals. Here, traditional organ technique expands to include clusters and cluster glissandos. Spatial separation of the sounds, possible on the Hill Auditorium organ and on many encased mechanical action organs, enhances the musical effect. In the preface to *Organbook III* (1977–8), Albright writes 'although in origin intended for organs of limited resources . . . *Organbook III* may be adapted to larger instruments'. A set of twelve études, *Organbook III* marks the intersection of his work and the contemporary American mechanical action organ. As in his earlier Organbooks, Albright juxtaposes extremes of all musical parameters. For example, as the organist co-ordinates metrical and non-metrical material among the hands and feet, fleeting diatonic harmonies emerge from the densely chromatic, glutinous sound created by over-legato touch in *Underground Stream.* In stark

Ex. 20.5 Albright, *Benediction*

Ex. 20.6 Albright, Finale from *Organbook III*

contrast, *Finale – The Offering* features a 'syncopated and delirious' savage dance which recalls American ragtime rhythm (Example 20.6).

Organbook III, performable without compromise on nearly any recent or earlier organ type, would find a suitable home on the Taylor & Boody organ at the Mount St Joseph Ursuline Motherhouse at Maple Mount, Kentucky:

Mount St Joseph Ursuline Motherhouse, Maple Mount, Kentucky
Taylor & Boody, Opus 25, 1995

Manual compass: C–g^3 (56 notes)
Pedal compass: C–f^1 (30 notes)

Great: 8.8.8.4.2.III.8
Choir: 8.4.3.II.2.8
Pedal: 16.8.8

For a more noble and dramatic voice, it could be adapted to the large concert organ built by C. B. Fisk, Inc. for the Myerson Symphony Center, Dallas, Texas:

The Lay Family Concert Organ, Meyerson Symphony Center, Dallas, Texas
C. B. Fisk, Inc., Opus 100, 1992

Manual compass: C–c^4 (61 notes)
Pedal compass: C–g^1 (32 notes)

Résonance (I and/or IV)		Positive (II)		Tuba (IV)	
		Bourdon	16′	Tuba Magna	16′
Prestant	32′	Principal	8′	Tuba	8′
Montre	16′	Dulcian	8′	Royal Trumpet	8′
Montre	8′	Gedackt	8′	Tuba Clarion	4′
Violoncelle	8′	Octave	4′		
Flûte harmonique	8′	Baarpijp	4′	**Pedal**	
Bourdon	8′	Nazard	2$\frac{2}{3}$′	Prestant	32′
Quinte	5$\frac{1}{3}$′	Doublette	2′	Untersatz	32′
Prestant	4′	Tierce	2′ and 1$\frac{3}{5}$′	Prestant	16′
Octave	4′	Sharp	VI–VIII	Contrebasse	16′
Quinte	2$\frac{2}{3}$′	Trompette	8′	Montre	16′
les Octaves	III	Cromorne	8′	Bourdon	16′
les Quintes	VI	Trechterregal	8′	Quinte	10$\frac{2}{3}$′
Plein jeu	VIII			Montre	8′+
Bombarde	16′	**Swell (III)**		Flûte	8′
Trompette	8′	Flûte traversière	8′	Violoncelle	8′+
Clairon	4′	Viole de gambe	8′	Flûte harmonique	8′+
		Voix céleste	8′	Bourdon	8′+
Great (I)		Bourdon	8′	Quinte	5$\frac{1}{3}$′+
Principal	16′	Prestant	4′	Prestant	4′+
Quintadehn	16′	Flûte octaviante	4′	Octave	4′+
Octava	8′	Octavin	2′	Quinte	2$\frac{2}{3}$′+
Spillpfeife	8′	Cornet	III	Mixture	VI+
Octava	4′	Basson	16′	Tuba Profunda	32′
Rohrflöte	4′	Trompette	8′	Bombarde	16′+
Superoctava	2′	Hautbois	8′	Tuba Magna	16′
Mixtur	VIII–XII	Voix humaine	8′	Posaune	16′

Trommeten	16'	Clairon	4'	Trompette	8'+
Trommeten	8'			Tuba	8'
				Royal Trumpet	8'
Couplers		**Ventils**		Clairon	4'+
Great to Résonance		Pedal reeds off			
Positive to Résonance		Résonance reeds off			
Swell to Résonance		Great reeds off			
Tuba to Résonance		Positive reeds off			
Résonance octaves graves		Swell reeds off			
Positive to Great		Résonance off			
Swell to Great					
Tuba to Great					
Swell to Positive					
Résonance to Pedal					
Great to Pedal					
Positive to Pedal					
Swell to Pedal					
Swell 4' to Pedal					

General Tremulant, Résonance Flue Tremulant
Mechanical key action, electric stop action, combination action by SSL

+ Alternating stops may be used in either the Résonance or the Pedal but not both simultaneously unless the Résonance to Pedal coupler is drawn.

The action, placement, scaling, winding, voicing, eclectic stop list and many other details of the Meyerson organ spring from European and American historical models. C. B. Fisk's highly refined synthesis of diverse elements presents an appropriate medium for historic repertoire, contemorary composition and improvisation.

Albright's eight-movement suite *Flights of Fancy* (1991–2), commissioned for the 1992 Atlanta American Guild of Organists National Convention, juxtaposes various dance types including the tango and the shimmy. The work climaxes with the 'A.G.O. Fight Song', which has been transcribed for a new carousel band organ in Missoula, Montana (1995).

Since 1985 several new organ method books have addressed issues of performance practice raised both by recent composition and by early music research (Brock 1988; Gleason and Crozier 1996; Soderlund 1986; Ritchie and Stauffer 1992). In response to recent renewed interest in the art of improvisation, several new improvisation method books have been published, the most auspicious by Gerre Hancock (Hancock 1994). The American Guild of Organists is a major force in the creation of new organ repertoire. The Guild published a major anthology of contemporary American organ music on the occasion of its ninetieth anniversary (AGO Anthology 1986); during its centennial year, it has initiated the publication of a second anthology, the ECS/AGO African-American Organ Series. The AGO has commissioned leading American composers, such as George Crumb (b. 1929) for its regional and national conventions. Since 1986, the AGO has sponsored an annual Composer of the Year programme which has recognised Samuel Adler (b. 1927), William Albright (b. 1944), Dominick Argento (b. 1927), Emma Lou Diemer (b. 1927), Don Locklair (b. 1949), Daniel Pinkham (b. 1923), Ned Rorem (b. 1923), Conrad Susa (b. 1935) and Virgil Thomson (1896–1989). In association with the AGO, the Holtkamp Organ Company provides an annual Holtkamp–AGO Award in Organ Composition. At the dawn of the twenty-first century, North American organ repertoire reflects a possible emerging ideal of a balanced emphasis on (1) informed performance of historic repertoire on church and concert hall instruments inspired by historic building practice, (2) fostering the composition of new organ repertoire, and (3) the art of improvisation.

Editions

Performing editions are available from Boosey & Hawkes (Copland, Rorem); Canadian Music Centre (Hambraeus); Elkan–Vogel Company (Albright, Persichetti); H. W. Gray/Belwin (Sowerby, Thomson); Jobert (Albright, Bolcom); Wayne Leupold Editions, Inc./ECS Publishing (Bates, Foote, Paine, Parker); Edward B. Marks/Hal Leonard (Bolcom); McAfee Music Corporation (Buck, Foote, Paine); Mercury Music (Ives); Oxford University Press (Sowerby, Willan); C. F. Peters Corp./Henmar Press, Inc. (Albright, Crumb, Finney, Hovhaness, Pinkham); Theodore Presser Company/Merion Music, Inc. (Hodkinson); E. C. Schirmer Publishing (Pinkham); G. Schirmer, Inc. (Barber). Anthologies are available from Oxford University Press (*AGO Anthology of American Organ Music*), H. W. Gray/Belwin (*Contemporary Masterworks for Organ* and *A Century of American Organ Music, Vols. I–IV*).

Appendix
The modes (toni) and their attributes according to Zarlino

Summary by Christopher Stembridge

The following summary may serve as an introduction to the modes, the basis of all organ music through to the seventeenth century. The voice-ranges of the twelve modes are given, the white note being the key-note. All are in their untransposed state with the exception of modes II and XI, which have been transposed respectively up a fourth and down a fifth, reflecting common usage. All pairs of modes function regularly: in the odd-numbered modes Tenor (and Soprano) use the authentic scale, Alto and Bass the plagal scale. In the even-numbered modes the roles are reversed except in the case of mode IV, which is often almost indistinguishable from mode III, having sometimes a smaller range, sometimes a larger one, especially at the upper end of the Soprano. In all cases it is quite normal to extend the voice-range occasionally by one or possibly two notes. For further reading see Meier 1992 and the present writer's introduction to his edition of Giovanni de Macque's *Ricercari sui Dodici Toni*. Unless otherwise stated, the descriptions represent a *précis* of the widely-known account of the modes given by Gioseffo Zarlino in his *Le istitutioni harmoniche* of 1558.

Mode I:

The sound of this mode, since it has a minor third above both d and a, is about mid-way between being sad and being cheerful. It is good for setting a serious text.

Mode II:

Traditionally used for laments and sad subjects. However, it is nearly always transposed up a fourth.

Mode III:

This mode has been used for lamentations and texts of a doleful nature. Its essentially rather hard character is normally tempered by cadences on a, which bring it close to Mode IX.

Mode IV:

This is wonderfully suited to lamentations, entreaties and texts full of flattery. It is rather sadder than Mode II, especially when it has a falling melodic line and a slow tempo.

Mode V*:

As this mode is considered harsh, it is little used today [1558]. Solace, happiness, triumph are some of its attributes.

Mode VI*:

Not very cheerful or elegant. Serious and devout.

Mode VII:

Cheerfulness, but lust and anger also.

Mode VIII:

This mode has a natural grace and sweetness, filling the listener with pure joy.

Mode IX:

Since this mode combines simplicity with an unusual soft sweetness, it is suitable for setting lyric poetry.

Mode X:

Similar to Modes II and IV. According to Diruta (Diruta 1609: IV/22), somewhat sad.

Mode XI*:

By nature very suitable for dance music. There is also much church music in this mode.

Mode XII*:

A certain sadness, suitable for plaints and love-songs.

*There is some confusion about these modes: V and VI as described by Glareanus and Zarlino are based on a Lydian scale (i.e. F–F with the raised fourth B♭ natural), However, many composers, including Claudio Merulo and both Gabrielis, used exclusively B♭ in these modes, so that they become identical with modes XI and XII respectively. The 'harsh' Lydian version is however used by, amongst others, Frescobaldi in both his *Fantasie* (1608) and his *Ricercari* (1615). (In the latter he does not in fact use XI or XII.)

While it became normal in Germany to use the 'ancient' names for the modes in the wake of Glarean's *Dodecachordon*, this nomenclature was rejected in sixteenth-century Italy and elsewhere since the modes understood by these names were not identical to those referred to by the same names in ancient music theory. The numerical system was more generally used and is simple to grasp. For those who are more familiar with the modes by these names, the following list may be helpful:

I   Dorian
II   Hypodorian
III   Phrygian
IV   Hypophrygian
V   Lydian
VI   Hypolydian
VII   Mixolydian
VIII Hypomixolydian
IX   Aeolian
X   Hypoaeolian
XI   Ionian
XII   Hypoionian

Notes

5 The organ case

1 Practical experiments show clearly that this is true; for example, in results of tests carried out by the American builder B. Batty, communicated privately to the author in May 1996.

10 Italian organ music to Frescobaldi

1 For further discussion of the music by this composer, the reader is encouraged to consult Judd 1995, Apel 1972 and Hammond l983.

2 This organ was still extant in the mid eighteenth century. Mattheson (Mattheson 1739: 466, §62) gives a second-hand description of it. He assumed that the small number of stops implied a small instrument, a basic mistake perpetuated even in recent publications.

3 This assumes that mean-tone temperament was being used at such an early date. It is interesting to note that an organ keyboard in an intarsia in Assisi, Basilica of San Francesco, shows an extra natural key between E and F. Since other details in this intarsia, such as the proportion of the pipes, suggest accuracy on the part of the artist (Apollonio da Ripatransone, 1471), this extra key, which is shown in both octaves of the two-octave keyboard, cannot easily be dismissed as an error. It would seem to the author that the purpose of such a key might have been to provide a solution for the wolf-fifth in Pythagorean tuning – albeit in an unusual place (i.e. a second e or f).

4 Unfortunately no music written for such a registration has survived. Antegnati also mentions that a similar arrangement existed at San Marco, Milan, where, at the request of Ottavio Bariolla and Ruggiero Trofeo the principale, the VIII and the f1auto in VIII were divided into treble and bass. Antegnati was unused to divided stops; he relates how he was taken by surprise when he encountered the divided principale at S. Giuseppe in Brescia.

5 In the Turin manuscript Giordano II, Merulo's *Toccata Ottava del Quarto tono* appears in an untransposed form – i.e. a fourth lower than the version in the 1598 print of Merulo's Toccatas.

6 It would, for instance, seem to the present writer a rather pointless exercise to play a Toccata by Merulo on an instrument tuned in equal temperament. The light and shade occasioned by passing from one chord to another would be reduced to a monotonous grey, like a poor photocopy of an artist's photograph. The musical line would be lost as cadences become non-events.

7 Diruta states that the beginning of any ricercar or canzona should be embellished, as should any voice given as a solo to one hand (Diruta 1593: 10v). In Spain a similar practice is clearly implied by Correa de Arauxo (Correa 1626: 16v), who states that a minim may occasionally be left unembellished.

8 A 4' organ generally reputed to have been built by Merulo himself is preserved at Parma Conservatory. (Doubt has however been expressed concerning its authenticity.) At Parma there were two claviorgana at the Farnese court according to an inventory dated 1587 – the year after Merulo took up duties as organist to the Duke. (I am indebted to Robert Judd for passing on this information to me.)

11 Iberian organ music before 1700

1 See the anthology *Spain and Portugal c.1550–1620* (Faber Early Organ Series 4, ed. J. Dalton, 1987), nos. 6, 7, 12, 13 and 14, for some indication of the system.

2. See J. Cabanilles, *Musici Organici Opera Omnia* 1, ed. H. Anglès (1927).

14 Catholic Germany and Austria 1648–c 1800

1 Gottlieb Muffat's *alternatim* Masses in F and C (incomplete), ed. Rudolf Walter (Doblinger 1980) and Poglietti's *Toccatina per l'Introito* (Faber Early Organ Series 15, no. 5) are rare examples of Mass music. The Muffat works give valuable insight into the role the organ could play at Mass. In addition, the large-scale toccatas and contrapuntal forms of the period (or sections of them) were evidently used as introits, graduals, offertories, elevations and communions along lines familiar from Frescobaldi's *Fiori musicali* (1635). A promising southern cantus firmus tradition, exemplified by Christian Erbach (Corpus of Early Keyboard Music 36) and Johann Ulrich Steigleder (CEKM 13), did not survive the Thirty Years War.

2 See Faber Early Organ Series 14, p. 15 for a fine example by Pachelbel's Nuremberg predecessor, Kindermann. Catholic aspects of

Pachelbel's training included study with a Kerll pupil, Kaspar Prenz, while in Catholic Regensburg at the Protestant Gymnasium there from 1670, and the post of deputy organist at St Stephen's Cathedral, Vienna in 1673–7, most of the time under Kerll himself. The Nuremberg organ Magnificat practice varied between the preludial and the *alternatim* according to liturgical occasion. The exact relationship of Pachelbel's ninety-five Magnificat fugues to the Nuremberg liturgy remains uncertain. Nolte's excellent article in *The New Grove Dictionary* remains the only readily available overview of Pachelbel in English.

3 The FbWV numbering in Johann Jacob Froberger, *New Edition of the Complete Keyboard and Organ Works,* ed. S. Rampe (Bärenreiter 1994–) adopts the item numbering of Guido Adler's historic 1897–1903 edition for *Denkmäler der Tonkunst in Österreich,* adding a centesimal digit according to genre: toccatas 101–, fantasias 201–, canzonas 301–, ricercars 401–, capriccios 501–.

4 The third note of Rampe's edition of the Ricercar FbVW 411 should be corrected to f[1].

5 Silbiger evaluates the authenticity of the non-autograph works contained in the first printed Froberger anthologies, of 1693, 1697 (Mainz) and 1698 (Amsterdam), and the posthumous manuscript copies. He also assesses the relative authority of the sources. A fascinating example of Froberger's (and south German) influence in England can be seen in *John Blow's Anthology* ed. Thurston Dart rev. Davitt Moroney (Stainer & Bell, 1978), which in addition to much Froberger also includes music by Fischer and Strungk. Webber 1986 illustrates aspects of north German assimilation.

6 Though Poglietti's twelve ricercars circulated widely as a complete set, Ricercar IV was in fact printed as early as 1650 in Rome in Kircher's *Musurgia Universalis,* attributed to Kerll. The attribution of Ricercar XI is also doubtful.

7 Wollenberg's article on Georg Muffat for *The New Grove Dictionary* remains the only authoritative general consideration of the composer in English – likewise her articles on Fischer and Gottlieb Muffat.

8 Six capriccios and one ricercar by Strungk are published in *Denkmäler der Tonkunst in Österreich,* xiii, 2 (vol. 27, 1906) erroneously attributed to Georg Reutter the elder (see Apel 1972: 575–6). The *Capriccio sopra Ich dank dir schon* and the ricercar on the death of his mother are published in Kistner & Siegel's *Organum* Series IV, No. 2, ed. M. Seiffert. Sections from both works were 'borrowed' by Handel for *Israel in Egypt* and *Saul* respectively. A good complete edition of Strungk's keyboard works is badly needed.

9 *Classical Organ Music,* vol. 1, ed. R. Langley (Oxford University Press 1986) gives another good example of Seger and a fine introduction to this troubled period for the organ.

15 The north German organ school

1 Michael Praetorius's treatise of 1619 is the most important single document regarding the north German organ in the early seventeenth century, containing specifications of thirty-four contemporary organs from all over Germany.

2 For a general survey of the duties and social position of the north German organist during the seventeenth century, see Edler 1985.

3 The work is included in the complete edition of Sweelinck's works (see under Editions, p. 234).

4 This registration associated with Jacob Praetorius is taken from an account of Matthias Weckmann's audition for the post of organist at the Jakobikirche in Hamburg, as recorded by Johann Kortkamp in his 'Organistenchroniek'. For details see Davidsson 1991: 51.

5 Scheidt's instructions can be found in the edition of his *Tabulatura nova* (1624), and for a general guide to registrations in the cantus firmus repertoire see Davidsson 1991: 47–58.

6 The practice of playing a single chorale verse before the congregation begins to sing the chorale is specifically mentioned in a Braunschweig–Lüneburg church book of 1709 (see Glabbatz 1909: 18).

7 Radeck's Canzona is included in Beckmann's collection of miscellaneous free compositions: *Freie Orgelwerke des norddeutschen Barocks* (Wiesbaden 1988).

8 For a more thorough survey of Buxtehude's organ works, see Snyder 1987: 227–73.

17 German organ music after 1800

1 Immanuel Kant defined *Aufklärung* as the courage to use one's reason to think independently and critically, refusing to accept the tutelage of another's authority. *Empfindsamkeit* was a cultural movement focusing on inner experience and individual development, seen as having its origins in Pietism. See M. Fulbrook, *A Concise History of Germany* (Cambridge 1990), pp. 88 and 92.

2 Literally, 'useful' music; by implication, music which served a functional purpose.

3 They were often marked *ad libitum.* This may have been pragmatic on the part of composers, especially in South Germany and Austria. Many organs had a short octave and compass (up to a[2]).

4 This information and specification are given by Ewald Kooiman in the Preface to his edition of Hesse's Variations on 'God Save the King!' (Harmonia 1995).

5 A full survey of the nineteenth- and twentieth-

century organ sonata is beyond the scope of this essay. The reader is directed to examples by composers, *inter alia*, in the following chronological list: Johann Georg Herzog, Johann Gottlob Töpfer, Franz Lachner, August Gottfried Ritter, Jan Albert van Eyken, Gustav Merkel, Christian Fink, Rudolf Bibl, Julius Reubke, Josef Rheinberger, Josef Labor, Ludwig Neuhoff, Hans Fährmann, Ludwig Thuille, Max Reger, Camillo Schumann, Sigfrid Karg-Elert (Sonatina in A minor), Josef Haas, Heinrich Kaminski (*Choralsonate* 1925), Gottfried Rüdinger, Paul Hindemith, Ernst Krenek, Conrad Beck, Günther Raphael, Hermann Schroeder, Helmut Bornefeld, Hugo Distler, Kurt Hessenberg, Harald Genzmer, Johannes Driessler, Anton Heiller, Wolfgang Stockmeier. A comprehensive list of organ sonatas written between 1960 and 1983 is given in Dorfmüller 1983: 199–240. See also Weyer 1969, Lucas 1986 and Beckmann 1994. In addition to the sonata composers continued to write other types of extended, free-form piece throughout the nineteenth and twentieth centuries – prelude and fugue, fantasy and fugue, toccata and fugue, passacaglia and fugue, theme and variations – as well as short, occasional pieces of a mainly functional nature.
6 Liszt's monumental Piano Sonata in B minor (1852–3) was also to prove one of the most influential works of the period. In his *Sonata on the 94th Psalm* Julius Reubke (1834–58) adopts his mentor's single-movement, monothematic procedure, subjecting an angular, chromatic theme to a series of arresting metamorphoses.
7 Further examples of the chorale fantasy are: Heinrich Karl Breidenstein, *Ein' feste Burg ist unser Gott*; Christian Heinrich Fink, *Ein' feste Burg ist unser Gott* Op. 23; Heinrich von Herzogenberg, *Nun komm, der heiden Heiland* Op. 39 and *Nun danket alle Gott* Op. 46; Hans Fährmann, *Ein' fest Burg ist unser Gott* Op. 28; Hugo Kaun, *Morgenglanz der Ewigkeit*; Arno Landmann, *Herzliebster Jesu, was hast du verbrochen*.
8 Well-crafted examples may be found in the works of Johann Gottlob Töpfer, Carl Ferdinand Becker, Ernst Friedrich Richter, August Gottfried Ritter, Jan Albert van Eyken, Wilhelm Rust, Robert Papperitz, Gustav Merkel, Christian Fink, Johannes Brahms, Heinrich von Herzogenberg, Carl Piutti, Theophil Forchhammer, Arnold Mendelssohn, Felix Woyrsch, Max Reger, Franz Schmidt, Sigfrid Karg-Elert, Alfred Sittard, Josef Haas, Johanna Senfter, Karl Hasse, Hermann Ernst Koch, Arno Landmann and Karl Hoyer.
9 Other pupils of Reger were Johanna Senfter, Hermann Ernst Koch, Gottfried Rüdinger, Hermann Grabner, Arno Landmann, Fritz Lubrich (jun.) and Rudolf Moser.

10 The leading protagonists have been Hermann Grabner, Heinrich Kaminski, Arno Landmann, Johann Nepomuk David, Günther Ramin, Willy Burkhard, Ernst Pepping, Hans Friedrich Micheelsen, Gunther Raphael, Josef Ahrens, Helmut Bornefeld, Karl Höller, Helmut Walcha, Hugo Distler, Kurt Hessenberg, Harald Genzmer, Siegfried Rega, Johannes Driessler, Anton Heiller and Wolfgang Stockmeier.
11 Notably by Hermann Grabner, Ernst Pepping, Georg Trexler, Hermann Schroeder and Joseph Ahrens.

19 British organ music after 1800
1 British Library, Add. MS 27953.
2 The worklist for Wesley's organ compositions in *The New Grove Dictionary* has since been thoroughly revised; see Langley 1993: 102–16. Langley's preface to his selected edition of Wesley's organ music *Six Voluntaries and Fugues for Organ* (Oxford University Press 1981) also gives further details of sources and the original publication of some of the works.
3 For an over-view of the eighteenth and early nineteenth-century organ concerto, see Cudworth 1953: 51–60.
4 Wesley's Bach duet is in the British Library, Add. MS 14340. For an early résumé of Bach's music in Britain, see Edwards 1896: 585–7, 652–7, 722–6, 797–800. Williams (1963: 140–51) gives an excellent critique of the impact of Bach on composers for organ, and Dirst (1995: 64–8) details Wesley's propagation of Bach's music. Thistlethwaite (1990: 163–80) also investigates the burgeoning interest in Bach during the opening decades of the nineteenth century.
5 *Henry Smart's Organ Book* (Boosey 1873), reissued by Edwin Lemare in 1911 as Henry Smart's *Twelve Pieces* (Boosey), and Novello's conflation of its previous Smart edition with pieces from *The Organist's Quarterly Journal* (ed. Spark) as Henry Smart's *Original Compositions for Organ*, provide a good picture of Smart's work.
6 Published by Novello under the general title of *Arrangements from the Scores of the Masters*, stretching to 100 numbers.
7 Forgotten in recent times (not helped by its absence from the worklists currently available), this work appeared originally in William Spark's *The Organist's Quarterly Journal* (no. 29) and was later republished by Novello (1887) in their series *Original Compositions for the Organ* (no. 89).
8 The increasing impact of overseas recitalists in Britain during the twentieth century and the not inconsiderable influence of recorded sound should not be overlooked.

Bibliography

Aaron, P. 1523, *Thoscanello de la musica*, Venice (repr. 1969; English translation by P. B. Bergquist, Colorado Springs 1970).

[Adamoli, I., Bentini, J., Krauss, E., Mischiati, O., Tagliavini, L. F.] 1982, *Il restauro degli organi di S. Petronio*, Bologna.

Adlung, J. 1768, *Musica mechanica organoedi*, ed. J. L. Albrecht and J. F. Agricola, Berlin (repr. Kassel 1961).

Ammerbach, E. N. 1571, *Orgel oder Instrument Tabulatur*, Leipzig, repr. Nuremberg 1583 (English translation by C. Jacobs, Oxford 1984).

Andersen, P.-G. 1956, *Orgelbogen*, Copenhagen (English translation, *Organ Building and Design*, London 1969).

Antegnati, C. 1608, *L'arte organica*, Brescia (facsimile repr. Bologna 1971).

Anthony, J. 1997, *French Baroque Music*, London (3rd edn).

Apel, W. 1972, *The History of Keyboard Music to 1700* (transl. and rev. H. Tischler), Bloomington and London.

Archbold, L. and Peterson, W. J. (eds.) 1995, *French Organ Music from the Revolution to Franck and Widor*, New York.

Armstrong, W. H. 1967, *Organs for America: The Life and Work of David Tannenberg*, Philadelphia.

Arnold, C. R. 1984, *Organ Literature: A Comprehensive Survey* (2 vols.), Metuchen, NJ and London.

Audsley, G. A. 1905, *The Art of Organ-Building*, New York.

Bach, C. P. E. 1753, 1762, *Versuch über die wahre Art das Clavier zu spielen*, Berlin (Part I rev. 1787) (English translation by W. J. Mitchell, *The True Art of Playing the Keyboard*, New York 1949).

Banchieri, A. 1605, 4/1638, *L'organo suonarino*, Venice (facsimile repr. of 4th edn Bologna 1978).

  1609, *Conclusioni nel suono dell'organo*, Bologna (facsimile repr. Milan 1934; English translation by L. R. Garrett, *Conclusions for Playing the Organ*, Colorado Springs 1982).

Barber, G. 1989, ' "Symphonic Metamorphosis": Karg-Elert's Symphony for Organ', *The Musical Times* 130: 769–71.

Barbour, J. M. 1951, *Tuning and Temperament: A Historical Survey*, East Lansing, MI.

Beckmann, K. 1987, 'Was Buxtehude's E Major Prelude Originally in C Major? Transposition Hypotheses regarding Organ Works by D. Buxtehude and V. Lübeck', *Kirchenmusiker* 27/3: 77–84 and 27/4: 122–7.

  1994, *Repertorium Orgelmusik 1150–1992*, Moos am Bodensee.

Bédos de Celles, Dom F. (OSB) 1766–78, *L'Art du Facteur d'Orgues* (4 vols.), Paris.

Bermudo, J. 1549, *Libro llamado declaracion de instrumentos musicales*, Osuna (repr. 1555).

Bernhard, C. *c*1660, 'Tractatus compositionis augmentatus', ed. J. M. Müller-Blattau in *Die Kompositionslehre Heinrich Schützens in der Fassung seines Schülers Christoph Bernhard*, Kassel 1926, repr. Kassel 1963 (English translation by W. Hilse, 'The Treatises of Christoph Bernhard', *Music Forum* 3 (1973)).

Bicknell, S. 1982, 'The Organ in Wollaton Hall', *BIOS Journal (British Institute of Organ Studies Journal)* 6: 43–57.

1996, *The History of the English Organ*, Cambridge.

Blanchard, H. D. 1975, *Organs of our Time*, Delaware, OH.

1981, *Organs of our Time II*, Delaware, OH.

Blanton, J. E. 1957, *The Organ in Church Design*, Albany, NY.

1965, *The Revival of the Organ Case*, Albany, NY.

Blume, F. 1975, *Protestant Church Music – A History*, London.

Bovicelli, G. B. 1594, *Regole Passaggi di Musica Madrigali*, Venice (facsimile repr. Kassel 1957).

Bower, R. 1995, 'A Holdich Temperament', *The Organbuilder* 13: 22.

Brock, J. 1988, *Introduction to Organ Playing in 17th & 18th Century Style*, Knoxville, TN.

Buchner, H., 'Fundamentum sive ratio vera, quae docet quemvis cantum planum', Zurich, Zentralbibliothek MS 284, ed. C. Paesler, 'Das Fundamentbuch von Hans von Constanz', *Vierteljahrsschrift für Musikwissenschaft* 5 (1889): 1–192. Also published in *Hans Buchner: Sämtliche Orgelwerke*, ed. J. H. Schmidt, *Das Erbe Deutscher Musik* 54–5, Frankfurt 1974.

Buelow, G. J. 1985, 'Johann Jacob Froberger', *The New Grove: North European Baroque Masters*, London, pp. 151–70.

Burchell, D. 1992, '"The Psalms Set full for the organ" by John Reading', *BIOS Journal* 16: 14–28.

Butt, J. 1995, 'Germany and the Netherlands', *Keyboard Music before 1700*, ed. A. Silbiger, New York, pp. 147–234.

Cabezón, H. de. 1578, *Obras de música*, Madrid, ed. H. Anglès, *Monumentos de música española* 27–9, 1966.

Caffi, F. 1854–5, *Storia della musica sacra nella già cappella ducale di San Marco in Venezia dal 1318 al 1797*, Venice, repr. Milan 1931.

Caldwell, J. 1965, 'Keyboard Plainsong Settings in England, 1500–1660', *Musica Disciplina* 19: 129–53 (addenda and corrigenda in *Musica Disciplina* 34 (1980): 215–19).

1970, 'The Pitch of Early Tudor Organ Music', *Music and Letters* 51: 156–63.

1973, *English Keyboard Music Before the Nineteenth Century*, Oxford, repr. New York 1985.

Callahan, C. 1990, *The American Classic Organ: A History in Letters*, Richmond, VA.

Campbell, D. M. and Greated, C. A. 1987, *The Musician's Guide to Acoustics*, New York.

Clark, J. B. 1974, *Transposition in 17th-century English Organ Accompaniments and the Transposing Organ*, Detroit.

Clark, R. 1994, 'Transcriptions', *BIOS Journal* 18: 126–36.

Coltman, J. W. 1969, 'Sound Radiation from the Mouth of an Organ Pipe', *Journal of the Acoustical Society of America* 46: 477.

Correa de Arauxo, F. 1626, *Facultad organica*, Alcalá (facsimile repr. Geneva 1981).

Couperin, F. 1717, *L'Art de toucher le clavecin*, Paris.

Cox, G. 1983, 'John Blow and the Earliest English Cornet Voluntaries', *BIOS Journal* 7: 4–17.

    1989, *Organ Music in Restoration England: A Study of Sources, Styles and Influences* (2 vols.), New York.

    1995, 'The English Trumpet Voluntary at the time of Henry Purcell', *BIOS Journal* 19: 30–45.

Crociata, F. 1995, 'Leo Sowerby: The 100th Anniversary Celebration of an American Original', *The American Organist* 29/5: 50–3.

Crüger, J. 1660, *Musicae practicae praecepta brevia: Der rechte Weg zur Singekunst*, Berlin.

Cudworth, C. L. 1953, 'The English Organ Concerto', *The Score* 8: 51–60.

Dähnert, U. 1962, *Der Orgel- und Instrumentenbauer Zacharias Hildebrandt*, Leipzig.

    1970, 'Johann Sebastian Bach's Ideal Organ', *Organ Yearbook* 1: 21–37.

    1980, *Historische Orgeln in Sachsen*, Frankfurt am Main.

    1986, 'Organs Played and Tested by J. S. Bach', *J. S. Bach as Organist*, ed. G. Stauffer and E. May, London.

Dart, T. 1954, 'A New Source of Early English Organ Music', *Music and Letters* 35: 201–4.

David, H. and Mendel, A. (eds.) 1945, *The Bach Reader*, New York (rev. 1966).

Davidsson, H. 1991, *Matthias Weckmann: The Interpretation of his Organ Music*, vol. I, Göteborg.

Diruta, G. 1593, *Il transilvano dialogo sopra il vero modo di sonar organi et istromenti da penna*, Venice (facsimile repr. Bologna 1969; English translation by M. C. Bradshaw and E. J. Soehlen, Henryville, PA).

Dirst, M. 1995, 'Samuel Wesley and The Well-Tempered Clavier: A Case Study in Bach Reception', *The American Organist* 29/5 1995: 64–8.

Donat, F. W. 1933, *Christian Heinrich Rinck und die Orgelmusik seiner Zeit*, Bad Oeynhausen.

Donati, P. P. 1993, '1470–1490 organi di cartone degli studioli dei principi', *La musica a Firenze al tempo di Lorenzo il Magnifico*, ed. P. Gargiulo, Florence, pp. 275–81.

    1995, ' "Spicco" e tocco organistico', *Musicus Perfectus – studi in onore di Luigi Ferdinando Tagliavini*, Bologna, pp. 107–13.

Donington, R. 1992, *The Interpretation of Early Music*, rev. edn, New York.

Dorfmüller, J. 1983, *Zeitgenössische Orgelmusik 1960–1983*, Wolfenbüttel and Zurich.

Douglass, F. 1969, *The Language of the Classical French Organ*, New Haven and London (2nd edn 1995).

Downes, R. 1983, *Baroque Tricks*, Oxford.

Dufourcq, N. 1972 *Le livre d'orgue français*, vol. IV *La Musique*, Paris.

Edler, A. 1985, 'Organ Music within the Social Structure of North German Cities in the Seventeenth Century', *Church, Stage and Studio: Music and Its Contexts in Seventeenth-Century Germany*, ed. P. Walker, Ann Arbor, pp. 23–41.

Edwards, F. G. 1896, 'Bach's Music in England', *Musical Times* 37: 585–7, 652–7, 722–6, and 797–800.

Edwards, L. (ed.) 1992, *The Historical Organ in America: A Documentary of Recent Organs Based on European & American Models*, Easthampton, MA.

Ellis, A. J. 1880, see Mendel, A. 1968, below.

Engramelle, M.-D.-J. 1775, *La tonotechnie ou l'art de noter les cylindres*, Paris (facsimile repr. Geneva 1971).

Erig, R. 1979, *Italian Diminutions*, Zurich.

Ferguson, H. 1975, *Keyboard Interpretation from the 14th to the 19th Century: An Introduction*, New York and London.

Ferguson, J. A. 1979, *Walter Holtkamp, American Organ Builder*, Kent, OH.

Fesperman, J. 1962, *The Organ as Musical Medium*, New York.
    1982, *Flentrop in America: An Account of the Work and Influence of the Dutch Organ Builder D. A. Flentrop in the United States, 1939–1977*, Raleigh, NC.

Fischer, H. and Wohnhaas, T. 1982, *Historische Orgeln in Schwaben*, Munich and Zurich.

Fletcher, N. H. and Rossing, T. D. 1991, *The Physics of Musical Instruments*, New York and London.

Fletcher, N. H. and Thwaites, S. 1983, 'The Physics of Organ Pipes', *Scientific American* 248: 94–103.

Freeman, A. and Rowntree, J. 1977, *Father Smith: Otherwise Bernard Smith, Being an Account of a Seventeenth Century Organ Maker*, Oxford.

Fuller, D. 1986, 'Commander-in-Chief of the American Revolution in Organbuilding: Emerson Richards', *Charles Brenton Fisk, Organ Builder – Essays in His Honor*, ed. F. Douglass, O. Jander and B. Owen, Easthampton, MA, pp. 55–84.

Gallat-Morin, E. 1988, *Le livre d'orgue de Montréal*, Paris and Montreal.

Geer, E. H. 1957, *Organ Registration in Theory and Practice*, Glen Rock, NJ.

Gerlach, S. 1984, *Sigfrid Karg-Elert – Verzeichnis Sämtlicher Werke*, Odenthal.

Glabbatz, H. 1909, *Der Organist einst und jetzt*, Göttingen.

Göllner, M. L. 1982. *Eine neue Quelle zur italienischen Orgelmusik des Cinquecento*, Tutzing.

Gleason, H. 1988, *Method of Organ Playing* (7th edn), Englewood Cliffs, NJ.
    1996, *Method of Organ Playing* (8th edn, ed. C. Crozier), Englewood Cliffs, NJ.

Gorenstein, N. 1993, *L'Orgue post-classique français*, Paris.

Graaf, G. A. C. de 1982, 'The Gothic Organ in the Chapel of St. Bartholomew in Salamanca', *ISO Information* 22: 9–34.

Grace, H. 1926–7, 'Modern English Organ Composers', *The Rotunda* 1/2: 41–8; 1/3: 25–31; 1/4: 11–17.

Graves, C. L. 1926, *Hubert Parry* (2 vols.), London.

Gwynn, D. 1985, 'Organ Pitch in Seventeenth Century England' *BIOS Journal* 9: 65–78.

Hammond, F. 1983, *Girolamo Frescobaldi*, Cambridge, MA and London.

Hancock, G. 1994, *Improvising: How to Master the Art*, New York.

Hantz, E. 1973, 'An Introduction to the Organ Music of William Albright', *The Diapason* 5 (May): 1–5.

Hase-Koehler, E. von (ed.) 1928, *Max Reger: Briefe eines deutschen Meisters –
Ein Lebensbild*, Leipzig.

Heuren, J. van, 1804, *De Orgelmaker* (3 vols.), Dordrecht 1804–5.

Herbst, J. A. 1653, *Musicae moderna prattica*, Frankfurt.

Higginbottom, E. 1976, 'French Classical Organ Music and the Liturgy', *Proceedings
of the Royal Musical Association* 103: 19–40.

    1981, 'Ecclesiastical Prescription and Musical Style in French Classical Organ
Music', *Organ Yearbook* 12: 31–54.

Hilgemann, W. and Kinder, H. 1978, *The Penguin Atlas of World History, Volume II:
From the French Revolution to the Present* (English translation by E. Menze),
London.

Hill, A. G. 1883–91, *The Organ-Cases and Organs of the Middle Ages and Renaissance:
A Comprehensive Essay* (2 vols.), London.

Hilmes, O. 1996, 'Karl Hoyer (1891–1936)', *Mitteilungen der Karg-Elert Gesellschaft*
8: 51–61.

Holden, D. J. 1985, *The Life and Work of Ernest M. Skinner*, Richmond.

Holmes, E. 1828, *A Ramble among the Musicians of Germany*, London.

Hopkins, E. J. and Rimbault, E. F. 1855, *The Organ, Its History and Construction*,
London.

Horton, P. (ed.) 1963, S. S. Wesley, *Anthems II*, Musica Britannica 63, London.

Houle, G. 1987, *Meter in Music, 1600–1800*, Bloomington.

Howell, A. C. 1958, 'French Baroque Organ Music and the Eight Church Tones',
Journal of the American Musicological Society 11: 106–18.

Hunter, D. 1992, 'My Ladye Nevells Book and the Art of Gracing', *Byrd Studies*,
ed. A. Brown and R. Turbet, Cambridge, pp. 174–92.

Hurford, P. 1988, *Making Music on the Organ*, Oxford.

Jakob, F. *et al.* 1991, *Die Valeria Orgel: ein gothisches Werk in der Burgkirche zu
Sitten/Sion*, Zurich.

Jancke, R. 1977, *The Planning and Realisation of Contemporary Organs*
(*ISO Information* 16).

Jeppesen, K. 1960, *Die italienische Orgelmusik am Anfang des Cinquecento* (2nd edn),
Copenhagen.

Joy, R. (ed.) 1953, *Music in the Life of Albert Schweitzer*, London.

Judd, R. F. 1995, 'Italy', *Keyboard Music before 1700*, ed. A. Silbiger, New York,
pp. 235–311.

Kee, P. 1988, *Number and Symbolism in the Passacaglia and Ciacona*, Buckfastleigh.

Kent, C. 1990, 'Tuning and Temperament and the British Organ 1750–1850: A
Century of Change Viewed through the Repertoire', *BIOS Journal* 14: 21–34.

Kienzle, M. J. M. 1988, *The Life and Work of John Brombaugh, Organ Builder*, Ann
Arbor (University Microfilms International).

Kjersgaard, M. 1987, 1988, 'Technical Aspects of Swedish Organ-building during the
Middle Ages', *ISO Information* 27 (1987): 5–118; *ISO Information* 29 (1988):
29–30.

Klais, H.-G. 1975, *Reflections on the Organ Stoplist*, Delaware, OH.

    1990, *Design Principles in the Planning of Organ Cases*, Bonn.

Kooiman, E. 1995, 'Jacques Lemmens, Charles-Marie Widor, and the French Bach

Tradition' (English translation by J. Brock), *The American Organist* 29/3: 56–64.

Kollmann, A. F. C. 1812, *The Quarterly Musical Register* 1 (Jan 1812).

Kratzenstein, M. 1980, *Survey of Organ Literature and Editions.*

Kroeger, E. (ed.) 1904, *Alexandre Guilmant's Organ Recitals: The Forty Programs Rendered by M. Alexandre Guilmant at Festival Hall, World's Fair, St. Louis Together with Annotations by Mr. Ernest R. Kroeger,* St Louis (repr. by The Organ Historical Society, Inc. 1985).

Langley, R. 1993, 'Samuel Wesley's Contribution to the Development of English Organ Literature', *BIOS Journal* 17: 102–16.

Le Cerf de la Viéville 1725, *Comparaison de la musique italienne et de la musique françoise,* Paris 1706, repr. in P. Bourdet and J. Bonnet, *Histoire de la musique,* 2nd edn, Amsterdam 1725.

Le Huray, P. G. 1981, 'English Keyboard Fingering', *Source Materials and the Interpretation of Music,* ed. I. Bent, London, pp. 251–7.

Lemmens, J. N. 1862, *Ecole d'orgue basée sur le plainchant,* Brussels.

Levy, B. A. 1983, 'The Organ at Mechanics Hall', *The Diapason* 6 (June): 13–15.

Lindley, M. 1980, 'Temperaments', *The New Grove Dictionary of Music and Musicians,* London.

1985, 'Bach's Tunings', *The Musical Times* 126: 721–6.

1993, *Ars ludendi: Early German Keyboard Fingerings, c. 1525–c. 1625,* Neuhof.

Lindley, M. and Boxall, M. *c*1992, *Early Keyboard Fingerings: A Comprehensive Guide,* Mainz.

Lucas, V. 1986, *Reclams Orgelmusikführer* (5th edn), Stuttgart (English translation by A. Wyburd, *A Guide to Organ Music,* Portland, OR 1989).

Mackenzie, A. C. 1979, 'The Well-Tuned Organ: An Introduction to Keyboard Temperaments in 18th and 19th Century England', *BIOS Journal* 3: 56–72.

Mackey, D. (ed.) 1981, *L'Orgue à notre époque: Papers and Proceedings of the Symposium Held at McGill University, May 26–28, 1981,* Montreal.

Mainstone, J. S. 1992, 'Young Mr Newton and the overblown pipe', *BIOS Journal* 16: 44–9.

Marpurg, F. W. 1756, *Principes du clavecin,* Berlin (facsimile repr. Bologna 1971).

1776, *Versuch über die musikalische Temperatur,* Breslau.

Mattheson, J. 1735, *Kleine General-Bass-Schule,* Hamburg (facsimile repr., *Dokumente früher Musik und Musikliteratur im Faksimile* 2, Laaber 1980).

1739, *Der vollkommene Capellmeister,* Hamburg (facsimile repr. Kassel 1954; English translation by E. C. Harris, Ann Arbor 1981).

Meier, B. 1992, *Alte Tonarten dargestellt an der Instrumentalmusik des 16. und 17. Jahrhunderts,* Kassel (an English translation by C. Collins Judd and R. Judd is to be published by Oxford University Press under the title *The Modes of Early Instrumental Music*).

Mendel, A. ed. 1968, *Studies in the History of Musical Pitch,* Amsterdam.

1978, 'Pitch in Western Music since 1500 – A Re-examination', Kassel.

Mersenne, M. 1636–7, *Harmonie universelle,* Paris (facsimile repr. 1963).

Mizler, L. C. 1754, *Neu eröffnete musikalische Bibliothek,* vol. 4, Leipzig.

Monette, L. G. 1992, *The Art of Organ Voicing,* Kalamazoo, MI.

Morehen, J. 1995, 'The Organ in the Post-Reformation English Liturgy', *The Royal College of Organists Journal* 3: 40–50.

Neenan, T. A. 1987, 'Ornamentation in the Music of Dieterich Buxtehude and His Contemporaries', *The American Organist* 21/5: 72–4.

Neighbour, O. 1979, *The Consort and Keyboard Music of William Byrd*, London.

Nivers, G.-G. 1665, *Livre d'orgue contenant cent pièces de tous les tons de l'église*, Paris (facsimile repr. 1987).

Noack, F. 1978, *Trends in American Organ Building in 1976* (*ISO Information* 15).

Ochse, O. 1975, *The History of the Organ in the United States*, Bloomington and London.

Oldham, G. 1960, 'Louis Couperin, a New Source of French Keyboard Music of the Mid-17th Century', *Recherches sur la musique française classique* 1: 51–60.

Owen, B. 1979, *The Organ in New England: An Account of its Use and Manufacture to the End of the Nineteenth Century*, Raleigh, NC.

Owen, B. (ed.) 1975–1991, *A Century of American Organ Music* (prefaces to vols. 1–4), Miami.

Padgham, C. A. 1986, *The Well-Tempered Organ*, Oxford.

Padgham, C. A., Collins, P. D. and Parker, C. A. 1979, 'A Trial of Unequal Temperaments on the Organ', *BIOS Journal* 3: 73–92.

Pape, U. 1978, *The Tracker Organ Revival in America*, Berlin.

Parkins, R. 1983, 'Keyboard Fingering in Early Spanish Sources', *Early Music* 11/3: 323–31.

Parratt, Sir W. 1892, 'On Musical Instruments and Music: II, the Organ', *The Victorian Magazine* January 1892: 105–7.

Pascall, R. 1995, 'Brahms's Solo Organ Works', *The Royal College of Organists Journal* 3: 97–120.

Peeters, F. and Vente, M. A. 1971, *The Organ and Its Music in the Netherlands*, Antwerp.

Perrot, J. 1971, *The Organ, from Its Invention in the Hellenistic Period to the End of the Thirteenth Century*, London.

Phelps, L. I. 1967, *A Short History of the Organ Revival*, St Louis.

Praetorius, M. 1619, *Syntagma Musicum*, vol. II *De organographia*, Wolfenbüttel (facsimile ed. W. Gurlitt, Kassel 1985); vol. III *Termini musici*, Wolfenbüttel (facsimile ed. W. Gurlitt, Kassel 1954).

Radulescu, M. 1980, 'Die 12 Toccaten von Georg Muffat', *Die süddeutsch-österreichische Orgelmusik im 17. und 18. Jahrhundert*, ed. W. Salmen, Innsbruck, pp. 169–84.

Radulescu, M. (ed.) 1993, *Nicolaus Bruhns: Orgelwerke*, vol. 2, Vienna.

Rameau, J.-P. 1724, *Pièces de clavecin*, Paris (ed. K. Gilbert, Paris 1979). 1737, *Génération harmonique*, Paris.

Reed, D. 1976, *The Organ Works of William Albright: 1965–75*, Ann Arbor (University Microfilms International). 1993, 'William Albright: Organ Music of the 80s', *The American Organist* 27/4: 60–3.

Riemann, H. 1898, *Geschichte der Musiktheorie*, Leipzig (English translation by Raymond H. Haggh, *History of Music Theory*, Lincoln, NE 1962).

Rinck, J. C. 1818, *Praktische Orgel-Schule*, Op. 55, Bonn and Cologne (English translation by W. T. Best, *Rink's Organ School*, Boston 1870)

Ritchie, G. and Stauffer, G. 1992, *Organ Technique: Modern and Early*, Englewood Cliffs, NJ.

Röhring, K. (ed.) 1974, *Max Reger 1873–1973 – Ein Symposion*, Wiesbaden.

Routh, F. 1973, *Early English Organ Music from the Middle Ages to 1837*, London.

Rowntree, J. 1979, 'Organ Reform in England – Some Influences', *BIOS Journal* 3: 5–16.

　1996, *Organs in Britain 1990–1995*, Basingstoke.

Rowntree, J. P. and Brennan J. F. 1975, *The Classical Organ in Britain 1955–1974*, Oxford.

　1979, *The Classical Organ in Britain Volume Two 1975–78*, Oxford.

　1993, *The Classical Organ in Britain Volume Three 1979–1990*, Oxford.

Sachs, B. and Ife, B. 1981, *Anthology of Early Keyboard Methods (Diruta, Santa Maria, Ammerbach, Banchieri, Buchner, H. de Cabezón, Venegas)*, Cambridge.

Sadie, J. A. (ed.) 1990, *Companion to Baroque Music*, London.

Saint-Lambert, Monsieur de 1702, *Les Principes du clavecin*, Paris (English translation by R. Harris-Warrick, *Principles of the Harpsichord*, Cambridge 1984).

Santa María, Fr. T. de 1565, *Libro llamada arte de tañer fantasia*, Valladolid (facsimile repr. Heppenheim 1972; English translation by A. C. Howell and W. E. Hultberg, *The Art of Playing the Fantasia*, Pittsburgh 1991).

Scheidt, S. 1624, *Tabulatura nova*, Hamburg (Part 1 ed. H. Vogel, Wiesbaden 1994).

Schlick, A. 1511, *Spiegel der Orgelmacher und Organisten*, Mainz (facsimile with English translation by E. B. Barber, Buren 1980).

Scholes, P. (ed.) 1944, *The Mirror of Music*, London.

Schweitzer, A. 1906, *Deutsche und französische Orgelbaukunst und Orgelkunst*, Leipzig.

　1931, *Aus meinem Leben und Denken*, Leipzig.

Servières, G. 1928, *La Décoration Artistique du Buffet de l'Orgue*, Paris

Silbiger, A. 1993, 'Tracing the Contents of Froberger's Lost Autographs', *Current Musicology* 54: 5–23.

Skinner, E. M. and R. H. 1981, *The Composition of the Organ*, Ann Arbor.
[no date], *The Modern Organ*, Braintree.

Snyder, K. J. 1987, *Dieterich Buxtehude: Organist in Lübeck*, New York and London.

Soderlund, S. 1986, *Organ Technique: An Historical Approach*, Chapel Hill 1980, 2nd edn 1986.

Spark, W. 1881, *Henry Smart: His Life and Works*, London.

Stembridge, C. 1993, 'The Cimbalo Cromatico and other Italian Keyboard Instruments with Nineteen or More Divisions to the Octave', *Performance Practice Review* 6: 33–59.

　1994, see under Wraight, D. and Stembridge.

Stevens, D. 1969, *Early Tudor Organ Music II: Music for the Mass* (*Early English Church Music* 10), London.

Sumner, W. L. 1973, *The Organ: Its Evolution, Principles of Construction and Use*, London (4th edn).

Tagliavini, L. F. 1986, 'Notes on Tuning Methods in Fifteenth-century Italy', *Charles Brenton Fisk, Organ Builder – Essays in His honor*, ed. F. Douglass, O. Jander and B. Owen, Easthampton, MA, pp. 191–9.

Tagliavini, L. F. 1992, 'Note sull'uso del pedale nella prassi organo-cembalistica italiana', *Livro de homenagem a Macario Santiago Kastner*, Lisbon.

Thistlethwaite, N. 1990, *The Making of the Victorian Organ*, Cambridge.

Türk, D. G. 1789, *Klavierschule*, Leipzig (English translation by R. H. Haggh, *School of Clavier Playing, or Instructions in Playing the Clavier for Teachers and Students*, Lincoln, NE and London 1982).

Van Pelt, W. 1991, *The Hook Opus List, 1829–1916 in Facsimile*, Richmond, VA.

Van Wye, B. 1980, 'The Ritual Use of the Organ in France', *Journal of the American Musicological Society*, 33: 287–325.

Venegas de Henestrosa, L. 1557, *Libro de cifra nueva para tecla, harpa, y vihuela*, Alcalá, ed. H. Anglès, *Monumentos de música española* 2, 1944.

Vente M. A. and Flentrop D. A. 1970, 'The Renaissance Organ of Evora Cathedral, Portugal', *The Organ Yearbook* 1: 5–19.

Vente M. A. and Kok W. 1970, 'Organs in Spain and Portugal', *The Organ* 139: 136–42.

Vogel, H. 1986a, 'Tuning and Temperament in the North German School of the Seventeenth and Eighteenth Centuries', *Charles Brenton Fisk, Organ Builder – Essays in His Honor*, ed. F. Douglass, O. Jander and B. Owen, Easthampton, MA, pp. 237–65.

    1986b, 'North German Organ Building of the Late Seventeenth Century: Registration and Tuning', *J. S. Bach as Organist*, ed. G. Stauffer and E. May, London, pp. 31–40.

Walter, R. 1990, *Johann Caspar Ferdinand Fischer: Hofkapellmeister der Markgrafen von Baden*, Frankfurt and New York.

Warren, J. 1842, *Hamilton's Catechism of the Organ* (2nd edn), London.

Webber, G. 1986, 'New Evidence Concerning the Transmission of Styles in Seventeenth-Century German Organ Music: MS Berlin, Amalien-Bibliothek 340', *Organ Yearbook* 17: 81–7.

    1992, 'Organ or Orphanage? Religious Controversy Surrounding the Role of Organ Music in German Lutheran Worship in the Baroque Era', *BIOS Journal* 16: 19–38.

Weyer, M. 1969, *Die deutsche Orgelsonate von Mendelssohn bis Reger*, Regensburg.

Wilkes, J. O. 1995, *Pipe Organs of Ann Arbor*, Ann Arbor.

Williams, P. F. 1963, 'J. S. Bach and English Organ Music', *Music and Letters* 44: 140–51.

    1966, *The European Organ, 1450–1850*, London.

    1968, 'Equal Temperament and the English Organ, 1675–1825', *Acta Musicologica* 40/1: 53–65.

    1980, *A New History of the Organ*, London.

    1984, *The Organ Music of J. S. Bach*, vol. III, *A Background*, Cambridge.

    1993, *The Organ in European Culture, 750–1250*, Cambridge.

Williams, P. F. and Owen, B. 1988, *The Organ*, London.

Wilson, M. I. 1979, *Organ Cases of Western Europe*, London.

Wraight, D. and Stembridge, C. 1994, 'Italian Split-keyed Instruments with Fewer than Nineteen Divisions to the Octave', *Performance Practice Review* 7: 150–77.

Wulstan, D. 1985, *Tudor Music*, London.

Zachariassen, S. 1969, *Current Organ Building* (essay 1952, published in *ISO Information* 1).

Zarlino, G. 1558, *Le istitutioni harmoniche*, Venice (facsimile repr. New York 1965).

Index

Italicised entries refer to figures.